In the
FOOTSTEPS
of *Jesus*

A chronological journey through the gospels set in the geography,
politics, people, power, culture and history of the day

HON STUART ROBERT MP

I0225299

Unless otherwise noted, all scripture is from the New English Translation (NET) Bible. This is a wonderful contemporary but rigorously exact translation that I know you will thoroughly enjoy reading.

Within copyright statements or in discussion about the NET Bible, the following is preferred: Scripture quoted by permission. Quotations designated (NET) are from the NET Bible® copyright ©1996-2016 by Biblical Studies Press, L.L.C. http://netbible.org All rights reserved.

The names: THE NET BIBLE®, NEW ENGLISH TRANSLATION COPYRIGHT (c) 1996 BY BIBLICAL STUDIES PRESS, L.L.C. NET Bible® IS A REGISTERED TRADEMARK THE NET BIBLE® LOGO, SERVICE MARK COPYRIGHT (c) 1997 BY BIBLICAL STUDIES PRESS, L.L.C. ALL RIGHTS RESERVED. SATELLITE IMAGERY COPYRIGHT (c) RØHR PRODUCTIONS LTD. AND CENTRE NATIONAL D'ÉTUDES SPATIALES PHOTOGRAPHS COPYRIGHT (c) RØHR PRODUCTIONS LTD.

ISBN 978-0-97575-671-3

Published by the Honourable Stuart Robert MP

Copyright © 2017 Hon Stuart Robert MP

Coverart: Miguel S. Kilantang Jr
Cover design: Miguel S. Kilantang Jr
Photographs: used by permission from the Hon Stuart Robert MP
                     used by permission from the Library of Congress (public domain)
                     front cover image is used by permission from istockphotos.com
Maps: used by permission the American bible society 1888 (public domain)
                     used by permission from God's Word First International Biblical Research and Teaching Ministry
                     used by permission, J. T. Barclay 'City of the Great King' 1858 (public domain)
Edit: The Expert Editor
Printed in: Createspace
Comments: inthefootstepsofjesus@robert.com.au

To my amazing wife, Chantelle. Thank you for your patience in this great gospel journey of discovery.

To our three beautiful sons, Caleb, Isaac and Jacob. May you grow and learn to love the Saviour of the world, Jesus, and the holy land of Israel He lived and died in, as much as we do.

To readers young and old. May you walk through the gospel story of Jesus afresh and marvel at the scandal of grace that has been afforded to you.

Contents

Contents

Prologue

Many have attempted to provide a chronology of the key events from Jesus' life sourced from the four gospels. Early attempts, starting with the 'Diatessaron' by the Assyrian Christian Tatian in the 2nd century erroneously tried to merge the gospels into a single narrative and remove repetition. Many subsequently tried and all ultimately failed. The gospel accounts of Jesus are too rich and varied to harmonise into a simple, lone account.

Though this is a single book, this chronological attempt does not resort to a single narrative. Every word of the gospels is included and put in a chronological order to try to build a flowing picture of Jesus' life and ministry. It is important to note that every attempt, including this one include leaps of logic, numerous assumptions and a few flat out guesses. Every attempt is cognisant of geography, archeology, historical documents and the odd local legend. All are well meaning and there is no conclusive proof that one chronological attempt is better than another.

The four gospels were written as different accounts to different audiences and there was never an attempt to harmonise them geographically or chronologically within the Bible. Jesus probably spoke in Aramaic, but the gospels are written in Greek, which helps explains different versions of the same stories. Matthew, Mark and Luke are called 'synoptic' gospels because they seek to present the events of Jesus' life with the same intent (synoptic literally means 'together sight'). Nearly 90 percent of Mark's content is found in Matthew, and 50 percent of Mark is in Luke. All of the parables of Christ are found in the synoptic gospels, whilst John's gospel contains no parables (the vine and the branches in John 15:1-8 is not considered a parable). Some of the authors tended to arrange materially topically, which explains all of Jesus' recorded miracles in Matthew being contained in just a few chapters. Jesus travelled extensively and used similar analogies and phrases to communicate His message at different times, in much the same way itinerant preachers do today. This explains why different gospels have similar content used in different circumstances.

What is refreshing about this clear lack of coordination and chronology, is that it is one of the best examples of the independence of the gospels. The differing accounts of the same activity and different order they appear in the gospels put to flight any criticism of gospel plagiarism from any 'unnamed' source.

This book's chronological attempt, however flawed, tends to follow the order of the gospel of Luke. Luke was writing an historical account for his benefactor and thus tended to be more concerned with timing of events. Luke was a doctor in his time and it's fair to say that order was a little more up his alley. He was also keen to emphasis Jesus' compassion to Gentiles and Samaritans so that the travel diaries of Jesus in His final months on earth (Luke 10-20) is largely unique to that gospel.

Matthew was writing to a predominantly Jewish audience so his focus was not necessarily logical but more spiritual. He quotes extensively from the Old Testament and his often-used phrase (in fact thirty-two times), 'the kingdom of heaven' is not found anywhere else in scripture.

Both Luke and Mathew are also much longer than Mark's gospel. Mark was writing from the teaching of Peter and to a predominantly Gentile (Roman) audience, so his account is fast paced, punchy and full of activity. A bit like Peter.

John's gospel is different again. Many of the important events in the synoptic gospels are omitted: the temptation of Jesus, the sermon on the mount, Jesus' transfiguration, the Lord's prayer and the institution of communion (the Lord's supper). You won't find Jesus casting out a demon in John, yet only John mentions Jesus' early Galilean ministry. In fact, it is John's gospel that gives us the three year view of time in ministry and the number of visits to Jerusalem. The synoptic gospels appear to describe only one journey of Jesus to Jerusalem (the final one), and concentrate predominantly on just one year of Jesus' ministry in Galilee. John also tends to write in more dialogue and discourses, rather than statement of events, leading some to argue his gospel is a more reflective style of writing[1].

Suffice to say that every effort has been made to present the chronology of the gospels with as much rigour as possible. Likewise every effort has been made to present the dates accurately. All dates are based on the crucifixion of Jesus on Friday 3rd April 33 AD (14th Nisan 3793 in the Hebrew calendar). There are equally compelling arguments for the date being Friday 7th April 30AD (16th Nisan 3790 in the Hebrew calendar) however like the chronology, a timeline has to be chosen, so for this book it is 33 AD.

Please note that if there are errors, they are mine and mine alone and I apologise for them if they appear. My only caution is not to jump to conclusions too readily. Archaeological evidence seems compelling at

---

[1]   W. Hall Harris III is Professor of New Testament Studies at Dallas Theological Seminary in https://bible.org/seriespage/2-major-differences-between-john-and-synoptic-gospels (accessed 22 Oct 2016)

first until the fifth century piece of pottery turns up in the undisturbed pristine first century living room. Above all, enjoy the rollicking read of the greatest story every told. Jesus, the Son of God, through whom the universe was made, came to earth to die for you and I to reconcile us back to God. Separated by the first man Adam, we are made right with our God because of the second Adam, Jesus.

Hon Stuart Robert

Introduction

The Bible speaks of a scarlet thread woven through human history, in the form of the continuing theme of Jesus the Christ (Messiah) the Son of God. Beginning as the Creator of the world before time began, continuing through creation, walking in Eden, enduring the fall, coming as a baby, growing into a man and laying down His life as a final and complete sacrifice for all, Jesus was, is and always will be.

The story of the scarlet thread is one like no other, because it began before time. God the Father, Jesus the Son and the person of the Holy Spirit, the triune nature of God has always been. Then they created us. That's right, they created this world and all that is in it. They created the first man and woman, Adam and Eve, with the intent that the world would be filled with people who know and love God. People who would know no sin, no shame, no guilt, no fear. A people in perfection.

The problem, as it still often is, was people. Adam and Eve could do whatever they wanted in the Garden of Eden except for one thing, just one, stay away from the tree of the knowledge of good and evil. History tells us that that one thing was one thing too many, and sin subsequently entered the world through the first fruity bite. As sin entered, we became separated from that beautiful, perfect relationship with God. Shame, guilt and fear came flooding in where previously only love, joy and peace resided.

Yet even at that instant, God had already planned a path to restore everyone back to Him. A perfect path that would restore that perfect righteous relationship. Except this time it would not be based on the knowledge of good and evil in the form of a tree, it would be based on a perfect sacrifice to satisfy the righteous judgement of a perfect God. God himself would step down from eternity in the form of His son Jesus, would live amongst us, would die amongst us and would rise again amongst us. We would be given the opportunity to choose Jesus as our path to eternal life, our restoration of the perfect righteous relationship with God.

All of this planned in an instant, and because God is omniscient (all-knowing), all of this was known in the beginning. Such perfect love to create the universe knowing all this, to create our world knowing all this, to create us in His image knowing all this, to allow Adam and Eve to do that one thing knowing all this. Knowing all this, God still created....

We know all this because of the inspired, innerant, infallible Word of God, the 'Bible', an incredible picture of the creation, fall and redemption of mankind. It is actually a book of sixty-six books written by forty authors on three continents in three languages over a period of 2000 years. The authors ranged from princes to prophets, from shepherds to scholars, writing from palaces and prisons and everywhere in between. They recorded history, recited poetry, delivered prophecy, offered proverbs, sang psalms, recorded laws and ultimately presented grace. It is a book of two covenants, 'the old and the new' one that leads to death and one that leads to life. It is a book of law and of grace. The Old Covenant was handed down from God in the form of the

Ten Commandments at Mount Sinai where 3000 people would die (Exodus 32:28). The New Covenant of Grace was purchased with the blood of Jesus and 3000 people would be saved the day the promised Holy Spirit came at Pentecost on Mount Zion (Acts 2:41).

The law was given on Mount Sinai but grace was given on Mount Zion.

For you have not come to something that can be touched, to a burning fire and darkness and gloom and a whirlwind..... But you have come to Mount Zion, the city of the living God, the heavenly Jerusalem, and to myriads of angels, to the assembly. Hebrews 12:18 and 22

Woven through all of this scripture like a scarlet thread is the person of Jesus Christ, the promised Messiah, the Son of God. Jesus appears in the very first verse of the Bible (chronologically) John 1:1, "In the beginning was the Word, and the Word was with God, and the Word was fully God", and the end of the Bible in Revelation 22:20, "Yes, I am coming soon", and everywhere in between.

It is this Jesus, the sinless Son of God, that was born as a man, lived as a man and died as a man to pay the penalty for our sin. It is this Jesus that took our trespasses and gave us His right standing with God. It is this Jesus that ushered in the New Covenant of Grace, of unmerited, undeserved, unfathomable favour upon the lives of all who believe in the finished redemptive power of the cross. It is this Jesus that made us completely righteous, not because of anything we did, but because of everything He did. It is this Jesus that crawled as a baby, walked as a man and died as a Saviour amongst us.

Jesus lived on earth for just thirty-three years and travelled no more than a couple of hundred kilometres in any direction. He lived at the time of seemingly ultimate power, that of the Roman Empire, yet He discussed politics only once, when the issue of taxation was used to try and trap him (Matthew 22:17-22). He penned no letters and left no monuments, leaving that to His disciples and the church.

The only recognised reliable account that exists of the Saviour of the World, the Son of God, Jesus the Christ, amongst us on earth is the four gospels in the Bible named Matthew, Mark, Luke and John, after their authors. Whilst there are numerous authenticating secular letters, the gospel accounts offer four unique and different pictures of Jesus, written to different audiences for different purposes. The gospels contain 64,766 words in total with each containing the same and different stories. Of the almost 400 stories, events and accounts of Jesus in the gospels, very few accounts are contained in all four gospels, testimony to their differences. The gospel of Mark doesn't even contain the miracle of the birth of Jesus.

The gospels are not chronological and at times contain different accounts of the same event, as if a number of people were witnesses but each saw and concentrated on something unique in the same encounter. There is something endearingly human about different authors focussing their attentions on what they perhaps thought was the most important facet within a certain event. That still doesn't explain Mark's gospel missing the virgin birth though! I must speak to him about that when my race here on earth is run.

There is such richness in the gospel accounts of Jesus, that bring the author and perfector of our faith to life (Hebrews 12:2). It is a story unparalleled in the history of the world. A story of love so divine and of grace so deep that it deserves to be told in many different ways, as the gospels do so beautifully. The Bible will always be an open and flowing conversation with us today. If we want to find out what Jesus would do, go find out what He said. For Jesus doesn't just bring life, He is life and the Bible brings this to our life.

Indeed one of the four gospels, that of Luke, was written for his bene-factor, Theophilus, so that he would know the certainty of what he had been taught.

> *Now many have undertaken to compile an account of the things*
> *that have been fulfilled among us, like the accounts passed on to*
> *us by those who were eyewitnesses and servants of the word from*
> *the beginning. So it seemed good to me as well, because I have*
> *followed all things carefully from the beginning, to write an*
> *orderly account for you, most excellent Theophilus, so that you*
> *may know for certain the things you were taught. Luke 1:1-4*

Whilst there are thousands of books on the gospels and each has been a blessing, there is space for yet one more book to build on this certainty. A harmonised, chronologically presented gospel account of Jesus, set in the geography, politics, people, power, culture and history of the day so the reader can walk with Jesus over his thirty-three years as he crawled, walked and died on earth. This book is not meant as a commentary or an academic treatise, merely an opportunity to read every word of the four gospels woven into the time and setting of the historical truth of the Saviour of the world.

Professor Beitzel, the chief consultant for the amazing 'Biblica' Bible Atlas reinforces the values of such an approach, writing that where Jesus was when He taught brings His message to life. "Jesus talks about liv-ing water while at Jacob's well; He calls himself the bread of life while at Capernaum where basaltic grain mills were manufactured; and he talks about faith that can move a mountain while on the road to Bethphage, from where His disciples could easily have looked southward and phys-ically seen evidence of a mountain that had been moved by Herod the Great in order to construct his fortress site of Herodium."[2]

---

[2]   Beitzel, B., 'Biblica' Barron's Educational Services, USA, 2007, Foreward.

CHAPTER 1

The scarlet thread

There has never been a time when Jesus has not been with God the Father and the third person of the Godhead, the person of the Holy Spirit. Jesus was there when our world was created, and more, everything was created through Him.

> *In the beginning was the Word, and the Word was with God,*
> *and the Word was fully God. The Word was with God in the*
> *beginning. All things were created by him, and apart from him*
> *not one thing was created that has been created. In him was life,*
> *and the life was the light of mankind. And the light shines on in*
> *the darkness, but the darkness has not mastered it. John 1:1-5*

This is literally the first verse of the Bible, the opening scene of our history. It is the moment when the God of the universe commenced His great act of creation that is recorded in the book of Genesis. Furthermore, this opening scene tells us that Jesus is the author of life and the light of mankind. It is through Jesus that we can see the truth of where we came from, where we're going and how we're going to get there. That's what light does – it illuminates the path.

A witness to this light, a man named John the Baptist, was sent to announce the coming of the Light of the world, Jesus. Chapter 3 will discuss the work of John in more detail, suffice to say he was the last of the prophetic witnesses to Jesus as the light of the world. The last prophet sent by God to herald the coming Jesus, and the first prophet to actually see Jesus.

A man came, sent from God, whose name was John. He came as a witness to testify about the light, so that everyone might believe through him. He himself was not the light, but he came to testify about the light. The true light, who gives light to everyone, was coming into the world. He was in the world, and the world was created by him, but the world did not recognize him. He came to what was his own, but his own people did not receive him. But to all who have received him-those who believe in his name-he has given the right to become God's children -children not born by human parents or by human desire or a husband's decision, but by God. Now the Word became flesh and took up residence among us. We saw his glory-the glory of the one and only, full of grace and truth, who came from the Father. John testified about him and shouted out, "This one was the one about whom I said, 'He who comes after me is greater than I am, because he existed before me.'" For we have all received from his fullness one gracious gift after another. For the law was given through Moses, but grace and truth came about through Jesus Christ. No one has ever seen God. The only one, himself God, who is in closest fellowship with the Father, has made God known. John 1:6-18

Whilst Jesus was fully God, He was also born fully man in fulfilment of the promise first given to Abraham and again to King David. Thus, Jesus has a human legal lineage through His earthly father Joseph that traces right back to Abraham as listed in Matthew's gospel. This lineage lists three lots of fourteen generations from Abraham to King David, King David to the final exile of the Israelites from Jerusalem and then from the exile to the coming of Jesus. As an aside, there are only 41 names in the list, yet three lots of fourteen is 42. This is awkward, until you explore a little deeper. Excluded from the list is Jehoiakim (also known as 'Eliakim'), who was Josiah's son and Jeconiah's father (1 Chronicles 3:15-16). The reason for his exclusion may be that he was a puppet king, given his rule by Pharaoh King of Egypt. The first phase of the captivity of Judah by Babylon began at the end of Jehoiakim's reign, prior to his son Jeconiah coming into power. Thus, the three groupings of 14 generations would include Abraham to David, Solomon to Jehoiakim (he is not mentioned, but was among the first to be carried off into Babylon) and Jeconiah to Jesus. This is the wonder of the treasure trove of the Bible. At almost every page there is fascinating history, hidden gems and profound truths.

This is the record of the genealogy of Jesus Christ, the son of David, the son of Abraham. Abraham was the father of Isaac, Isaac the father of Jacob, Jacob the father of Judah and his brothers, Judah the father of Perez and Zerah (by Tamar), Perez the father of Hezron, Hezron the father of Ram, Ram the father of Amminadab, Amminadab the father of Nahshon, Nahshon the father of Salmon, Salmon the father of Boaz (by Rahab), Boaz the father of Obed (by Ruth), Obed the father of Jesse, and Jesse the father of David the king. David was the father of Solomon (by the wife of Uriah), Solomon the father of Rehoboam, Rehoboam the father of Abijah, Abijah the father of Asa, Asa the father of Jehoshaphat, Jehoshaphat the father of Joram, Joram the father of Uzziah, Uzziah the father of Jotham, Jotham the father of Ahaz, Ahaz the father of Hezekiah, Hezekiah the father of Manasseh, Manasseh the father of Amon, Amon the father of Josiah, and Josiah the father of Jeconiah and his brothers, at the time of the deportation to Babylon. After the deportation to Babylon, Jeconiah became the father of Shealtiel, Shealtiel the father of Zerubbabel, Zerubbabel the father of Abiud, Abiud the father of Eliakim, Eliakim the father of Azor, Azor the father of Zadok, Zadok the father of Achim, Achim the father of Eliud, Eliud the father of Eleazar, Eleazar the father of Matthan, Matthan the father of Jacob, and Jacob the father of Joseph, the husband of Mary, by whom Jesus was born, who is called Christ. So all the generations from Abraham to David are fourteen generations, and from David to the deportation to Babylon, fourteen generations, and from the deportation to Babylon to Christ, fourteen generations.... Matthew 1:1-17

The second account of Jesus' genealogy in Luke's gospel takes his human lineage back to the first man, Adam, and his creator God. Considering the first part of this chapter states clearly that Jesus and God are one, this genealogy takes Jesus literally back to Himself in the Godhead. This genealogy however, goes back through the line of Mary, the birth mother of Jesus. Thus, it is the same as that for Joseph above, up to King David where it diverges. Mary is from the line of King David's son 'Nathan', born to Bathsheba, whilst Joseph is from the line of King David's son 'Solomon', also born to Bathsheba (1 Chron 3:5).

He was the son (as was supposed) of Joseph, the son of Heli, the son of Matthat, the son of Levi, the son of Melchi, the son of Jannai, the son of Joseph, the son of Mattathias, the son of Amos, the son of Nahum, the son of Esli, the son of Naggai, the son of Maath, the son of Mattathias, the son of Semein, the son of Josech, the son of Joda, the son of Joanan, the son of Rhesa, the son of Zerubbabel, the son of Shealtiel, the son of Neri, he son of Melchi, the son of Addi, the son of Cosam, the son of Elmadam, the son of Er, the son of Joshua, the son of Eliezer, the son of Jorim, the son of Matthat, the son of Levi, the son of Simeon, the son of Judah, the son of Joseph, the son of Jonam, the son of Eliakim, the son of Melea, the son of Menna, the son of Mattatha, the son of Nathan, the son of David, the son of Jesse, the son of Obed, the son of Boaz, the son of Sala, the son of Nahshon, the son of Amminadab, the son of Admin, the son of Arni, the son of Hezron, the son of Perez, the son of Judah, the son of Jacob, the son of Isaac, the son of Abraham, the son of Terah, the son of Nahor, the son of Serug, the son of Reu, the son of Peleg, the son of Eber, the son of Shelah, the son of Cainan, the son of Arphaxad, the son of Shem, the son of Noah, the son of Lamech, the son of Methuselah, the son of Enoch, the son of Jared, the son of Mahalalel, the son of Kenan, the son of Enosh, the son of Seth, the son of Adam, the son of God. Luke 3:23b-38

Thus, Jesus is indeed the promised King from the line of Abraham and King David, both on His Father and Mother's side. He is the 42nd generation from Abraham. It is interesting to note that the Israelites when they came out of captivity also passed through 42 camps[3], the last being at the Jordan River, where Jesus would be baptised. This is the beauty of the gospel account of Jesus that we will walk through. The scarlet thread begins in the Old Testament and points at every twist and turn to the coming Messiah, Jesus. Whether it is in camps stayed at during the wilderness years or the number of fish Peter caught at the end of John's gospel, it all points to Jesus.

Jesus proclaimed...

When Jesus was to be born, God sent His messenger angel, Gabriel, to Jerusalem, now under Roman occupation, to announce His coming. The question is, why Jerusalem? A little bit of history will start to unpack that question, for Jerusalem is one of the most controversial cities on earth. In the last 3000 years this city has been destroyed at least twice, besieged twenty-three times, attacked an additional fifty-two times, and captured and recaptured forty-four times.[4] Christian and Jewish history draw heavily upon the city, and Islam views Jerusalem as its the third holiest site (after Mecca and Medina) believing that Mohammed ascended to heaven from the city in the seventh century. Clearly there is something about this city.

---

[3] http://www.betemunah.org/stages.html#_Toc454392386 accessed on 7 October 2016. Noting there is considerable dispute about this number

[4] Eric H. Cline 'Jerusalem Besieged' as reproduced at https://web.archive.org/web/20080603214950/http://www.momentmag.com/Exclusive/2008/2008-03/200803-Jerusalem.html accessed on 7 October 2016.

In the temporal, it is difficult to understand why Jerusalem has any importance. It does not lie on any major trade routes and there is no easily discernible reason why this city should be one of the most significant places in the world. Geographically, Jerusalem lies at the crest of a low range of hills, forty-eight kilometres inland from the Mediterranean Sea. Turn east and you are confronted with the Judean Hills and a descending landscape that drops rapidly to the Dead Sea that sits at 427m below sea level, the lowest body of water on earth and completely undrinkable.

The maps below, printed by the American Bible Society in 1888, show the city of Jerusalem with its walls at the time of Jesus and the existing walls built from 1537 to 1541 by Sultan Suleiman the Magnificent after the Ottoman conquest of Israel. The topography of the land is also displayed. It shows the northern and highest part of the city being the peak of Mount Moriah, that extends south as a ridge line, ending where the Kidron and Hinnom valleys meet. This is where the current excavations are occurring at the site of the ancient City of David. The land fall from Mount Moriah, at 777 metres high, to the intersection of the two valleys is 177 metres, with the valley floor being 600 metres above sea level.

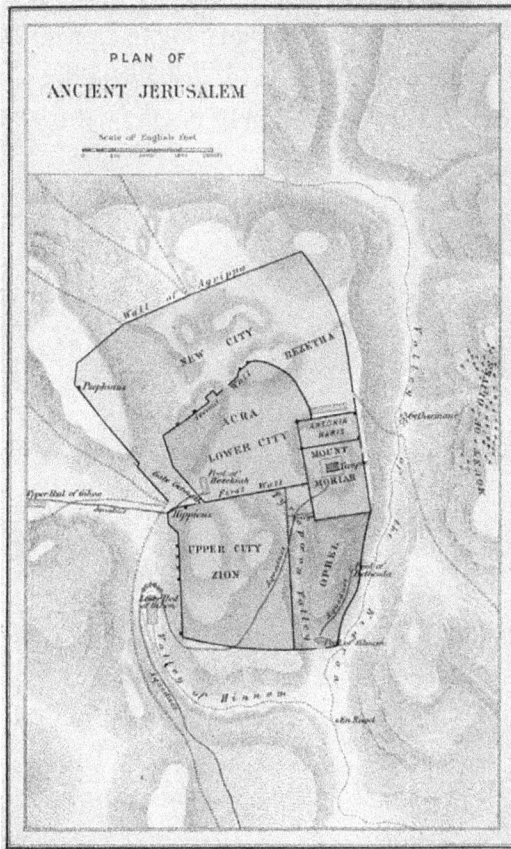

The walls of Jerusalem in different times courtesy
the American Bible Society 1888

600 metres to the west of Mt Moriah at 772 metres is Mount Zion. At the time of Jesus the deep Tyropean Valley separated Mount Zion from Mount Moriah; today however, the valley is completely filled with many layers of ruined city rubble from Jerusalem's many destructions.[5] As will be discussed in the section on the Temple, almost half of the western retaining wall of the Temple Mount lies below the present ground level, because the wall started at the bottom of this ancient valley. East of Mount Moriah across the Kidron Valley is the Mount of

---

[5]   http://www.templemount.org/moriah2.html accessed on 7 October 2016

Olives which is 100 meters higher than Mount Zion or Mount Moriah. At the bottom of the Mount of Olives just above the Kidron Valley is the historical location of the Garden of Gethsemane.

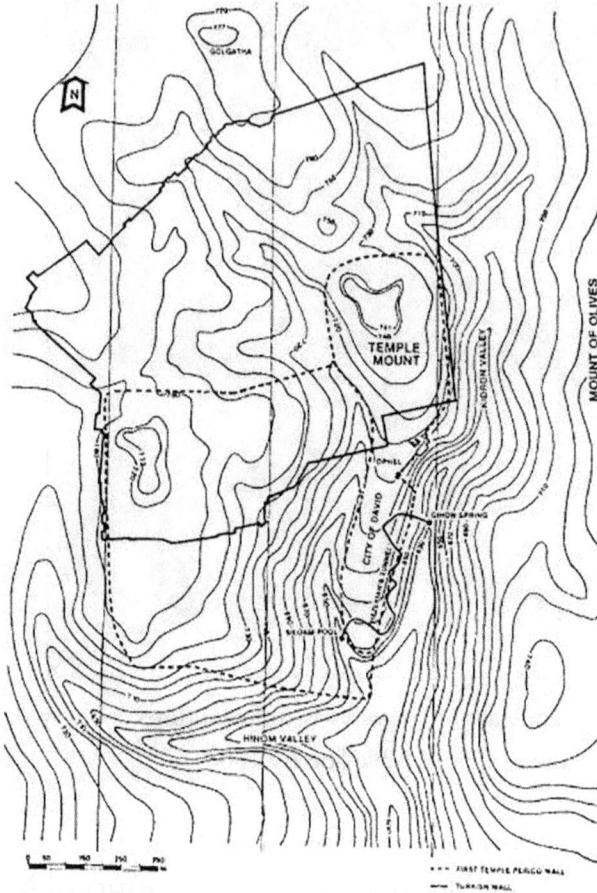

The geographical relief of Jerusalem courtesy the American Bible Society 1888

Whilst all this is fascinating, none of it explains the biblical significance of Jerusalem and why the announcement of the coming Messiah would be made in this city. To gain this understanding, we have to go back to the first book of the Bible, Genesis, and read the story of Abraham, yes the same Abraham in both Joseph's and Mary's genealogy of Jesus.

Abraham was originally from modern day Iraq. He was born in the city of Ur of the Chaldeans on the Euphrates River in ancient Mesopotamia (Genesis 11:27-32) and left with his father to live in Harran in northwest Mesopotamia (literally the land between the rivers). At Harran, God called Abraham to go to the land of Canaan (Genesis 12:1-9) where He promised He would make Abraham into a great nation and would give his ancestors that land. Abraham leaves Harran for Canaan (much of modern day Israel) and subsequently flees to Egypt due to a famine (Genesis 12:10) and then later returns to the southern part of Israel, to Hebron in the Negev (a desert and semi-desert region of southern Israel). Abraham would have to rescue his cousin 'Lot' who was inadvertently caught up in a tribal fight (Genesis 14:1-17) and Abraham would then be blessed by Melchizedek, King of Salem (modern day Jerusalem) and priest of the most high God who met Abraham with bread and wine. Abraham would give Melchizedek ten percent of all that he had (Genesis 14:18). What makes this account fascinating is that it is one of the many linkages between the Old and New Testaments that point to Jesus. Abraham, the ancestor of Jesus, meets a priest of God residing in Jerusalem who blesses him with bread and wine, the same items that Jesus asked to be remembered with on the night before he was crucified (Luke 22:19-20). Melchizedek as a priest of the most high God, living and serving in what became Jerusalem, is an arch-type figure of Jesus.

Abraham then went back to the Negev and was living at modern day Beersheba (Genesis 21:22-34) when God tested him by asking him to sacrifice his son Isaac, yes the same Abraham and Isaac in the genealogy of both earthy parents of Jesus.

God said, "Take your son-your only son, whom you love, Isaac-and go to the land of Moriah! Offer him up there as a burnt offering on one of the mountains which I will indicate to you." Genesis 22:2

So Abraham goes to Mount Moriah, the same Mount Moriah that stands 777 metres high in modern-day Jerusalem (at that time called 'Salem'). Suffice to say Isaac was not sacrificed in the way the pagans commonly did at that time. God provided a ram, caught in the thickets, to end up getting the chop on Mount Moriah instead of Isaac. At the time the ram was symbolic of many of the pagan gods in the area, thus the one true God was literally saying, 'I AM not like all the other gods that demand child sacrifice, I AM the God who saves.' Jerusalem's significance only grows from there.

King David, the same King David in the genealogy of both Joseph and Mary, captured the city, named it Jerusalem and made it the capital of the Jewish people. The city was later chosen as the site for the Temple that was subsequently built by his son Solomon, the same Solomon in the genealogy of Jesus. In fact, the city of Jerusalem is referenced in the Bible using many different names, titles and designations. In ancient times the city was referred to as Salem (Genesis 14:18), Jebus (Joshua 18:28 and Judges 19:10), Zion (1 Kings 8:1 and Zechariah 9:13), the city of David (2 Samuel 5:7 and Isaiah 22:9), the city of God (Psalm 46:4), the city of the great King (Psalm 48:2), God's holy mountain (Daniel 9:16, 20) and the holy city (Matthew 4:5). Are you starting to get a feel for why Jerusalem has been historically so significant?

It is in this incredible city, with its rich history built around Mount Moriah where Abraham was about to sacrifice Isaac, upon which the third Jewish Temple stood, that the coming of Jesus was proclaimed.

A little bit of history and geography about this Jewish Temple will further set the scene and cement the importance of Jerusalem as a city. The first Temple built by Solomon was on Mount Moriah. This Temple was completed in circa 964 BC[6] and destroyed by the Babylonians in 586

---

6   http://www.kingscalendar.com/cgi-bin/index.cgi?action=view-news&id=569 accessed on 6 October 2016

BC in response to the disobedience of God's people the Jews. It was rebuilt in circa 515 BC by the leader of the returning exiled Jews, a man called 'Zerubbabel', the same Zerubbabel in the line of Jesus. It appears this Temple fell into disrepair over time and the third Temple was built by Herod the great. Herod did not build the third Temple on top of Mount Moriah as it was. He constructed a whole new raised platform that enlarged the Temple Mount area to some thirty-five acres (1,555,000 square feet) with four huge walls to support the new platform. The walls were constructed of massive limestones and were some 1500 feet long, 90 feet high and went 60 feet into the ground. The current western wall in Jerusalem, that is the scene of much Jewish prayer and celebration, is the remains of the western supporting wall for this platform. It is this raised platform on Mount Moriah that visitors see today in Jerusalem and upon which the Islamic Dome of the Rock was completed in 691 AD and the Al-Asqa Mosque was built centuries later.

The third Temple, like the two before it, was apparently magnificent. The actual Temple building sat in the middle of the massive raised platform that was itself surrounded by an outer wall and on the far northwest corner sat the imposing Antonia Fortress, the home of the temple garrison that stayed alert for disturbances in the Temple.

Inside the walls around the raised platform ran cloisters or roofed walkways with their backs to the outer walls and rows of tall marble pillars or colonnades holding up the roof. There is limited historical material that describes the Temple, though the first century Jewish historian scholar, Josephus does use glowing terms as he described this outer Temple area.

'All the cloisters were double, and the pillars to them belonging were
twenty-five cubits in height, and supported the cloisters. These pillars
were of one entire stone each of them, and that stone was white

marble; and the roofs were adorned with cedar, curiously graven. The natural magnificence, and excellent polish, and the harmony of the joints in these cloisters, afforded a prospect that was very remarkable; nor was it on the outside adorned with any work of the painter or engraver. The cloisters (of the outmost court) were in breadth thirty cubits, while the entire compass of it was by measure six furlongs, including the tower of Antonia; those entire courts that were exposed to the air were laid with stones of all sorts. [7]

There were apparently eight gates leading into the Temple complex and then further gates within the complex to separate different areas. Like many things in Jerusalem, there remains some dispute about detail. It appears that there were two gates which provided entry into the Temple court from the south, four from the west, one (the Golden Gate) from the east, and one gate to the north. There also appeared to be an underground tunnel from the Antonia fortress into the Temple complex.

The four western gates, according to Josephus were…

'Now in the western quarters of the enclosure of the temple there were four gates; the first led to the king's palace, and went to a passage over the intermediate valley; two more led to the suburbs of the city; and the last led to the other city, where the road descended down into the valley by a great number of steps, and from there up again by the ascent for the city… [8]

---

[7] Jewish War 5. 5. 2
[8] Josephus, Antiquities 15. 11

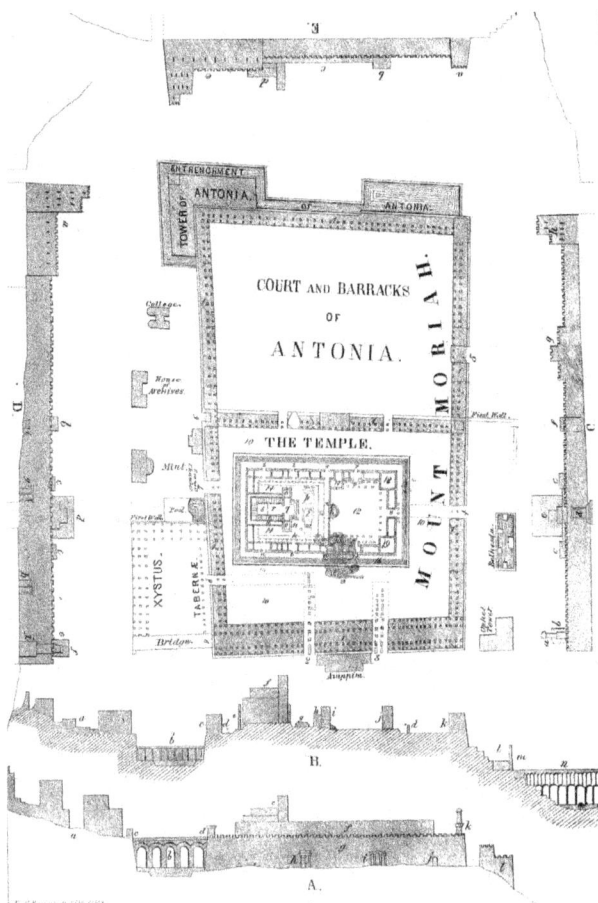

The above map is from J. T Barclay's book 'City of the great King, published in 1858, page 290.

One of the four western gates, 'The Gate of Coponius' named after the first procurator, was the main gate from the west. It was apparently decorated by Herod with the golden eagle as a sign that the Temple had been placed under the protection of Rome. Read the word 'protection' more as 'occupation': the Romans and/or Herod clearly had a sense of humour.

The southern gates, called the double Huldah and the triple Huldah, were the most frequently used, although a ravine lined the southern wall, so great staircases led to the actual gates. The eastern portico along the wall was named after King Solomon, and it was somewhere along this wall that the twelve-year old Jesus debated with the scholars (Luke 2:46). It's possible that the highest corner of the eastern wall was where satan took Jesus (Matthew 4:5) during the temptation in the wilderness.

Of all the gates, it was the eastern Golden Gate that faces the Mount of Olives, that the Old Testament prophets prophesied the Messiah would use (Nehemiah 3:29 and Ezekiel 44:1–3). Indeed Jesus would ride through this gate on a donkey (Luke 19:28–48). The gate is still visible today and is the only original gate on the Temple Mount.

The eight gates led worshippers to the outer area called the 'Court of the Gentiles' since anyone was allowed to go there. Within fourteen steps of the eastern Golden Gate was another gate called the Beautiful Gate to the court of the women where the poor boxes were. It was into one of these boxes that the widow cast her two small coins (Luke 21:1-4). Another fifteen steps led up to the famous Gate of Nicanor, through which Mary brought the child Jesus at the time of his presentation. This led through the Court of Men to the Court of Priests, which had in its centre the altar for the burnt offerings. To the left of the altar was a large basin, called the Bronze Sea, resting upon twelve bulls cast in bronze. Further steps led up to the actual Temple, a comparatively small building. A priceless curtain, embroidered with a map of the known world, concealed from view what lay beyond, and no one except the priest on duty was allowed to go inside.

The Temple contained the golden altar on which incense was offered and next to it the seven-branched candelabrum and the table with the twelve loaves of bread, which were replaced by fresh loaves every Sabbath. Beyond it, behind another large curtain, lay the Holy of Holies, which no one except the priest was allowed to enter; and he only once a year, chosen by lot on the Day of Atonement. The Holy of Holies was the place where the Ark of the Covenant once rested, where God would meet His holy people, the Jews. The Ark went missing after the sacking of Jerusalem sometime between the first fall of Jerusalem in 607 BC and the third fall in 586 BC, so a stone sat in its place at the time of Jesus.

Having given the briefest of histories of the most complex of places, we now return to the gospel story. It picks up with Zechariah the priest, the cousin by marriage to Mary (the soon-to-be mother of Jesus) going into the Temple to conduct his duty. He is confronted by the very messenger of God telling him he will have a son (John the Baptist) who will herald the Messiah (the Saviour of the world, Jesus). So yes, confronting is the right word.

During the reign of Herod king of Judea, there lived a priest named Zechariah who belonged to the priestly division of Abijah, and he had a wife named Elizabeth, who was a descendant of Aaron. They were both righteous in the sight of God, following all the commandments and ordinances of the Lord blamelessly. But they did not have a child, because Elizabeth was barren, and they were both very old. Now while Zechariah was serving as priest before God when his division was on duty, he was chosen by lot, according to the custom of the priesthood, to enter the holy place of the Lord and burn incense. Now the whole crowd of people were praying outside at the hour of the incense offering. An angel of the Lord, standing on the right side of the altar of incense, appeared to him. And Zechariah, visibly shaken when he saw the angel, was seized with fear. But the angel said to him, "Do not be afraid, Zechariah, for your prayer has been heard, and your wife Elizabeth will bear you a son; you will name him John. Joy and gladness will come to you, and many will rejoice at his birth, for he will be great in the sight of the Lord. He must never drink wine or strong drink, and he will be filled with the Holy Spirit, even before his birth. He will turn many of the people of Israel to the Lord their God. And he will go as forerunner before the Lord in the spirit and power of Elijah, to turn the hearts of the fathers back to their children and the disobedient to the wisdom of the just, to make ready for the Lord

*a people prepared for him." Zechariah said to the angel, "How can I be
sure of this? For I am an old man, and my wife is old as well." The angel
answered him, "I am Gabriel, who stands in the presence of God, and
I was sent to speak to you and to bring you this good news. And now,
because you did not believe my words, which will be fulfilled in their time,
you will be silent, unable to speak, until the day these things take place."
Now the people were waiting for Zechariah, and they began to wonder
why he was delayed in the holy place. When he came out, he was not
able to speak to them. They realized that he had seen a vision in the holy
place, because he was making signs to them and remained unable to speak.
When his time of service was over, he went to his home. Luke 1:5-23*

The first message of the coming Jesus is delivered with power by God's
messenger and affirmed with the miracle of muteness for Zechariah and
the promise of an opened womb for Elizabeth, the cousin of Mary (the
future mother of Jesus). Zechariah would remain in Jerusalem, silently,
until his time of service was complete and then he would return to his
home in the Judean Hill country (Luke 1:39) and Elizabeth would fall
pregnant in her old age. The Judean Hill country is a series of mountain ranges rising to 1000 metres that separates the Jordan valley from
the coastal plains. The Hills include the towns of Jerusalem, Bethlehem
and Hebron. Whilst today they are a wilderness of little vegetation, in
the time of Jesus they were more heavily forested.

*After some time his wife Elizabeth became pregnant, and for five
months she kept herself in seclusion. She said, "This is what the
Lord has done for me at the time when he has been gracious to
me, to take away my disgrace among people." Luke 1:24-25*

It appears that Elizabeth did indeed remain behind closed doors during
the early stages of her pregnancy. Gabriel's message to Mary (see below),
is the first time Mary had heard about the blessing on her cousin
Elizabeth's life. You would have thought with children being seen as

such a blessing in ancient Jewish culture and the lack of children as a 'disgrace among the people' (Luke 1:25b), that Elizabeth would have told everyone. It appears not, for as soon as Mary hears the news she rushes to Elizabeth's home and stays until the birth of the baby John.

From Jerusalem to the Judean Hills, this amazing story now moves to Nazareth, a town in the hills rising about the Jezreel valley in the area called Galilee. Galilee is located in the north-west part of Israel with its southern boundary the Jezreel valley, its northern boundary Lebanon, its eastern boundary the Sea of Galilee and the Jordan valley and to the west the Mediterranean. The Galilee region was the home of Jesus for the majority of his life.

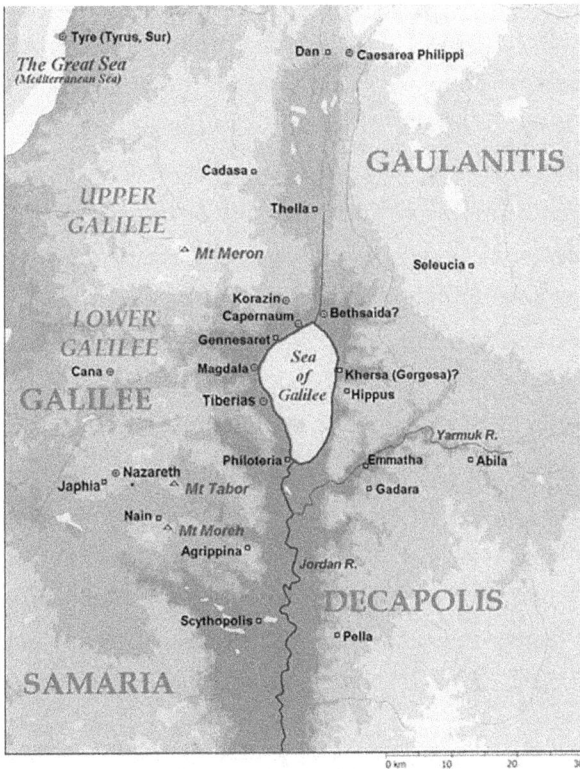

The location of Galilee courtesy God's Word First International Biblical Research and Teaching Ministry

In Nazareth at this time, lived two descendants of King David, Joseph and Mary. They were pledged to be married (the western mindset would call it 'engaged') and Mary was a virgin, thus not pregnant. The same messenger angel, Gabriel who had appeared six months previously to Zechariah in Jerusalem, now appears to Mary in Nazareth. The opening words of Gabriel are similar in that they contain the phrase, 'do not be afraid'. Gabriel must have been awesome in appearance and overpowering in presence.

In the sixth month of Elizabeth's pregnancy, the angel Gabriel was sent by God to a town of Galilee called Nazareth, to a virgin engaged to a man whose name was Joseph, a descendant of David, and the virgin's name was Mary. The angel came to her and said, "Greetings, favored one, the Lord is with you!" But she was greatly troubled by his words and began to wonder about the meaning of this greeting. So the angel said to her, "Do not be afraid, Mary, for you have found favor with God! Listen: You will become pregnant and give birth to a son, and you will name him Jesus. He will be great, and will be called the Son of the Most High, and the Lord God will give him the throne of his father David. He will reign over the house of Jacob forever, and his kingdom will never end." Mary said to the angel, "How will this be, since I have not had sexual relations with a man?" The angel replied, "The Holy Spirit will come upon you, and the power of the Most High will overshadow you. Therefore the child to be born will be holy; he will be called the Son of God. "And look, your relative Elizabeth has also become pregnant with a son in her old age-although she was called barren, she is now in her sixth month! For nothing will be impossible with God." So Mary said, "Yes, I am a servant of the Lord; let this happen to me according to your word." Then the angel departed from her. Luke 1:26-38

This account of the coming of the Messiah is almost too overwhelming to unpack. There are too many questions unanswered. Why was Mary favoured? What was she thinking and feeling when Gabriel spoke to her? How did she think she would get pregnant? What did she think about Elizabeth pregnant in her old age? What would Joseph say? What would people think? Why me? These and a hundred more questions must have raced through this young girl's mind. Yet in her simplicity of faith she quietly accepted God's 'devine' plan and will and said, 'I am the Lord's servant' (Luke 1:38a). What an extraordinary girl!

Faced with this amazing revelation, it appears she did the one thing she could: race to be with her much older and wiser cousin Elizabeth. Perhaps Elizabeth, her elder, may have some answers.

In those days Mary got up and went hurriedly into the hill country, to a town of Judah, and entered Zechariah's house and greeted Elizabeth. When Elizabeth heard Mary's greeting, the baby leaped in her womb, and Elizabeth was filled with the Holy Spirit. She exclaimed with a loud voice, "Blessed are you among women, and blessed is the child in your womb! And who am I that the mother of my Lord should come and visit me? For the instant the sound of your greeting reached my ears, the baby in my womb leaped for joy. And blessed is she who believed that what was spoken to her by the Lord would be fulfilled." Luke 1:39-45

And answers Elizabeth indeed had. The second the voice of Mary rang out, Elizabeth's unborn child 'leaped' and she was filled with the Holy Spirit and practically yelled 'the mother of the Messiah has just walked through my front door!' Remember this is a dignified, elderly and pregnant Jewish woman married to a respected priest. A much, much younger cousin has just come to see her and here Elizabeth is exclaiming loudly, 'Why am I so favoured, that the mother of my Lord should come to me?' (Luke 1:43) Elizabeth then dispels any doubt for Mary and frankly for anyone in ear shot saying, 'blessed is she who has believed that the Lord would fulfil His promises to her!' (Luke 1:45)

Two cousins, one elderly, one very young, both stand in awesome wonder as they confess, loudly, that they are the two central figures in bringing the Messiah into the world. The older carries the messenger, the younger, the Messiah. Mary's response shows her belief, her acceptance and her understanding of what it all means, as much as one could understand such wonder.

And Mary said, "My soul exalts the Lord, and my spirit has begun to rejoice in God my Savior, because he has looked upon the humble state of his servant. For from now on all generations will call me blessed, because he who is mighty has done great things for me, and holy is his name; from generation to generation he is merciful to those who fear him. He has demonstrated power with his arm; he has scattered those whose pride wells up from the sheer arrogance of their hearts. He has brought down the mighty from their thrones, and has lifted up those of lowly position; he has filled the hungry with good things, and has sent the rich away empty. He has helped his servant Israel, remembering his mercy, as he promised to our ancestors, to Abraham and to his descendants forever." Luke 1:46-55

Mary would stay in the Judean Hills with Elizabeth for the next three months, until the birth of Elizabeth's child, John the Baptist, and then Mary would return home to Nazareth probably after the child's circumcision ceremony.

So Mary stayed with Elizabeth about three months and then returned to her home. Now the time came for Elizabeth to have her baby, and she gave birth to a son. Her neighbors and relatives heard that the Lord had shown great mercy to her, and they rejoiced with her. On the eighth day they came to circumcise the child, and they wanted to name him Zechariah after his father. But his mother replied, "No! He must be named John." They said to her, "But none of your relatives bears this name." So they made signs to the baby's father, inquiring what he wanted to name his son. He asked for a writing tablet and wrote, "His

*name is John." And they were all amazed. Immediately Zechariah's
mouth was opened and his tongue released, and he spoke, blessing God.
All their neighbors were filled with fear, and throughout the entire
hill country of Judea all these things were talked about. All who heard
these things kept them in their hearts, saying, "What then will this
child be?" For the Lord's hand was indeed with him. Luke 1:56-66*

Once more the Holy Spirit, the third person of the triune nature of
God enters the equation through the lips of Zechariah, after baby John
has been circumcised on the eighth day. The scene would likely be in
the family home in the Judean Hills with lots of friends and neighbours
present. It is highly likely, considering the importance of the circumcision ceremony in the law of Moses and in naming the child, that Mary
would still have been present. With so many witnesses, the Holy Spirit
comes upon Zechariah in power, loosening his tongue as he prophesies
both the coming Messiah and the role of baby John in heralding the
Messiah. This is the first public message from God, through the Holy
Spirit, that the Messiah is coming in that generation and that those
present who are younger, would likely see him. How apt that the message was delivered by one in the priestly line.

*Then his father Zechariah was filled with the Holy Spirit and
prophesied,"Blessed be the Lord God of Israel, because he has come
to help and has redeemed his people. For he has raised up a horn of
salvation for us in the house of his servant David, as he spoke through
the mouth of his holy prophets from long ago, that we should be saved
from our enemies, and from the hand of all who hate us. He has
done this to show mercy to our ancestors, and to remember his holy
covenant- the oath that he swore to our ancestor Abraham. This oath
grants that we, being rescued from the hand of our enemies, may
serve him without fear, in holiness and righteousness before him for as
long as we live. And you, child, will be called the prophet of the Most
High. For you will go before the Lord to prepare his ways, to give his*

*people knowledge of salvation through the forgiveness of their sins.
Because of our God's tender mercy the dawn will break upon us from
on high to give light to those who sit in darkness and in the shadow
of death, to guide our feet into the way of peace." Luke 1:67-79*

If Mary was there, listening and watching, as she probably was, I
wonder what she was thinking? Three months prior, the Holy Spirit
through Elizabeth had affirmed that she, Mary, was going to bear the
Messiah and now this is affirmed publicly by the priest Zechariah,
authenticated (if it needed it) by the loosening of his tongue. It could
have been overwhelming, though I gather for the last three months,
Elizabeth and Mary had walked and worked together every day talking
about, discussing over and praising God for all that was to come. It was
probably the preparation Mary needed.

When Mary returned to Galilee, after three months, she was probably
beginning to show her pregnancy. Her husband to be, Joseph, knew he
had not been intimate with her, especially as she has been in the Judean
Hills with Elizabeth. Yet he knew, in his earthy wisdom, that someone
must have been, since she was pregnant.

*Now the birth of Jesus Christ happened this way. While his mother
Mary was engaged to Joseph, but before they came together, she was
found to be pregnant through the Holy Spirit. Matthew 1:18*

The Jewish law was very clear on what Joseph was to do if consensual
adultery was evident, and the resultant action was not pretty.

*If a man commits adultery with his neighbor's wife, both the
adulterer and the adulteress must be put to death. Leviticus 20:10*

Perhaps Joseph thought that Mary may have been raped whilst in the Judean Hills, the countryside if you will, and that therefore meant there was no penalty under the Mosaic law.

> *But if the man came across the engaged woman in the field and*
> *overpowered her and raped her, then only the rapist must die.*
> *You must not do anything to the young woman-she has done*
> *nothing deserving of death. Deuteronomy 22:25-26a*

However Joseph viewed the situation and the requirements of the law, he felt he had to act. He had choices and he determined to be as honourable as possible. Such was the measure of the man who upheld the paternal lineage of the Son of God. He decided to quietly walk away from Mary, he decided not to marry her, though this meant abandoning her to public disgrace.

> *Because Joseph, her husband to be, was a righteous*
> *man, and because he did not want to disgrace her, he*
> *intended to divorce her privately. Matthew 1:19*

It is reasonable to suggest that Joseph and Mary had a conversation or two when Mary returned from Elizabeth's home. It is likely that Mary did not discuss Gabriel's visit with Joseph before she left in a hurry to see Elizabeth three months earlier, but it's likely when confronted by Joseph with her pregnancy she told Joseph everything. Clearly Joseph didn't believe her – do you blame him?

Before we all beat up on Joseph, let's understand the geo-strategic circumstances. God promised to deliver his chosen people the Jews, yet 586 years previously Israel went into captivity and the Temple was destroyed. Sure Herod the Great had rebuilt the Temple, but the new occupier was the Roman Empire and Jewish hope of salvation was waning. The law had been taken to its zenith with differing religious sects vying for control and Jewish scribes and legalists had turned their faith into a regulatory nightmare. Everyone was waiting for a political and military restoration of Israel in the form of a king like David, and here a young girl was saying she was carrying the Saviour of the world, miraculously impregnated by the Holy Spirit of God. I feel for Joseph, as I feel for the vulnerability of a young Galilean girl who would have felt very alone. Luckily God intervened at the eleventh hour.

> *When he had contemplated this, an angel of the Lord appeared to him in a dream and said, "Joseph, son of David, do not be afraid to take Mary as your wife, because the child conceived in her is from the Holy Spirit. She will give birth to a son and you will name him Jesus, because he will save his people from their sins." This all happened so that what was spoken by the Lord through the prophet would be fulfilled: "Look! The virgin will conceive and give birth to a son, and they will name him Emmanuel," which means "God with us." When Joseph awoke from sleep he did what the angel of the Lord told him. He took his wife, but did not have marital relations with her until she gave birth to a son, whom he named Jesus. Matthew 1:20-25*

The morning dawn brings a polar opposite scene. Joseph awakes and ponders the magnitude of what he has just been told. Mary, oblivious to this revelation during the night, has probably endured a horrible night's sleep as she contemplated rejection, public disgrace and wondering how God will work out this mess. Joseph amazed, Mary downcast. I wonder how long it took Joseph to run to Mary's place with the good news.

I'm sure his first words were, 'I'm sorry I didn't believe you, when you said you were miraculously carrying the Saviour of the world.' If Mary's response was 'I told you so', Joseph's retort of 'an angel told me so' may have settled it. Mary had had three months to reconcile the revelation that she was carrying the Son of God, the creator and Saviour of the world. Joseph had five minutes. I hope they had coffee in Nazareth.

Yet the question remains why it took God over three months to let Joseph know? Why did God allow Joseph to question Mary, to consider divorce, for Mary to feel so rejected. Sometimes we are shipwrecked on God's omnipotence and marooned on His faithfulness. Suffice to say, Joseph in obedience took Mary as his wife and they remained celibate for the final six months of her pregnancy until after Jesus was born.

My wife and I have three beautiful sons and I well remember preparing for them all. Painting walls, decorating rooms, buying even more stuffed toys and stocking up on supplies. It was a wonderfully expectant time. There were discussions about names, hopes and dreams as to what our children would do and be. Joseph and Mary may have had a slightly different preparation. They were told their child would be a son and that his name would be Jesus. They were told he was the Son of God and He would claim King David's throne and rule forever and save the people from their sins. I don't know how you prepare to receive such a child into the world. I guess you just paint the walls blue, make a stuffed donkey, shear a sheep for a blanket and try not to think too hard about it all.

And what happened to John, the son of Zechariah and Elizabeth, the cousin of the soon-to-be Jesus the Christ, the Saviour of the world?

And the child kept growing and becoming strong in spirit, and he was in the wilderness until the day he was revealed to Israel. Luke 1:80

Thirty-odd years in the wilderness, growing strong, developing mentally and spiritually to be the prophesied type of Elijah, the one calling in the desert, to make straight paths for the coming Lord.

CHAPTER 2

Time is split

Jesus' birth and early years (circa 1 BC - 30 AD)

Time is about to be split

Jesus, the Saviour of the world, is to be born in a stable because those in palaces wanted to count their subjects. Prophecies over hundreds of years that pointed to this moment, would be realised in an instant. Celestial stars would guide wise men, angelic hosts would proclaim to less wise men and earthly rulers would tremble in fear. God's messenger angels would work overtime, God's prophets would see salvation and be dismissed from service, and Christmas would be engrained in our collective cultures. A stable would become a nursery, three gifts would become legend and the earthly mother of Jesus would quietly ponder what it all meant.

Time is split

Then just as quickly as time stopped and restarted, thirty years of quietness descended. The toddler, teenage and early man-hood years of Jesus would be silent, apart from the account of the twelve year old 'lost' in the Temple. There would be no mention of the first shaky steps of a little boy, the perfection of the eldest brother's behaviour or the vocation of the young man Jesus. Matthew 13:55 and Mark 6:3 point to Joseph being a carpenter and Jesus following in His earthly dad's footsteps, yet nothing more is mentioned about the work of the tradesman of Nazareth.

Silence

Mary the mother of Jesus would be present at the Cross and Jesus would ask the apostle John to care for her, but Joseph is not mentioned after Jesus was missing in the Temple at age twelve. It is reasonable to assume that Joseph died before Jesus' ministry began, as the gospels mention Mary and Jesus' brothers a number of times, but not Joseph. Jesus, as the eldest brother, would therefore have been instrumental in the funeral and as a carpenter probably made the casket or the litter on which His dad was carried and/or buried. I bet Jesus wept at the funeral of His dad, just as He wept at the burial site of His friend Lazarus, before He raised him from the dead. Nothing of Joseph is mentioned. With Joseph gone, Jesus would have taken on the role of the literal 'father' in the house as the eldest male. He would have had to continue to work and provide for the family and may well have taught His younger brothers the carpentry vocation. Yet nothing of this is mentioned.

Time is miraculously and powerfully split as Jesus is born then time goes silent as Jesus grows up.

The last six months of Mary's pregnancy in Nazareth passed with locals probably thinking the child was a result of the marriage between Joseph and Mary. There is no indication that anyone in the village knew of the awesome blessing that was in their midst. At the time of the impending birth of Jesus, Nazareth was a simple hill side town in Galilee. Now Nazareth is not just remembered, it is a global pilgrimage destination.

The birth at their home in Nazareth, customary in those times, was not to be. The Roman Caesar Augustus had other plans and it involved a count of those living under the dominion of Rome. Such was the heel of Rome, that a valid excuse of an expectant mother would not wash, and each family had to go to their ancestral home for the obligatory count.

Now in those days a decree went out from Caesar Augustus to register all the empire for taxes. This was the first registration, taken when Quirinius was governor of Syria. Everyone went to his own town to be registered. So Joseph also went up from the town of Nazareth in Galilee to Judea, to the city of David called Bethlehem, because he was of the house and family line of David. He went to be registered with Mary, who was promised in marriage to him, and who was expecting a child. Luke 2:1-5

As is the case at busy times, accommodation was at a premium. In this case there was none, and the expectant couple could only find lodging in a stable with the animals. It was a roof, but not the most hygienic or appropriate lodging to give birth, let alone to the Saviour of the world.

While they were there, the time came for her to deliver her child. And she gave birth to her firstborn son and wrapped him in strips of cloth and laid him in a manger, because there was no place for them in the inn. Luke 2:6-7

So the Son of God was born in the humblest of surrounds; the greatest of Kings in the simplest of settings. If ever there was a comparison between the self-appointed kings of the earth and the God-ordained king of the ages, this was it. Caesar in a palace demanding to know the number of his subjects, Jesus the servant king born in a stable. However the glory of the birth could not be contained.

Now there were shepherds nearby living out in the field, keeping guard over their flock at night. An angel of the Lord appeared to them, and the glory of the Lord shone around them, and they were absolutely terrified. But the angel said to them, "Do not be afraid! Listen carefully, for I proclaim to you good news that brings great joy to all the people: Today your Savior is born in the city of David. He is Christ the Lord. This will be a sign for you: You will find a baby wrapped in strips of cloth and lying in a manger." Suddenly a vast, heavenly army appeared with the angel, praising God and saying, "Glory to God in the highest, and on earth peace among people with whom he is pleased!" Luke 2:8-14

The angels of God now make a fourth appearance to foretell the coming Messiah, following Gabriel visiting firstly Zechariah and then Mary, and then another angel visiting Joseph in a dream. This fourth appearance is both public and powerful, involving a host of heaven descending loudly to proclaim the birth of the King of Kings. Yet they didn't appear to Caesar or Herod the Great or the religious elite. They appeared to the common man, the shepherds, to proclaim the birth of Jesus –the birth of the shepherd of the people of Israel (Micah 5:2-4) was first proclaimed to the humble shepherds of the flock.

Scripture only records the shepherds saying to each other, 'let's go to Bethlehem'. I think there is a space in time before this where the shepherds stare at each other in amazement. Many of them would have had to recover from the prostrate position to which they had fallen on the ground and the rest of them probably sat down in awe and wonder. What started as a single angel speaking to them with the fully glory of the Lord surrounding them, would turn into a great company of the host of heaven praising God. Thousands of angels resplendent and reflective of the glory of God saying 'glory to God in the highest heaven'. I think it might have been a little while before the poor shepherds got moving. Best not to think about who was looking after the sheep whilst they were gone, because I doubt any of them wanted to stay behind in the fields after such an invitation.

How did the shepherds know which stable to go to? Did they go through each stable one at a time or did the inspiration of God guide them, as the Magi were so guided afterwards? The answer is unknown, suffice to say they found Mary, Joseph and baby Jesus. They then proceeded to tell everyone in Bethlehem and surrounds about what they had seen. Praise was on their lips, glory was on their tongues, for they had been the first to see the Saviour of the world. They, like all who meet Jesus for the first time, would never forget it and would be changed for all time. Did anyone go back for the sheep I hear you ask? Good question, well asked.

When the angels left them and went back to heaven, the shepherds said to one another, "Let us go over to Bethlehem and see this thing that has taken place, that the Lord has made known to us." So they hurried off and located Mary and Joseph, and found the baby lying in a manger. When they saw him, they related what they had been told about this child, and all who heard it were astonished at what the shepherds said. But Mary treasured up all these words, pondering in her heart what they might mean. So the shepherds returned, glorifying and praising God for all they had heard and seen; everything was just as they had been told. Luke 2:15-20

Evidently the family either stayed in or around Bethlehem, a town only ten kilometres south of Jerusalem, because Jesus was circumsized and named on the eighth day.

At the end of eight days, when he was circumcised, he was named Jesus, the name given by the angel before he was conceived in the womb. Luke 2:21

Thirty-three days after the seven day wait for uncleanliness (forty days in total), Jesus was presented in the Temple as required by the law (Leviticus 12:1-8). Walking a 300 kilometre round trip back to Nazareth and then to Jerusalem was probably not wise, hence the next thirty-two days after the circumcision would probably have been spent in and around the Judean Hills, specifically Bethlehem. Let's hope the young family found more suitable lodging.

> *Now when the time came for their purification according to the law of Moses, Joseph and Mary brought Jesus up to Jerusalem to present him to the Lord (just as it is written in the law of the Lord, "Every firstborn male will be set apart to the Lord"), and to offer a sacrifice according to what is specified in the law of the Lord, a pair of doves or two young pigeons. Luke 2:22-24*

As devote followers of the law, Mary and Joseph would have presented baby Jesus to the priest on duty in the Temple on Mount Moriah on the fortieth day.

> *"When the days of her purification are completed for a son or for a daughter, she must bring a one year old lamb for a burnt offering and a young pigeon or turtledove for a sin offering to the entrance of the Meeting Tent, to the priest. The priest is to present it before the LORD and make atonement on her behalf, and she will be clean from her flow of blood. This is the law of the one who bears a child, for the male or the female child. If she cannot afford a sheep, then she must take two turtledoves or two young pigeons, one for a burnt offering and one for a sin offering, and the priest is to make atonement on her behalf, and she will be clean." Leviticus 12:6-8*

Because Luke 2:39 says that Joseph and Mary did everything required by the law, it is safe to say that Jesus was presented to the priest and the requisite offering was made. A pair of doves or two young pigeons were offered, though not a lamb. Evidently Jesus' natural family were quite poor and could not afford a lamb as an offering. There is also something beautiful running through this scene. A lamb was not offered for Jesus' birth, perhaps because Jesus would Himself become the final Passover lamb for us all at His death. Only one lamb would die, Jesus

Himself. None of this is presented in the gospel account, it is simply inferred. Since Jesus came to complete the law by ushering in grace, it is a fair assumption though.

What transpires in the Temple is nothing short of amazing and a sad indictment on the state of the Jewish faith at the time. The central part of the story should have been the presentation of Jesus to the priest, who was meant to represent God and His law. Nothing is mentioned about the priest's reaction so it is highly likely that when Jesus was presented to the priest, this 'servant' of God had no idea who it was that was being presented to him, or the gospels would have recorded his surprise and wonder. I think the priest took the two birds and did his religious duty with no insight, blinded to the reality of who it was in front of him. God also made no effort to open the priest's eyes. This is the first glimpse of God's rejection of the religious elite's interpretation of the law, a rejection that Jesus continued, ultimately leading to those same religious elite calling for Jesus to be crucified thirty-three years later. It is a sad story of a focus on religious rules rather than a relationship with God. A story of the priest in the Temple who did not recognise God amongst them, the very Messiah that they had all waited for. Tragic!

This religious ignorance is contrast with the living breathing relationship that Simeon and Anna have with God. They were the first of the prophets to divinely recognise Jesus. They who lived a life of worship, were given the opportunity to worship their Saviour that they had waited so long to see. Jesus was presented to a male priest who didn't recognise Him. Two prophets, one male and one female, presented themselves to the parents, recognising and proclaiming the Messiah. This is a beautiful picture of the impending grace of God coming equally to all people without the need for a priest to intercede. This is the first glimpse of grace (Simeon and Anna) completing and replacing the law (priest).

Now there was a man in Jerusalem named Simeon who was righteous and devout, looking for the restoration of Israel, and the Holy Spirit was upon him. It had been revealed to him by the Holy Spirit that he would not die before he had seen the Lord's Christ. So Simeon, directed by the Spirit, came into the temple courts, and when the parents brought in the child Jesus to do for him what was customary according to the law, Simeon took him in his arms and blessed God, saying, "Now, according to your word, Sovereign Lord, permit your servant to depart in peace. For my eyes have seen your salvation that you have prepared in the presence of all peoples: a light, for revelation to the Gentiles, and for glory to your people Israel." So the child's father and mother were amazed at what was said about him. Then Simeon blessed them and said to his mother Mary, "Listen carefully: This child is destined to be the cause of the falling and rising of many in Israel and to be a sign that will be rejected. Indeed, as a result of him the thoughts of many hearts will be revealed-and a sword will pierce your own soul as well!" There was also a prophetess, Anna the daughter of Phanuel, of the tribe of Asher. She was very old, having been married to her husband for seven years until his death. She had lived as a widow since then for eighty-four years. She never left the temple, worshiping with fasting and prayer night and day. At that moment, she came up to them and began to give thanks to God and to speak about the child to all who were waiting for the redemption of Jerusalem. Luke 2:25-38

It is likely after the ceremony in the Temple, the young family went back to Bethlehem and enjoyed an extended stay in the town, which is where the Magi found them some time later. Evidence for this includes the story below of the Magi finding the child in 'a house' not a stable. The word for 'child' in the Greek text, 'paidion', does not refer to a newborn baby (as the word 'brephos' does in Luke 2:12). This also points to the belief that the Magi did not come to Bethlehem immediately after the shepherds. The Magi's visit occurred a relatively short time before the death of King Herod, and from the mention that

Herod sought to kill all male children of an age 'two years and under' it is reasonable to believe that Jesus was no longer a newborn baby.

After Jesus was born in Bethlehem in Judea, in the time of King Herod, wise men from the East came to Jerusalem saying, "Where is the one who is born king of the Jews? For we saw his star when it rose and have come to worship him." When King Herod heard this he was alarmed, and all Jerusalem with him. After assembling all the chief priests and experts in the law, he asked them where the Christ was to be born. "In Bethlehem of Judea," they said, "for it is written this way by the prophet: 'And you, Bethlehem, in the land of Judah, are in no way least among the rulers of Judah, for out of you will come a ruler who will shepherd my people Israel.'" Then Herod privately summoned the wise men and determined from them when the star had appeared. He sent them to Bethlehem and said, "Go and look carefully for the child. When you find him, inform me so that I can go and worship him as well." After listening to the king they left, and once again the star they saw when it rose led them until it stopped above the place where the child was. When they saw the star they shouted joyfully. As they came into the house and saw the child with Mary his mother, they bowed down and worshiped him. They opened their treasure boxes and gave him gifts of gold, frankincense, and myrrh. After being warned in a dream not to return to Herod, they went back by another route to their own country. Matthew 2:1-12

Who are these Magi from the east that came to see Jesus? All sorts of church tradition has grown up concerning who they are, but the bottom line is we don't know. Due east of Jerusalem is modern day Jordan, Saudi Arabia, Iraq, Iran, Afghanistan, Pakistan, India and China, depending on how far east you go, so take your pick of possible home countries. We don't even know how many of them there were, however three gifts were given, so it's fair to say there were three Magi. There is clearly more than one, or Matthew's gospel would have said 'a', meaning single Magus arrived. Two Magi is a strange number to give three gifts. If there were four Magi, the idea that one of the three would travel all that way and not give a gift to the creator and Saviour of the world is almost unimaginable, so three Magi remains the best guess. Having said that, travel in those times could be dangerous, so a retinue of some substantial numbers would have accompanied them making the travelling group quite large.

This substantial retinue followed a star and this star led them first to Jerusalem and then right to the place that Jesus was staying. This doesn't sound like any astrological star I've seen. Considering we have already had four angelic encounters, including the Host of Heaven surrounded by the Glory of God, it doesn't take much to believe God sent a sign to wise men of the earth so they could worship Jesus.

King Herod received the Magi so they were clearly significant in stature or perhaps the story of being led by a star caught his attention. Their message of the birth of the King of the Jews in Bethlehem was verified by the chief priests and teachers of the law who confirmed what the scriptures said about that city. It is interesting that a star led the Magi to Jerusalem, but it was scripture that led them to Bethlehem and to Jesus. It's probably more interesting that the religious elite knew where the Messiah was to be born but couldn't be bothered walking the ten kilometres to Bethlehem to check on it. Matthew's gospel said all of Jerusalem was abuzz about the Magi's visit; all except the religious elite who thought they knew best and thought that God only spoke through them.

How the religious elite missed the birth of Jesus is beyond me. Surely they would have heard the excited stories of the shepherds about how the angels appeared to them? The shepherds went and told everyone so word must have filtered back. They must have known the story of Zechariah and at the very least the arrival of the Magi must have provoked some thought. Apparently not. If you think you know best and you 'use people and care for things', as was their custom, your level of connectedness with people will be limited. If you think nothing great can occur without your involvement and perhaps imprimatur, you will miss every move of God, 'who opposes the proud but shows favour to the humble' (James 4:6b). If you 'care for people and use things' God can use you, as He used shepherds and Magi to herald the King of Kings.

The Magi then commenced their final ten kilometre trip to Bethlehem to find Jesus, and as they took their steps in faith, the star moved to above where Jesus was staying. I guess faith moves mountains, and stars. When they arrived they presented three gifts: gold, the metal of God for the new born King; frankincense, a fragrance for a priest; and myrrh, an anointing oil commonly used in burials. This later gift was a sign of the suffering servant to come, noting that Jesus would later have an alabaster jar of fragrant perfume poured on him to prepare him for his death (Matthew 26:6-13). Gifts for a priestly king whose purpose was ultimately to die to connect us back to God.

The Magi probably stayed the night as they were warned in a dream, unless they were day dreaming, not to go back the ten kilometres to Jerusalem to see King Herod but to return to their country by another route. So from Bethlehem they headed back to where they had come from, touched and changed by being with Jesus. Whatever route their life had been on before, they returned home via and to a different route. No one knows why these men had been called by a sign. Maybe others were called and only these men answered. Maybe others contemplated the journey and thought it possible but too difficult, whereas these Magi thought it may be difficult, but it is possible. What we do know is that once called, they followed the sign. At Jerusalem they were instructed by scripture and when they returned home, it was at the prompting of the living God. It literally took the resources of heaven to move the wisdom of the world to see Jesus. As it was then, so it is today.

As Max Lucado notes, 'God uses every possible means to communicate with you. The wonders of nature call to you. The promises and prophecies of scripture speak to you. God Himself reaches out to you.'[9] So let God's signs and wonders, nature all around, the vastness of the heavens lead you to His Word. Let His Word soak your soul and lead you to worship His son, Jesus. As you're changed like the Magi, know that God will lead you home. For that is true wisdom, as opposed to what followed in Herod's court in Jerusalem.

Clearly Herod the Great was as furious as he was vain, as he was not going to allow any other King to arise in Israel. So he ordered the destruction of all boys that met any of the possible time lines of Jesus' birth, a staggering two year period. God's plans can never be frustrated though, as an angel appears a sixth time (the fifth time was to warn the Magi not to return to Herod) to warn the young family to flee to Egypt.

After they had gone, an angel of the Lord appeared to Joseph in a dream and said, "Get up, take the child and his mother and flee to Egypt, and stay there until I tell you, for Herod is going to look for the child to kill him." Then he got up, took the child and his mother during the night, and went to Egypt. He stayed there until Herod died. In this way what was spoken by the Lord through the prophet was fulfilled: "I called my Son out of Egypt." When Herod saw that he had been tricked by the wise men, he became enraged. He sent men to kill all the children in Bethlehem and throughout the surrounding region from the age of two and under, according to the time he had learned from the wise men. Then what was spoken by Jeremiah the prophet was fulfilled: "A voice was heard in Ramah, weeping and loud wailing, Rachel weeping for her children, and she did not want to be comforted, because they were gone." After Herod had died, an angel of the Lord appeared in a dream

---

9   Lucado, Max, 'Because of Bethlehem' Thomas Nelson.

*to Joseph in Egypt saying, "Get up, take the child and his mother, and go
to the land of Israel, for those who were seeking the child's life are dead."
So he got up and took the child and his mother and returned to the land
of Israel. But when he heard that Archelaus was reigning over Judea in
place of his father Herod, he was afraid to go there. After being warned
in a dream, he went to the regions of Galilee. He came to a town called
Nazareth and lived there. Then what had been spoken by the prophets
was fulfilled, that Jesus would be called a Nazarene. Matthew 2:13-23*

*So when Joseph and Mary had performed everything
according to the law of the Lord, they returned to Galilee,
to their own town of Nazareth. Luke 2:39*

It is not known how long the little family stayed in Egypt or where in
Egypt they stayed. The stay was no longer than two - five years though,
the gap between the census and Herod the Great's death. Dating these
events gets a little interesting and there is continued contention and
scholarly debate as to which date is accurate. Considering this is one
of the major inputs into whether Jesus was crucified in 30 AD or 33
AD the debate will continue. 'Hang on,' I hear you say, 'the birth of
Jesus split time between Before Christ (BC) and Anno Domini (AD)
literally 'the year of the Lord', thus Jesus had to be born in '0 BC / 0
AD'. All of that is true, except the lads doing the modern calendar got
it a few years out of date, so that Jesus was probably born sometime
between 1 BC and 4 BC. Does any of this make any difference to salvation through grace? Not one iota, but interesting none the less.

In brief, Caesar Augustus (Publius Sulpicius Quirinius), a legendary
soldier and former Consul was appointed Imperial Legate (governor)
of the province of Roman Syria in about 6 BC. Judea was declared a
Roman province in the same twelve-month period and a census was
undertaken of the new territory for taxation purposes. This all makes
sense and this was the census time in which Jesus was born, sometime

after 4 BC as these things take time to organise and be communicated. Death and taxes, you can't escape them.

However, when did Herod die and thus when did Jesus return from Egypt? Herod's death is based on Josephus's writings[10] where he states that Herod died shortly before Passover and that his death was preceded by a lunar eclipse. There were only two visible lunar eclipses shortly before Passover during the possible range of Herod's death, one in 4 BC and the other in 1 BC. Therefore these are the two date options. The eclipse on 13 March 4 BC, was apparently only visible very late at night in Judea and then there were two eclipses in 1 BC that were far more visible. This book is going with the eclipses in 1 BC as being when Herod left this mortal coil. This then feeds into the date for Jesus' death being 3rd April 33 AD.

Since an angel appeared in a dream to Joseph after Herod died, it is fair to state that Jesus headed back to Nazareth sometime after 1 BC. Either way, the family intended to return to the region of Judea (Matthew 2:22) but were dissuaded by the reign of Herod Archelaus, son of Herod the Great and so they journeyed to Galilee, back to Nazareth. Josephus writing in 'Antiquities' quotes Archelaus as cruel and as treacherous as his father, citing a case within a few months after his accession of sending horsemen to disperse a crowd and slaying 3,000 men in the process. Antipas on the other hand was seen as milder. This, and possibly Antipas's absence from Galilee on a visit to Rome at the time, may well have led Joseph to return to Galilee as a safer prospect. As an aside, when Jesus was approximately nine years old, the oppression of Archelaus became so intolerable that both Jews and Samaritans complained of him to the Emperor, and he was deposed and banished

---

[10]   Josephus, 'Antiquities of the Jews', book 17, chapter 6.4, and 'Wars of the Jews', book 1, chapter 33

to Gaul (modern day France).[11] Great for the Jews, not so great for the French.

Jesus in Nazareth

Very little is known about Jesus for the next twenty-eight to thirty years. He clearly grew and became strong, wise and full of stature and the grace of God. We know he never knew sin, so He was literally the perfect child. Consequently I always feel for his younger brothers and sisters (born biologically to Joseph and Mary), because how would they ever be able to live up to the perfection of their elder brother? Colloquially, I can hear Mary disciplining the smaller children saying, 'why can't you be more like your eldest brother, he wouldn't have pulled your sisters hair?' True, though in defence of the smaller children, their older brother was the Son of God. At the same time I envy those siblings, decades spent daily with their 'brother' the lamb of God.

And the child grew and became strong, filled with wisdom,
and the favor of God was upon him. Luke 2:40

However one story recorded in the Bible gives a glimpse of the preteen Jesus that is both prescient of the purpose for which Jesus came and problematic for very worried parents. The law required all Jews to celebrate three festivals each year in Jerusalem: Passover; Pentecost and Tabernacles (Exodus 23:14-17, 34:22-23 and Deuteronomy 16:16). But by the first century, Josephus records that God fearing Jews made only one journey a year for the Passover because of the distances involved.[12]

The Passover was the major feast celebrated at the beginning of the Jewish year, 15th of Nisan, which falls in March or April in our cur-

---

[11]   Josephus, Antiquities. xvii. 2, 5, 6, 8, 9.
[12]   Josephus, Life 345-54; Antiquities 17.9.3 213-14; Jewish Wars 2.1.3
        10-12; 2.14.3 280

rent calendar. Only men were required to make the journey, however it appears Jesus' whole family went, leading some to conclude that Mary's presence shows her commitment and zealousness for the law.[13] Presumably Jesus may have had some biological brothers and sisters at this stage so they also would have gone for the ride.

Now Jesus' parents went to Jerusalem every year for the feast of the Passover. When he was twelve years old, they went up according to custom. But when the feast was over, as they were returning home, the boy Jesus stayed behind in Jerusalem. His parents did not know it, but (because they assumed that he was in their group of travelers) they went a day's journey. Then they began to look for him among their relatives and acquaintances. When they did not find him, they returned to Jerusalem to look for him. After three days they found him in the temple courts, sitting among the teachers, listening to them and asking them questions. And all who heard Jesus were astonished at his understanding and his answers. When his parents saw him, they were overwhelmed. His mother said to him, "Child, why have you treated us like this? Look, your father and I have been looking for you anxiously." But he replied, "Why were you looking for me? Didn't you know that I must be in my Father's house?" Yet his parents did not understand the remark he made to them. Then he went down with them and came to Nazareth, and was obedient to them. But his mother kept all these things in her heart. Luke 2:41-51

Jesus is twelve years old. Around this age the oral Torah (laws, statutes, and legal interpretations that were not recorded in the five books of Moses) is imparted through more intense religious instruction, thus finding Jesus in the Temple at this age is appropriate[14]. The custom of

---

13   Preisker, H,. Theological dictionary of the New Testament, translated and edited by Geoffrey Bromiley, 10 volumes (Grand Rapids: Eerdmans, 1964-76), p. 373.

14   Jewish Mishna, (Niddah 5:6; Megilla 4:6; Avot 5:12)

bar mitzvah for a thirteen-year-old Jewish boy was not in place at this time.[15]

There is no mention in the Temple of dear Simeon and Anna the prophets who announced Jesus' arrival. Perhaps they had been called to Glory, their race having been run and won. The priests and teachers of the law are still there and still ignorant of who Jesus is, though amazed at His knowledge. Perhaps they should have paid more attention to Simeon and Anna.

I feel for Jesus' earthly parents, as they are clearly frantic, as you would expect. I've lost one child for five minutes in a busy street and it is gut-wrenching. Losing a child for days is generally a state emergency. Not only had Joseph and Mary lost their child, though at twelve under Jewish law he was a man, they had literally lost the Son of God. That is not a good look.

As an historical aside, it had happened once before. What you say, Jesus had been previously lost? Well an arch-type of Jesus in the form of the Ark of the Covenant had been lost twice. Firstly after the battle at Ebenezer when the Ark was captured by the Philistines (1 Samuel 4-6) and remained with the Philistines for seven months. God ensured the Ark's return by closing the wombs of every Philistine woman and giving the nation a dose of haemorrhoids. And people say God has no sense of humour. The second time was more unforgivable. The Ark was returned to Beth Shemesh in Israel (1 Samuel 6:13) and then almost immediately moved to Kiriath Jearim (1 Samuel 7:1) where it remained for somewhere between 40 and 100 years (noting that King Saul's 40 year reign is in the middle of this period) before David bought the Ark up to Jerusalem. The Psalms say that the Ark was 'found' in the fields of Jearim (Psalm 132:6). You can only find something that is lost, so

---

15   Fitzmyer, J., The Gospel According to Luke: Introduction, Translation, and Notes, Volume 1; Volume 28, Doubleday, 1981, p. 440

it is probable that the people forgot that the Ark was hiding up in the hills of Kiriath Jearim. The Tabernacle was still at Shiloh and was then moved to Nob, but apparently no one bothered to find the Ark to put in the Tabernacle.

Yet the grace of God always shines through. The Ark was found in the woods and taken to Jerusalem and Jesus was found in Jerusalem and taken home to the woods. Jesus returns to Nazareth and sets the example for all children in obedience to His earthly parents and the ire of every younger sibling for being the perfect brother.

And Jesus increased in wisdom and in stature, and in favor with God and with people. Luke 2:52

CHAPTER 3

Inauguration

Baptism - Cana (30 AD)

Jesus' ministry now formally commences – a ministry of only three years, culminating in Jesus laying down His life as a sacrifice, once and for all, for the sin of mankind. The Day of Atonement, that annual sacrifice in the Temple where the priest would sprinkle the blood of the lamb on the mercy seat of the Ark to atone for the people's sin (Exodus 30:10), replaced once and for all by the shed blood of Jesus, the ultimate lamb of God. These life-changing, history-shattering events commenced with the voice of one calling in the wilderness, 'prepare the way for the Lord'.

Thirty years prior it was John the Baptist's father, Zechariah pointing to the coming Jesus and calling his son out as the prophet that would go before the Lord. (Luke 1:67-79). Now thirty years later that prophecy will be fulfilled and Jesus, and his cousin, John the Baptist would meet at the waters of baptism. Jesus would commence His ministry and become greater, and cousin John, having fulfilled his mission, would become lesser.

Thirty-one years prior, the angel Gabriel came to Zechariah in the Temple, in front of the curtain that separated the Most Holy Place from the Holy Place (Luke 1:5-22). John had been chosen by lot (randomly) to burn incense on the altar in front of where the Ark should have been behind the curtain (remember the Ark disappeared when the first Temple was destroyed by the Babylonians in 586 BC so a stone sat in its place in the Most Holy Place behind the curtain). Gabriel would proclaim to Zechariah that his son John would herald the Messiah. Six months later the same angel Gabriel would come to Mary to proclaim that she would be the earthly mother of the Messiah.

Now that angelic message of herald and Messiah would meet, the prophecy would be fulfilled and the earthly mission of the Saviour of the world would commence.

Our story now starts anew. Jesus is approximately thirty years old and his cousin John, son of Elizabeth and Zechariah, affectionately known as 'John the Baptist' commences his God-ordained ministry to pave the way for the coming Messiah.

> *In the fifteenth year of the reign of Tiberius Caesar, when Pontius Pilate was governor of Judea, and Herod was tetrarch of Galilee, and his brother Philip was tetrarch of the region of Iturea and Trachonitis, and Lysanias was tetrarch of Abilene, during the high priesthood of Annas and Caiaphas, the word of God came to John the son of Zechariah in the wilderness. Luke 3:1-2*

> *The beginning of the gospel of Jesus Christ, the Son of God. Mark 1:1*

God had foretold through the prophets of old that a messenger would come before Jesus to herald the coming Messiah. John was that man with a message of repentance and water immersion, or baptism, as a sign of that repentance. Dunking under water as an outward sign of an inward change was a little novel to the Jews. They were use to ceremonial washing before going to the Temple but few had been called to be fully immersed. Indeed the last person called to be immersed in the Jordan River was Naaman, the Aramian General covered in leprosy (2 Kings 5) but that was over 700 years prior and he had to be dunked seven times. Yet the people of Jerusalem and Judea and those who lived along the Jordan River came down to hear John and went under the waters as a sign of their repentance and change of heart.

In those days John the Baptist came into the wilderness of Judea proclaiming, "Repent, for the kingdom of heaven is near." For he is the one about whom Isaiah the prophet had spoken: "The voice of one shouting in the wilderness, 'Prepare the way for the Lord, make his paths straight.'" Now John wore clothing made from camel's hair with a leather belt around his waist, and his diet consisted of locusts and wild honey. Then people from Jerusalem, as well as all Judea and all the region around the Jordan, were going out to him, and he was baptizing them in the Jordan River as they confessed their sins. Matthew 3:1-6

As it is written in Isaiah the prophet, "Look, I am sending my messenger ahead of you, who will prepare your way, the voice of one shouting in the wilderness, 'Prepare the way for the Lord, make his paths straight.'" In the wilderness John the baptizer began preaching a baptism of repentance for the forgiveness of sins. People from the whole Judean countryside and all of Jerusalem were going out to him, and he was baptizing them in the Jordan River as they confessed their sins. John wore a garment made of camel's hair with a leather belt around his waist, and he ate locusts and wild honey. Mark 1:2-6

He went into all the region around the Jordan River, preaching a baptism of repentance for the forgiveness of sins. As it is written in the book of the words of Isaiah the prophet, "The voice of one shouting in the wilderness: 'Prepare the way for the Lord, make his paths straight. Every valley will be filled, and every mountain and hill will be brought low, and the crooked will be made straight, and the rough ways will be made smooth,

and all humanity will see the salvation of God.'"
Luke 3:3-6

As the people flocked to hear the new message, the religious elite who controlled the Jewish faith and enforced the strict laws, notably the Pharisees and the Sadducees, also came down to see what was drawing the people. John was typically blunt and preached the law at them, reminding them of their responsibilities under the all encompassing law.

But when he saw many Pharisees and Sadducees coming to his baptism, he said to them, "You offspring of vipers! Who warned you to flee from the coming wrath? Therefore produce fruit that proves your repentance, and don't think you can say to yourselves, 'We have Abraham as our father.' For I tell you that God can raise up children for Abraham from these stones! Even now the ax is laid at the root of the trees, and every tree that does not produce good fruit will be cut down and thrown into the fire. Matthew 3:7-10

So John said to the crowds that came out to be baptized by him, "You offspring of vipers! Who warned you to flee from the coming wrath? Therefore produce fruit that proves your repentance, and don't begin to say to yourselves, 'We have Abraham as our father.' For I tell you that God can raise up children for Abraham from these stones! Even now the ax is laid at the root of the trees, and every tree that does not produce good fruit will be cut down and thrown into the fire." So the crowds were asking him, "What then should we do?" John answered them, "The person who has two tunics must share with the person who has none, and the person who has food must do likewise." Tax collectors also came to be baptized, and they said to him, "Teacher, what should we do?" He told them, "Collect no more than you are required to." Then some soldiers also asked him, "And as for us-what

should we do?" He told them, "Take money from no one by violence
or by false accusation, and be content with your pay." Luke 3:7-14

The Pharisees and the Sadducees will feature heavily in every chapter from this point so its worthwhile giving a brief synopsis of these 'brood of vipers' or main religious parties, as they are the players in the Jewish religious hierarchy and politics of the day. Like all politics there are also minor parties or groups in Israel at the time including elders, scribes, teachers of the law, Herodians, Essenes, Zealots and the list goes on.

The main Jewish ruling body or council was referred to as the Sanhedrin and was an assembly of twenty-three judges appointed in every city in Israel. The 'Supreme Court' of the Sanhedrin was referred to as the Great Sanhedrin and was located in Jerusalem. It had seventy-one members[16], made up predominantly by the two main religious parties, the Pharisees and the Sadducees.

The Sadducees were the wealthy, powerful upper class that held the majority of the seats in the Sanhedrin, including that of chief priest and high priest. They were also collaborators as they worked hard to keep the peace by basically agreeing with the decisions of the Roman occupiers. They were not well regarded by the common man however, who preferred the leaders from the party of the Pharisees. Though the Sadducees held the majority of seats in the Sanhedrin, it appears they had little choice but to acquiesce with the policy positions of the Pharisaic minority, due to the Pharisees popularity with the people.

The Pharisees (Hebrew word meaning 'separate') gave oral tradition equal authority to the written Word of God, the Torah (being the first five books of the Old Testament) and they strictly followed the Torah and their tradition, and demanded as such from everyone else. The

---

[16] http://www.jewishvirtuallibrary.org/the-sanhedrin, accessed on 30 November 2016.

Sadducees considered only the Torah, making them more conservative. The two groups also differed on other issues of doctrine including whether angels and demons existed and whether the dead will rise in the last days (Acts 23:6-8). You wouldn't see any differences between major schools of faith today I'm sure?

Suffice to say, John didn't have a lot of time for these religious elite, and, as we'll discover, nor did Jesus. One of the reasons was that these religious elite had been teaching the people to expect the coming Messiah to be a worldly political and religious leader who would re-establish King David's throne in Israel, in other words, evict the Romans. With such a prospect, it is no wonder the people asked John if he was the prophesied Messiah.

John was typically blunt in stating his job was to baptise in water for repentance in preparation for the Messiah who would baptise with the Holy Spirit. This was the first time that any of the people would have heard of the Holy Spirit. The families of Jesus and John had experienced the Holy Spirit and felt the power of the third person of the Godhead, but this was new to the common man. Indeed it would be fifty days after Passover, when Jesus was crucified, that the person of the Holy Spirit, first alluded to here by John the Baptist and promised by Jesus, would arrive in power (Acts 2:1-13).

While the people were filled with anticipation and they all wondered whether perhaps John could be the Christ, John answered them all, "I baptize you with water, but one more powerful than I am is coming-I am not worthy to untie the strap of his sandals. He will baptize you with the Holy Spirit and fire. His winnowing fork is in his hand to clean out his threshing floor and to gather the wheat into his storehouse, but the chaff he will burn up with inextinguishable fire." And in this way, with many other exhortations, John proclaimed good news to the people. Luke 3:15-18

He proclaimed, "One more powerful than I am is coming after me; I am not worthy to bend down and untie the strap of his sandals. I baptize you with water, but he will baptize you with the Holy Spirit." Mark 1:7-8

"I baptize you with water, for repentance, but the one coming after me is more powerful than I am-I am not worthy to carry his sandals. He will baptize you with the Holy Spirit and fire. His winnowing fork is in his hand, and he will clean out his threshing floor and will gather his wheat into the storehouse, but the chaff he will burn up with inextinguishable fire." Matthew 3:11-12

John the Baptist did exactly what he had been called to do. Remember in chapter 1 when the angel Gabriel appeared to John's father Zechariah and said to him…

He will turn many of the people of Israel to the Lord their God. And he will go as forerunner before the Lord in the spirit and power of Elijah, to turn the hearts of the fathers back to their children and the disobedient to the wisdom of the just, to make ready for the Lord a people prepared for him." Luke 1:16-17

I often wonder whether John the Baptist and Jesus, whose respective mothers were cousins and thus so were they, hung out together. Elizabeth, John's mother was very old when she had him, so it was likely Jesus went with His parents to Elizabeth's funeral and probably to Zechariah's as well. Mary and Elizabeth were both joined through the incredible prophecy from the angel Gabriel so it would be natural for them both to hang out, especially as the elderly Elizabeth approached her final years. They were both observant families in the Jewish tradition so each Passover, both families would have been in Jerusalem together. It seems entirely possible and almost self-evident that John and Jesus, of the same age and cousins, had a relationship. They may have been friends. Yet at some point they each took on various roles as adults, Jesus became a carpenter and John headed into the wilderness, clothed in camel hair and eating simply. Their reunion though, was filled with power.

As John was baptising at the Jordan River, Jesus came from his home in Nazareth in Galilee to be baptised, marking the beginning of His ministry. There is conjecture about where on the Jordan River John was baptising as it is likely he used multiple sites to reach as many people as possible, including inland from the Jordan River when John was baptising at Aenon near Salim (John 3:23). Scripture records that people came from Jerusalem and Galilee to be baptised by John.

As good an argument as any is that Jesus was baptised at the place where the Israelites under Joshua crossed the Jordan to enter the promised land. If this was the case, the stones that John the Baptist was referring to in Luke 3:8 could have been the twelve stones placed on Israelite soil after the crossing of the Jordan River (Joshua 4:1-9). Or it could have just been a pile of rocks John pointed to. It's worth thinking about. What matters is that Jesus commenced his public ministry as He rose from the waters of baptism.

Then Jesus came from Galilee to John to be baptized by him in the Jordan River. But John tried to prevent him, saying, "I need to be baptized by you, and yet you come to me?" So Jesus replied to him, "Let it happen now, for it is right for us to fulfill all righteousness." Then John yielded to him. After Jesus was baptized, just as he was coming up out of the water, the heavens opened and he saw the Spirit of God descending like a dove and coming on him. And a voice from heaven said, "This is my one dear Son; in him I take great delight." Matthew 3:13-17

Now in those days Jesus came from Nazareth in Galilee and was baptized by John in the Jordan River. And just as Jesus was coming up out of the water, he saw the heavens splitting apart and the Spirit descending on him like a dove. And a voice came from heaven: "You are my one dear Son; in you I take great delight." Mark 1:9-11

Now when all the people were baptized, Jesus also was baptized. And while he was praying, the heavens opened, and the Holy Spirit descended on him in bodily form like a dove. And a voice came from heaven, "You are my one dear Son; in you I take great delight." So Jesus, when he began his ministry, was about thirty years old. Luke 3:21-23a

The moment Jesus revealed Himself as the Son of God and commenced His ministry, the devil (also known as satan, lucifer, or the prince of darkness) came hunting him. A fallen angel who once led the worship in Heaven until he wanted the praise himself and was cast out by God, he is the personification of evil.

The devil wants nothing more than the destruction of God's people, who are made in the image of God. His plan was to destroy Jesus, for he thought with Jesus gone, God's plan fails. The devil didn't realise that God's plan was always for Jesus to willingly lay down His life. Jesus came to earth to be the sinless lamb of God, to pay the price you and I deserved for our sins and for us to have His righteousness and inherit eternal life. That is the gospel of salvation. It is for that purpose that Jesus was born as a child, lived as a man and died as our Saviour. The devil didn't quite get that. In fact he didn't quite get a lot of things, which is why as a fallen angel, he is the devil.

Enough of getting to the end of the story before we've even begun it. The Holy Spirit of God led Jesus into the Judean wilderness to allow him to be tempted by the devil. For as the Bible says…

For since he himself suffered when he was tempted, he is able to help those who are tempted. Hebrews 2:18

*For we do not have a high priest incapable of sympathizing
with our weaknesses, but one who has been tempted in every
way just as we are, yet without sin. Hebrews 4:15*

Jesus fasted for forty days in the Judean wilderness before the devil
came to tempt Him. As an aside, life revolves around the three laws of
four. Four minutes without air, four days without water and forty days
without food and we as humans are dead. Jesus, very much a man, is
on the edge of death through starvation, at His maximum physical
weakness when the devil comes. This is not a spiritual fast or a divine
sustainment of life like Moses on Mount Sinai. This is Jesus as a man,
suffering as a man, at the absolute point of starvation and death like
any other man in such circumstances. This was Jesus being tempted at
his point of greatest weakness, so it could be said for us later on:

*No trial has overtaken you that is not faced by others. And God
is faithful: He will not let you be tried beyond what you are
able to bear, but with the trial will also provide a way out so
that you may be able to endure it. 1 Corinthians 10:13*

This is no pleasant fast for forty days. This is the scorching, treeless
desert of the Judean wilderness with little water, shade or respite from
the elements.

*Then Jesus, full of the Holy Spirit, returned from the Jordan River
and was led by the Spirit in the wilderness, where for forty days he
endured temptations from the devil. He ate nothing during those
days, and when they were completed, he was famished. Luke 4:1-2*

*Then Jesus was led by the Spirit into the wilderness to
be tempted by the devil. After he fasted forty days and
forty nights he was famished. Matthew 4:1-2*

The Spirit immediately drove him into the wilderness. He was in the wilderness forty days, enduring temptations from Satan. He was with wild animals, and angels were ministering to his needs.
Mark 1:12-13

The devil tempted Jesus with the same things he tempts us all with today: lust of the flesh, pride of life and lust of the eyes (1 John 2:16).

Temptation 1 - lust of the flesh

The tempter came and said to him, "If you are the Son of God, command these stones to become bread." But he answered, "It is written, 'Man does not live by bread alone, but by every word that comes from the mouth of God." Matthew 4:3-4

The devil said to him, "If you are the Son of God, command this stone to become bread." Jesus answered him, "It is written, 'Man does not live by bread alone." Luke 4:3-4

Jesus was hungry and the devil tempts Him to turn stone into bread. Jesus responded by pointing back to the forty years the Jews wandered in the desert and how God fed them through the miracle of manna, referring to the following Word of God:

So he humbled you by making you hungry and then feeding you with unfamiliar manna. He did this to teach you that humankind cannot live by bread alone, but also by everything that comes from the LORD's mouth. Deuteronomy 8:3

Temptation 2 - the pride of life

Then the devil took him to the holy city, had him stand on the highest point of the temple, and said to him, "If you are the Son of God, throw yourself down. For it is written, 'He will command his angels concerning you' and 'with their hands they will lift you up, so that you will not strike your foot against a stone.'" Jesus said to him, "Once again it is written: 'You are not to put the Lord your God to the test." Matthew 4:5-7

Then the devil brought him to Jerusalem, had him stand on the highest point of the temple, and said to him, "If you are the Son of God, throw yourself down from here, for it is written, 'He will command his angels concerning you, to protect you,' and 'with their hands they will lift you up, so that you will not strike your foot against a stone.'" Jesus answered him, "It is said, 'You are not to put the Lord your God to the test." Luke 4:9-12

The devil quotes scripture (Psalm 91:11-12) to tempt Jesus to use his power. Again Jesus responded by referring to the following Word of God:

You must not put the LORD your God to the test..... Deuteronomy 6:16

Temptation 3 - lust of the eyes

Again, the devil took him to a very high mountain, and showed him all the kingdoms of the world and their grandeur. And he said to him, "I will give you all these things if you throw yourself to the ground and worship me." Then Jesus said to him, "Go away, Satan! For it is written: 'You are to worship the Lord your God and serve only him.'" Matthew 4:8-10

Then the devil led him up to a high place and showed him in a flash all the kingdoms of the world. And he said to him, "To you I will grant this whole realm-and the glory that goes along with it, for it has been relinquished to me, and I can give it to anyone I wish. So then, if you will worship me, all this will be yours." Jesus answered him, "It is written, 'You are to worship the Lord your God and serve only him." Luke 4:5-8

The devil suggests to Jesus a quick route to Messiahship devoid of the cross. The devil already has control of the world (Ephesians 2:2) but was now ready to give everything to Christ in return for allegiance and servitude. Again Jesus responds by referring to the following Word of God:

You must revere the LORD your God, serve him....Deuteronomy 6:13

What is remarkable is that Jesus didn't quote Deuteronomy back to the devil word for word. Jesus dismissed satan, not by quoting the law that said *'fear the Lord your God'*, but by quoting the fulfilled law that His death would bring about on the cross reflected by the words *'worship the Lord your God'*. Even at His moment of absolute weakness, Jesus still reflected His true purpose, to journey towards the cross to lay down His life and usher in the New Covenant of Grace. A covenant where there is no fear, for fear would be beaten at the cross.

Faced with the greatest of temptations and trials by the most wicked of schemers, satan, who himself is a charlatan and a fraud *'And no wonder, for even Satan disguises himself as an angel of light.'* (2 Corinthians 11:14), Jesus, through the word of God, prevails. Since He prevailed and we who believe *'so that in Him we would become the righteousness of God'* (2 Corinthians 5:21) we also can prevail.

Then the devil left him, and angels came and began
ministering to his needs. Matthew 4:11

So when the devil had completed every temptation, he departed
from him until a more opportune time. Luke 4:13

Through these tumultuous days, John would keep preaching, calling Jews to repentance and baptising in different locations. After Jesus had finished His wilderness experience, the Pharisees and Jewish religious elite came down from their ivory towers in Jerusalem to question John on what he was doing. The location is a village called Bethany on the east of the Jordan River. This is not Bethany near Jerusalem, it is another village. Local tradition, with nothing to support it, cites the location as Bethabara[17]. What is probable is that the location was within easy reach of Galilee as the following day Jesus commences calling disciples in that area and on the third day Jesus performs His first miracle at a wedding in Cana in Galilee. So an area close to the southern border of Galilee, around the Sea of Galilee makes some sense.

Now this was John's testimony when the Jewish leaders sent priests and Levites from Jerusalem to ask him, "Who are you?" He confessed-he did not deny but confessed-"I am not the Christ!" So they asked him, "Then who are you? Are you Elijah?" He said, "I am not!""Are you the Prophet?" He answered, "No!" Then they said to him, "Who are you? Tell us so that we can give an answer to those who sent us. What do you say about yourself?" John said, "I am the voice of one shouting in the wilderness, 'Make straight the way for the Lord,' as Isaiah the prophet said." (Now they had been sent from the Pharisees.) So they asked John, "Why then are you baptizing if you are not the Christ, nor Elijah, nor the Prophet?" John answered them, "I baptize with water. Among you stands one whom you do not recognize, who is coming after me. I am not worthy to untie the strap of his sandal!" These things happened in Bethany across the Jordan River where John was baptizing. John 1:19-28

Jesus shows up the day after John told the religious elite that he was heralding the way for the Saviour of the world, who was now amongst them. He had finished in the wilderness and after being attended to by angels, which evidently included something to eat, Jesus walks back to the Jordan River, somewhere close to Galilee. I bet Jesus looked thin when John saw Him walking towards him.

---

[17] Ellicott C. J., A Bible commentary for English Readers (8 vols), Cassell and Company, 1905, Chronology and Geography Introduction p. 93.

On the next day John saw Jesus coming toward him and said, "Look, the Lamb of God who takes away the sin of the world! This is the one about whom I said, 'After me comes a man who is greater than I am, because he existed before me.' I did not recognize him, but I came baptizing with water so that he could be revealed to Israel." Then John testified, "I saw the Spirit descending like a dove from heaven, and it remained on him. And I did not recognize him, but the one who sent me to baptize with water said to me, 'The one on whom you see the Spirit descending and remaining-this is the one who baptizes with the Holy Spirit.' I have both seen and testified that this man is the Chosen One of God." John 1:29-34

If only the Pharisees, Priests and Levites had stayed the extra day to hear John's testimony about Jesus and to meet Jesus. They didn't, and Jesus walks past this area of the Jordan River near 'Bethabara' where John was baptising. John sees Jesus and can do nothing but again cry out and point to Jesus as the 'Lamb of God that takes away the sin of the earth', the first public statement that Jesus would indeed lay down his life so we could receive eternal life.

What Jesus did for the rest of that day is unknown. The next day, Jesus goes back to that same spot where John is baptising, this time with some of His disciples and again John can do nothing but cry out and point to Jesus as the 'Lamb of God'.

Again the next day John was standing there with two of his disciples. Gazing at Jesus as he walked by, he said, "Look, the Lamb of God!" When John's two disciples heard him say this, they followed Jesus. Jesus turned around and saw them following and said to them, "What do you want?" So they said to him, "Rabbi" (which is translated Teacher), "where are you staying?" Jesus answered, "Come and you will see." So they came and saw where he was staying, and they stayed with him that day. Now it was about four o'clock in the afternoon. Andrew, the brother of Simon Peter, was one of the two disciples who heard what John said and followed

Jesus. He first found his own brother Simon and told him, "We have found the Messiah!" (which is translated Christ). Andrew brought Simon to Jesus. Jesus looked at him and said, "You are Simon, the son of John. You will be called Cephas" (which is translated Peter). John 1:35-42

This time, two of John's disciples, Andrew and an unknown disciple, hear the declaration of Jesus as the 'Lamb of God' and instantly follow Jesus. I feel a bit sorry for John the Baptist, he just had two of his disciples pinched. However as John the Baptist says twice:

This is the one about whom I said, "After me comes a man who is greater than I am, because he existed before me." John 1:30

He must become more important while I become less important. John 3:30

Scripture is silent on who this unknown disciple is, though I think there is a case for the author of this gospel, John the beloved as being this 'unknown disciple' as he's the only one who references the account. The first thing Andrew does is find his brother, Simon Peter, to tell him he has found Jesus the Messiah, and it appears the two of them and the 'unknown disciple' spend that day and night with Jesus. What also supports the 'unknown disciple being John argument, is that Jesus' three closest friends through His ministry years were the first three He called and spent time with. Only these three were on the mount of transfiguration, in the room when Jarius's daughter was raised from the dead and in the centre of the Garden of Gethsemane with Jesus. These three closest of friends were the first called by Jesus.

On the next day Jesus wanted to set out for Galilee. He found Philip and said to him, "Follow me." (Now Philip was from Bethsaida, the town of Andrew and Peter.) Philip found Nathanael and told him, "We have found the one Moses wrote about in the law, and the prophets also wrote about-Jesus of Nazareth, the son of Joseph." Nathanael replied, "Can anything good come out of Nazareth?" Philip replied, "Come and see." Jesus saw Nathanael coming toward him and exclaimed, "Look, a true Israelite in whom there is no deceit!" Nathanael asked him, "How do you know me?" Jesus replied, "Before Philip called you, when you were under the fig tree, I saw you." Nathanael answered him, "Rabbi, you are the Son of God; you are the king of Israel!" Jesus said to him, "Because I told you that I saw you under the fig tree, do you believe? You will see greater things than these." He continued, "I tell all of you the solemn truth-you will see heaven opened and the angels of God ascending and descending on the Son of Man." John 1:43-51

The next day, Jesus leaves this village of 'Bethabara' with the first three disciples and heads to the region of Galilee. He enlists Philip en route who goes and grabs his friend Nathanael, who is a resident of Cana (John 21:2). Considering Nathanael is from Cana and Jesus and the disciples were heading to Cana for a wedding the next day, it is probable that the group spent the day walking to Cana and Jesus and his now five disciples overnighted in the town. Such a walk would have been twenty - thirty kilometres from the northern part of the Jordan River.

The first recorded miracle - power over the elements

Jesus has now arrived in Galilee, the region where He grew up, and is in the town of Cana to attend a wedding. The town is six kilometres north-east from Nazareth and is considered to be the modern day town of Kfar-Cana. There is nothing especially noteworthy about Cana. It was a typical little village in the lower part of Galilee. What is significant is that Jesus apparently has strong family connections to this town and its proximity to Nazareth would indicate Jesus would have been here many times growing up.

The wedding at Cana is the first recorded miracle of Jesus. Mary, Jesus' mother, His brothers and His first five disciples were all in attendance.

It appears that Mary is more than an attendee as Jesus' disciples are quickly invited at the last minute and she gets personally involved in the issue of wine running out. This suggests more of a family wedding affair, perhaps even the wedding of one of Jesus' sisters or relatives to a local from Cana, though this is only interesting speculation. If it was one of Jesus' family being married, Jesus as the head of the house may well have had a role in proceedings. I bet He gave a great speech!

Jewish weddings of the era took place over seven days, and to run out of wine would have been a major embarrassment to the organising family. If this wedding was connected in some way to Jesus' earthly family, this would explain Mary coming to Jesus for help. This embarrassing issue was probably at the end of the week's celebration, so perhaps Jesus and His disciples only attended for the last day or two. I know, there are lots of 'what ifs' here.

Now on the third day there was a wedding at Cana in Galilee. Jesus' mother was there, and Jesus and his disciples were also invited to the wedding. When the wine ran out, Jesus' mother said to him, "They have no wine left." Jesus replied, "Woman, why are you saying this to me? My time has not yet come." His mother told the servants, "Whatever he tells you, do it." Now there were six stone water jars there for Jewish ceremonial washing, each holding twenty or thirty gallons. Jesus told the servants, "Fill the water jars with water." So they filled them up to the very top. Then he told them, "Now draw some out and take it to the head steward," and they did. When the head steward tasted the water that had been turned to wine, not knowing where it came from (though the servants who had drawn the water knew), he called the bridegroom and said to him, "Everyone serves the good wine first, and then the cheaper wine when the guests are drunk. You have kept the good wine until now!" Jesus did this as the first of his miraculous signs, in Cana of Galilee. In this way he revealed his glory, and his disciples believed in him. John 2:1-11

Jesus' response to His Mother's request for help would indicate that perhaps He was not prepared for His first miracle to be performed at a wedding. Yet the prophet Jeremiah had foretold that in the Messianic age *they will be radiant with joy over the good things the LORD provides, the grain, the fresh wine...* '(Jeremiah 31:12). Food, or maybe wine for thought.

What is fascinating is that Jesus turned the six stone jars full of water into the highest quality wine. These stone jars contained water for ceremonial washing, so Jesus effectively created between 444 and 666 litres of superior, host-stunning wine (read that as Australian Penfolds Grange, the finest red Shiraz in the world. Yes I'm an Australian author with a heavy bias to Australian produce and wine and I won't hear another word about my scriptural interpretation that Jesus turned Galilean water into Australian red wine). Apart from a prophetic portend of how great Australian wine is, it would appear to be far more wine that any of the guests could consume in the last day or two of the feast. This is over abundance, unmerited favour, more than enough – a powerful symbol of grace being ushered in by Jesus.

As an aside, have you ever wondered what the waiter thought as he dipped his ladle into the ceremonial water jar and drew forth sparkling red wine? I can imagine him stumbling dumbfounded to the host and pouring his glass in wide-eyed wonder. I think the miracle would also have made a strong impression on Jesus' new disciples, teaching them from the start that He is indeed the Son of Jehovah Jireh, their provider.

> *Even when you are old, I will take care of you, even when you have gray hair, I will carry you. I made you and I will support you; I will carry you and rescue you. Isaiah 46:4*

It is also reasonable to read into the text the significance of marriage between a man and a woman as the setting for the first miracle. Jesus placed His stamp of approval on the covenant of marriage through His attendance and His miracle certainly added to the joy of the wedding, as His presence adds joy to our lives (Luke 2:10).

After this he went down to Capernaum with his mother and brothers and his disciples, and they stayed there a few days. John 2:12

Once the wedding was complete, Jesus, His mother, brothers and five disciples travelled for a day (forty kilometres) from Cana to Capernaum where they stayed for a few days. There is no mention of Jesus' earthy father, Joseph. Considering the wedding was possibly some type of family affair, it is reasonable to suggest that Joseph had possibly died earlier, never to see the revolution of love His earthly son would bring. The fact that in a further two years, Jesus, hanging on the cross, asked the disciple John to take care of Mary, Jesus' mother, is further proof that Joseph was no longer alive (John 19:26-27).

Capernaum

A little bit about Capernaum. This small town was a fishing village on the northern shore of the Sea of Galilee. It is mentioned in all four gospels and became the centre for Jesus' ministry in Galilee. Peter, Andrew, James, John and Matthew were all from here. Considering the first four were fishermen and Matthew was a 'despised' tax collector, this group of five of the eventual twelve disciples probably didn't hang out before Jesus called them. What a great picture of the unity the gospel of grace brings.

Capernaum is part of the evangelical triangle that included the villages of Bethsaida and Chorazin. These three villages were visited often by Jesus and He healed literally everyone sick, possessed or diseased. Three villages of very healthy people. Yet apparently their hearts weren't healthy, prompting Jesus' condemnation of them (Matthew 11:21-23). There was a synagogue in Capernaum made from the black basalt that defines the area and consequently everything else in the town was built from black basalt. The ruins of this first-century synagogue still exist today, with the ruins of a later fourth-century white stone synagogue sitting on top. It is an interesting contrast to see the black basalt buildings in Capernaum compared to the whitish sandstone structures everywhere else in Israel including in Jerusalem where almost everything was, and continues to be, built from Jerusalem sandstone. This just demonstrates the different geological properties of Galilee which are also seen further east towards the modern Golan heights, a rich fertile area popular for vineyards.

Josephus also referred to Capernaum as a fertile spring and apparently stayed the night there after bruising his wrist in a riding accident at Bethsaida.[18] Clearly he should have been more careful. Oil and grain mills have been discovered in the area which brings to life Jesus' statement that He is the bread of life. The remains of harbours have also been identified, that point to fishing as a mayor source of activity for the region. Suffice to say that this town appeared to be a smaller regional hub of sorts for Galilee, sitting on the northern shore of the Sea of Galilee and away from the Roman city of Tiberius to the west of the Sea.

---

[18] Josephus, 'The Life of Flavius Josephus' 94AD, p. 72.

CHAPTER 4

Death threats

Passover - seventh disciple (30 - 31 AD)

Passover Friday 7th - Sunday 10th April 30 AD
Jesus' first visit to Jerusalem during His ministry (three years to the cross)

The wedding in Cana was close to the time of the Jewish Passover. We learnt in the previous chapter that Jesus' family went to Jerusalem every year for the Passover as was the custom of devout families. It is fair to say that this is His thirtieth Passover in Jerusalem. This one though will be different. Jesus now travels to Jerusalem not as part of the family, but as the Son of God who has officially entered His ministry years. For decades Jesus would have observed the religious elite, especially the Pharisees and the Sadducees, ply their version of the law over the people. For decades Jesus would have been obedient to the law. Now Jesus starts His ministry to fulfil the law, thus confrontation with the religious elite is both inevitable and immediate.

> *Now the Jewish feast of Passover was near, so*
> *Jesus went up to Jerusalem. John 2:13*

It is a 136 kilometre walk from Capernaum on the northern tip of the Sea of Galilee via the Jordan Valley, past Jericho to Jerusalem. This is just short of a week's journey with his five disciples and perhaps family

81

members in tow. There is plenty of time for Jesus to contemplate His actions. Remember Jesus had been to Jerusalem and the Temple for at least twenty-nine previous Passovers, so he has often seen the perversion of the sacrifice of the lamb to God being turned into a money-making scheme through differential exchange rates, all in the Temple courts. Arriving at the Temple at the start of His ministry, Jesus made a whip from cords and drove the money makers out of the Temple. Even the process of making a whip takes time, so this was no rash action, but a considered act of zeal for the house of prayer.

He found in the temple courts those who were selling oxen and sheep and doves, and the money changers sitting at tables. So he made a whip of cords and drove them all out of the temple courts, with the sheep and the oxen. He scattered the coins of the money changers and overturned their tables. To those who sold the doves he said, "Take these things away from here! Do not make my Father's house a marketplace!" His disciples remembered that it was written, "Zeal for your house will devour me." So then the Jewish leaders responded, "What sign can you show us, since you are doing these things?" Jesus replied, "Destroy this temple and in three days I will raise it up again." Then the Jewish leaders said to him, "This temple has been under construction for forty-six years, and are you going to raise it up in three days?" But Jesus was speaking about the temple of his body. So after he was raised from the dead, his disciples remembered that he had said this, and they believed the scripture and the saying that Jesus had spoken.Now while Jesus was in Jerusalem at the feast of the Passover, many people believed in his name because they saw the miraculous signs he was doing. But Jesus would not entrust himself to them, because he knew all people. He did not need anyone to testify about man, for he knew what was in man. John 2:14-25

Interestingly, the first words Jesus spoke to the religious elite in the Temple pointed them to His exact purpose for life – to replace the Temple as the centre of worship and the sacrifice of animals as atonement, with His own body as the final sacrifice, once and for all, for the sin of mankind by rising from the dead after three days. It was fitting that Jesus spoke these words about His own impending sacrifice on the day of Passover when the lamb was sacrificed. It is also clear that His five disciples had no idea what He was talking about (John 2:22) although He evidently performed a range of signs and wonders to accompany His words and people believed in Him as the impending new earthly king of Israel. Jesus would always reject the people's overt desire to make him a physical king in the line and order of King David, for that was never His intent. That was never the purpose of scandalous grace for which He came.

During Jesus' stay in Jerusalem for the Passover, a Pharisee called Nicodemus from the Jewish ruling council, a member of the Great Sanhedrin and one of the seventy-one senior leaders of Israel, came to see Jesus. He was motivated by the unbelievable and the unexplained miracles of Jesus. He was so worried about being seen meeting Jesus though, he came secretly at night, sneaking through the back alleys – but hey, at least he turned up. The dialogue between the two is fascinating and it is easy to see how this Pharisee, the first to come to see Jesus, would also be one of the two to bury Jesus as his life changed through this encounter and perhaps through these words:

> *For this is the way God loved the world: He gave his*
> *one and only Son, so that everyone who believes in him*
> *will not perish but have eternal life. John 3:16*

Nicodemus, like all who hear or read this conversation was different from that moment on. The final time we read about him, was when he accompanied Joseph of Arimathea (John 19:39) to speak to the Roman prefect, Pilate, to get Jesus' body and bury Him. Only a man changed by an encounter with Jesus would risk everything to do such a thing. Sadly, it appears that only Nicodemus and Joseph were changed by meeting Jesus. The other sixty-nine members of the Great Sanhedrin simply crucified His body and missed His message.

Now a certain man, a Pharisee named Nicodemus, who was a member of the Jewish ruling council, came to Jesus at night and said to him, "Rabbi, we know that you are a teacher who has come from God. For no one could perform the miraculous signs that you do unless God is with him."Jesus replied, "I tell you the solemn truth, unless a person is born from above, he cannot see the kingdom of God." Nicodemus said to him, "How can a man be born when he is old? He cannot enter his mother's womb and be born a second time, can he?" Jesus answered, "I tell you the solemn truth, unless a person is born of water and spirit, he cannot enter the kingdom of God. What is born of the flesh is flesh, and what is born of the Spirit is spirit. Do not be amazed that I said to you, 'You must all be born from above.' The wind blows wherever it will, and you hear the sound it makes, but do not know where it comes from and where it is going. So it is with everyone who is born of the Spirit." Nicodemus replied, "How can these things be?" Jesus answered, "Are you the teacher of Israel and yet you don't understand these things? I tell you the solemn truth, we speak about what we know and testify about what we have seen, but you people do not accept our testimony. If I have told you people about earthly things and you don't believe, how will you believe if I tell you about heavenly things? No one has ascended into heaven except the one who descended from heaven— the Son of Man. Just as Moses lifted up the serpent in the wilderness, so must the Son of Man be lifted up, so that everyone who believes in him may have eternal life." For this is the way God loved the world: He gave his one and only Son, so that everyone who believes in him will not perish but have eternal life. For God did not send his Son into the world to condemn the world, but that the world should be saved through him. The one who believes in him is not condemned. The one who does not believe has been condemned already, because he has not believed in the name of the one and only Son of God. Now this is the basis for judging: that the light has come into the world and people loved the darkness rather than the light, because their deeds were evil. For everyone who does evil deeds hates the light and does not come to the light, so that their deeds will not be exposed. But the one who practices the truth comes to the light, so that it may be plainly evident that his deeds have been done in God. John 3:1-21

Judean countryside

After the Passover festival had concluded, Jesus and His five disciples headed into the Judean countryside where Jesus taught His disciples, who then baptised those who came to see and hear Jesus (John 4:2).

After this, Jesus and his disciples came into Judean territory, and there he spent time with them and was baptizing. John 3:22

John the Baptist was also preaching and baptising at the same time at Aenon nears Salim. 'Ænon' or Aenon is the Greek form of the Semitic word for 'spring' or 'natural fountain'. It is only mentioned once in the Bible and it is conjecture where the location is. A good guess is west of the Jordan River near a naturally occurring water source.

John was also baptizing at Aenon near Salim, because water was plentiful there, and people were coming to him and being baptized. (For John had not yet been thrown into prison.) Now a dispute came about between some of John's disciples and a certain Jew concerning ceremonial washing. So they came to John and said to him, "Rabbi, the one who was with you on the other side of the Jordan River, about whom you testified — see, he is baptizing, and everyone is flocking to him!" John replied, "No one can receive anything unless it has been given to him from heaven. You yourselves can testify that I said, 'I am not the Christ,' but rather, 'I have been sent before him.' The one who has the bride is the bridegroom. The friend of the bridegroom, who stands by and listens for him, rejoices greatly when he hears the bridegroom's voice. This then is my joy, and it is complete. He must become more important while I become less important." The one who comes from above is superior to all. The one who is from the earth belongs to the earth and speaks about earthly things. The one who comes from heaven is superior to all. He testifies about what he has seen and heard, but no one accepts his testimony. The one who has accepted his testimony has confirmed clearly that God is truthful. For the one whom God has sent speaks the words of God, for he does not give the Spirit sparingly. The Father loves the Son and has placed all things under his authority. The one who believes in the Son has eternal life. The one who rejects the Son will not see life, but God's wrath remains on him. John 3:23-36

The words of John the Baptist herald the end of his ministry of announcing Jesus, now that Jesus has formally appeared in Jerusalem at Passover. John the Baptist would be summarily arrested and later murdered to please the puerile antics of a pre-pubescent girl.

"He must become more important while I become less important." John 3:30

But when John rebuked Herod the tetrarch because of Herodias, his brother's wife, and because of all the evil deeds that he had done, Herod added this to them all: He locked up John in prison. Luke 3:19-20

Now when Jesus heard that John had been imprisoned, he went into Galilee. Matthew 4:12

*Now after John was imprisoned, Jesus went into Galilee and proclaimed the gospel of God.
Mark 1:14*

Samaria
Having attended Passover and withdrawn with His five disciples to the Judean countryside, Jesus now walks the 135 kilometre journey back to

Galilee heading north through the countryside via Samaria, stopping at a village called Sychar. When Jesus walked from Galilee to Jerusalem, Samaria wasn't mentioned, so why is it now? The answer lies in history – doesn't it always – and in this case the bitter history between the northern kingdom of the Jews (Israel) and the southern kingdom of the Jews (Judah). Such was the enmity in the time of Jesus, that Jews walking from Galilee to Jerusalem would take the longer route through the Jordan Valley, which Jesus did on his way to Jerusalem, rather than walk the shorter route directly south through Samaria.

Firstly a bit of history. Nine hundred years earlier, after the death of King Solomon in 975 BC, the nation of Israel split into north and south on the basis of taxation without representation (1 Kings 11:26-39 and 1 Kings 12:1-24). Oh how much agony has been caused by this issue of taxation! The northern tribes of Israel were collectively called Israel, and their capital city was Samaria (1 Kings 16:24). The southern tribes of Judah, Benjamin and Simeon were collectively called Judah, and their capital city was Jerusalem. Jerusalem and Samaria are fifty kilometres apart.

All the resultant Kings of Israel were frankly quite evil and failed to follow God, who subsequently thrust them from His presence in the form of the Assyrian invasion and sacking in 722 BC. The Old Testament, especially Kings and Chronicles lists their failings ad nauseum. The Assyrians deported many of the people of the northern tribes and forced their assimilation into indigenous populations in modern day Iraq, Iran and perhaps even as far as Afghanistan (2 Kings 17:5-6) literally creating the lost tribes of Israel. The Assyrians then sent five foreign non-Jewish eastern groups of people to settle in northern Israel (2 Kings 17:22-41) to replace the Israelite tribes that had been deported. These five foreign groups brought with them their own religions and customs and diminished the remanent northern Israelite identity and culture. The eastern foreigners intermarried with the remaining much-depleted Israelite population and consequently, a hybrid people group became the foundation of the Samaritan people.

Throughout the next 700 years the Samaritans developed their own version of Judaism. They still believed in the God of Israel, but they worshipped at Mount Gerizim (instead of Jerusalem) with their own-adapted worship practices. The Samaritans had their own Torah in Aramaic, which differed from the Hebrew Torah in places, and the Samaritans did not accept the poetic and prophetic books of the Hebrew scriptures. Around 400 BC the Samaritans built a temple on Mount Gerizim, causing hostility between Jews and Samaritans. The Jews ultimately destroyed the Samaritan temple in 128–129 BC.

Consequently most Jews regarded the Samaritans as inbred, ignorant, superstitious, and outside of God's favour. That was until Jesus took the short road home and bought the good news to the little, insignificant, Samaritan village of Sychar. The whereabouts of Sychar is unknown, although the scripture reference referring to land Jacob gave to Joseph points to it being near Shechem (modern day Nablus). The block of ground would be the one that Abraham bought and passed down through Isaac to Jacob, who gave it to Joseph, and where Joseph was buried (Genesis 33:19, Genesis 48:22 and Joshua 24:32). So Jesus stops at the well dug by Jacob (hence it is called 'Jacob's Well') near the ground where the original Patriachs, those called of God – indeed Jesus' own earthly legal relatives – were buried. He stops to draw water from Jacob's Well and speak to the locals about Himself as the living water. The analogy was not lost on them.

The photo above was taken by the American colony photo department in approximately 1898 and shows Mount Gerizim taken from Jacob's well.

Now when Jesus knew that the Pharisees had heard that he was winning and baptizing more disciples than John (although Jesus himself was not baptizing, but his disciples were), he left Judea and set out once more for Galilee. But he had to pass through Samaria. Now he came to a Samaritan town called Sychar, near the plot of land that Jacob had given to his son Joseph. Jacob's well was there, so Jesus, since he was tired from the journey, sat right down beside the well. It was about noon. A Samaritan woman came to draw water. Jesus said to her, "Give me some water to drink." (For his disciples had gone off into the town to buy supplies.) So the Samaritan woman said to him, "How can you—a

Jew-ask me, a Samaritan woman, for water to drink?" (For Jews use nothing in common with Samaritans.) Jesus answered her, "If you had known the gift of God and who it is who said to you, 'Give me some water to drink,' you would have asked him, and he would have given you living water.""Sir," the woman said to him, "you have no bucket and the well is deep; where then do you get this living water? Surely you're not greater than our ancestor Jacob, are you? For he gave us this well and drank from it himself, along with his sons and his livestock." Jesus replied, "Everyone who drinks some of this water will be thirsty again. But whoever drinks some of the water that I will give him will never be thirsty again, but the water that I will give him will become in him a fountain of water springing up to eternal life." The woman said to him, "Sir, give me this water, so that I will not be thirsty or have to come here to draw water." He said to her, "Go call your husband and come back here." The woman replied, "I have no husband." Jesus said to her, "Right you are when you said, 'I have no husband,' for you have had five husbands, and the man you are living with now is not your husband. This you said truthfully!" The woman said to him, "Sir, I see that you are a prophet. Our fathers worshiped on this mountain, and you people say that the place where people must worship is in Jerusalem." Jesus said to her, "Believe me, woman, a time is coming when you will worship the Father neither on this mountain nor in Jerusalem. You people worship what you do not know. We worship what we know, because salvation is from the Jews. But a time is coming-and now is here-when the true worshipers will worship the Father in spirit and truth, for the Father seeks such people to be his worshipers. God is spirit, and the people who worship him must worship in spirit and truth." The woman said to him, "I know that Messiah is coming" (the one called Christ); "whenever he comes, he will tell us everything." Jesus said to her, "I, the one speaking to you, am he." Now at that very moment his disciples came back. They were shocked because he was speaking with a woman. However, no one said, "What do you want?" or "Why are you speaking with her?" Then the woman left her water jar, went off into the town and said to the people, "Come, see a man who told me everything I ever did. Surely he can't be the Messiah, can he?" So they left the town and began coming to him. Meanwhile the disciples were urging him, "Rabbi, eat something." But he said to them, "I have food to eat that you know nothing about." So the disciples began to say to one another, "No one brought him anything to eat, did they?" Jesus said to them, "My food is to do the will of the one who sent me and to complete his work. Don't you say, 'There are four more months and then comes the harvest?' I tell you, look up and see that the fields are already white for harvest! The one who reaps receives pay and gathers fruit for eternal life, so that the one who sows and the one who reaps can rejoice together. For in this instance the saying is true, 'One sows and another reaps.' I sent you to reap what you did not work for; others have labored and you have entered into their labor." Now many Samaritans from that town believed in him because of the report of the woman who testified, "He told me everything I ever did." So when the Samaritans came to him, they began asking him to stay with them. He stayed there two days, and because of his word many more believed. They said to the woman, "No longer do we believe because of your words, for we have heard for ourselves, and we know that this one really is the Savior of the world." John 4:1-42

What a beautiful image of Jesus reaching out to a people despised as half-breeds and to a woman held in low esteem in that hated community; It is an image of Jesus demonstrating to His disciples that salvation is for everyone and that opportunities to share the good news are abundant. Jesus then seals that message by staying in the village for two days.

After the two days he departed from there to Galilee. John 4:43

Jesus starts His Galilee ministry

After his short stay in Samaria, Jesus continues on his way north to Galilee. He heads to His home town, Nazareth, via numerous other towns; then on to Cana – the scene of the wedding miracle –and, finally, Capernaum.

It is probable that Jesus' first five disciples did not accompany Him to the surrounds of Galilee, which include Nazareth and Cana. There is no mention of the disciples, and they next appear back in Capernaum doing what they had grown up doing, fishing. If they had remained with Jesus after the Samaria visit, it is likely that Simon Peter and Andrew would not have been found in their father's boat.

> *Then Jesus, in the power of the Spirit, returned to Galilee, and news about him spread throughout the surrounding countryside. He began to teach in their synagogues and was praised by all. Luke 4:14-15*

> *Jesus went into Galilee and proclaimed the gospel of God. He said, "The time is fulfilled and the kingdom of God is near. Repent and believe the gospel!" Mark 1:14b-15*

Nazareth

Fresh from the miracle at the wedding in Cana and the multiple signs at the Passover in Jerusalem you would have thought that Jesus would receive a right royal hometown welcome in Nazareth. Everyone would have known Him since birth and would have known that there was something different about Him. Now that He has demonstrated with signs and wonders the grace upon His life as the Son of God, surely the town would have been waiting in humility and awe. Surely? They would have all heard about the miracles... palm branches would be laid on the ground for sure...

The photo above of Nazareth was taken by the American colony photo department between 1898 and 1946.

Now Jesus came to Nazareth, where he had been brought up, and went into the synagogue on the Sabbath day, as was his custom. He stood up to read, and the scroll of the prophet Isaiah was given to him. He unrolled the scroll and found the place where it was written, "The Spirit of the Lord is upon me, because he has anointed me to proclaim good news to the poor. He has sent me to proclaim release to the captives and the regaining of sight to the blind, to set free those who are oppressed, to proclaim the year of the Lord's favor." Then he rolled up the scroll, gave it back to the attendant, and sat down. The eyes of everyone in the synagogue were fixed on him. Then he began to tell them, "Today this scripture has been fulfilled even as you heard it being read." All were speaking well of him, and were amazed at the gracious words coming out of his mouth. They said, "Isn't this Joseph's son?" Jesus said to them, "No doubt you will quote to me the proverb, 'Physician, heal yourself!' and say, 'What we have heard that you did

in Capernaum, do here in your hometown too.'" And he added, "I tell
you the truth, no prophet is acceptable in his hometown. But in truth
I tell you, there were many widows in Israel in Elijah's days, when the
sky was shut up three and a half years, and there was a great famine
over all the land. Yet Elijah was sent to none of them, but only to a
woman who was a widow at Zarephath in Sidon. And there were
many lepers in Israel in the time of the prophet Elisha, yet none of them
was cleansed except Naaman the Syrian." When they heard this, all
the people in the synagogue were filled with rage. They got up, forced
him out of the town, and brought him to the brow of the hill on which
their town was built, so that they could throw him down the cliff. But
he passed through the crowd and went on his way. Luke 4:16-30

Humility and awe was apparently not the order of the day. Jesus tells
His community that He is the promised Messiah and they respond by
trying to throw Him off a cliff. How's that for a local home-grown hero
welcome? Jesus then leaves Nazareth for Cana and Capernaum. Sadly
the gospels only record one other later instance of Jesus going back to
His home town. This rejection of Jesus and the attempt to kill Him
by those seemingly closest to Him is one of the saddest stories in the
gospel. The rejection of the Saviour of the world by those who knew
Him best.

The second recorded miracle – power over sickness

This rejection is contrast with the humility and desperation of a royal
official from Capernaum, probably a high-ranking official in the service of the Tetrarch of Galilee and Perea, Herod Antipas (who inci-
dentally would put John the Baptist to death). Jesus' second recorded
miracle is the first that touches the physical life of people. The royal
official makes a thirty kilometre dash from Capernaum to Cana to beg
Jesus to heal his son, something every father can relate to. Jesus simply
speaks and the father simply believes, in stark contrast to the previous
situation in Nazareth. The scene is instructive for us also, to simply

believe. No special words, no laying on of special hands, no special oil, just believe!

> *(For Jesus himself had testified that a prophet has no honor in his own country.) So when he came to Galilee, the Galileans welcomed him because they had seen all the things he had done in Jerusalem at the feast (for they themselves had gone to the feast). Now he came again to Cana in Galilee where he had made the water wine. In Capernaum there was a certain royal official whose son was sick. When he heard that Jesus had come back from Judea to Galilee, he went to him and begged him to come down and heal his son, who was about to die. So Jesus said to him, "Unless you people see signs and wonders you will never believe!" "Sir," the official said to him, "come down before my child dies." Jesus told him, "Go home; your son will live." The man believed the word that Jesus spoke to him, and set off for home. While he was on his way down, his slaves met him and told him that his son was going to live. So he asked them the time when his condition began to improve, and they told him, "Yesterday at one o'clock in the afternoon the fever left him." Then the father realized that it was the very time Jesus had said to him, "Your son will live," and he himself believed along with his entire household. Jesus did this as his second miraculous sign when he returned from Judea to Galilee. John 4:44-54*

Capernaum

Jesus now chooses to settle in Capernaum, a Galilean seaside town thirty kilometres from His hometown of Nazareth, and there officially starts to call His disciples, noting that He had been travelling with five 'disciples' already. The first two, Andrew and Peter, were two of the original five disciples that Jesus called after He returned from the wilderness. They had been with Jesus for the miracle at Cana, and had travelled to Jerusalem and then back through Samaria. So when Jesus called them to 'follow him' they dropped everything. The second two to be called were John and his brother James. If John was indeed the 'unknown disciple' and had therefore also been at Cana, Jerusalem and in Samaria, that would explain his rapid following of Jesus, grabbing his brother James and both of them leaving their father.

While in Galilee, he moved from Nazareth to make his home in Capernaum by the sea, in the region of Zebulun and Naphtali, so that what was spoken by Isaiah the prophet would be fulfilled: "Land of Zebulun and land of Naphtali, the way by the sea, beyond the Jordan, Galilee of the Gentiles-the people who sit in darkness have seen a great light, and on those who sit in the region and shadow of death a light has dawned." From that time Jesus began to preach this message: "Repent, for the kingdom of heaven is near." Matthew 4:13-17

So he went down to Capernaum, a town in Galilee, and on the Sabbath he began to teach the people. They were amazed at his teaching, because he spoke with authority. Luke 4:31-32

As he was walking by the Sea of Galilee he saw two brothers, Simon (called Peter) and Andrew his brother, casting a net into the sea (for they were fishermen). He said to them, "Follow me, and I will turn you into fishers of people." They left their nets immediately and followed him. Going on from there he saw two other brothers, James the son of Zebedee and John his brother, in a boat with Zebedee their father, mending their nets. Then he called them. They immediately left the boat and their father and followed him. Matthew 4:18-22

As he went along the Sea of Galilee, he saw Simon and Andrew, Simon's brother, casting a net into the sea (for they were fishermen). Jesus said to them, "Follow me, and I will turn you into fishers of people." They left their nets immediately and followed him. Going on a little farther, he saw James, the son of Zebedee, and John his brother in their boat mending nets. Immediately he called them, and they left their father Zebedee in the boat with the hired men and followed him. Mark 1:16-20

The third recorded miracle – power over provision

Jesus stepped into Simon Peter's boat and asked if He could use the vessel as a platform. Simon Peter evidently agreed and took the boat into the water to allow Jesus to speak. I'm sure Simon Peter would have listened to Jesus' words and they were enough to convince him to row the boat further out to sea, at Jesus' request, to go fishing. Simon Peter and the others in the boat heard Jesus' words but did not fully believe in the power behind the word. This miracle, shown only to the few men in the boat, was intended only for those few. It was a miracle to authenticate the word of Jesus and to demonstrate His power when He said 'follow me'.

Now Jesus was standing by the Lake of Gennesaret, and the crowd was pressing around him to hear the word of God. He saw two boats by the lake, but the fishermen had gotten out of them and were washing their nets. He got into one of the boats, which was Simon's, and asked him to put out a little way from the shore. Then Jesus sat down and taught the crowds from the boat. When he had finished speaking, he said to Simon, "Put out into the deep water and lower your nets for a catch." Simon answered, "Master, we worked hard all night and caught nothing! But at your word I will lower the nets." When they had done this, they caught so many fish that their nets started to tear. So they motioned to their partners in the other boat to come and help them. And they came and filled both boats, so that they were about to sink. But when Simon Peter saw it, he fell down at Jesus' knees, saying, "Go away from me, Lord, for I am a sinful man!" For Peter and all who were with him were astonished at the catch of fish that they had taken, and so were James and John, Zebedee's sons, who were Simon's business partners. Then Jesus said to Simon, "Do not be afraid; from now on you will be catching people." So when they had brought their boats to shore, they left everything and followed him. Luke 5:1-11

The fourth recorded miracle – power over the demonic

Now that Andrew, Peter, James and John were 'formally' called as disciples, they joined Philip and Nathaniel to be the first six disciples. Jesus and these six then go to the Capernaum synagogue on the Sabbath (Saturday). Here in the synagogue is the first recorded casting out of a demon by Jesus. Without going into the fundamentals of demonology and whether or not the demonic can oppress, possess, repress, or all of the above, in this case a fallen angel, a demon, was possessing (indwelling and controlling) a person. Now demons (fallen angels) had been around since satan tempted Adam and Eve in the garden. They are unclean, impure, evil spirits that like satan seek to torment mankind who are made in the image of God. These fallen angels were once in heaven as angelic beings serving God before they rebelled and were thrown down to earth. Now they exist on earth and this encounter shows clearly the power imbalance between the Son of God and the demonic, and it is all Jesus' way.

What drove a possessed man into the synagogue is unknown, although it sets the scene for this massive imbalance of power to be demonstrated. Jesus speaks with authority and His words alone contain the power over the demonic by casting out the evil spirit that had possessed and controlled the man. Interestingly, the demon automatically recognised the 'Holy One of God' and also recognised that its end is destruction hence why the demon asks Jesus whether the time for their destruction had come. This encounter also establishes the pattern between Jesus and the forces of darkness. The word of Christ triumphs over all, every time, without fail.

> *Then they went to Capernaum. When the Sabbath came, Jesus went into the synagogue and began to teach. The people there were amazed by his teaching, because he taught them like one who had authority, not like the experts in the law. Just then there was a man in their synagogue with an unclean spirit, and he cried out, "Leave us alone, Jesus the*

Nazarene! Have you come to destroy us? I know who you are-the Holy One of God!" But Jesus rebuked him: "Silence! Come out of him!" After throwing him into convulsions, the unclean spirit cried out with a loud voice and came out of him. They were all amazed so that they asked each other, "What is this? A new teaching with authority! He even commands the unclean spirits and they obey him." So the news about him spread quickly throughout all the region around Galilee. Mark 1:21-28

Now in the synagogue there was a man who had the spirit of an unclean demon, and he cried out with a loud voice, "Ha! Leave us alone, Jesus the Nazarene! Have you come to destroy us? I know who you are-the Holy One of God." But Jesus rebuked him: "Silence! Come out of him!" Then, after the demon threw the man down in their midst, he came out of him without hurting him. They were all amazed and began to say to one another, "What's happening here? For with authority and power he commands the unclean spirits, and they come out!" So the news about him spread into all areas of the region. Luke 4:33-37

The fifth recorded miracle – power over sickness

Following the synagogue, Jesus and his presumably six disciples went to Peter's house. The remains of the house have been identified and the location is only a few hundred metres from the synagogue, so it is a short walk down towards the lake. Again the first thing Jesus does is heal and again, the first response is adoration and service.

Now when Jesus entered Peter's house, he saw his mother-in-law lying down, sick with a fever. He touched her hand, and the fever left her. Then she got up and began to serve them.
Matthew 8:14-15

Now as soon as they left the synagogue, they entered Simon and Andrew's house, with James and John. Simon's mother-in-law was lying down, sick with a fever, so they spoke to Jesus at once about

her. He came and raised her up by gently taking her hand. Then
the fever left her and she began to serve them. Mark 1:29-31

After Jesus left the synagogue, he entered Simon's house. Now Simon's
mother-in-law was suffering from a high fever, and they asked Jesus
to help her. So he stood over her, commanded the fever, and it left her.
Immediately she got up and began to serve them. Luke 4:38-39

The sixth recorded miracle – power over everything

The response from the community to Jesus' teaching and healing of Simon's mother-in-law was instant, in contrast with that of the residents of Nazareth. In Capernaum the entire community came to be healed, released from demonic torment and restored. It must have been an extraordinary evening of praise and thanksgiving, as all were set free – not some, but all. I wonder what the demonically possessed, the sick and the infirm were doing that night in Nazareth? For they had had the opportunity to embrace the Saviour of the world, but had rejected Jesus. Imagine the difference in their lives if they had responded as the citizens of Capernaum had.

When it was evening, many demon-possessed people were brought to
him. He drove out the spirits with a word, and healed all who were
sick. In this way what was spoken by Isaiah the prophet was fulfilled:
"He took our weaknesses and carried our diseases." Matthew 8:16-17

As the sun was setting, all those who had any relatives sick with various
diseases brought them to Jesus. He placed his hands on every one of them
and healed them. Demons also came out of many, crying out, "You
are the Son of God!" But he rebuked them, and would not allow them
to speak, because they knew that he was the Christ. Luke 4:40-41

When it was evening, after sunset, they brought to him all who
were sick and demon-possessed. The whole town gathered by the

*door. So he healed many who were sick with various diseases
and drove out many demons. But he would not permit the
demons to speak, because they knew him. Mark 1:32-34*

Prayer

The next morning reveals a beautiful scene that is repeated time and
time again. Jesus rising early, to spend the first hours of the day with
His - and our - Heavenly Father. Jesus knew the source of His power,
peace and authority, that of God the Father. Jesus had spent the previous night meeting the needs of the entire community; and now, in
the predawn stillness, He draws upon the power of life itself, through
prayer, to His Heavenly father.

*Then Jesus got up early in the morning when it was still very dark,
departed, and went out to a deserted place, and there he spent time
in prayer. Simon and his companions searched for him. When they
found him, they said, "Everyone is looking for you." He replied, "Let
us go elsewhere, into the surrounding villages, so that I can preach
there too. For that is what I came out here to do." Mark 1:35-38*

*The next morning Jesus departed and went to a deserted place.
Yet the crowds were seeking him, and they came to him and
tried to keep him from leaving them. But Jesus said to them, "I
must proclaim the good news of the kingdom of God to the other
towns too, for that is what I was sent to do." Luke 4:42-43*

Jesus walked throughout northern Israel in the Galilee, teaching, healing and restoring. People came from hundreds of kilometres away,
from all over Israel and further afield to receive a touch from Jesus.
People came from the Decapolis, an area of ten cities (nine of which
were east of the Jordan River), that according to Pliny the Elder in his

work *Natural History*[19] included the modern day cities of Damascus in Lebanon, Amman in Jordan, and Hippos in Syria. People of different faiths, backgrounds, colour and language came from everywhere to see Jesus and Jesus met their needs, healed their bodies and shared the love of the Father.

> *Jesus went throughout all of Galilee, teaching in their synagogues, preaching the gospel of the kingdom, and healing all kinds of disease and sickness among the people. So a report about him spread throughout Syria. People brought to him all who suffered with various illnesses and afflictions, those who had seizures, paralytics, and those possessed by demons, and he healed them. And large crowds followed him from Galilee, the Decapolis, Jerusalem, Judea, and beyond the Jordan River. Matthew 4:23-25*

> *So he went into all of Galilee preaching in their synagogues and casting out demons. Mark 1:39*

> *So he continued to preach in the synagogues of Judea. Luke 4:44*

The seventh recorded miracle – power over disease

The gospels give account after account of Jesus healing people. Everyone was apparently healed in Capernaum and non-Jewish people were walking hundreds of kilometres from east of the Jordan River to see Jesus. The seventh individually recorded miracle is that of Jesus physically touching a man with leprosy. In the time of Christ, a person with leprosy was an outcast, dressed in rags and would not have felt the touch of another human being since their condition materialised. This could have been decades. They were alone, isolated, marginalised and desperate. Jesus was not afraid of exposing Himself to the disease when He touched the man in this story, for Jesus wanted to love him and let

---

[19]   Pliny the Elder (Gaius Plinius Secundus), Naturalis Historia (Natural Histories), 77-79 AD, book 5, Chapter 18.

him know how much he mattered. Jesus wanted to do more than heal him physically – Jesus wanted to touch the man's soul, just as He had touched the man's skin. Jesus could have spoken and the disease would have left, like the royal servant's son at Cana in the second recorded miracle. Jesus wanted to heal more than just the disease, He wanted to heal the whole man. So Jesus touched the man and I bet He looked at him with great compassion and smiled.

And a leper approached, and bowed low before him, saying, "Lord, if you are willing, you can make me clean." He stretched out his hand and touched him saying, "I am willing. Be clean!" Immediately his leprosy was cleansed. Then Jesus said to him, "See that you do not speak to anyone, but go, show yourself to a priest, and bring the offering that Moses commanded, as a testimony to them." Matthew 8:2-4

Now a leper came to him and fell to his knees, asking for help. "If you are willing, you can make me clean," he said. Moved with compassion, Jesus stretched out his hand and touched him, saying, "I am willing. Be clean!" The leprosy left him at once, and he was clean.Immediately Jesus sent the man away with a very strong warning. He told him, "See that you do not say anything to anyone, but go, show yourself to a priest, and bring the offering that Moses commanded for your cleansing, as a testimony to them." But as the man went out he began to announce it publicly and spread the story widely, so that Jesus was no longer able to enter any town openly but stayed outside in remote places. Still they kept coming to him from everywhere. Mark 1:40-45

While Jesus was in one of the towns, a man came to him who was covered with leprosy. When he saw Jesus, he bowed down with his face to the ground and begged him, "Lord, if you are willing, you can make me clean." So he stretched out his hand and touched him, saying, "I am willing. Be clean!" And immediately the leprosy left him. Then he ordered the man to tell no one, but commanded him,

"Go and show yourself to a priest, and bring the offering for your cleansing, as Moses commanded, as a testimony to them." But the news about him spread even more, and large crowds were gathering together to hear him and to be healed of their illnesses. Yet Jesus himself frequently withdrew to the wilderness and prayed. Luke 5:12-16

The eighth recorded miracle – power over paralysis

A few days after healing the man with leprosy, Jesus is again teaching in Capernaum, having arrived by boat, and the religious elite have again gathered. Jesus continues to heal people, but there is a wider issue now being taught. Jesus is presenting himself as the forgiver of sins – literally as the Messiah. Jesus is confronting the religious elite, who thought their animal sacrifice was the means to forgive sin. But Jesus was offering Himself as the ultimate sacrifice for the forgiveness once and for all of sin. First Jesus heals to demonstrate His power and authority, then He teaches the purpose of this power and authority.

Now after some days, when he returned to Capernaum, the news spread that he was at home. So many gathered that there was no longer any room, not even by the door, and he preached the word to them. Some people came bringing to him a paralytic, carried by four of them. When they were not able to bring him in because of the crowd, they removed the roof above Jesus. Then, after tearing it out, they lowered the stretcher the paralytic was lying on. When Jesus saw their faith, he said to the paralytic, "Son, your sins are forgiven." Now some of the experts in the law were sitting there, turning these things over in their minds: "Why does this man speak this way? He is blaspheming! Who can forgive sins but God alone?" Now immediately, when Jesus realized in his spirit that they were contemplating such thoughts, he said to them, "Why are you thinking such things in your hearts? Which is easier, to say to the paralytic, 'Your sins are forgiven,' or to say, 'Stand up, take your stretcher, and walk'? But so that you may know that the Son of Man has authority on earth to forgive sins,"-he said to the paralytic- "I tell you, stand up, take your stretcher, and go home." And immediately the man stood up, took his stretcher, and went out in front of them all. They were all amazed and glorified God, saying, "We have never seen anything like this!" Mark 2:1-12

After getting into a boat he crossed to the other side and came to his own town. Just then some people brought to him a paralytic lying on a stretcher. When Jesus saw their faith, he said to the paralytic, "Have courage, son! Your sins are forgiven." Then some of the experts in the law said to themselves, "This man is blaspheming!" When Jesus perceived their thoughts he said, "Why do you respond with evil in your hearts? Which is easier, to say, 'Your sins are forgiven' or to say, 'Stand up and walk'? But so that you may know that the Son of Man has authority on earth to forgive sins"-then he said to the paralytic-"Stand up, take your stretcher, and go home." And he stood up and went home. When the crowd saw this, they were afraid and honored God who had given such authority to men. Matthew 9:1-8

Now on one of those days, while he was teaching, there were Pharisees and teachers of the law sitting nearby (who had come from every village of Galilee and Judea and from Jerusalem), and the power of the Lord was with him to heal. Just then some men showed up, carrying a paralyzed man on a stretcher. They were trying to bring him in and place him before Jesus. But since they found no way to carry him in because of the crowd, they went up on the roof and let him down on the stretcher through the roof tiles right in front of Jesus. When Jesus saw their faith he said, "Friend, your sins are forgiven." Then the experts in the law and the Pharisees began to think to themselves, "Who is this man who is uttering blasphemies? Who can forgive sins but God alone?" When Jesus perceived their hostile thoughts, he said to them, "Why are you raising objections within yourselves? Which is easier, to say, 'Your sins are forgiven,' or to say, 'Stand up and walk'? But so that you may know that the Son of Man has authority on earth to forgive sins"-he *said to the paralyzed man—"I tell you, stand up, take your stretcher and go home." Immediately he stood up before them, picked up the stretcher he had been lying on, and went home, glorifying God. Then astonishment seized them all, and they glorified God. They were filled with awe, saying, "We have seen incredible things today." Luke 5:17-26*

The seventh disciple

After the healing of the paralysed man in front of the religious elite, Jesus went to the Sea of Galilee to teach the people and, whilst there, He called the seventh disciple — a despised tax collector called Mathew (Levi son of Alphaeus), who would eventually author the gospel named after him.

After this, Jesus went out and saw a tax collector named Levi sitting at the tax booth. "Follow me," he said to him. And he got up and followed him, leaving everything behind. Luke 5:27-28

As Jesus went on from there, he saw a man named Matthew sitting at the tax booth. "Follow me," he said to him. And he got up and followed him. Matthew 9:9

Jesus went out again by the sea. The whole crowd came to him, and he taught them. As he went along, he saw Levi, the son of Alphaeus, sitting at the tax booth. "Follow me," he said to him. And he got up and followed him. Mark 2:13-14

Matthew invites Jesus and presumably the existing six disciples to dinner. It was evidently a large affair as the religious elite turned up, as did the disciples of John the Baptist. Importantly, there were also many ordinary people in attendance, people the religious elite looked down upon as 'sinners'. Jesus uses this opportunity to draw attention again to His impending personal sacrifice and the New Covenant of Grace that would result. Jesus now starts teaching in parables (stories) to present

His message in the most impactful and memorable way. In this case He used three parables concerning feasting with the bridegroom, new cloth and new wine to emphasise that the New Covenant of Grace will complete the Old Covenant of Law. This is a theme that Jesus returns to often.

Then Levi gave a great banquet in his house for Jesus, and there was a large crowd of tax collectors and others sitting at the table with them. But the Pharisees and their experts in the law complained to his disciples, saying, "Why do you eat and drink with tax collectors and sinners?" Jesus answered them, "Those who are well don't need a physician, but those who are sick do. I have not come to call the righteous, but sinners to repentance." Then they said to him, "John's disciples frequently fast and pray, and so do the disciples of the Pharisees, but yours continue to eat and drink." So Jesus said to them, "You cannot make the wedding guests fast while the bridegroom is with them, can you? But those days are coming, and when the bridegroom is taken from them, at that time they will fast." He also told them a parable: "No one tears a patch from a new garment and sews it on an old garment. If he does, he will have torn the new, and the piece from the new will not match the old. And no one pours new wine into old wineskins. If he does, the new wine will burst the skins and will be spilled, and the skins will be destroyed. Instead new wine must be poured into new wineskins. No one after drinking old wine wants the new, for he says, 'The old is good enough.'" Luke 5:29-39

As Jesus was having a meal in Matthew's house, many tax collectors and sinners came and ate with Jesus and his disciples. When the Pharisees saw this they said to his disciples, "Why does your teacher eat with tax collectors and sinners?" When Jesus heard this he said, "Those who are healthy don't need a physician, but those who are sick do. Go and learn what this saying means: 'I want mercy and not sacrifice.' For I did not come to call the righteous, but sinners." Then John's disciples came to Jesus and asked, "Why do we and the Pharisees fast often, but your disciples don't fast?" Jesus said to them, "The wedding guests cannot mourn while the bridegroom is with them, can they? But the days are coming when the bridegroom will be taken from them, and then they will fast. No one sews a patch of unshrunk cloth on an old garment, because the patch will pull away from the garment and the tear will be worse. And no one pours new wine into old wineskins; otherwise the skins burst and the wine is spilled out and the skins are destroyed. Instead they put new wine into new wineskins and both are preserved." Matthew 9:10-17

As Jesus was having a meal in Levi's home, many tax collectors and sinners were eating with Jesus and his disciples, for there were many who followed him. When the experts in the law and the Pharisees saw that he was eating with sinners and tax collectors, they said to his disciples, "Why does he eat with tax collectors and sinners?" When Jesus heard this he said to them, "Those who are healthy don't need a physician, but those who are sick do. I have not come to call the righteous, but sinners." Now John's disciples and the Pharisees were fasting. So they came to Jesus and said, "Why do the disciples of John and the disciples of the Pharisees fast, but your disciples don't fast?" Jesus said to them, "The wedding guests cannot fast while the bridegroom is with them, can they? As long as they have the bridegroom with them they do not fast. But the days are coming when the bridegroom will be taken from them, and at that time they will fast. No one sews a patch of unshrunk cloth on an old garment; otherwise, the patch pulls away from it, the new from the old, and the tear becomes worse. And no one pours new wine into old wineskins; otherwise, the wine will burst the skins, and both the wine and the skins will be destroyed. Instead new wine is poured into new wineskins." Mark 2:15-22

CHAPTER 5

Popularity

Passover - Galilee (31 AD)

The second year of the ministry of Jesus is one defined by popularity. All of Israel is stirred by His teaching and the accompanying signs and wonders, especially healings, that are performed to validate the message of grace. At the start of Jesus' ministry, at His baptism, three disciples were called and at the end of the first year of ministry, seven disciples were with Jesus. Many more are also following, including presumably many of John the Baptist's former disciples.

Jesus has been through Galilee, down to Jerusalem, and then taken the short road through Samaria. He has healed, taught, confronted and challenged. The north is astir, the south is perplexed and the ruling elite are only thinking of themselves and their positions. Jesus has reached out to the Jews, the 'half-bred' Samaritans and healed many from other nations that came to see Him. Jesus has shown that the New Covenant of Grace He will bring in through His blood is for everyone, Jews and non-Jews alike.

Now that the second year has commenced, Jesus goes back to Jerusalem for the Passover and then seeks to formalise his discipleship arrangement by choosing the twelve that will be by His side for the next two years. Eleven of the twelve would ultimately take the gospel forward from Jerusalem, to Samaria and then to the whole world.

Passover Wednesday 25th April 31 AD

Jesus now travels to Jerusalem for a Jewish festival.

> *After this there was a Jewish feast, and Jesus*
> *went up to Jerusalem. John 5:1*

It is reasonable to suggest that this was the second Passover in Jerusalem that Jesus attended post baptism and it effectively commences his second year of ministry. Jesus was a devout Jew who didn't come to replace the law but to complete it. He could only do this if He fulfilled the law, so attending Passover was important. There is also an argument that this festival is one of the other two major festivals that devout Jews were expected to go to Jerusalem for, perhaps Tabernacles. No one knows for sure, however Passover seems to make the most sense.

The ninth miracle – power over disability

Whilst in Jerusalem, Jesus goes to the pool of Bethesda, just outside the old city walls near the Sheep Gate. (As an aside, the pool is now inside the current walls of Jerusalem within the Muslim quarter next to the Church of St Anne). Whilst Jesus has healed countless numbers of people, including literally everyone in Capernaum, the story focuses on one man who has been crippled for thirty eight years. Jesus then has the temerity to heal the man on the Jewish holy day of the Sabbath, a day where 'work' was prohibited and the religious elite had evidently decided that healing was classed as 'work'. And He did this in Jerusalem in the shadow of the Temple. Apparently this was outrageous. I bet the crippled man didn't think so.

The photo above of the pool of Bethesda was taken
by the American colony photo department between
1898 and 1934.

*Now there is in Jerusalem by the Sheep Gate a pool called Bethzatha in
Aramaic, which has five covered walkways. A great number of sick, blind,
lame, and paralyzed people were lying in these walkways. Now a man
was there who had been disabled for thirty-eight years. When Jesus saw
him lying there and when he realized that the man had been disabled
a long time already, he said to him, "Do you want to become well?"
The sick man answered him, "Sir, I have no one to put me into the pool
when the water is stirred up. While I am trying to get into the water,
someone else goes down there before me." Jesus said to him, "Stand up!
Pick up your mat and walk." Immediately the man was healed, and he
picked up his mat and started walking. (Now that day was a Sabbath.)
So the Jewish leaders said to the man who had been healed, "It is the*

Sabbath, and you are not permitted to carry your mat." But he answered them, "The man who made me well said to me, 'Pick up your mat and walk.'" They asked him, "Who is the man who said to you, 'Pick up your mat and walk'?" But the man who had been healed did not know who it was, for Jesus had slipped out, since there was a crowd in that place. After this Jesus found him at the temple and said to him, "Look, you have become well. Don't sin any more, lest anything worse happen to you." The man went away and informed the Jewish leaders that Jesus was the one who had made him well. Now because Jesus was doing these things on the Sabbath, the Jewish leaders began persecuting him. So he told them, "My Father is working until now, and I too am working." For this reason the Jewish leaders were trying even harder to kill him, because not only was he breaking the Sabbath, but he was also calling God his own Father, thus making himself equal with God. John 5:2-18

This is one more occasion where Jesus healed on the holy day of the Sabbath (Saturday) in direct contradiction to the Jewish religious leader's interpretation of the law. The religious elite continue to take their eyes off the miracles that confirm Jesus' claim to being the Messiah and place their sights on persecuting and killing Jesus because He is not conforming to their view of who and what the Messiah would be and do. This is what the law does, it kills. Compare this to the grace that Jesus brings – very life itself.

So Jesus answered them, "I tell you the solemn truth, the Son can do nothing on his own initiative, but only what he sees the Father doing. For whatever the Father does, the Son does likewise. For the Father loves the Son and shows him everything he does, and will show him greater deeds than these, so that you will be amazed. For just as the Father raises the dead and gives them life, so also the Son gives life to whomever he wishes. Furthermore, the Father does not judge anyone, but has assigned all judgment to the Son, so that all people will honor the Son just as they honor the Father. The one who does not honor the Son does not honor the Father who sent him. "I tell you the solemn truth, the one who hears my message and believes the one who sent me has eternal life and will not be condemned, but has crossed over from death to life. I tell you the solemn truth, a time is coming-and is now here-when the dead will hear the voice of the Son of God, and those who hear will live. For just as the Father has life in himself, thus he has granted the Son to have life in himself, and he has granted the Son authority to execute judgment, because he is the Son of Man. "Do not be amazed at this, because a time is coming when all who are in the tombs will hear his voice and will come out-the ones who have done what is good to the resurrection resulting in life, and the ones who have done what is evil to the resurrection resulting in condemnation. I can do nothing on my own initiative. Just as I hear, I judge, and my judgment is just, because I do not seek my own will, but the will of the one who sent me. "If I testify about myself, my testimony is not true. There is another who testifies about me, and I know the testimony he testifies about me is true. You have sent to John, and he has testified to the truth. (I do not accept human testimony, but I say this so that you may be saved.) He was a lamp that was burning and shining, and you wanted to rejoice greatly for a short time in his light. "But I have a testimony greater than that from John. For the deeds that the Father has assigned me to complete-the deeds I am now doing-testify about me that the Father has sent me. And the Father who sent me has himself testified about me. You people have never heard his voice nor seen his form at any time, nor do you have his word residing in you, because you do not believe the one whom he sent. You study the scriptures thoroughly because you think in them you possess eternal life, and it is these same scriptures that testify about me, but you are not willing to come to me so that you may have life. "I do not accept praise from people, but I know you, that you do not have the love of God within you. I have come in my Father's name, and you do not accept me. If someone else comes in his own name, you will accept him. How can you believe, if you accept praise from one another and don't seek the praise that comes from the only God? "Do not suppose that I will accuse you before the Father. The one who accuses you is Moses, in whom you have placed your hope. If you believed Moses, you would believe me, because he wrote about me. But if you do not believe what Moses wrote, how will you believe my words?"... John 5:19-47

Return to Galilee

Jesus now walks back from Jerusalem to Galilee, probably via the Jordan Valley as there is no reference to Samaria. As He journeys, He stops in various towns and confronts the issue of religious rules in defiance of those who care more for their laws than the lives of people. Keeping the Sabbath day holy was one of the Ten Commandments and was thus religiously observed. Jesus begins to change the people's view of this observance, not through disobedience, but by fulfilling the law through His own sacrifice and ushering in the New Covenant of Grace. It was this covenant transition that the religious elite could not see and were unwilling to accept. Jesus was making the point that He would replace the Old Covenant, the law, with the New Covenant, grace and replace religious observance with joyful relationship.

At that time Jesus went through the grain fields on a Sabbath. His disciples were hungry, and they began to pick heads of wheat and eat them. But when the Pharisees saw this they said to him, "Look, your disciples are doing what is against the law to do on the Sabbath." He said to them, "Haven't you read what David did when he and his companions were hungry – how he entered the house of God and they ate the sacred bread, which was against the law for him or his companions to eat, but only for the priests? Or have you not read in the law that the priests in the temple desecrate the Sabbath and yet are not guilty? I tell you that something greater than the temple is here. If you had known what this means: 'I want mercy and not sacrifice,' you would not have condemned the innocent. For the Son of Man is lord of the Sabbath."...Matthew 12:1-8

Jesus was going through the grain fields on a Sabbath, and his disciples
began to pick some heads of wheat as they made their way. So the
Pharisees said to him, "Look, why are they doing what is against the law
on the Sabbath?" He said to them, "Have you never read what David
did when he was in need and he and his companions were hungry –
how he entered the house of God when Abiathar was high priest and
ate the sacred bread, which is against the law for any but the priests to
eat, and also gave it to his companions?" Then he said to them, "The
Sabbath was made for people, not people for the Sabbath. For this
reason the Son of Man is lord even of the Sabbath." Mark 2:23-28

Jesus was going through the grain fields on a Sabbath, and his disciples
picked some heads of wheat, rubbed them in their hands, and ate them.
But some of the Pharisees said, "Why are you doing what is against the
law on the Sabbath?" Jesus answered them, "Haven't you read what
David did when he and his companions were hungry – how he entered
the house of God, took and ate the sacred bread, which is not lawful for
any to eat but the priests alone, and gave it to his companions?" Then
he said to them, "The Son of Man is lord of the Sabbath." Luke 6:1-5

The tenth miracle – power over the body

Jesus continues his journey north and continues his pattern of chal-
lenging the Sabbath, this time with a healing in front of the religious
elite. Jesus has upped the ante. He started with healing people generally
and now openly challenges the sacredness of the Sabbath by healing on
the Sabbath in their synagogue, right in front of them.

Then Jesus left that place and entered their synagogue. A man was
there who had a withered hand. And they asked Jesus, "Is it lawful to
heal on the Sabbath?" so that they could accuse him. He said to them,
"Would not any one of you, if he had one sheep that fell into a pit on the
Sabbath, take hold of it and lift it out? How much more valuable is a
person than a sheep! So it is lawful to do good on the Sabbath." Then he

said to the man, "Stretch out your hand." He stretched it out and it was restored, as healthy as the other. But the Pharisees went out and plotted against him, as to how they could assassinate him. Matthew 12:9-14

On another Sabbath, Jesus entered the synagogue and was teaching. Now a man was there whose right hand was withered. The experts in the law and the Pharisees watched Jesus closely to see if he would heal on the Sabbath, so that they could find a reason to accuse him. But he knew their thoughts, and said to the man who had the withered hand, "Get up and stand here." So he rose and stood there. Then Jesus said to them, "I ask you, is it lawful to do good on the Sabbath or to do evil, to save a life or to destroy it?" After looking around at them all, he said to the man, "Stretch out your hand." The man did so, and his hand was restored. But they were filled with mindless rage and began debating with one another what they would do to Jesus. Luke 6:6-11

Then Jesus entered the synagogue again, and a man was there who had a withered hand. They watched Jesus closely to see if he would heal him on the Sabbath, so that they could accuse him. So he said to the man who had the withered hand, "Stand up among all these people." Then he said to them, "Is it lawful to do good on the Sabbath, or evil, to save a life or destroy it?" But they were silent. After looking around at them in anger, grieved by the hardness of their hearts, he said to the man, "Stretch out your hand." He stretched it out, and his hand was restored. So the Pharisees went out immediately and began plotting with the Herodians, as to how they could assassinate him. Mark 3:1-6

What is extraordinary is that the religious elite witness a miracle that is beyond understanding, yet their response is to join with their hated enemy, the Herodians, to kill Jesus. The Herodians were a third political force (after the Pharisees and the Sadducees) and were loyal to the dynastic family of the Herods and popular with hellenistic Jews. They weren't big fans of anyone who came against the Herods, so Jesus was not in their good books.

So blinded were the religious authorities regarding their view of God that they missed God's repeated attempts to show them who He really was. No wonder Jesus went and withdrew from that place and continued north. It must have done His head in to see such blinkered unbelief and intransigence, followed by murderous threats. The crowds still followed though, as Jesus healed them, taught them, encouraged them and loved them.

Now when Jesus learned of this, he went away from there. Great crowds followed him, and he healed them all. But he sternly warned them not to make him known. This fulfilled what was spoken by Isaiah the prophet: "Here is my servant whom I have chosen, the one I love, in whom I take great delight. I will put my Spirit on him, and he will proclaim justice to the nations. He will not quarrel or cry out, nor will anyone hear his voice in the streets. He will not break a bruised reed or extinguish a smoldering wick, until he brings justice to victory. And in his name the Gentiles will hope." Matthew 12:15-21

Then Jesus went away with his disciples to the sea, and a great multitude from Galilee followed him. And from Judea, Jerusalem, Idumea, beyond the Jordan River, and around Tyre and Sidon a great multitude came to him when they heard about the things he had done. Because of the crowd, he told his disciples to have a small boat ready for him so the crowd would not press toward him. For he had healed many, so that all who were afflicted with diseases pressed toward him in order to touch him. And whenever the unclean spirits saw him, they fell down before him and cried out, "You are the Son of God." But he sternly ordered them not to make him known. Mark 3:7-12

The twelve disciples

Back in Galilee, at the start of the second year of ministry, Jesus' first priority was to call his team of twelve disciples, through whom He would change the world. It's a big decision choosing a team such as this, which may explain why Jesus spent the whole night praying about it. This is the first time we read of Jesus spending this much time on His knees.

Now it was during this time that Jesus went out to the mountain to pray, and he spent all night in prayer to God. When morning came, he called his disciples and chose twelve of them, whom he also named apostles: Simon (whom he named Peter), and his brother Andrew; and James, John, Philip, Bartholomew, Matthew, Thomas, James the son of Alphaeus, Simon who was called the Zealot, Judas the son of James, and Judas Iscariot, who became a traitor. Luke 6:12-16

Now Jesus went up the mountain and called for those he wanted, and they came to him. He appointed twelve (whom he named apostles), so that they would be with him and he could send them to preach and to have authority to cast out demons. He appointed twelve: To Simon he gave the name Peter; to James and his brother John, the sons of Zebedee, he gave the name Boanerges (that is, "sons of thunder"); and Andrew, Philip, Bartholomew, Matthew, Thomas, James the son of Alphaeus, Thaddaeus, Simon the Zealot, and Judas Iscariot, who betrayed him. Mark 3:13-19

What a motley crew Jesus chose. Eleven of the disciples were from Galilee and only one was from Judea, Judas Iscariot, son of Simon Iscariot (John 6:71 and John 13:26) – Iscariot meaning 'man of Kerioth' (Joshua 15:25). One was a nationalistic Zealot, another a despised tax collector and another a courageous doubter. There were two and potentially three lots of brothers, and at least five fishermen. Surely that can't be the gun team to change the world?

Think about the circumstances of your call, brothers and sisters. Not many were wise by human standards, not many were powerful, not many were born to a privileged position. But God chose what the world thinks foolish to shame the wise, and God chose what the world thinks weak to shame the strong. God chose what is low and despised in the world, what is regarded as nothing, to set aside what is regarded as something, so that no one can boast in his presence. He is the reason you have a relationship with Christ Jesus, who became for us wisdom from God, and righteousness and sanctification and redemption, so that, as it is written, "Let the one who boasts, boast in the Lord." 1 Corinthians 1:26-31

This is the beauty of being on God's team, for it is never about me. Our skills, our abilities, our righteousness are rubbish. Jesus' perfect righteousness flowing effortlessly through us to be the salt and light in the world is what matters. This is what we see in the following twelve disciples.

Simon (Peter). Simon Peter, son of Jonas, was a fisherman who lived in Bethsaida and Capernaum. At the time of Christ, the common language was Greek and the family language was Hebrew, so his Greek name was Simon (Mark 1:16 and John 1:40-41) and his Hebrew name was Cephas (1 Corinthians 1:12, 3:22; 9:5 and Galatians 2:9). The Greek meaning of Simon is 'rock' as is the Arabic meaning of Cephas. Peter did evangelistic and missionary work among the Jews, going as far as Babylon. He was a member of Jesus' inner circle and authored the two New Testament epistles which bear his name, and most of Mark's gospel appears to be from Peter's teachings. Tradition says that Peter was crucified upside down in Rome, considering himself not worthy to be crucified in the same manner as Jesus. In every gospel list, the name Peter is mentioned first and it appears he was the only married disciple (1 Corinthians 9:5). Any guesses as to his wife's name, what became of her and whether they had children?

Andrew. Andrew, Peter's brother and Jonas's son, lived in Bethsaida and Capernaum, and was a fisherman. Andrew was a disciple of John the Baptist before being called by Jesus (Mark 1:16-18). Andrew brought his brother, Peter, to Jesus (John 1:40).

John. John Boanerges (son of thunder), son of Zebedee and brother of James is the apostle known as the beloved disciple, which is what he called himself in his gospel. A fisherman who lived in Bethsaida, Capernaum and Jerusalem, John was also a member of Jesus' inner circle. He wrote the gospel of John; the three letters known as I John, 2 John and 3 John; and the book of Revelations. He preached among the churches of Asia Minor and would finish his life banished to the Isle of Patmos – the only disciple to die a natural death. John was one of the prominent apostles and is mentioned in many places in the New Testament.

James. James Boanerges (son of thunder), son of Zebedee and brother of John the apostle, was a fisherman who lived in Bethsaida, Capernaum and Jerusalem. He preached in Jerusalem and Judea and was beheaded by Herod in 44 AD (Acts 12:1-2). He was the third member of Jesus' inner circle. His name only ever appears with that of his brother John, as they were an inseparable pair (Mark 1:19-20, Matthew 4:21 and Luke 5:1-11).

Philip. Philip came from Bethsaida, the town from which Peter and Andrew came from (John 1:44). It is likely that he was also a fisherman. Although the first three gospels and the book of Acts record his name (Matthew 10:3, Mark 3:18, Luke 6:14 and Acts 1:13), it is the gospel of John that states Philip was one of the first to whom Jesus addressed the words, "follow me". When Philip met Christ, he immediately found Nathanael and told him that "we have found him, of whom Moses… and the prophets, did write." Nathanael was sceptical, but Philip didn't argue with him; he simply answered, "come and see".

In Acts 6:5, a man called Philip is named as one of the seven ordained deacons and many argue this is the same Philip. If this is the case, then he led the Ethiopian eunuch to Christ (Acts 8:26), stayed with Paul in Ceasarea (Acts 21:8) and was one of the major figures in the missionary enterprise of the early church.

Bartholomew. Bartholomew Nathanael, son of Talmai, lived in Cana of Galilee. His name means son of Tolmai or Talmai(2 Samuel 3:3). Talmai was King of Geshur whose daughter, Maacah, was the wife of King David, mother of Absalom. This has led a number of scholars to believe that he was the only one of the twelve disciples who came from royal blood, or noble birth[20]. Bartholomew's name appears with every list of the disciples (Matthew 10:3, Mark 3:18, Luke 6:14 and Acts 1:13). This was not his first name, however, it was his second. His first name was Nathanael, whom Jesus said of him in John 1:47, "Here truly is an Israelite in whom there is no deceit."

Matthew. Matthew, or Levi, son of Alpheus, lived in Capernaum. He was a publican or tax collector and wrote the gospel that bears his name. Jesus' call of Matthew is mentioned in Mark 2:14, Matthew 9:9 and Luke 5:27-28. It was a common custom in the Middle East at the time of Christ for men to have two names. Matthew's names mean 'a gift of God'. It is possible that the disciple James, son of Alpheus, was Matthew's brother. What is of note is that the Jewish people disliked tax collectors, thinking many of them corrupt, believing that only God was the one to whom tax should be paid. To many Jews, tax collectors were criminals. In New Testament times they were classified with harlots, Gentiles and sinners (Matthew 18:17, Matthew 21:31 and 33, Matthew 9:10, Mark 2:15-16 and Luke 5:30).

---

[20] http://www.bibleinfo.com/en/questions/who-were-twelve-disciples#bartholomew-nathanael as accessed on 19 October 2016.

Thomas. Thomas was his Hebrew name and Didymus his Greek name. He lived in Galilee, though tradition says after the resurrection of Jesus, Thomas was a missionary in Parthia, Persia, and India, and suffered martyrdom at Mt. St. Thomas, India (near Madras) having planted many churches through that area. Thomas appeared at the raising of Lazarus (John 11:2-16) and at the Last Supper (John 14:1-6) where he wanted to know where Jesus was going and the way to get there. In John 20:25, he said that unless he saw the nail prints in Jesus' hand and the gash of the spear in His side he would not believe. That's why Thomas became known as doubting Thomas. I prefer to see Thomas in a different light as the courageous disciple, "Then Thomas (also known as Didymus) said to the rest of the disciples, 'Let us also go, that we may die with him [Jesus]'" (John 11:16).

James son of Alphaeus. James, the younger, son of Alpheus lived in Galilee. Some argue he was the brother of either Matthew or Thaddaeus. According to tradition he wrote the Epistle of James, preached in Palestine and Egypt and was crucified in Egypt.

Thaddaeus. Jerome called him 'Trinomious', which means 'a man with three names', as he is called Thaddeus (Mark 3:18), Lebbeus (Matthew 10:3) and Judas son of James (Luke 6:16 and Acts 1:13) in different gospel accounts. Some argue he was the brother of James son of Alphaeus. Thaddeus wasalso referred to as Judas the Zealot as he was keen to make Jesus known to the world (John 14:22) asking Jesus at the Last Supper, "But Lord, why do you intend to show yourself to us and not to the world?"

Simon the Zealot. The gospels tell us very little about Simon except that he was a member of the Zealots. These were fanatical Jewish nationalists who had heroic disregard for the suffering involved in the struggle for what they regarded as the purity of their faith. The Zealots hated the Romans, and this hatred would lead in many ways to the destruction of Jerusalem in 70 AD. Josephus says the Jewish high priest had to restrain the madness of those that had the name of zealots; but their violence was too hard for him'[21] which gives an idea of their level of zeal.

Judas Iscariot. Judas was the son of Simon Iscariot (John 6:71). The name 'Judas' is the Greek transliteration of the Hebrew name 'Judah' and means 'praise Yahweh [God]'. Iscariot, probably means 'man of Kerioth', a town described in Joshua 15:25 as in the southern part of Judah, thought to be the ruins of el-Kureitein, which lies twenty-five kilometres south of Hebron. If this is the case that would make him the only disciple who was not from Galilee.

Sermon on the Mount

Having chosen His team, Jesus commences his longest recorded teaching session, known globally as the Sermon on the Mount. The setting is probably one of the hills between Tiberius and Capernaum to the north of the Sea of Galilee. As was His habit, Jesus firstly healed those who were ill and then taught them. That would certainly have caught the crowd's attention.

> *Then he came down with them and stood on a level place. And a large number of his disciples had gathered along with a vast multitude from all over Judea, from Jerusalem, and from the seacoast of Tyre and Sidon. They came to hear him and to be healed of their diseases, and those who suffered from unclean spirits were cured. The whole crowd was trying to touch him, because power was coming out from him and healing them all.... Luke 6:17-19*

---

[21]   Josephus, *War of the Jews*, Chapter 22.

When he saw the crowds, he went up the mountain.
After he sat down his disciples came to him. Then he
began to teach them by saying: Matthew 5:1-2

Having met the physical needs of the listeners, Jesus now moves to meet the spiritual needs through His amazing teaching – words that have revolutionised societies for 2000 years and have become the basis for the morality of much of the world's secular legal systems. More importantly, Jesus taught about the coming kingdom, the gift of righteousness that His death would bring, and what it means to live a victorious life clothed in His righteousness.

Blessings for those who will inherit the kingdom of God

Then he looked up at his disciples and said: "Blessed are you who are
poor, for the kingdom of God belongs to you. "Blessed are you who
hunger now, for you will be satisfied. "Blessed are you who weep now,
for you will laugh. "Blessed are you when people hate you, and when
they exclude you and insult you and reject you as evil on account of
the Son of Man! Rejoice in that day, and jump for joy, because your
reward is great in heaven. For their ancestors did the same things to
the prophets. "But woe to you who are rich, for you have received your
comfort already. "Woe to you who are well satisfied with food now, for
you will be hungry. "Woe to you who laugh now, for you will mourn
and weep. "Woe to you when all people speak well of you, for their
ancestors did the same things to the false prophets. Luke 6:20-26

"Blessed are the poor in spirit, for the kingdom of heaven belongs
to them. "Blessed are those who mourn, for they will be comforted.
"Blessed are the meek, for they will inherit the earth. "Blessed are those
who hunger and thirst for righteousness, for they will be satisfied.
"Blessed are the merciful, for they will be shown mercy. "Blessed are
the pure in heart, for they will see God. "Blessed are the peacemakers,

for they will be called the children of God. "Blessed are those who are persecuted for righteousness, for the kingdom of heaven belongs to them. "Blessed are you when people insult you and persecute you and say all kinds of evil things about you falsely on account of me. Rejoice and be glad because your reward is great in heaven, for they persecuted the prophets before you in the same way. Matthew 5:3-12

Responsibilities whilst waiting for the Kingdom of God

"You are the salt of the earth. But if salt loses its flavor, how can it be made salty again? It is no longer good for anything except to be thrown out and trampled on by people. You are the light of the world. A city located on a hill cannot be hidden. People do not light a lamp and put it under a basket but on a lampstand, and it gives light to all in the house. In the same way, let your light shine before people, so that they can see your good deeds and give honor to your Father in heaven. Matthew 5:13-16

Law, righteousness and the kingdom

"Do not think that I have come to abolish the law or the prophets. I have not come to abolish these things but to fulfill them. I tell you the truth, until heaven and earth pass away not the smallest letter or stroke of a letter will pass from the law until everything takes place. So anyone who breaks one of the least of these commands and teaches others to do so will be called least in the kingdom of heaven, but whoever obeys them and teaches others to do so will be called great in the kingdom of heaven. For I tell you, unless your righteousness goes beyond that of the experts in the law and the Pharisees, you will never enter the kingdom of heaven. Matthew 5:17-20

The full impact of the law, and why it can never be kept

"You have heard that it was said to an older generation, 'Do not murder,' and 'whoever murders will be subjected to judgment.' But I say to you that anyone who is angry with a brother will be subjected to judgment. And whoever insults a brother will be brought before the council, and whoever says 'Fool' will be sent to fiery hell. So then, if you bring your gift to the altar and there remember that your brother has something against you, leave your gift there in front of the altar. First go and be reconciled to your brother and then come and present your gift. Reach agreement quickly with your accuser while on the way to court, or he may hand you over to the judge, and the judge hand you over to the warden, and you will be thrown into prison. I tell you the truth, you will never get out of there until you have paid the last penny! "You have heard that it was said, 'Do not commit adultery.' But I say to you that whoever looks at a woman to desire her has already committed adultery with her in his heart. If your right eye causes you to sin, tear it out and throw it away! It is better to lose one of your members than to have your whole body thrown into hell. If your right hand causes you to sin, cut it off and throw it away! It is better to lose one of your members than to have your whole body go into hell. "It was said, 'Whoever divorces his wife must give her a legal document.' But I say to you that everyone who divorces his wife, except for immorality, makes her commit adultery, and whoever marries a divorced woman commits adultery. "Again, you have heard that it was said to an older generation, 'Do not break an oath, but fulfill your vows to the Lord.' But I say to you, do not take oaths at all-not by heaven, because it is the throne of God, not by earth, because it is his footstool, and not by Jerusalem, because it is the city of the great King. Do not take an oath by your head, because you are not able to make one hair white or black. Let your word be 'Yes, yes' or 'No, no.' More than this is from the evil one. "You have heard that it was said, 'An eye for an eye and a tooth for a tooth.' But I say to you, do not resist the evildoer. But whoever strikes you on the right cheek, turn the other to him as well. And if someone

wants to sue you and to take your tunic, give him your coat also. And if anyone forces you to go one mile, go with him two. Give to the one who asks you, and do not reject the one who wants to borrow from you. "You have heard that it was said, 'Love your neighbor' and 'hate your enemy.' But I say to you, love your enemy and pray for those who persecute you, so that you may be like your Father in heaven, since he causes the sun to rise on the evil and the good, and sends rain on the righteous and the unrighteous. For if you love those who love you, what reward do you have? Even the tax collectors do the same, don't they? And if you only greet your brothers, what more do you do? Even the Gentiles do the same, don't they? So then, be perfect, as your heavenly Father is perfect. Matthew 5:21-48

"But I say to you who are listening: Love your enemies, do good to those who hate you, bless those who curse you, pray for those who mistreat you. To the person who strikes you on the cheek, offer the other as well, and from the person who takes away your coat, do not withhold your tunic either. Give to everyone who asks you, and do not ask for your possessions back from the person who takes them away. Treat others in the same way that you would want them to treat you. "If you love those who love you, what credit is that to you? For even sinners love those who love them. And if you do good to those who do good to you, what credit is that to you? Even sinners do the same. And if you lend to those from whom you hope to be repaid, what credit is that to you? Even sinners lend to sinners, so that they may be repaid in full. But love your enemies, and do good, and lend, expecting nothing back. Then your reward will be great, and you will be sons of the Most High, because he is kind to ungrateful and evil people. Be merciful, just as your Father is merciful. Luke 6:27-36

Hypocritical 'acts of righteousness' to be avoided

"Be careful not to display your righteousness merely to be seen by people. Otherwise you have no reward with your Father in heaven. Thus whenever you do charitable giving, do not blow a trumpet before you, as

the hypocrites do in synagogues and on streets so that people will praise them. I tell you the truth, they have their reward. But when you do your giving, do not let your left hand know what your right hand is doing, so that your gift may be in secret. And your Father, who sees in secret, will reward you. "Whenever you pray, do not be like the hypocrites, because they love to pray while standing in synagogues and on street corners so that people can see them. Truly I say to you, they have their reward. But whenever you pray, go into your room, close the door, and pray to your Father in secret. And your Father, who sees in secret, will reward you. When you pray, do not babble repetitiously like the Gentiles, because they think that by their many words they will be heard. Do not be like them, for your Father knows what you need before you ask him. So pray this way: Our Father in heaven, may your name be honored, may your kingdom come, may your will be done on earth as it is in heaven. Give us today our daily bread, and forgive us our debts, as we ourselves have forgiven our debtors. And do not lead us into temptation, but deliver us from the evil one. "For if you forgive others their sins, your heavenly Father will also forgive you. But if you do not forgive others, your Father will not forgive you your sins. "When you fast, do not look sullen like the hypocrites, for they make their faces unattractive so that people will see them fasting. I tell you the truth, they have their reward. When you fast, put oil on your head and wash your face, so that it will not be obvious to others when you are fasting, but only to your Father who is in secret. And your Father, who sees in secret, will reward you. Matthew 6:1-18

Three prohibitions

"Do not judge, and you will not be judged; do not condemn, and you will not be condemned; forgive, and you will be forgiven. Give, and it will be given to you: A good measure, pressed down, shaken together, running over, will be poured into your lap. For the measure you use will be the measure you receive." He also told them a parable: "Someone who is blind cannot lead another who is blind, can he? Won't they both

fall into a pit? A disciple is not greater than his teacher, but everyone when fully trained will be like his teacher. Why do you see the speck in your brother's eye, but fail to see the beam of wood in your own? How can you say to your brother, 'Brother, let me remove the speck from your eye,' while you yourself don't see the beam in your own? You hypocrite! First remove the beam from your own eye, and then you can see clearly to remove the speck from your brother's eye. Luke 6:37-42

"Do not accumulate for yourselves treasures on earth, where moth and rust destroy and where thieves break in and steal. But accumulate for yourselves treasures in heaven, where moth and rust do not destroy, and thieves do not break in and steal. For where your treasure is, there your heart will be also. "The eye is the lamp of the body. If then your eye is healthy, your whole body will be full of light. But if your eye is diseased, your whole body will be full of darkness. If then the light in you is darkness, how great is the darkness! "No one can serve two masters, for either he will hate the one and love the other, or he will be devoted to the one and despise the other. You cannot serve God and money. "Therefore I tell you, do not worry about your life, what you will eat or drink, or about your body, what you will wear. Isn't there more to life than food and more to the body than clothing? Look at the birds in the sky: They do not sow, or reap, or gather into barns, yet your heavenly Father feeds them. Aren't you more valuable than they are? And which of you by worrying can add even one hour to his life? Why do you worry about clothing? Think about how the flowers of the field grow; they do not work or spin. Yet I tell you that not even Solomon in all his glory was clothed like one of these! And if this is how God clothes the wild grass, which is here today and tomorrow is tossed into the fire to heat the oven, won't he clothe you even more, you people of little faith? So then, don't worry saying, 'What will we eat?' or 'What will we drink?' or 'What will we wear?' For the unconverted pursue these things, and your heavenly Father knows that you need them. But above all pursue his kingdom and righteousness, and all these things will be given to you

as well. So then, do not worry about tomorrow, for tomorrow will worry about itself. Today has enough trouble of its own. Matthew 6:19-34

"Do not judge so that you will not be judged. For by the standard you judge you will be judged, and the measure you use will be the measure you receive. Why do you see the speck in your brother's eye, but fail to see the beam of wood in your own? Or how can you say to your brother, 'Let me remove the speck from your eye,' while there is a beam in your own? You hypocrite! First remove the beam from your own eye, and then you can see clearly to remove the speck from your brother's eye. Do not give what is holy to dogs or throw your pearls before pigs; otherwise they will trample them under their feet and turn around and tear you to pieces. Matthew 7:1-6

Application

"Ask and it will be given to you; seek and you will find; knock and the door will be opened for you. For everyone who asks receives, and the one who seeks finds, and to the one who knocks, the door will be opened. Is there anyone among you who, if his son asks for bread, will give him a stone? Or if he asks for a fish, will give him a snake? If you then, although you are evil, know how to give good gifts to your children, how much more will your Father in heaven give good gifts to those who ask him! In everything, treat others as you would want them to treat you, for this fulfills the law and the prophets. "Enter through the narrow gate, because the gate is wide and the way is spacious that leads to destruction, and there are many who enter through it. How narrow is the gate and difficult the way that leads to life, and there are few who find it! "Watch out for false prophets, who come to you in sheep's clothing but inwardly are voracious wolves. You will recognize them by their fruit. Grapes are not gathered from thorns or figs from thistles, are they? In the same way, every good tree bears good fruit, but the bad tree bears bad fruit. A good tree is not able to bear bad fruit, nor a bad tree

to bear good fruit. Every tree that does not bear good fruit is cut down and thrown into the fire. So then, you will recognize them by their fruit. "Not everyone who says to me, 'Lord, Lord,' will enter into the kingdom of heaven-only the one who does the will of my Father in heaven. On that day, many will say to me, 'Lord, Lord, didn't we prophesy in your name, and in your name cast out demons and do many powerful deeds?' Then I will declare to them, 'I never knew you. Go away from me, you lawbreakers!' "Everyone who hears these words of mine and does them is like a wise man who built his house on rock. The rain fell, the flood came, and the winds beat against that house, but it did not collapse because it had been founded on rock. Everyone who hears these words of mine and does not do them is like a foolish man who built his house on sand. The rain fell, the flood came, and the winds beat against that house, and it collapsed; it was utterly destroyed!" Matthew 7:7-27

"For no good tree bears bad fruit, nor again does a bad tree bear good fruit, for each tree is known by its own fruit. For figs are not gathered from thorns, nor are grapes picked from brambles. The good person out of the good treasury of his heart produces good, and the evil person out of his evil treasury produces evil, for his mouth speaks from what fills his heart. "Why do you call me 'Lord, Lord,' and don't do what I tell you? "Everyone who comes to me and listens to my words and puts them into practice-I will show you what he is like: He is like a man building a house, who dug down deep, and laid the foundation on bedrock. When a flood came, the river burst against that house but could not shake it, because it had been well built. But the person who hears and does not put my words into practice is like a man who built a house on the ground without a foundation. When the river burst against that house, it collapsed immediately, and was utterly destroyed!" Luke 6:43-49

Response

When Jesus finished saying these things, the crowds were amazed by
his teaching, because he taught them like one who had authority,
not like their experts in the law.After he came down from the
mountain, large crowds followed him. Matthew 7:28 - 8:1

The eleventh miracle – the first non Jew to believe

After finishing His amazing teaching, the Sermon on the Mount, Jesus
walks back to His adopted hometown of Capernaum. In the town
Jesus was confronted with an extraordinary situation, the commander
of the Roman occupation force in the area, a Centurion, caring for an
ill servant. A Centurion is a commander of a group of 100 soldiers.
Because the 10th Roman Legion did not arrive in Israel until the revolt
that led to the Temple destruction in 70 AD, most of the soldiers of the
time were imported constabulary serving the governor Herod Antipas.
It appears there was a Roman detachment of professional fighting men
in Galilee, led by a professional soldier, a Roman Centurion. It further appears that this occupying Roman commander was not only well
thought of but had a love for God's holy chosen Jewish people and had
built the black basalt synagogue in the city. The Centurion clearly cares
for his servant and the local Jewish elders clearly think highly of him.

What is more amazing is that the Centurion had an insight into the
power and authority of Jesus that few in Israel had yet understood.
Remember that Jesus' second miracle was the healing of a royal official's son (John 4:43-54) and that it was done remotely, accompanied
by a rebuke of the people because of their lack of belief. Every other
healing by Jesus since then, had seen the infirm meet with Jesus and
receive His healing touch. The Centurion, who is not a Jew, demonstrated none of the unbelief of the royal official. Indeed the Centurion
comes right out and acknowledges Jesus' authority with certainty and
absolute belief, and receives that which he asks.

After Jesus had finished teaching all this to the people, he entered Capernaum. A centurion there had a slave who was highly regarded, but who was sick and at the point of death. When the centurion heard about Jesus, he sent some Jewish elders to him, asking him to come and heal his slave. When they came to Jesus, they urged him earnestly, "He is worthy to have you do this for him, because he loves our nation, and even built our synagogue." So Jesus went with them. When he was not far from the house, the centurion sent friends to say to him, "Lord, do not trouble yourself, for I am not worthy to have you come under my roof. That is why I did not presume to come to you. Instead, say the word, and my servant must be healed. For I too am a man set under authority, with soldiers under me. I say to this one, 'Go,' and he goes, and to another, 'Come,' and he comes, and to my slave, 'Do this,' and he does it." When Jesus heard this, he was amazed at him. He turned and said to the crowd that followed him, "I tell you, not even in Israel have I found such faith!" So when those who had been sent returned to the house, they found the slave well. Luke 7:1-10

When he entered Capernaum, a centurion came to him asking for help: "Lord, my servant is lying at home paralyzed, in terrible anguish." Jesus said to him, "I will come and heal him." But the centurion replied, "Lord, I am not worthy to have you come under my roof. Instead, just say the word and my servant will be healed. For I too am a man under authority, with soldiers under me. I say to this one, 'Go' and he goes, and to another 'Come' and he comes, and to my slave 'Do this' and he does it." When Jesus heard this he was amazed and said to those who followed him, "I tell you the truth, I have not found such faith in anyone in Israel! I tell you, many will come from the east and west to share the banquet with Abraham, Isaac, and Jacob in the kingdom of heaven, but the sons of the kingdom will be thrown out into the outer darkness, where there will be weeping and gnashing of teeth." Then Jesus said to the centurion, "Go; just as you believed, it will be done for you." And the servant was healed at that hour. Matthew 8:5-13

The twelve miracle – the dead are raised to life in Nain

Jesus then walks from Capernaum to Nain, a distance of forty-seven kilometres. Nain is a small village fourteen kilometres south of Nazareth on the northwestern slope of Jebel ed-Duchy (Hill of Moreh). The village has a beautiful view across the plain of Carmel, over the Nazareth hills, past Mount Tabor to the snow-capped peak of Mount Hermon. To the south are the heights of Gilboa and the uplands of Samaria. Nestled in the rocks to the east of this town were many ancient burial tombs, some of which remain today.

The photo above shows the village of Nain on the hill slope looking towards Mount Tabor (Mount of Transfiguration) and was taken by the American colony photo department between 1900 and 1920.

Jesus would have approached the village from the north-east and if He had walked all day from Capernaum He would have arrived at the town at dusk, which was a popular time for funerals. Jesus was not alone, but was with His disciples and a large crowd who were probably quite jubilant, but tired from the walk. This cavalcade of Messianic excitement runs straight into a funeral procession led by a lonely widow weeping before the body of her only son, who is being carried towards the burial tombs in the rocks. As was the custom, the body would have been wrapped in a burial shroud with the face exposed, and was most likely carried upon a bier, a type of wicker conveyance.[22]

This is a beautiful story of two people, the Saviour of the world and a heart-broken widow. No prayer is offered, no assistance sought, just the compassion of Jesus and the dead are raised to life. The impact on the disciples is equally breath-taking. For the first time, Luke refers to Jesus as, "the Lord" (Luke 7:13), and commonly thereafter. This Hebrew word 'Adonai' was the word the Jews spoke out loud when they read God's name 'Yahweh' in the Hebrew text. This was a defining moment, as Jesus proved His power over life and death and those around Him acknowledged it.

> *Soon afterward Jesus went to a town called Nain, and his disciples and a large crowd went with him. As he approached the town gate, a man who had died was being carried out, the only son of his mother (who was a widow), and a large crowd from the town was with her. When the Lord saw her, he had compassion for her and said to her, "Do not weep." Then he came up and touched the bier, and those who carried it stood still. He said, "Young man, I say to you, get up!" So the dead man sat up and began to speak, and Jesus gave him back to his mother. Fear seized them all, and they began to glorify God, saying, "A great prophet has appeared among us!" and*

---

22   Alfred Edersheim, Life & Times, vol. 1, chapter 20

"God has come to help his people!" This report about Jesus circulated throughout Judea and all the surrounding country. Luke 7:11-17

The prison cell

The gospel story now moves to the prison cell where John the Baptist lies rotting. John has heard that the Messiah is moving with power and he sends two of his disciples to ask Jesus, are you the one I baptised in the Jordan, the one who raises the dead to life, the one who is 'Adonai', literally God?

Now when John heard in prison about the deeds Christ had done, he sent his disciples to ask a question: "Are you the one who is to come, or should we look for another?" Jesus answered them, "Go tell John what you hear and see: The blind see, the lame walk, lepers are cleansed, the deaf hear, the dead are raised, and the poor have good news proclaimed to them. Blessed is anyone who takes no offense at me."... Matthew 11:2-6

John's disciples informed him about all these things. So John called two of his disciples and sent them to Jesus to ask, "Are you the one who is to come, or should we look for another?" When the men came to Jesus, they said, "John the Baptist has sent us to you to ask, 'Are you the one who is to come, or should we look for another?'" At that very time Jesus cured many people of diseases, sicknesses, and evil spirits, and granted sight to many who were blind. So he answered them, "Go tell John what you have seen and heard: The blind see, the lame walk, lepers are cleansed, the deaf hear, the dead are raised, the poor have good news proclaimed to them. Blessed is anyone who takes no offense at me." Luke 7:18-23

Jesus quotes Isaiah 35:5-6a, a clear Messianic prophesy as He points to Himself as the fulfilment of this prophesy.

Then blind eyes will open, deaf ears will hear. Then the lame will leap like a deer, the mute tongue will shout for joy. Isaiah 35:5-6a

Jesus uses this discussion again as a teaching opportunity about the Kingdom of God for the crowd that continued to flock around him.

While they were going away, Jesus began to speak to the crowd about John: "What did you go out into the wilderness to see? A reed shaken by the wind? What did you go out to see? A man dressed in fancy clothes? Look, those who wear fancy clothes are in the homes of kings! What did you go out to see? A prophet? Yes, I tell you, and more than a prophet. This is the one about whom it is written: 'Look, I am sending my messenger ahead of you, who will prepare your way before you.' "I tell you the truth, among those born of women, no one has arisen greater than John the Baptist. Yet the one who is least in the kingdom of heaven is greater than he is. From the days of John the Baptist until now the kingdom of heaven has suffered violence, and forceful people lay hold of it. For all the prophets and the law prophesied until John appeared. And if you are willing to accept it, he is Elijah, who is to come. The one who has ears had better listen! "To what should I compare this generation? They are like children sitting in the marketplaces who call out to one another, 'We played the flute for you, yet you did not dance; we wailed in mourning, yet you did not weep.' For John came neither eating nor drinking, and they say, 'He has a demon!' The Son of Man came eating and drinking, and they say, 'Look at him, a glutton and a drunk, a friend of tax collectors and sinners!' But wisdom is vindicated by her deeds." Matthew 11:7-19

When John's messengers had gone, Jesus began to speak to the crowds about John: "What did you go out into the wilderness to see? A reed shaken by the wind? What did you go out to see? A man dressed in fancy clothes? Look, those who wear fancy clothes and live in luxury are in kings' courts! What did you go out to see? A prophet? Yes, I tell you, and more than a prophet. This is the one about whom it is written, 'Look, I am sending my messenger ahead of you, who will prepare your way before you.' I tell you, among those born of women no one is greater than John. Yet the one who is least in the kingdom of God is greater than he is." (Now all the people who heard this, even the tax collectors, acknowledged God's justice, because they had been baptized with John's baptism. However, the Pharisees and the experts in religious law rejected God's purpose for themselves, because they had not been baptized by John.) "To what then should I compare the people of this generation, and what are they like? They are like children sitting in the marketplace and calling out to one another, 'We played the flute for you, yet you did not dance; we wailed in mourning, yet you did not weep.' For John the Baptist has come eating no bread and drinking no wine, and you say, 'He has a demon!' The Son of Man has come eating and drinking, and you say, 'Look at him, a glutton and a drunk, a friend of tax collectors and sinners!' But wisdom is vindicated by all her children." Luke 7:24-35

Jesus rebukes three cities

Jesus then rebukes three northern Galilean Jewish cities in which He had performed miracles during the previous twelve months: Chorazin, Bethsaida and Capernaum. He compares them to three non-Jewish cities: the two Phoenician cities of Tyre and Sidon to the north of Israel on the Mediterranean and the biblical city of perversion, Sodom that was destroyed by the Lord in the Jordan Valley (Genesis 19).

Firstly a little about Chorazin and Bethsaida as Capernaum has already been discussed. Chorazin (Korazin or Korazim) is located on the side of a hill four kilometres north of Capernaum and is only mentioned in this curse and that of Luke's curse later on. Now that's a sad indictment on a town. Bethsaida, the birthplace of some of the apostles notably – Andrew, Peter and Philip (John 1:44) is four kilometres north-east of Capernaum, near where the Jordan River enters the Sea of Galilee. All three towns formed the 'evangelical triangle' where most of Jesus' recorded miracles occurred. Yet it appears that whilst the people were overjoyed to be made whole, no tangible longer-term change resulted in their lives. Indeed in Capernaum everyone in the village who was infirm, diseased or demonically possessed was healed and set free and considering the closeness of Chorazin and Bethsaida it's a fair bet their citizens also experienced the healing power of the Messiah. Yet sadly it appears the hearts of the town folk may have been hard like those of the residents of Nazarath. They saw Jesus, they experienced the power, signs and wonders of Jesus, but unlike the widow at Nain, they did not see the 'Lordship' of the Messianic Jesus and perhaps only saw a prophet powerful in word and deed.

Then Jesus began to criticize openly the cities in which he had done many of his miracles, because they did not repent. "Woe to you, Chorazin! Woe to you, Bethsaida! If the miracles done in you had been done in Tyre and Sidon, they would have repented long ago in sackcloth and ashes. But I tell you, it will be more bearable for Tyre and Sidon on the day of judgment than for you! And you, Capernaum, will you be exalted to heaven? No, you will be thrown down to Hades! For if the miracles done among you had been done in Sodom, it would have continued to this day. But I tell you, it will be more bearable for the region of Sodom on the day of judgment than for you!" Matthew 11:20-24

At that time Jesus said, "I praise you, Father, Lord of heaven and earth, because you have hidden these things from the wise and intelligent, and revealed them to little children. Yes, Father, for this was your gracious will. All things have been handed over to me by my Father. No one knows the Son except the Father, and no one knows the Father except the Son and anyone to whom the Son decides to reveal him. Come to me, all you who are weary and burdened, and I will give you rest. Take my yoke on you and learn from me, because I am gentle and humble in heart, and you will find rest for your souls. For my yoke is easy to bear, and my load is not hard to carry." Matthew 11:25-30

The photo above of the northern view of Bethsaida was taken by the American colony photo department between 1898 and 1914.

CHAPTER 6

Parables
(31 AD)

Jesus is now approaching the end of the second year of ministry that would culminate in Passover in Jerusalem. He is focussing more on teaching, evidenced by the substantial number and depth of parables being taught and continues to authenticate His message with signs and wonders. These include taking command of the very elements themselves, confronting the demonic, healing the rejected and shamed and raising the dead.

Jesus, the God of second chances also returns to Nazareth for the second time to reach those He knew the best and probably loved the most. I don't think we appreciate the anguish of heart Jesus must have felt being rejected twice by those who knew him intimately. The book of Acts and subsequent books, such as James, demonstrates that some in Jesus' family did eventually come to see Him as Saviour. I wonder how many stubbornly refused, knowing Him the most, yet truly knowing Him the least.

That of course could not be said of the disciples, who were sent out in pairs to the lost sheep of Israel to proclaim the simple truth that the kingdom of God had arrived. They were to heal the sick, raise the dead, cleanse those who have leprosy, and drive out demons as signs of this truth. What joy they shared with Jesus on their return, excited by how the kingdom of God was growing. I gather this joy was also communicated by Judas who later betrayed Jesus. How Judas could lay his hands on people to heal the sick and cast out the demonic, and then deny the Saviour, whose name he called upon to do the impossible, is unbelievable. That sadness for another day. This day's sadness was the fate of John the Baptist, whose message of preparation was done, whose service was complete and who had run his last race on earth.

Dinner with Simon the Pharisee

Jesus is now somewhere in Galilee, possibly still in Nain. The setting in the Pharisee's house is what is important and Jesus' interaction with a local woman, quite possibly a prostitute. The picture is that of an ungracious religious leader who did not offer Jesus the normal courtesy of water for His feet (the roads were dusty), oil for his head and the shalom kiss of peace, and a penitent woman who offered all three at Jesus' feet with her tears.

Now one of the Pharisees asked Jesus to have dinner with him, so he went into the Pharisee's house and took his place at the table. Then when a woman of that town, who was a sinner, learned that Jesus was dining at the Pharisee's house, she brought an alabaster jar of perfumed oil. As she stood behind him at his feet, weeping, she began to wet his feet with her tears. She wiped them with her hair, kissed them, and anointed them with the perfumed oil. Now when the Pharisee who had invited him saw this, he said to himself, "If this man were a prophet, he would know who and what kind of woman this is who is touching him, that she is a sinner." So Jesus answered him, "Simon, I have something to say to you." He replied, "Say it, Teacher." "A certain creditor had two debtors; one owed him five hundred silver coins, and the other fifty. When they could not pay, he canceled the debts of both. Now which of them will love him more?" Simon answered, "I suppose the one who had the bigger debt canceled." Jesus said to him, "You have judged rightly." Then, turning toward the woman, he said to Simon, "Do you see this woman? I entered your house. You gave me no water for my feet, but she has wet my feet with her tears and wiped them with her hair. You gave me no kiss of greeting, but from the time I entered she has not stopped kissing my feet. You did not anoint my head with oil, but she has anointed my feet with perfumed oil. Therefore I tell you, her sins, which were many, are forgiven, thus she loved much; but the one who is forgiven little loves little." Then Jesus said to her, "Your sins are forgiven." But those who were at the table with him began to say among themselves, "Who is this, who even forgives sins?" He said to the woman, "Your faith has saved you; go in peace." Luke 7:36-50

As Jesus finished this episode in Nain, He continued to move from village to village, telling the good news of salvation.

Some time afterward he went on through towns and villages, preaching and proclaiming the good news of the kingdom of God. The twelve were with him, and also some women who had been healed of evil spirits and disabilities: Mary (called Magdalene), from whom seven demons had gone out, and Joanna the wife of Cuza (Herod's household manager), Susanna, and many others who provided for them out of their own resources. Luke 8:1-3

It appears that a number of women made up the travelling party and wore the financial burden of support and would continue to do so for the next two years. They include:

Mary Magdalene. Mary is from the Galilean seaside village of Magdala, five kilometres from Capernaum. She is mentioned fourteen times in the gospels, and had a horrific early life as Jesus cast out seven demons from her (Mark 16:9 and Luke 8:2). A notable feature in eight of the fourteen passages is that Mary is named with other women, but she is always at the head of the list. Therefore, one could conclude she occupied a place of leadership amongst the Godly women. In the five times where she is mentioned alone, the connection is with the death and resurrection of Christ (Mark 16:9; John 20:1, 11, 16 and 18). In one instance her name comes after that of the mother and the aunt of Jesus, where she stood close by the cross with these women (John 19:25). It is fair to say that no woman, except perhaps the mother of Jesus, superseded Mary in her utter devotion to Jesus.

Joanna. Joanna was the wife of Chuza, the manager of Herod's household. It is generally accepted the household belonged to Herod Antipas, the Tetrarch of Galilee. Some assert that Chuza was the royal official who came to Jesus in Cana (John 4:46-54) and whose son was the recipient of Jesus' first recorded healing. If that is the case it further explains Joanna's devotion, her son was healed by Jesus. It's possible, though unknown. Arguably, if Chuza was not the royal official he and Joanna would have known who was and would have known what Jesus did. Joanna, like Mary Magdalene and Susanna had experienced a tormented upbringing, noting that Luke 8:2 says these women had been cured of evil spirits and diseases. Having been cured and set free they were devoted to Jesus and Jesus to them, as He appeared first to these woman after He rose from the grave (Luke 24:1-12).

Susanna. Susanna is another of the devoted women that Jesus set free from demonic oppression and diseases (Luke 8:2). It's interesting the two seem to go together, demonic oppression and disease. Nothing more is known of Susanna, except that she is a woman of means, supporting Jesus, and clearly devoted to Him. Nothing is known of the 'other' women generously supporting Jesus and nothing said of any men financially supporting Jesus. I'm just saying…

Jesus unjustly accused

Jesus continued to travel around Galilee, healing and teaching and evidently within walking distance of Nazareth as his family turns up to the village He is in. There is irony in this scene. Evidently the family was happy for Jesus to perform a miracle at the wedding in Cana to prevent embarrassment, but is not happy for Him to continue with signs and wonders to authenticate His message as the Saviour of the world. The gospels say that Jesus' mother, Mary, was also present. I wonder if she thought 'He is out of his mind' or was that more likely some jealous brothers? And what was Jesus' family doing agreeing with the religious elite, or is it merely guilty by association?

Now Jesus went home, and a crowd gathered so that they were not able to eat. When his family heard this they went out to restrain him, for they said, "He is out of his mind." The experts in the law who came down from Jerusalem said, "He is possessed by Beelzebul," and, "By the ruler of demons he casts out demons." So he called them and spoke to them in parables: "How can Satan cast out Satan? If a kingdom is divided against itself, that kingdom will not be able to stand. If a house is divided against itself, that house will not be able to stand. And if Satan rises against himself and is divided, he is not able to stand and his end has come. But no one is able to enter a strong man's house and steal his property unless he first ties up the strong man. Then he can thoroughly plunder his house. I tell you the truth, people will be forgiven for all sins, even all the blasphemies they utter. But whoever blasphemes against the Holy Spirit will never be forgiven, but is guilty of an eternal sin" (because they said, "He has an unclean spirit"). Mark 3:20-30

The thirteenth miracle – casting out the demonic
The maddening crowds continue to press upon Jesus, desperate for the healing touch of the Messiah, and with them a blind and mute man caused by demonic possession. Jesus healed the man, casting the demon out, only to be rebuked by the religious elite who couldn't find it in themselves to question their own man-made rules, so they accuse the Son of God of being demonic. It would be ridiculous if not so seri-

ous that the nation's leaders were so blind. Jesus calls them to account for their words and by default calls us to account.

Then they brought to him a demon-possessed man who was blind and mute. Jesus healed him so that he could speak and see. All the crowds were amazed and said, "Could this one be the Son of David?" But when the Pharisees heard this they said, "He does not cast out demons except by the power of Beelzebul, the ruler of demons!" Now when Jesus realized what they were thinking, he said to them, "Every kingdom divided against itself is destroyed, and no town or house divided against itself will stand. So if Satan casts out Satan, he is divided against himself. How then will his kingdom stand? And if I cast out demons by Beelzebul, by whom do your sons cast them out? For this reason they will be your judges. But if I cast out demons by the Spirit of God, then the kingdom of God has already overtaken you. How else can someone enter a strong man's house and steal his property, unless he first ties up the strong man? Then he can thoroughly plunder the house. Whoever is not with me is against me, and whoever does not gather with me scatters. For this reason I tell you, people will be forgiven for every sin and blasphemy, but the blasphemy against the Spirit will not be forgiven. Whoever speaks a word against the Son of Man will be forgiven. But whoever speaks against the Holy Spirit will not be forgiven, either in this age or in the age to come. "Make a tree good and its fruit will be good, or make a tree bad and its fruit will be bad, for a tree is known by its fruit. Offspring of vipers! How are you able to say anything good, since you are evil? For the mouth speaks from what fills the heart. The good person brings good things out of his good treasury, and the evil person brings evil things out of his evil treasury. I tell you that on the day of judgment, people will give an account for every worthless word they speak. For by your words you will be justified, and by your words you will be condemned." Matthew 12:22-37

Now he was casting out a demon that was mute. When the demon had gone out, the man who had been mute began to speak, and the crowds were amazed. But some of them said, "By the power of Beelzebul, the ruler of demons, he casts out demons." Others, to test him, began asking for a sign from heaven. But Jesus, realizing their thoughts, said to them, "Every kingdom divided against itself is destroyed, and a divided household falls. So if Satan too is divided against himself, how will his kingdom stand? I ask you this because you claim that I cast out demons by Beelzebul. Now if I cast out demons by Beelzebul, by whom do your sons cast them out? Therefore they will be your judges. But if I cast out demons by the finger of God, then the kingdom of God has already overtaken you. When a strong man, fully armed, guards his own palace, his possessions are safe. But when a stronger man attacks and conquers him, he takes away the first man's armor on which the man relied and divides up his plunder. Whoever is not with me is against me, and whoever does not gather with me scatters. "When an unclean spirit goes out of a person, it passes through waterless places looking for rest but not finding any. Then it says, 'I will return to the home I left.' When it returns, it finds the house swept clean and put in order. Then it goes and brings seven other spirits more evil than itself, and they go in and live there, so the last state of that person is worse than the first." As he said these things, a woman in the crowd spoke out to him, "Blessed is the womb that bore you and the breasts at which you nursed!" But he replied, "Blessed rather are those who hear the word of God and obey it!" Luke 11:14-28

Nineveh, Jonah and the Queen of the South

Not content with accusing Jesus of being the devil, the religious elite then demand a sign. Apparently the innumerable healings, restorations, demonic expulsions and command over the elements weren't enough for those blinded by their own self-righteousness. Jesus points the religious elite to the sign of Jonah going to Nineveh as symbolic of his impending death and resurrection and to the Queen of the South as emulating how people should be, eagerly searching out the truth of the Messiah. To give this context, a little bit about Nineveh, Jonah and the Queen of the South.

The story of Jonah and the whale is recorded in the Old Testament book of Jonah. Jonah is sent as a prophet to warn the people in the ancient capital of the Assyrian empire, Nineveh, to repent and turn to God. Jonah runs away from God on a ship heading west towards Spain, nice try, so God sends a storm and a whale and Jonah gets swallowed and belched onto the shore of modern day Lebanon three days later. He then walks 400 kilometres west to the Euphrates River and then onto to the capital of the Assyrian empire, Nineveh (the modern day city of Mosul in Iraq) to say 'repent'. The Jews all knew this story about Jonah's three days avoiding whale mucus sitting in its dark stomach. Jesus used this knowledge to point to Himself spending three days in the ground, physically dead, before He rises again.

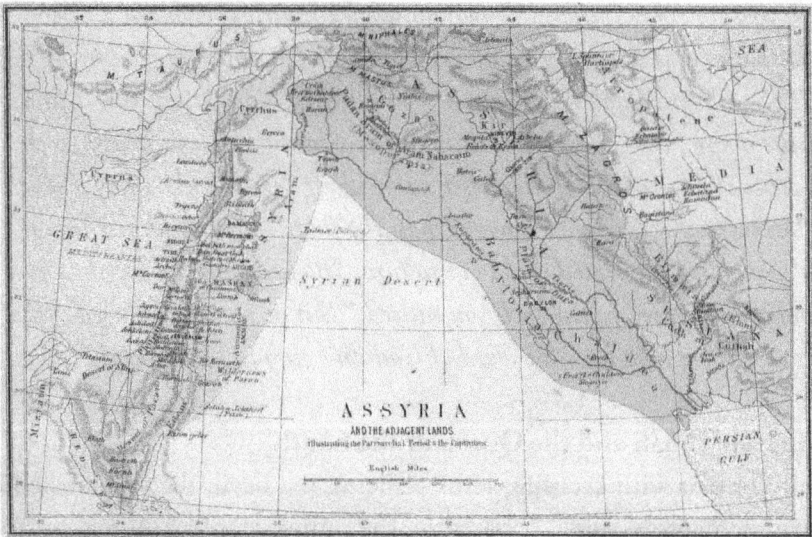

The location of Israel and Mesopotamia courtesy the American Bible Society 1888

The Queen of the South is better known as the Queen of Sheba or Queen of modern day Ethiopia. She came with enormous pomp to visit King Solomon and seek his wisdom (2 Chronicles 9:1-12 and

1 Kings 10:1-13). She gave Solomon almost four and a half tonnes of gold (120 talents), and large amounts of spices and gem stones in appreciation for the opportunity to sit at the feet of such wisdom. That is a large retinue to bring all those gifts. Yet what did the religious elite do and bring? They brought nothing, accused Jesus of everything and believed nothing. What a contrast.

Then some of the experts in the law along with some Pharisees answered him, "Teacher, we want to see a sign from you." But he answered them, "An evil and adulterous generation asks for a sign, but no sign will be given to it except the sign of the prophet Jonah. For just as Jonah was in the belly of the huge fish for three days and three nights, so the Son of Man will be in the heart of the earth for three days and three nights. The people of Nineveh will stand up at the judgment with this generation and condemn it, because they repented when Jonah preached to them-and now, something greater than Jonah is here! The queen of the South will rise up at the judgment with this generation and condemn it, because she came from the ends of the earth to hear the wisdom of Solomon-and now, something greater than Solomon is here!" When an unclean spirit goes out of a person, it passes through waterless places looking for rest but does not find it. Then it says, 'I will return to the home I left.' When it returns, it finds the house empty, swept clean, and put in order. Then it goes and brings with it seven other spirits more evil than itself, and they go in and live there, so the last state of that person is worse than the first. It will be that way for this evil generation as well!" Matthew 12:38-45

As the crowds were increasing, Jesus began to say, "This generation is a wicked generation; it looks for a sign, but no sign will be given to it except the sign of Jonah. For just as Jonah became a sign to the people of Nineveh, so the Son of Man will be a sign to this generation. The queen of the South will rise up at the judgment with the people of this generation and condemn them, because she came from the ends of the earth to hear the wisdom of Solomon-and now, something greater than

Solomon is here! The people of Nineveh will stand up at the judgment with this generation and condemn it, because they repented when Jonah preached to them-and now, something greater than Jonah is here! "No one after lighting a lamp puts it in a hidden place or under a basket, but on a lampstand, so that those who come in can see the light. Your eye is the lamp of your body. When your eye is healthy, your whole body is full of light, but when it is diseased, your body is full of darkness. Therefore see to it that the light in you is not darkness. If then your whole body is full of light, with no part in the dark, it will be as full of light as when the light of a lamp shines on you." Luke 11:29-36

Announcement of a new spiritual kingship

Not content with calling their brother Jesus 'out of his mind', His brothers send someone to call for Him, only to be met with what must have seemed an opaque answer. The answer was more illuminating than they thought, for it showed an amazing aspect of the coming New Covenant of Grace. That we would be reconciled to God and would, at the cross, inherit the very righteousness of God because Jesus would pay the penalty for our sin. This righteousness qualifies us to be adopted as sons of God (Romans 8:15, 8:23, 9:4, Galatians 4:5 and Ephesians 1:5), and thus quite literally brothers and sisters of Christ. Wow!

Then Jesus' mother and his brothers came. Standing outside, they sent word to him, to summon him. A crowd was sitting around him and they said to him, "Look, your mother and your brothers are outside looking for you." He answered them and said, "Who are my mother and my brothers?" And looking at those who were sitting around him in a circle, he said, "Here are my mother and my brothers! For whoever does the will of God is my brother and sister and mother." Mark 3:31-35

While Jesus was still speaking to the crowds, his mother and brothers came and stood outside, asking to speak to him. Someone told him, "Look, your mother and your brothers are standing outside wanting to speak to you." To the one who had said this, Jesus replied, "Who is my mother and who are my brothers?" And pointing toward his disciples he said, "Here are my mother and my brothers! For whoever does the will of my Father in heaven is my brother and sister and mother." Matthew 12:46-50

Now Jesus' mother and his brothers came to him, but they could not get near him because of the crowd. So he was told, "Your mother and your brothers are standing outside, wanting to see you." But he replied to them, "My mother and my brothers are those who hear the word of God and do it." Luke 8:19-21

The parables

As more and more people started to come and hear Jesus, He commences another series of teaching, again in parables (stories) to illustrate truths. The setting is once again the Sea of Galilee and the crowds are huge.

Again he began to teach by the lake. Such a large crowd gathered around him that he got into a boat on the lake and sat there while the whole crowd was on the shore by the lake. He taught them many things in parables, and in his teaching said to them: Mark 4:1-2

On that day after Jesus went out of the house, he sat by the lake. And such a large crowd gathered around him that he got into a boat to sit while the whole crowd stood on the shore. He told them many things in parables, saying:... Matthew 13:1-3a

While a large crowd was gathering and people were coming to Jesus from one town after another, he spoke to them in a parable:..... Luke 8:4

Interestingly Jesus' disciples didn't quite understand why He spoke in parables and would later ask Him the purpose of these parables. The purpose is probably a good place to start to understand where Jesus was going with His teaching.

Then his disciples asked him what this parable meant. He said, "You have been given the opportunity to know the secrets of the kingdom of God, but for others they are in parables, so that although they see they may not see, and although they hear they may not understand. Luke 8:9-10

When he was alone, those around him with the twelve asked him about the parables. He said to them, "The secret of the kingdom of God has been given to you. But to those outside, everything is in parables, so that although they look they may look but not see, and although they hear they may hear but not understand, so they may not repent and be forgiven." Mark 4:10-12

Then the disciples came to him and said, "Why do you speak to them in parables?" He replied, "You have been given the opportunity to know the secrets of the kingdom of heaven, but they have not. For whoever has will be given more, and will have an abundance. But whoever does not have, even what he has will be taken from him. For this reason I speak to them in parables: Although they see they do not see, and although they hear they do not hear nor do they understand. And concerning them the prophecy of Isaiah is fulfilled that says: 'You will listen carefully yet will never understand, you will look closely yet will never comprehend. For the heart of this people has become dull; they are hard of hearing, and they have shut their eyes, so that they would not see with their eyes and hear with their ears and understand with their hearts and turn, and I would heal them.' "But your eyes are blessed because they see, and your ears because they hear. For I tell you the truth, many prophets and righteous people longed to see what you see but did not see it, and to hear what you hear but did not hear it. Matthew 13:10-17

Once Jesus finished teaching the nine parables listed below (six of them in public, the last three given to the disciples indoors), He asks His disciples if they understood what He had said and then encourages them as teachers to bring forth the fulfilment of the truth, the message of grace. It's the same encouragement to us. To teach the history and background of the gospels but also the new treasure of the New Covenant of Grace.

"Have you understood all these things?" They replied, "Yes." Then he said to them, "Therefore every expert in the law who has been trained for the kingdom of heaven is like the owner of a house who brings out of his treasure what is new and old." Matthew 13:51-52

Jesus spoke all these things in parables to the crowds; he did not speak to them without a parable. This fulfilled what was spoken by the prophet: "I will open my mouth in parables, I will announce what has been hidden from the foundation of the world." Matthew 13:34-35

So with many parables like these, he spoke the word to them, as they were able to hear. He did not speak to them without a parable. But privately he explained everything to his own disciples. Mark 4:33-34

Parable one - the sower

"A sower went out to sow his seed. And as he sowed, some fell along the path and was trampled on, and the wild birds devoured it. Other seed fell on rock, and when it came up, it withered because it had no moisture. Other seed fell among the thorns, and they grew up with it and choked it. But other seed fell on good soil and grew, and it produced a hundred times as much grain." As he said this, he called out, "The one who has ears to hear had better listen!" Luke 8:5-8

"Listen! A sower went out to sow. And as he sowed, some seed fell along the path, and the birds came and devoured it. Other seed fell on rocky ground where it did not have much soil. It sprang up at once because the soil was not deep. When the sun came up it was scorched, and because it did not have sufficient root, it withered. Other seed fell among the thorns, and they grew up and choked it, and it did not produce grain. But other seed fell on good soil and produced grain, sprouting and growing; some yielded thirty times as much, some sixty, and some a hundred times." And he said, "Whoever has ears to hear had better listen!" Mark 4:3-9

"Listen! A sower went out to sow. And as he sowed, some seeds fell along the path, and the birds came and devoured them. Other seeds fell on rocky ground where they did not have much soil. They sprang up quickly because the soil was not deep. But when the sun came up, they were scorched, and because they did not have sufficient root, they withered.Other seeds fell among the thorns, and they grew up and choked them. But other seeds fell on good soil and produced grain, some a hundred times as much, some sixty, and some thirty. The one who has ears had better listen!" *Matthew 13:3b-9*

"Now the parable means this: The seed is the word of God. Those along the path are the ones who have heard; then the devil comes and takes away the word from their hearts, so that they may not believe and be saved. Those on the rock are the ones who receive the word with joy when they hear it, but they have no root. They believe for a while, but in a time of testing fall away. As for the seed that fell among thorns, these are the ones who hear, but as they go on their way they are choked by the worries and riches and pleasures of life, and their fruit does not mature. But as for the seed that landed on good soil, these are the ones who, after hearing the word, cling to it with an honest and good heart, and bear fruit with steadfast endurance. Luke 8:11-15

He said to them, "Don't you understand this parable? Then how will
you understand any parable? The sower sows the word. These are
the ones on the path where the word is sown: Whenever they hear,
immediately Satan comes and snatches the word that was sown in
them. These are the ones sown on rocky ground: As soon as they hear
the word, they receive it with joy. But they have no root in themselves
and do not endure. Then, when trouble or persecution comes because
of the word, immediately they fall away. Others are the ones sown
among thorns: They are those who hear the word, but worldly cares,
the seductiveness of wealth, and the desire for other things come in and
choke the word, and it produces nothing. But these are the ones sown
on good soil: They hear the word and receive it and bear fruit, one
thirty times as much, one sixty, and one a hundred." Mark 4:13-20

"So listen to the parable of the sower: When anyone hears the word about
the kingdom and does not understand it, the evil one comes and snatches
what was sown in his heart; this is the seed sown along the path. The seed
sown on rocky ground is the person who hears the word and immediately
receives it with joy. But he has no root in himself and does not endure;
when trouble or persecution comes because of the word, immediately
he falls away. The seed sown among thorns is the person who hears the
word, but worldly cares and the seductiveness of wealth choke the word,
so it produces nothing. But as for the seed sown on good soil, this is the
person who hears the word and understands. He bears fruit, yielding a
hundred, sixty, or thirty times what was sown." Matthew 13:18-23

Parable two - the lamp

"No one lights a lamp and then covers it with a jar or puts it under
a bed, but puts it on a lampstand so that those who come in can see
the light. For nothing is hidden that will not be revealed, and nothing
concealed that will not be made known and brought to light. So listen

carefully, for whoever has will be given more, but whoever does not have, even what he thinks he has will be taken from him." Luke 8:16-18

He also said to them, "A lamp isn't brought to be put under a basket or under a bed, is it? Isn't it to be placed on a lampstand? For nothing is hidden except to be revealed, and nothing concealed except to be brought to light. If anyone has ears to hear, he had better listen!" And he said to them, "Take care about what you hear. The measure you use will be the measure you receive, and more will be added to you. For whoever has will be given more, but whoever does not have, even what he has will be taken from him." Mark 4:21-25

Parable three - the seed

He also said, "The kingdom of God is like someone who spreads seed on the ground. He goes to sleep and gets up, night and day, and the seed sprouts and grows, though he does not know how. By itself the soil produces a crop, first the stalk, then the head, then the full grain in the head. And when the grain is ripe, he sends in the sickle because the harvest has come." Mark 4:26-29

Parable four - the weeds

He presented them with another parable: "The kingdom of heaven is like a person who sowed good seed in his field. But while everyone was sleeping, an enemy came and sowed weeds among the wheat and went away. When the plants sprouted and bore grain, then the weeds also appeared. So the slaves of the owner came and said to him, 'Sir, didn't you sow good seed in your field? Then where did the weeds come from?' He said, 'An enemy has done this.' So the slaves replied, 'Do you want us to go and gather them?' But he said, 'No, since in gathering the weeds you may uproot the wheat with them. Let both grow together until the harvest. At harvest time I will tell the reapers, "First collect the weeds and tie them in bundles to be burned, but then gather the wheat into my barn."" Matthew 13:24-30

Jesus would specifically explain this parable to His disciples at their request, quite possibly because this was the first time they had heard about the impending end of ages. The spiritual word for the study of what comes next is eschatology and, apparently, it was as interesting then as it is now.

And his disciples came to him saying, "Explain to us the parable of the weeds in the field." He answered, "The one who sowed the good seed is the Son of Man. The field is the world and the good seed are the people of the kingdom. The weeds are the people of the evil one, and the enemy who sows them is the devil. The harvest is the end of the age, and the reapers are angels. As the weeds are collected and burned with fire, so it will be at the end of the age. The Son of Man will send his angels, and they will gather from his kingdom everything that causes sin as well as all lawbreakers. They will throw them into the fiery furnace, where there will be weeping and gnashing of teeth. Then the righteous will shine like the sun in the kingdom of their Father. The one who has ears had better listen! Matthew 13:36b-43

Parable five - the mustard seed

He gave them another parable: "The kingdom of heaven is like a mustard seed that a man took and sowed in his field. It is the smallest of all the seeds, but when it has grown it is the greatest garden plant and becomes a tree, so that the wild birds come and nest in its branches." Matthew 13:31-32

He also asked, "To what can we compare the kingdom of God, or what parable can we use to present it? It is like a mustard seed that when sown in the ground, even though it is the smallest of all

*the seeds in the ground – when it is sown, it grows up, becomes
the greatest of all garden plants, and grows large branches so
that the wild birds can nest in its shade." Mark 4:30-32*

*Thus Jesus asked, "What is the kingdom of God like? To what
should I compare it? It is like a mustard seed that a man took
and sowed in his garden. It grew and became a tree, and
the wild birds nested in its branches." Luke 13:18-19*

Parable six - the yeast

*He told them another parable: "The kingdom of heaven is
like yeast that a woman took and mixed with three measures
of flour until all the dough had risen." Matthew 13:33*

*Again he said, "To what should I compare the kingdom of God?
It is like yeast that a woman took and mixed with three measures
of flour until all the dough had risen." Luke 13:20-21*

Parables seven, eight and nine - the hidden treasure, the costly pearl and the net

Jesus would deliver the last three parables only to the disciples. They all went into a house where Jesus explained the meaning of the parable of the weeds and its linkage to the end of time. Jesus then teaches the disciples what the Kingdom of God is like, by comparing it to things of immeasurable value.

Then he left the crowds and went into the house.... Matthew 13:36a

*"The kingdom of heaven is like a treasure, hidden in a field, that a
person found and hid. Then because of joy he went and sold all that
he had and bought that field. "Again, the kingdom of heaven is like*

a merchant searching for fine pearls. When he found a pearl of great value, he went out and sold everything he had and bought it. "Again, the kingdom of heaven is like a net that was cast into the sea that caught all kinds of fish. When it was full, they pulled it ashore, sat down, and put the good fish into containers and threw the bad away. It will be this way at the end of the age. Angels will come and separate the evil from the righteous and throw them into the fiery furnace, where there will be weeping and gnashing of teeth. Matthew 13:44-50

Now when Jesus finished these parables, he moved on from there. Matthew 13:53

The fourteenth miracle – power of the wind and waves

The scene now moves back to the Sea of Galilee as Jesus and his disciples, of which at least five of them have fished this lake all their lives, jump in a boat to go to the other side of the lake. There are other boats with them, it's evening, they are travelling just as they are and Jesus promptly falls asleep on a cushion at the front of the boat (the rocky part of the vessel). A storm whips up. Surely the professional fishermen who are now disciples have seen storms on the lake before, but this one scares them all literally to death. Yet Jesus sleeps, secure in the knowledge of being in the Father's hands. It must have been some storm.

As an aside, when the disciples wake Jesus to accuse Him of not caring that they were all going to die, they were only concerned about their own safety. Not once did the disciples say to Jesus, 'we and the people in the other boats are going to die' as presumably the woman caring for Jesus and the disciples' needs were travelling in the other boats. Faced with fear, they thought only of themselves. These lads still had a lot to learn, and learn they did when Jesus took command of the very elements themselves.

159

*Now when Jesus saw a large crowd around him, he gave
orders to go to the other side of the lake. Matthew 8:18*

*As he got into the boat, his disciples followed him. And a great storm
developed on the sea so that the waves began to swamp the boat. But he
was asleep. So they came and woke him up saying, "Lord, save us! We are
about to die!" But he said to them, "Why are you cowardly, you people
of little faith?" Then he got up and rebuked the winds and the sea, and
it was dead calm. And the men were amazed and said, "What sort of
person is this? Even the winds and the sea obey him!" Matthew 8:23-27*

*One day Jesus got into a boat with his disciples and said to them, "Let's
go across to the other side of the lake." So they set out, and as they sailed he
fell asleep. Now a violent windstorm came down on the lake, and the boat
started filling up with water, and they were in danger. They came and
woke him, saying, "Master, Master, we are about to die!" So he got up
and rebuked the wind and the raging waves; they died down, and it was
calm. Then he said to them, "Where is your faith?" But they were afraid
and amazed, saying to one another, "Who then is this? He commands
even the winds and the water, and they obey him!" Luke 8:22-25*

*On that day, when evening came, Jesus said to his disciples, "Let's go across
to the other side of the lake." So after leaving the crowd, they took him
along, just as he was, in the boat, and other boats were with him. Now
a great windstorm developed and the waves were breaking into the boat,
so that the boat was nearly swamped. But he was in the stern, sleeping on
a cushion. They woke him up and said to him, "Teacher, don't you care
that we are about to die?" So he got up and rebuked the wind, and said
to the sea, "Be quiet! Calm down!" Then the wind stopped, and it was
dead calm. And he said to them, "Why are you cowardly? Do you still
not have faith?" They were overwhelmed by fear and said to one another,
"Who then is this? Even the wind and sea obey him!" Mark 4:35-41*

The fifteenth miracle – healing of the demon possessed man

Fresh from seeing Jesus, the creator of the universe, give orders to the elements of the earth to cease their tirade, the party lands at Gerasenes (Luke and Mark) or Gadarenes (Matthew). They are the same place, somewhere close to the town of Gergesa, the modern Kersa, close by the eastern shore of the Sea of Galilee. Gergesa has a mountain behind it with ancient tombs. It is probable that Gergesa was a small town at the time and probably unrecognisable to the reader, hence the reference to the 'Region of the Gerasenes', named after its capital Gerasa (Luke and Mark), or 'Region of the Gadarenes', named after its largest city Gadara (Matthew).

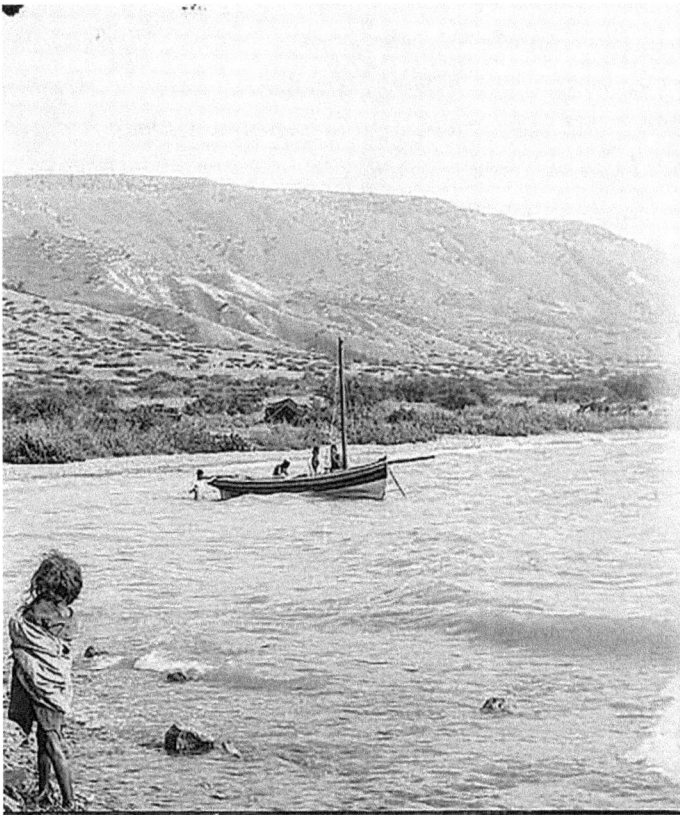

The photo above of the northern view of the region of Gerasenes / Gadarenes was taken by the American colony photo department between 1898 and 1914 and shows the mountain behind that contained the tombs.

Jesus is again faced with the demonic, yet not like He had previously seen or cast out. In this case it is one or two powerful, violent, naked, cut and bleeding men possessed by multiple demons. It must have been a frightening scene as the man (or men) met the travelling party as they stepped ashore. The man (or men) were screaming loudly but such was the power of Jesus that when he (they) saw Jesus, they fell at His feet and acknowledged Him as the Son of God. Such recognition was always followed by healing and restoration.

So they sailed over to the region of the Gerasenes, which is opposite Galilee. As Jesus stepped ashore, a certain man from the town met him who was possessed by demons. For a long time this man had worn no clothes and had not lived in a house, but among the tombs. When he saw Jesus, he cried out, fell down before him, and shouted with a loud voice, "Leave me alone, Jesus, Son of the Most High God! I beg you, do not torment me!" For Jesus had started commanding the evil spirit to come out of the man. (For it had seized him many times, so he would be bound with chains and shackles and kept under guard. But he would break the restraints and be driven by the demon into deserted places.) Jesus then asked him, "What is your name?" He said, "Legion," because many demons had entered him. And they began to beg him not to order them to depart into the abyss. Now a large herd of pigs was feeding there on the hillside, and the demonic spirits begged Jesus to let them go into them. He gave them permission. So the demons came out of the man and went into the pigs, and the herd of pigs rushed down the steep slope into the lake and drowned. When the herdsmen saw what had happened, they ran off and spread the news in the town and countryside. So the people went out to see what had happened, and they came to Jesus. They found the man from whom the demons had gone out, sitting at Jesus' feet, clothed and in his right mind, and they were afraid. Those who had seen it told them how the man who had been demon-possessed had been healed. Then all the people of the Gerasenes and the surrounding region asked Jesus to leave them alone, for they were seized with great fear. So he got into the boat and left. The man from whom the demons had gone out begged to go with him, but Jesus sent him away, saying, "Return to your home, and declare what God has done for you." So he went away, proclaiming throughout the whole town what Jesus had done for him. Luke 8:26-39

When he came to the other side, to the region of the Gadarenes, two demon-possessed men coming from the tombs met him. They were extremely violent, so that no one was able to pass by that way. They cried out, "Son of God, leave us alone! Have you come here to torment us before the time?" A large herd of pigs was feeding some distance from them. Then the demons begged him, "If you drive us out, send us into the herd of pigs." And he said, "Go!" So they came out and went into the pigs, and the herd rushed down the steep slope into the lake and drowned in the water. The herdsmen ran off, went into the town, and told everything that had happened to the demon-possessed men. Then the entire town came out to meet Jesus. And when they saw him, they begged him to leave their region. Matthew 8:28-34

So they came to the other side of the lake, to the region of the Gerasenes. Just as Jesus was getting out of the boat, a man with an unclean spirit came from the tombs and met him. He lived among the tombs, and no one could bind him anymore, not even with a chain. For his hands and feet had often been bound with chains and shackles, but he had torn the chains apart and broken the shackles in pieces. No one was strong enough to subdue him. Each night and every day among the tombs and in the mountains, he would cry out and cut himself with stones. When he saw Jesus from a distance, he ran and bowed down before him. Then he cried out with a loud voice, "Leave me alone, Jesus, Son of the Most High God! I implore you by God-do not torment me!" (For Jesus had said to him, "Come out of that man, you unclean spirit!") Jesus asked him, "What is your name?" And he said, "My name is Legion, for we are many." He begged Jesus repeatedly not to send them out of the region. There on the hillside, a great herd of pigs was feeding. And the demonic spirits begged him, "Send us into the pigs. Let us enter them." Jesus gave them permission. So the unclean spirits came out and went into the pigs. Then the herd rushed down the steep slope into the lake, and about two thousand were drowned in the lake. Now the herdsmen ran off and spread the news in the town and countryside, and the people went out to see what had happened. They came to Jesus and saw the demon-possessed man sitting there, clothed and in his right mind-the one who had the "Legion"-and they were afraid. Those who had seen what had happened to the demon-possessed man reported it, and they also told about the pigs. Then they began to beg Jesus to leave their region. As he was getting into the boat the man who had been demon-possessed asked if he could go with him. But Jesus did not permit him to do so. Instead, he said to him, "Go to your home and to your people and tell them what the Lord has done for you, that he had mercy on you." So he went away and began to proclaim in the Decapolis what Jesus had done for him, and all were amazed. Mark 5:1-20

I know what you're thinking, that was a sizeable economic loss the owners of the pigs just incurred. It does just show that the demonic loves to destroy and they don't mind what it is they kill. Hopefully the pig owners were insured.

The sixteenth and seventeenth miracles – twelve years of ordeal and joy

Our story now changes from the ferocious violence of the bloodied demon-possessed man (or men) now healed and restored, to another story of shed blood and beautiful restoration. Jesus jumped back in a boat and sailed to the north western side of the Sea of Galilee, probably back to Capernaum. The story that follows is a dichotomy of twelve years of joy and twelve years of sorrow. Joy for twelve years with a beautiful daughter and sorrow for twelve years for a desperate woman with uncontrolled bleeding who was not able to have children. Twelve years prior, joy came to a family through a child and hopelessness and despair came to a woman who could never, from that point, be a mother. Before Jesus arrives, both women are in pain, the daughter dying and finally dead and the woman hopeless and outcast. Then they both meet Jesus and, like the bloodied demon-possessed man (or men) on the other side of the lake, the women are left restored, whole and overjoyed.

In both instances of healing it was because of a touch of Jesus. The woman who was bleeding, intentionally went out to touch Jesus. When she heard that Jesus was coming, her faith said that if she just touched His clothes, she'd be healed (Mark 5:27-28). So she touched His cloak and was instantly healed. Jesus who was literally being mobbed – touched and grabbed by everyone – also knew she had been healed for He felt healing power, by faith, rush from Him.

Touching 'His cloak' is a strange place to grab Jesus. Surely, as you fought the crowds you'd grab His arm or shoulder or touch His back or cry out to Jesus. This poor woman, embarrassed, ashamed and most certainly shunned, did all her strength would allow her to – just reach out to Jesus. There is no audible prayer, laying on of hands or anointing oil. There is just a desperate cry of her heart to be made whole. Because of her outcast status, she had probably not felt the touch of others for over a decade and dared not touch a priest, prophet or doctor, nor probably wanted to after years of suffering at the hands of such as these. But she mustered the faith and strength to touch Jesus, even if it was just His cloak.

And the little girl...raised from the dead by a touch of Jesus. "Don't be afraid" the girl's father is told, "just believe'". Easy words to say, hard to accept when all that you love is being taken from you. Don't be afraid, just believe. What is interesting is that Mark 5:37 tells us that Jesus only took Peter, James and John into the house to see Jarius's daughter. This pattern would be repeated later on the Mount of Transfiguration and then at the olive press in the Garden of Gethsemane. Jesus had twelve disciples, but He included only the three closest to Him at key junctures and events. Jesus would later send out seventy-two 'disciples' to minister, and He would always have the crowds, but there is a pattern here for us to see. Jesus had some very close friends (the three), He had the group He was always around (the twelve), He had those He walked with as fellow travellers (the seventy-two) and there was always the maddening crowd.

Now when Jesus returned, the crowd welcomed him, because they were all waiting for him. Then a man named Jairus, who was a ruler of the synagogue, came up. Falling at Jesus' feet, he pleaded with him to come to his house, because he had an only daughter, about twelve years old, and she was dying. As Jesus was on his way, the crowds pressed around him. Now a woman was there who had been suffering from a hemorrhage for twelve years but could not be healed by anyone. She came up behind Jesus and touched the edge of his cloak, and at once the bleeding stopped. Then Jesus asked, "Who was it who touched me?" When they all denied it, Peter said, "Master, the crowds are surrounding you and pressing against you!" But Jesus said, "Someone touched me, for I know that power has gone out from me." When the woman saw that she could not escape notice, she came trembling and fell down before him. In the presence of all the people, she explained why she had touched him and how she had been immediately healed. Then he said to her, "Daughter, your faith has made you well. Go in peace." While he was still speaking, someone from the synagogue ruler's house came and said, "Your daughter is dead; do not trouble the teacher any longer." But when Jesus heard this, he told him, "Do not be afraid; just believe, and she will be healed." Now when he came to the house, Jesus did not let anyone go in with him except Peter, John, and James, and the child's father and mother. Now they were all wailing and mourning for her, but he said, "Stop your weeping; she is not dead but asleep." And they began making fun of him, because they knew that she was dead. But Jesus gently took her by the hand and said, "Child, get up." Her spirit returned, and she got up immediately. Then he told them to give her something to eat. Her parents were astonished, but he ordered them to tell no one what had happened. Luke 8:40-56

As he was saying these things, a ruler came, bowed low before him, and said, "My daughter has just died, but come and lay your hand on her and she will live." Jesus and his disciples got up and followed him. But a woman who had been suffering from a hemorrhage for twelve years came up behind him and touched the edge of his cloak. For she kept saying to herself, "If only I touch his cloak, I will be healed." But when Jesus turned and saw her he said, "Have courage, daughter! Your faith has made you well." And the woman was healed from that hour. When Jesus entered the ruler's house and saw the flute players and the disorderly crowd, he said, "Go away, for the girl is not dead but asleep." And they began making fun of him. But when the crowd had been put outside, he went in and gently took her by the hand, and the girl got up. And the news of this spread throughout that region. Matthew 9:18-26

When Jesus had crossed again in a boat to the other side, a large crowd gathered around him, and he was by the sea. Then one of the synagogue rulers, named Jairus, came up, and when he saw Jesus, he fell at his feet. He asked him urgently, "My little daughter is near death. Come and lay your hands on her so that she may be healed and live." Jesus went with him, and a large crowd followed and pressed around him. Now a woman was there who had been suffering from a hemorrhage for twelve years. She had endured a great deal under the care of many doctors and had spent all that she had. Yet instead of getting better, she grew worse. When she heard about Jesus, she came up behind him in the crowd and touched his cloak, for she kept saying, "If only I touch his clothes, I will be healed." At once the bleeding stopped, and she felt in her body that she was healed of her disease. Jesus knew at once that power had gone out from him. He turned around in the crowd and said, "Who touched my clothes?" His disciples said to him, "You see the crowd pressing against you and you say, 'Who touched me?'" But he looked around to see who had done it. Then the woman, with fear and trembling, knowing what had happened to her, came and fell down before him and told him the whole truth. He said to her, "Daughter, your faith has made you well. Go in peace, and be healed of your disease." While he was still speaking, people came from the synagogue ruler's house saying, "Your daughter has died. Why trouble the teacher any longer?" But Jesus, paying no attention to what was said, told the synagogue ruler, "Do not be afraid; just believe." He did not let anyone follow him except Peter, James, and John, the brother of James. They came to the house of the synagogue ruler where he saw noisy confusion and people weeping and wailing loudly. When he entered he said to them, "Why are you distressed and weeping? The child is not dead but asleep." And they began making fun of him. But he put them all outside and he took the child's father and mother and his own companions and went into the room where the child was. Then, gently taking the child by the hand, he said to her, "Talitha koum," which means, "Little girl, I say to you, get up." The girl got up at once and began to walk around (she was twelve years old). They were completely astonished at this. He strictly ordered that no one should know about this, and told them to give her something to eat. Mark 5:21-43

The eighteenth and nineteenth miracles – healing of two blind men and one mute man

As Jesus continued his journey through Capernaum en route to other towns and villages, He is confronted by two blind men and another man mute through demonic oppression. Jesus' compassion is evident and overflows in His timeless call for more workers to go into the field to reach more people. Compare this to the response of the religious elite who are more interested in strict observance to the rules than reaching the lost.

As Jesus went on from there, two blind men followed him, shouting, "Have mercy on us, Son of David!" When he went into the house, the blind men came to him. Jesus said to them, "Do you believe that I am able to do this?" They said to him, "Yes, Lord." Then he touched their eyes saying, "Let it be done for you according to your faith." And their eyes were opened. Then Jesus sternly warned them, "See that no one knows about this." But they went out and spread the news about him throughout that entire region. As they were going away, a man who could not talk and was demon-possessed was brought to him. After the demon was cast out, the man who had been mute spoke. The crowds were amazed and said, "Never has anything like this been seen in Israel!" But the Pharisees said, "By the ruler of demons he casts out demons." Matthew 9:27-34

Jesus returns to Nazareth for the last time

As Jesus went from town to town he eventually found himself back in His hometown of Nazareth. This was His second visit since the commencement of His ministry. Remember that when He returned the first time, the townsfolk – his friends – tried to kill Him (Luke 4:14-30). Despite this, Jesus, the God of the second chances, returns to His hometown. Unfortunately those who grew up with Jesus hadn't changed their view, which remains one of offence not acceptance. Jesus then simply moves on, quite probably sad at the intransigence of the Nazarites.

Then he came to his hometown and began to teach the people in their synagogue. They were astonished and said, "Where did this man get such wisdom and miraculous powers? Isn't this the carpenter's son? Isn't his mother named Mary? And aren't his brothers James, Joseph, Simon, and Judas? And aren't all his sisters here with us? Where did he get all this?" And so they took offense at him. But Jesus said to them, "A prophet is not without honor except in his hometown and in his own house." And he did not do many miracles there because of their unbelief. Matthew 13:54-58

Now Jesus left that place and came to his hometown, and his disciples followed him. When the Sabbath came, he began to teach in the synagogue. Many who heard him were astonished, saying, "Where did he get these ideas? And what is this wisdom that has been given to him? What are these miracles that are done through his hands? Isn't this the carpenter, the son of Mary and brother of James, Joses, Judas, and Simon? And aren't his sisters here with us?" And so they took offense at him. Then Jesus said to them, "A prophet is not without honor except in his hometown, and among his relatives, and in his own house." He was not able to do a miracle there, except to lay his hands on a few sick people and heal them. And he was amazed because of their unbelief. Mark 6:1-6a

Then Jesus went throughout all the towns and villages, teaching in their synagogues, preaching the good news of the kingdom, and healing every kind of disease and sickness. When he saw the crowds, he had compassion on them because they were bewildered and helpless, like sheep without a shepherd. Then he said to his disciples, "The harvest is plentiful, but the workers are few. Therefore ask the Lord of the harvest to send out workers into his harvest." Matthew 9:35-38

Then he [Jesus] went around among the villages and taught. Mark 6:6b

Twelve sent out

A very disappointed Jesus then moved on to other villages, never to return to His hometown and all that He knew for the first thirty years of His life. How His heart must have been burdened for those He grew up with — to know the saving power of grace was in their midst, but they were blind to it. What a tragic story. Jesus now sends the twelve disciples out in six teams of two to perform signs and wonders to authenticate the message of grace and salvation. Jesus had spent some twelve months with them, training them, and now they go out, alone.

Jesus called the twelve and began to send them out two by two. He gave them authority over the unclean spirits. He instructed them to take nothing for the journey except a staff-no bread, no bag, no money in their belts — and to put on sandals but not to wear two tunics. He said to them, "Wherever you enter a house, stay there until you leave the area. If a place will not welcome you or listen to you, as you go out from there, shake the dust off your feet as a testimony against them." So they went out and preached that all should repent. They cast out many demons and anointed many sick people with oil and healed them. Mark 6:7-13

After Jesus called the twelve together, he gave them power and authority over all demons and to cure diseases, and he sent them out to proclaim the kingdom of God and to heal the sick. He said to them, "Take nothing for your journey-no staff, no bag, no bread, no money, and do not take an extra tunic. Whatever house you enter, stay there until you leave the area. Wherever they do not receive you, as you leave that town, shake the dust off your feet as a testimony against them." Then they departed and went throughout the villages, proclaiming the good news and healing people everywhere. Luke 9:1-6

Jesus called his twelve disciples and gave them authority over unclean spirits so they could cast them out and heal every kind of disease and sickness. Now these are the names of the twelve apostles: first, Simon (called Peter), and Andrew his brother; James son of Zebedee and John his brother; Philip and Bartholomew; Thomas and Matthew the tax collector; James the son of Alphaeus, and Thaddaeus; Simon the Zealot and Judas Iscariot, who betrayed him. Matthew 10:1-4

Jesus sent out these twelve, instructing them as follows: "Do not go to Gentile regions and do not enter any Samaritan town. Go instead to the lost sheep of the house of Israel. As you go, preach this message: 'The kingdom of heaven is near!' Heal the sick, raise the dead, cleanse lepers, cast out demons. Freely you received, freely give. Do not take gold, silver, or copper in your belts, no bag for the journey, or an extra tunic, or sandals or staff, for the worker deserves his provisions. Whenever you enter a town or village, find out who is worthy there and stay with them until you leave. As you enter the house, give it greetings. And if the house is worthy, let your peace come on it, but if it is not worthy, let your peace return to you. And if anyone will not welcome you or listen to your message, shake the dust off your feet as you leave that house or that town. I tell you the truth, it will be more bearable for the region of Sodom and Gomorrah on the day of judgment than for that town! "I am sending you out like sheep surrounded by wolves, so be wise as serpents and innocent as doves. Beware of people, because they will hand you over to councils and flog you in their synagogues. And you will be brought before governors and kings because of me, as a witness to them and the Gentiles. Whenever they hand you over for trial, do not worry about how to speak or what to say, for what you should say will be given to you at that time. For it is not you speaking, but the Spirit of your Father speaking through you. "Brother will hand over brother to death, and a father his child. Children will rise against parents and have them put to death. And you will be hated by everyone because of my name. But the one who endures to the end will be saved. Whenever they persecute you in one place, flee to another. I tell you the truth, you will not finish going through all the towns of Israel before the Son of Man comes. "A disciple is not greater than his teacher, nor a slave greater than his master. It is enough for the disciple to become like his teacher, and the slave like his master. If they have called the head of the house 'Beelzebul,' how much more will they defame the members of his household! "Do not be afraid of them, for nothing is hidden that will not be revealed, and nothing is secret that will not be made known. What I say to you in the dark, tell in the light, and what is whispered in your ear, proclaim from the housetops. Do not be afraid of those who kill the body but cannot kill the soul. Instead, fear the one who is able to destroy both soul and body in hell. Aren't two sparrows sold for a penny? Yet not one of them falls to the ground apart from your Father's will. Even all the hairs on your head are numbered. So do not be afraid; you are more valuable than many sparrows. "Whoever, then, acknowledges me before people, I will acknowledge before my Father in heaven. But whoever denies me before people, I will deny him also before my Father in heaven. "Do not think that I have come to bring peace to the earth. I have not come to bring peace but a sword. For I have come to set a man against his father, a daughter against her mother, and a daughter-in-law against her mother-in-law, and a man's enemies will be the members of his household. "Whoever loves father or mother more than me is not worthy of me, and whoever loves son or daughter more than me is not worthy of me. And whoever does not take up his cross and follow me is not worthy of me. Whoever finds his life will lose it, and whoever loses his life because of me will find it. "Whoever receives you receives me, and whoever receives me receives the one who sent me. Whoever receives a prophet in the name of a prophet will receive a prophet's reward. Whoever receives a righteous person in the name of a righteous person will receive a righteous person's reward. And whoever gives only a cup of cold water to one of these little ones in the name of a disciple, I tell you the truth, he will never lose his reward." When Jesus had finished instructing his twelve disciples, he went on from there to teach and preach in their towns. Matthew 10:5 - 11:1

Killing of John the Baptist

Whilst Jesus and His disciples shared the gospel and healed the sick, a polar opposite evil event occurred behind closed doors. Herod Antipas had always wanted to kill John the Baptist but feared the people, so he had him imprisoned, all because John had said to Herod that taking his brother's wife Herodias as his own was wrong. Now at Herod's birthday party, in a drunken and rash promise in response to a 'pleasing' probably erotic dance, Herod orders John's death. What a contrast to the life brought by Jesus.

For Herod had arrested John, bound him, and put him in prison on account of Herodias, his brother Philip's wife, because John had repeatedly told him, "It is not lawful for you to have her." Although

Herod wanted to kill John, he feared the crowd because they accepted John as a prophet. But on Herod's birthday, the daughter of Herodias danced before them and pleased Herod, so much that he promised with an oath to give her whatever she asked. Instructed by her mother, she said, "Give me the head of John the Baptist here on a platter." Although it grieved the king, because of his oath and the dinner guests he commanded it to be given. So he sent and had John beheaded in the prison. His head was brought on a platter and given to the girl, and she brought it to her mother. Then John's disciples came and took the body and buried it and went and told Jesus. Matthew 14:3-12

For Herod himself had sent men, arrested John, and bound him in prison on account of Herodias, his brother Philip's wife, because Herod had married her. For John had repeatedly told Herod, "It is not lawful for you to have your brother's wife." So Herodias nursed a grudge against him and wanted to kill him. But she could not because Herod stood in awe of John and protected him, since he knew that John was a righteous and holy man. When Herod heard him, he was thoroughly baffled, and yet he liked to listen to John. But a suitable day came, when Herod gave a banquet on his birthday for his court officials, military commanders, and leaders of Galilee. When his daughter Herodias came in and danced, she pleased Herod and his dinner guests. The king said to the girl, "Ask me for whatever you want and I will give it to you." He swore to her, "Whatever you ask I will give you, up to half my kingdom." So she went out and said to her mother, "What should I ask for?" Her mother said, "The head of John the baptizer." Immediately she hurried back to the king and made her request: "I want the head of John the Baptist on a platter immediately." Although it grieved the king deeply, he did not want to reject her request because of his oath and his guests. So the king sent an executioner at once to bring John's head, and he went and beheaded John in prison. He brought his head on a platter and gave it to the girl, and the girl gave it to her mother. When John's disciples heard this, they came and took his body and placed it in a tomb. Mark 6:17-29

Herod's interest in Jesus

After almost two years of ministry that were accompanied by signs and wonders, it is understandable that the governor Herod Antipas would have developed an interest in events of the day. It is also understandable that reports about John the Baptist and/or Jesus were confusing. Considering that Joanna the wife of Chuza and the manager of Herod's household, supported Jesus (Luke 8:3) it is likely that there would have been a lot of discussion in Herod's household about Jesus. It appears that reports were also coming to Herod saying that Jesus was actually John the Baptist, raised from the dead. So a very confused Herod Antipas tried to see Jesus, an event that would only occur in Jesus' last hours on earth.

At that time Herod the tetrarch heard reports about Jesus,
and he said to his servants, "This is John the Baptist. He has
been raised from the dead! And because of this, miraculous
powers are at work in him." Matthew 14:1-2

Now King Herod heard this, for Jesus' name had become known.
Some were saying, "John the baptizer has been raised from the
dead, and because of this, miraculous powers are at work in him."
Others said, "He is Elijah." Others said, "He is a prophet, like
one of the prophets from the past." But when Herod heard this, he
said, "John, whom I beheaded, has been raised!" Mark 6:14-16

Now Herod the tetrarch heard about everything that was happening,
and he was thoroughly perplexed, because some people were saying that
John had been raised from the dead, while others were saying that Elijah
had appeared, and still others that one of the prophets of long ago had
risen. Herod said, "I had John beheaded, but who is this about whom I
hear such things?" So Herod wanted to learn about Jesus. Luke 9:7-9

CHAPTER 7

Opposition
Passover - Caesarea Philippi (32 AD)

Jesus now enters His third and final year of ministry, a year of mounting opposition. The previous year of popularity was marked by signs, wonders and teaching of grace. People's lives were touched and many were changed, although not all. The woe pronounced on Chorazin, Bethsaida and Capernaum demonstrated that many lives were externally changed but internally remained cold and hard. There is no doubt that people were amazed. Constantly the phrase of 'nothing like this has been seen before' was bandied around as people pondered the seemingly impossible, could this carpenter from Nazareth be the promised Messiah.

The problem was that the Israelites thought the promised Messiah, the King of the Jews, would be an earthly king in the line of King David. They were looking for the restoration of the promised land, the eviction of the Romans, the re-establishment of the kingdom that ended in 586 BC with the sacking of Jerusalem. Everyone saw the culmination of the prophecies of the Messiah as the veritable return of an earthly king.

This was the basis of the year of opposition, driven in many ways by disappointment that Jesus did not act and behave as they thought an earthly king should. Jesus was not swiftly restoring the Davidic kingdom, and the people didn't understand that Jesus was fulfilling the law (the Old Covenant) with His grace (and thus ushering in a New Covenant). The people didn't understand that Jesus was ending the daily sacrifices with His own sacrifice. The people didn't understand that Jesus was widening God's salvation from just the Jews to all of mankind. Jesus was fulfilling every promise and every prophecy made about the coming Messiah. Through Jesus' death, the world would have life and life ever lasting.

And surprisingly, not everyone was happy about this.

The twelve return

The third year begins with Jesus about to go to Jerusalem for His third Passover whilst ministering and catching up with His disciples. If you recall from the previous chapter, the disciples had been sent out by Jesus to proclaim the kingdom of God and heal the sick. They were evidently successful on this, their first solo missionary endeavour.

The third year also begins a process of withdrawal and continued teaching of the disciples. It begins with Jesus leaving Capernaum and taking the disciples to a solitary place near Bethsaida (discussed in chapter five as four kilometres northeast of Capernaum), so Jesus could teach and encourage them. This pattern would be repeated by Jesus time and again as this final year drew to an end.

Now the Jewish feast of the Passover was near. John 6:4

When the apostles returned, they told Jesus everything they had done. Then he took them with him and they withdrew privately to a town called Bethsaida. But when the crowds found out, they followed him. He welcomed them, spoke to them about the kingdom of God, and cured those who needed healing. Luke 9:10-11

Then the apostles gathered around Jesus and told him everything they had done and taught. He said to them, "Come with me privately to an isolated place and rest a while" (for many were coming and going, and there was no time to eat). So they went away by themselves in a boat to some remote place. But many saw them leaving and recognized them, and they hurried on foot from all the towns and arrived there ahead of them. As Jesus came ashore he saw the large crowd and he had compassion on them, because they were like sheep without a shepherd. So he taught them many things. Mark 6:30-34

Now when Jesus heard this he went away from there privately in a boat to an isolated place. But when the crowd heard about it, they followed him on foot from the towns. As he got out he saw the large crowd, and he had compassion on them and healed their sick. Matthew 14:13-14

After this Jesus went away to the other side of the Sea of Galilee (also called the Sea of Tiberias). A large crowd was following him because they were observing the miraculous signs he was performing on the sick. So Jesus went on up the mountainside and sat down there with his disciples. John 6:1-3

The twentieth miracle – feeding the 5000

The problem with withdrawing to a solitary place is that everywhere Jesus went, the crowds followed, somewhat like sheep looking for a leader. Jesus has previously rebuked the evangelical triangle of Chorazin, Capernaum and Bethsaida for their hard heartedness and lack of belief, yet still they came in their thousands. Regardless, Jesus was always filled with compassion for people and in this instance He healed them and then He fed them, multiplying a little boy's lunch. What is beautiful in this story is that out of the 5000 men and perhaps thousands more women and children, it was a little boy who offered to share his food. No one else is offering and I bet they had something to offer. Just a little boy who wanted to give to Jesus.

Now the day began to draw to a close, so the twelve came and said to Jesus, "Send the crowd away, so they can go into the surrounding villages and countryside and find lodging and food, because we are in an isolated place." But he said to them, "You give them something to eat." They replied, "We have no more than five loaves and two fish-unless we go and buy food for all these people." (Now about five thousand men were there.) Then he said to his disciples, "Have them sit down in groups of about fifty each." So they did as Jesus directed, and the people all sat down. Then he took the five loaves and the two fish, and looking up to heaven he gave thanks and broke them. He gave them to the disciples to set before the crowd. They all ate and were satisfied, and what was left over was picked up-twelve baskets of broken pieces. Luke 9:12-17

Then Jesus, when he looked up and saw that a large crowd was coming to him, said to Philip, "Where can we buy bread so that these people may eat?"(Now Jesus said this to test him, for he knew what he was going to do.) Philip replied, "Two hundred silver coins worth of bread would not be enough for them, for each one to get a little." One of Jesus' disciples, Andrew, Simon Peter's brother, said to him, "Here is a boy who has five barley loaves and two fish, but what good are these for so many people?" Jesus said, "Have the people sit down." (Now there was a lot of grass in that place.) So the men sat down, about five thousand in number. Then Jesus took the loaves, and when he had given thanks, he distributed the bread to those who were seated. He then did the same with the fish, as much as they wanted. When they were all satisfied, Jesus said to his disciples, "Gather up the broken pieces that are left over, so that nothing is wasted." So they gathered them up and filled twelve baskets with broken pieces from the five barley loaves left over by the people who had eaten. John 6:5-13

When it was already late, his disciples came to him and said, "This is an isolated place and it is already very late. Send them away so that they can go into the surrounding countryside and villages and buy something for themselves to eat." But he answered them, "You give them something to eat." And they said, "Should we go and buy bread for two hundred silver coins and give it to them to eat?" He said to them, "How many loaves do you have? Go and see." When they found out, they said, "Five—and two fish." Then he directed them all to sit down in groups on the green grass. So they reclined in groups of hundreds and fifties. He took the five loaves and the two fish, and looking up to heaven, he gave thanks and broke the loaves. He gave them to his disciples to serve the people, and he divided the two fish among them all. They all ate and were satisfied, and they picked up the broken pieces and fish that were left over, twelve baskets full. Now there were five thousand men who ate the bread. Mark 6:35-44

When evening arrived, his disciples came to him saying, "This is an isolated place and the hour is already late. Send the crowds away so that they can go into the villages and buy food for themselves." But he replied, "They don't need to go. You give them something to eat." They said to him, "We have here only five loaves and two fish.""Bring them here to me," he replied. Then he instructed the crowds to sit down on the grass. He took the five loaves and two fish, and looking up to heaven he gave thanks and broke the loaves. He gave them to the disciples, who in turn gave them to the crowds. They all ate and were satisfied, and they picked up the broken pieces left over, twelve baskets full. Not counting women and children, there were about five thousand men who ate. Matthew 14:15-21

The twenty-first miracle – Jesus walks on water

The excitement of the Galilean's has now reached fever pitch and, as scriptures tell us, the crowds intended to make Jesus king by force. Their hard hearts had not heard the true message of the kingdom of God. Jesus responded beautifully. He simply withdrew to a quiet place to spend time with His Heavenly Father. He took to prayer. He would then join His disciples a little later as they went to Capernaum, and in the process displays His full power and authority as the creator of the universe by walking on water.

Now when the people saw the miraculous sign that Jesus performed, they began to say to one another, "This is certainly the Prophet who is to come into the world." Then Jesus, because he knew they were going to come and seize him by force to make him king, withdrew again up the mountainside alone. Now when evening came, his disciples went down to the lake, got into a boat, and started to cross the lake to Capernaum. (It had already become dark, and Jesus had not yet come to them.) By now a strong wind was blowing and the sea was getting rough. Then, when they had rowed about three or four miles, they caught sight of Jesus walking on the lake, approaching the boat, and they were frightened. But he said to them, "It is I. Do not be afraid." Then they wanted to take him into the boat, and immediately the boat came to the land where they had been heading. John 6:14-21

Immediately Jesus made the disciples get into the boat and go ahead of him to the other side, while he dispersed the crowds. And after he sent the crowds away, he went up the mountain by himself to pray. When evening came, he was there alone. Meanwhile the boat, already far from land, was taking a beating from the waves because the wind was against it. As the night was ending, Jesus came to them walking on the sea. When the disciples saw him walking on the water they were terrified and said, "It's a ghost!" and cried out with fear. But immediately Jesus spoke to them: "Have courage! It is I. Do not be afraid." Peter said to him, "Lord, if it is you, order me to come to you on the water." So he said, "Come." Peter got out of the boat, walked on the water, and came toward Jesus. But when he saw the strong wind he became afraid. And starting to sink, he cried out, "Lord, save me!" Immediately Jesus reached out his hand and caught him, saying to him, "You of little faith, why did you doubt?" When they went up into the boat, the wind ceased. Then those who were in the boat worshiped him, saying, "Truly you are the Son of God." Matthew 14:22-33

*Immediately Jesus made his disciples get into the boat and go on ahead to the
other side, to Bethsaida, while he dispersed the crowd. After saying goodbye to
them, he went to the mountain to pray. When evening came, the boat was in
the middle of the sea and he was alone on the land. He saw them straining
at the oars, because the wind was against them. As the night was ending, he
came to them walking on the sea, for he wanted to pass by them. When they
saw him walking on the water they thought he was a ghost. They cried out, for
they all saw him and were terrified. But immediately he spoke to them: "Have
courage! It is I. Do not be afraid." Then he went up with them into the boat,
and the wind ceased. They were completely astonished, because they did not
understand about the loaves, but their hearts were hardened. Mark 6:45-52*

As Jesus took command of not just the elements but the created order
itself, our eyes are instantly drawn to Peter. Impetuous and in this
instance faithful enough to think that he also could do what Jesus did,
if Jesus called him. I love the picture of Peter. He kept his eyes on Jesus
and walked on the water. Then fear snuck in, he took his eyes off Jesus
and put them on his circumstances. You guessed it, he started to sink. He
didn't sink like a stone, just sunk slowly. Maybe there's a lesson there for
us all about where our eyes should be and what our faith should look like.

*I am able to do all things through the one who
strengthens me. Philippians 4:13*

The twenty-second miracle – healing everyone
The disciples were not sailing far and probably hugged the shore line as
they sailed to a tract of land five kilometres long on the western bank of
the Sea of Galilee, called Gennesaret. The region was well known to Jesus
as it included the towns of Capernaum and Bethsaida to the east, and was
therefore part of the evangelical triangle. Evidently Jesus didn't want to go
to either of these two centres, but landed to the west of Capernaum in this
fertile area. The result was the same, everyone flocked to Jesus to be healed.

*After they had crossed over, they came to land at Gennesaret.
When the people there recognized him, they sent word into all
the surrounding area, and they brought all their sick to him.
They begged him if they could only touch the edge of his cloak,
and all who touched it were healed....Matthew 14:34-36*

*After they had crossed over, they came to land at Gennesaret and
anchored there. As they got out of the boat, people immediately recognized
Jesus. They ran through that whole region and began to bring the sick
on mats to wherever he was rumored to be. And wherever he would
go-into villages, towns, or countryside-they would place the sick in
the marketplaces, and would ask him if they could just touch the edge
of his cloak, and all who touched it were healed. Mark 6:53-56*

The photo above shows the plain of Gennesaret taken from Bethsaida by the American colony photo department between 1900 and 1920.

The crowd of 5000 that Jesus fed on the north-east side of the lake woke up to find Jesus gone and they rapidly sought to locate Him. They found Jesus in the synagogue in Capernaum, after He walked back from the region of Gennesaret. Thousands of people then descended on Capernaum into a synagogue that could only hold hundreds. Maybe Jesus taught outside, maybe people queued at the door. What is known is that Jesus teaches them again, but this time finds hearts less open.

The next day the crowd that remained on the other side of the lake realized that only one small boat had been there, and that Jesus had not boarded it with his disciples, but that his disciples had gone away alone. Other boats from Tiberias came to shore near the place where they had eaten the bread after the Lord had given thanks. So when the crowd realized that neither Jesus nor his disciples were there, they got into the boats and came to Capernaum looking for Jesus. When they found him on the other side of the lake, they said to him, "Rabbi, when did you get here?" Jesus replied, "I tell you the solemn truth, you are looking for me not because you saw miraculous signs, but because you ate all the loaves of bread you wanted. Do not work for the food that disappears, but for the food that remains to eternal life-the food which the Son of Man will give to you. For God the Father has put his seal of approval on him." So then they said to him, "What must we do to accomplish the deeds God requires?" Jesus replied, "This is the deed God requires-to believe in the one whom he sent." So they said to him, "Then what miraculous sign will you perform, so that we may see it and believe you? What will you do? Our ancestors ate the manna in the wilderness, just as it is written, 'He gave them bread from heaven to eat.'" Then Jesus told them, "I tell you the solemn truth, it is not Moses who has given you the bread from heaven, but my Father is giving you the true bread from heaven. For the bread of God is the one who comes down from heaven and gives life to the world." So they said to him, "Sir, give us this bread all the time!" Jesus said to them, "I am the bread of life. The one who comes to me will never go hungry, and the one who believes in me will never be thirsty. But I told you that you have seen me and still do not believe. Everyone whom the Father gives me will come to me, and the one who comes to me I will never send away. For I have come down from heaven not to do my own will but the will of the one who sent me. Now this is the will of the one who sent me-that I should not lose one person of every one he has given me, but raise them all up at the last day. For this is the will of my Father-for everyone who looks on the Son and believes in him to have eternal life, and I will raise him up at the last day." John 6:22-40

What is staggering in the synagogue, and evidently outside, is that the Israelites grumbled against Jesus declaring Himself as the Messiah, even though they had all just been miraculously fed. Many of those present would also have been miraculously healed by Jesus and one of the synagogue leaders, Jarius, had seen Jesus raise his daughter from the dead. And yet they grumble…. are you kidding me? Miraculously healed, miraculously fed and miraculously raised from the dead and grumbling because their view of the Messiah was different to God's view. Are we as humans really that stiff necked? Has the fall, original sin, really made us that hard-hearted?

Then the Jews who were hostile to Jesus began complaining about him because he said, "I am the bread that came down from heaven," and they said, "Isn't this Jesus the son of Joseph, whose father and mother we know? How can he now say, 'I have come down from heaven'?" Jesus replied, "Do not complain about me to one another. No one can come to me unless the Father who sent me draws him, and I will raise him up at the last day. It is written in the prophets, 'And they will all be taught by God.' Everyone who hears and learns from the Father comes to me. (Not that anyone has seen the Father except the one who is from God-he has seen the Father.) I tell you the solemn truth, the one who believes has eternal life. I am the bread of life. Your ancestors ate the manna in the wilderness, and they died. This is the bread that has come down from heaven, so that a person may eat from it and not die. I am the living bread that came down from heaven. If anyone eats from this bread he will live forever. The bread that I will give for the life of the world is my flesh." Then the Jews who were hostile to Jesus began to argue with one another, "How can this man give us his flesh to eat?" Jesus said to them, "I tell you the solemn truth, unless you eat the flesh of the Son of Man and drink his blood, you have no life in yourselves. The one who eats my flesh and drinks my blood has eternal life, and I will raise him up on the last day. For my flesh is true food, and my blood is true drink. The one who eats my flesh and drinks my blood resides in me, and I in him. Just as the

*living Father sent me, and I live because of the Father, so the one who
consumes me will live because of me. This is the bread that came down
from heaven; it is not like the bread your ancestors ate, but then later
died. The one who eats this bread will live forever." Jesus said these things
while he was teaching in the synagogue in Capernaum. John 6:41-59*

Jesus presents His body as the final sacrifice, and tells us that by believing in His sacrifice we would inherit eternal life. Jesus would later institute the sacrament called 'communion' – the Lord's supper, the eucharist, the drinking of wine and eating of bread, symbols of Jesus' blood shed and body broken to remember and proclaim the New Covenant of Grace. Yet many of those who followed could not accept this. They could not accept that Jesus was not declaring himself the earthly Jewish King, so they left. This is certainly one way to separate the true followers from the hangers-on.

*Then many of his disciples, when they heard these things, said, "This
is a difficult saying! Who can understand it?" When Jesus was aware
that his disciples were complaining about this, he said to them, "Does
this cause you to be offended? Then what if you see the Son of Man
ascending where he was before? The Spirit is the one who gives life;
human nature is of no help! The words that I have spoken to you are
spirit and are life. But there are some of you who do not believe." (For
Jesus had already known from the beginning who those were who did
not believe, and who it was who would betray him.) So Jesus added,
"Because of this I told you that no one can come to me unless the Father
has allowed him to come." After this many of his disciples quit following
him and did not accompany him any longer. So Jesus said to the twelve,
"You don't want to go away too, do you?" Simon Peter answered him,
"Lord, to whom would we go? You have the words of eternal life. We
have come to believe and to know that you are the Holy One of God!"
Jesus replied, "Didn't I choose you, the twelve, and yet one of you is*

the devil?" (Now he said this about Judas son of Simon Iscariot, for
Judas, one of the twelve, was going to betray him.)...John 6:60-71

Jesus then continues to teach in northern Israel, staying away from the
south because His time had not yet come to lay down His life. The
tragedy of this statement is that so many towns in Judea never had the
opportunity to receive the touch of Jesus, because of the venom of the
religious elite, who were more concerned for their own welfare and not
that of the people they were supposed to serve.

> *After this Jesus traveled throughout Galilee. He stayed out of*
> *Judea because the Jewish leaders wanted to kill him. John 7:1*

Those Pharisees again

Jesus continues His ministry in Galilee, perhaps in the north-western
part of the region because his next journey is north into Phoenicia.
Whilst in Galilee, Pharisees and teachers of the law travelled over 150
kilometres north, from Jerusalem, to accuse Jesus of not keeping the
law. I can imagine them all riding their donkeys – they were far too
important to walk – reinforcing each other's biases as they journeyed
for a week to confront Jesus.

> *Then Pharisees and experts in the law came from Jerusalem to Jesus and*
> *said, "Why do your disciples disobey the tradition of the elders? For they*
> *don't wash their hands when they eat." He answered them, "And why do*
> *you disobey the commandment of God because of your tradition? For God*
> *said, 'Honor your father and mother' and 'Whoever insults his father*
> *or mother must be put to death.' But you say, 'If someone tells his father*
> *or mother, "Whatever help you would have received from me is given*
> *to God," he does not need to honor his father.' You have nullified the*
> *word of God on account of your tradition. Hypocrites! Isaiah prophesied*
> *correctly about you when he said, 'This people honors me with their lips,*
> *but their heart is far from me, and they worship me in vain, teaching as*

doctrines the commandments of men.'" Then he called the crowd to him and said, "Listen and understand. What defiles a person is not what goes into the mouth; it is what comes out of the mouth that defiles a person." Then the disciples came to him and said, "Do you know that when the Pharisees heard this saying they were offended?" And he replied, "Every plant that my heavenly Father did not plant will be uprooted. Leave them! They are blind guides. If someone who is blind leads another who is blind, both will fall into a pit." But Peter said to him, "Explain this parable to us." Jesus said, "Even after all this, are you still so foolish? Don't you understand that whatever goes into the mouth enters the stomach and then passes out into the sewer? But the things that come out of the mouth come from the heart, and these things defile a person. For out of the heart come evil ideas, murder, adultery, sexual immorality, theft, false testimony, slander. These are the things that defile a person; it is not eating with unwashed hands that defiles a person." Matthew 15:1-20

Now the Pharisees and some of the experts in the law who came from Jerusalem gathered around him. And they saw that some of Jesus' disciples ate their bread with unclean hands, that is, unwashed.(For the Pharisees and all the Jews do not eat unless they perform a ritual washing, holding fast to the tradition of the elders. And when they come from the marketplace, they do not eat unless they wash. They hold fast to many other traditions: the washing of cups, pots, kettles, and dining couches.) The Pharisees and the experts in the law asked him, "Why do your disciples not live according to the tradition of the elders, but eat with unwashed hands?" He said to them, "Isaiah prophesied correctly about you hypocrites, as it is written: 'This people honors me with their lips, but their heart is far from me. They worship me in vain, teaching as doctrine the commandments of men.' Having no regard for the command of God, you hold fast to human tradition." He also said to them, "You neatly reject the commandment of God in order to set up your tradition. For Moses said, 'Honor your father and your mother,' and, 'Whoever insults his father or mother must be put to death.' But you say that if anyone tells his father or mother, 'Whatever help you would have received from me is corban' (that is, a gift for God), then you no longer permit him to do anything for his father or mother. Thus you nullify the word of God by your tradition that you have handed down. And you do many things like this." Then he called the crowd again and said to them, "Listen to me, everyone, and understand. There is nothing outside of a person that can defile him by going into him. Rather, it is what comes out of a person that defiles him." Now when Jesus had left the crowd and entered the house, his disciples asked him about the parable. He said to them, "Are you so foolish? Don't you understand that whatever goes into a person from outside cannot defile him? For it does not enter his heart but his stomach, and then goes out into the sewer." (This means all foods are clean.) He said, "What comes out of a person defiles him. For from within, out of the human heart, come evil ideas, sexual immorality, theft, murder, adultery, greed, evil, deceit, debauchery, envy, slander, pride, and folly. All these evils come from within and defile a person." Mark 7:1-23

Phoenicia and the city states of Tyre and Sidon

Having rebuked the religious elite, again, Jesus walks between forty and fifty kilometres north-west into Phoenicia (modern day Lebanon) to the city of Tyre and a further thirty kilometres north to Sidon. Both cities lie on the Mediterranean and were part of Syria at the time. It appears Jesus was looking for an opportunity to connect with His disciples privately whilst avoiding opposition and the crowds, hence travelling to Phoenicia and then east to Caesarea Philippi and the Decapolis.

First a little about the ancient civilisation of Phoenicia. It's not actually a city but a cluster of independent city-states that lay along the east coast of the Mediterranean Sea from Syria, Lebanon and northern Israel. By virtue of their location by the sea, the cities and their people were considered a great maritime power and quickly became known for their ships adorned with horses' heads in honour of their god of the sea,

Yamm, the brother of Mot, the god of death.[23] The two most powerful cities were Tyre and Sidon while Byblos and Baalbek were the most important religious centres. The Phoenician city-states began around 3000 BC and were firmly established by 2750 BC, so they were old by the time of Christ.

The name Phoenicia (Greek Phoinikes for Tyranian purple) came from the special purple dye of the murex snail that was manufactured and used in Tyre for the robes of the Mesopotamian royalty. The Phoenicians were skilled at manufacturing purple cloth, along with other crafts (2 Chronicles 2:13-14). The Greek historian Herodotus also cites Phoenicia as the birthplace of the alphabet, stating that it was brought to Greece by the Phoenician Kadmus (sometime before the 8th century BC) and that prior to that the Greeks had no alphabet[24]. The Phoenician alphabet is the basis for most western languages today and the city of Byblos gave the Bible its name (from the Greek 'Ta Biblia', the books) as Byblos was the great exporter of papyrus used in writing in ancient Egypt and Greece. Thus, Phoenicia has had a significant impact on the biblical world.

The Phoenician city-state of Sidon, called Saida today (Arabic for 'fishing') is a port city, built on a promontory with a nearby offshore island that shelters the harbour from storms. It was named after Sidon, the firstborn son of Canaan, son of Ham, son of Noah (Genesis 10:15) and it's reasonable to assume it was settled by his descendants making Sidon a very early city in the life of the planet. The northern border of Canaan extended to Sidon (Genesis 10:19). When Jacob blessed his sons (Genesis 49:13) he spoke of Sidon as the boundary of Zebulun and when God spoke to Joshua in his later years, God promised the area of Sidon to Israel (Joshua 13:6). Sidon was subsequently included

---

23   http://www.ancient.eu/phoenicia accessed on 21 October 2016
24   Herodotus, Histories 5. 57-58

in the inheritance of Asher, on its northern boundary (Joshua 19:28), but it was never taken by that tribe in conquest (Judges 1:31, 3:3).

The Phoenician city-state of Tyre, called Sour today (Hebrew Sor, Arabic Sur, Babylonian Surru for 'rock') lies 30 kilometres south of Sidon in the middle of a coastal plain. Tyre was originally constructed on a rock island a few hundred metres out into the Mediterranean, though over time the city grew to include a mainland component. Tyre first appeared as part of Asher's western boundary and was specifically called a fortified city since it was such a significant landmark (Joshua 19:29). Tyre does not appear again in the Bible until Hiram, King of Tyre, sends cedar, carpenters, and masons to build King David's palace (2 Samuel 5:11).

The twenty-third miracle – healing of a Phoenician (non Jewish) woman

Entering the region of Phoenicia, Jesus is confronted by a Canaanite woman. The term Canaanite refers to the area the descendants of Canaan first settled in, noting Canaan was the son of Ham, the son of Noah (Genesis 10). Numbers 24 specifies the area of Canaan in greater detail as being from Lebanon (Sidon), south to the Wadi of Egypt, and from the Mediterranean to the Dead Sea, and so included various people groups, both settled and nomadic. The book of Joshua outlines the proposed conquest of the Canaanites by the Israelites and, apart from a time with King David and King Solomon, this goal was never achieved. Suffice to say the land of the Phoenicians was part of Canaan.

The story of Jesus in Phoenicia is the first recorded time that Jesus heals a Canaanite (having previously healed a Samaritan), though other non-Jewish healings are certainly inferred in the gospels when people east of the Jordan River from the region of the ten cities (Decapolis), came to Jesus (Matthew 4:25 and Mark 5:20). This case is different. A desperate woman in tears comes pleading to Jesus for her daughter's sake. Jesus is full of compassion, yet in this instance His response seems cold, especially compared with the grace in which he healed the foreigners from the Decapolis. What is happening here? The answer lies in a lesson to the disciples. The Jewish view was that the Canaanites were lower than the half bred Samaritans, if that was possible, so the disciples wanted Jesus to send the woman away. Jesus speaks the words that many of the Jews had spoken about their 'pagan' neighbours – 'they are dogs', they scream – yet a touch from Jesus shows they are of equal value. This is the miracle in Phoenicia, the continued demonstration of the inclusion of everyone in the Saviour's plan.

After going out from there, Jesus went to the region of Tyre and Sidon. A Canaanite woman from that area came and cried out, "Have mercy on me, Lord, Son of David! My daughter is horribly demon-possessed!" But he did not answer her a word. Then his disciples came and begged him, "Send her away, because she keeps on crying out after us." So he answered, "I was sent only to the lost sheep of the house of Israel." But she came and bowed down before him and said, "Lord, help me!" "It is not right to take the children's bread and throw it to the dogs," he said. "Yes, Lord," she replied, "but even the dogs eat the crumbs that fall from their masters' table." Then Jesus answered her, "Woman, your faith is great! Let what you want be done for you." And her daughter was healed from that hour. Matthew 15:21-28

After Jesus left there, he went to the region of Tyre. When he went into a house, he did not want anyone to know, but he was not able to escape notice. Instead, a woman whose young daughter had an unclean spirit immediately heard about him and came and fell at his feet. The woman was a Greek, of Syrophoenician origin. She asked him to cast the demon out of her daughter. He said to her, "Let the children be satisfied first, for it is not right to take the children's bread and to throw it to the dogs." She answered, "Yes, Lord, but even the dogs under the table eat the children's crumbs." Then he said to her, "Because you said this,

you may go. The demon has left your daughter." She went home and
found the child lying on the bed, and the demon gone. Mark 7:24-30

The twenty-fourth miracle – healing more 'pagans'

Jesus leaves Phoenicia as quickly as he arrived and walks to the Sea of Galilee, across the northern reaches of the Jordan and into the Decapolis, the region of ten cities, east of the Jordan River. That's a long walk of up to 100 kilometres. There He heals more 'pagans' this time tribes and groups that are not even Canaanites.

Then Jesus went out again from the region of Tyre and came through
Sidon to the Sea of Galilee in the region of the Decapolis. They brought
to him a deaf man who had difficulty speaking, and they asked him
to place his hands on him. After Jesus took him aside privately, away
from the crowd, he put his fingers in the man's ears, and after spitting,
he touched his tongue. Then he looked up to heaven and said with
a sigh, "Ephphatha" (that is, "Be opened"). And immediately the
man's ears were opened, his tongue loosened, and he spoke plainly.
Jesus ordered them not to tell anyone. But as much as he ordered
them not to do this, they proclaimed it all the more. People were
completely astounded and said, "He has done everything well. He
even makes the deaf hear and the mute speak." Mark 7:31-37

The twenty-fifth miracle – Jesus feeds 4000

Jesus is again on the move, this time completing His circuit back to the Sea of Galilee, healing and teaching as He goes. People again came to see and hear Jesus and stayed with Him for at least three days. Whilst water from the Sea of Galilee was plentiful, evidently food was not, as the place Jesus was staying in appeared remote. Luckily Jesus is the 'bread of life' metaphorically and at this time physically, as seven loaves and a few fish are miraculously multiplied to feed 4000.

When he left there, Jesus went along the Sea of Galilee. Then he went up a mountain, where he sat down. Then large crowds came to him bringing with them the lame, blind, crippled, mute, and many others. They laid them at his feet, and he healed them. As a result, the crowd was amazed when they saw the mute speaking, the crippled healthy, the lame walking, and the blind seeing, and they praised the God of Israel. Matthew 15:29-31

Then Jesus called the disciples and said, "I have compassion on the crowd, because they have already been here with me three days and they have nothing to eat. I don't want to send them away hungry since they may faint on the way." The disciples said to him, "Where can we get enough bread in this desolate place to satisfy so great a crowd?" Jesus said to them, "How many loaves do you have?" They replied, "Seven-and a few small fish." After instructing the crowd to sit down on the ground, he took the seven loaves and the fish, and after giving thanks, he broke them and began giving them to the disciples, who then gave them to the crowds. They all ate and were satisfied, and they picked up the broken pieces left over, seven baskets full. Not counting children and women, there were four thousand men who ate. After sending away the crowd, he got into the boat and went to the region of Magadan. Matthew 15:32-39

In those days there was another large crowd with nothing to eat. So Jesus called his disciples and said to them, "I have compassion on the crowd, because they have already been here with me three days, and they have nothing to eat. If I send them home hungry, they will faint on the way, and some of them have come from a great distance." His disciples answered him, "Where can someone get enough bread in this desolate place to satisfy these people?" He asked them, "How many loaves do you have?" They replied, "Seven." Then he directed the crowd to sit down on the ground. After he took the seven loaves and gave thanks, he broke them and began giving them to the disciples to serve. So they served the crowd. They also had a few small fish.

After giving thanks for these, he told them to serve these as well.
Everyone ate and was satisfied, and they picked up the broken pieces
left over, seven baskets full. There were about four thousand who ate.
Then he dismissed them. Immediately he got into a boat with his
disciples and went to the district of Dalmanutha. Mark 8:1-10

Show us a sign

Jesus now jumps back into the boat and travels to the region of
Dalmanutha (Mark) or Magadan (Matthew). It is reasonable to suggest both of these names are for the same place. Magadan is probably
the town of Magdala where Mary Magdalen came from, on the western side of the Sea of Galilee, close to Tiberius. As an aside, south
of the plain of Gennesareta, a cave has been found bearing the name
Talmanutha – perhaps the spot where Jesus landed[25].

---

[25] Hastings, J, "A Dictionary of the Bible: Volume III: (Part I: Kir --
Nympha)" p. 203.

The photo above is a view from the north of Magdala taken by the American colony photo department between 1900 and 1920.

Here we go again with the wretched religious elite, though this time the Pharisees and Sadducees come together to see Jesus, which is the first time the religious sects have acted in harmony. They came with an impure motive, however, which was to demand a sign. Apparently healing the sick; curing the leper; casting out the demonic; giving sight to the blind; hearing to the deaf; mobility to the lame and raising the dead weren't enough. Jesus does give them a hint, the sign of Jonah who spent three days in the belly of a whale only to be spat out on the shore (Jonah 1) though Jesus was referring to himself raising from the dead in three days.

Now when the Pharisees and Sadducees came to test Jesus, they asked him to show them a sign from heaven. He said, "When evening comes you say, 'It will be fair weather, because the sky is red,' and in the morning, 'It will be stormy today, because the sky is red and darkening.' You know how to judge correctly the appearance of the sky, but you cannot evaluate the signs of the times. A wicked and adulterous generation asks for a sign, but no sign will be given to it except the sign of Jonah." Then he left them and went away. Matthew 16:1-4

Then the Pharisees came and began to argue with Jesus, asking for a sign from heaven to test him. Sighing deeply in his spirit he said, "Why does this generation look for a sign? I tell you the truth, no sign will be given to this generation." Then he left them, got back into the boat, and went to the other side. Mark 8:11-13

Jesus and His disciples are again in a boat crossing over to the other side of the Sea of Galilee. There follows a wonderful discourse where Jesus warns His disciples against the teachings of the religious elite, which are based on false law and precedent. It's almost amusing that His disciples thought Jesus was complaining about not enough bread.

Now they had forgotten to take bread, except for one loaf they had with them in the boat. And Jesus ordered them, "Watch out! Beware of the yeast of the Pharisees and the yeast of Herod!" So they began to discuss with one another about having no bread. When he learned of this, Jesus said to them, "Why are you arguing about having no bread? Do you still not see or understand? Have your hearts been hardened? Though you have eyes, don't you see? And though you have ears, can't you hear? Don't you remember? When I broke the five loaves for the five thousand, how many baskets full of pieces did you pick up?" They replied, "Twelve.""When I broke the seven loaves for the four thousand, how many baskets full of pieces did you pick up?" They replied, "Seven." Then he said to them, "Do you still not understand?" Mark 8:14-21

When the disciples went to the other side, they forgot to take bread. "Watch out," Jesus said to them, "beware of the yeast of the Pharisees and Sadducees." So they began to discuss this among themselves, saying, "It is because we brought no bread." When Jesus learned of this, he said, "You who have such little faith! Why are you arguing among yourselves about having no bread? Do you still not understand? Don't you remember the five loaves for the five thousand, and how many baskets you took up? Or the seven loaves for the four thousand and how many baskets you took up? How could you not understand that I was not speaking to you about bread? But beware of the yeast of the Pharisees and Sadducees!" Then they understood that he had not told them to be on guard against the yeast in bread, but against the teaching of the Pharisees and Sadducees. Matthew 16:5-12

The twenty-sixth miracle – healing sight

Jesus and the disciples arrive back to Bethsaida, one of the towns of the evangelical triangle where Jesus heals a blind man in an interesting manner. Sometimes Jesus just spoke and the person was healed, at other times He prayed or laid hands on them, or touched their eyes or tongues, and at other times people just touched Him. God is certainly the God of variety.

Then they came to Bethsaida. They brought a blind man to Jesus and asked him to touch him. He took the blind man by the hand and brought him outside of the village. Then he spit on his eyes, placed his hands on his eyes and asked, "Do you see anything?" Regaining his sight he said, "I see people, but they look like trees walking." Then Jesus placed his hands on the man's eyes again. And he opened his eyes, his sight was restored, and he saw everything clearly. Jesus sent him home, saying, "Do not even go into the village." Mark 8:22-26

Peter's confession

Jesus and his disciples now head north out of Galilee to the Roman city of Caesarea Philippi and its surrounds. Undistracted there is a moment of clarity for the disciples when Peter, the head spokesman, openly declares that Jesus is the Messiah the Son of God. This is the first and only time that Jesus is recorded heading this far north. By the time that Jesus finishes this journey He would have been through the non-Jewish cities of Tyre and Sidon, the Roman city of Caesarea Philippi, and the Roman settlements of the Decapolis east of the Jordan River. In all these locations Jesus has met the physical and spiritual needs of the people as He demonstrated that salvation is available to everyone. It is also noteworthy that where Jesus walked is still within the original land boundaries given by God to the Israelites. Just because the Jews didn't obediently claim the land God gave them at the time, doesn't mean God's plan has changed.

The Roman city of Caesarea Philippi was originally called Paneas (the ancient name survives today as Banias) in honour of the Greek god Pan, whose shrine was located there. The region was pagan to its core and after Roman occupation the city was rebuilt by Herod's son Philip, who named it after Tiberius Caesar and himself. How's that for humility? It was north of the Sea of Galilee near one of the three sources of the Jordan River.

When Jesus came to the area of Caesarea Philippi, he asked his disciples, "Who do people say that the Son of Man is?" They answered, "Some say John the Baptist, others Elijah, and others Jeremiah or one of the prophets." He said to them, "But who do you say that I am?" Simon Peter answered, "You are the Christ, the Son of the living God." And Jesus answered him, "You are blessed, Simon son of Jonah, because flesh and blood did not reveal this to you, but my Father in heaven! And I tell you that you are Peter, and on this rock I will build my church, and the gates of Hades will not overpower it. I will give you the keys of the kingdom of heaven. Whatever you bind on earth will have been bound in heaven, and whatever you release on earth will have been released in heaven." Then he instructed his disciples not to tell anyone that he was the Christ. Matthew 16:13-20

Then Jesus and his disciples went to the villages of Caesarea Philippi. On the way he asked his disciples, "Who do people say that I am?" They said, "John the Baptist, others say Elijah, and still others, one of the prophets." He asked them, "But who do you say that I am?" Peter answered him, "You are the Christ." Then he warned them not to tell anyone about him. Mark 8:27-30

Once when Jesus was praying by himself, and his disciples were nearby, he asked them, "Who do the crowds say that I am?" They answered, "John the Baptist; others say Elijah; and still others that one of the prophets of long ago has risen." Then he said to them, "But who do you say that I am?" Peter answered, "The Christ of God." But he forcefully commanded them not to tell this to anyone. Luke 9:18-21

Jesus brings His disciples into the loop

Now that the disciples have finally heard – I don't know about grasped – who Jesus is, the Messiah, the Son of God, it is time for Jesus to bring them into the loop. Jesus communicates the grand plan that He is not on earth to restore the Davidic kingdom but to usher in a New Covenant of Grace through His death and resurrection as the final blood sacrifice. The conversation didn't go that well and Peter goes from hero to zero; to acknowledging Jesus as the Messiah to trying to rebuke Him for His plan.

saying, "The Son of Man must suffer many things and be rejected by the elders, chief priests, and experts in the law, and be killed, and on the third day be raised." Luke 9:22

From that time on Jesus began to show his disciples that he must go to Jerusalem and suffer many things at the hands of the elders, chief priests, and experts in the law, and be killed, and on the third day be raised. So Peter took him aside and began to rebuke him: "God forbid, Lord! This must not happen to you!" But he turned and said to Peter, "Get behind me, Satan! You are a stumbling block to me, because you are not setting your mind on God's interests, but on man's." Matthew 16:21-23

Then Jesus began to teach them that the Son of Man must suffer many things and be rejected by the elders, chief priests, and experts in the law, and be killed, and after three days rise again. He spoke openly about this. So Peter took him aside and began to rebuke him. But after turning and looking at his disciples, he rebuked Peter and said, "Get behind me, Satan. You are not setting your mind on God's interests, but on man's." Mark 8:31-33

Jesus then finishes this discussion with His disciples by pointing them to the cross. This is the first time that the Roman weapon of death, crucifixion, is raised by Jesus. Doubtless everyone had seen some poor soul crucified by the Romans as it was the customary way to both punish an offence and send a message to the populous to behave. This discussion by Jesus has a dual meaning. It points to the cross where He is going and metaphorically it points to rebirth through faith, death to self and life with Jesus.

Then Jesus said to his disciples, "If anyone wants to become my follower, he must deny himself, take up his cross, and follow me. For whoever wants to save his life will lose it, but whoever loses his life for my sake will find it. For what does it benefit a person if he gains the whole world but forfeits his life? Or what can a person give in exchange for his life? For the Son of Man will come with his angels in the glory of his Father, and then he will reward each person according to what he has done. I tell you the truth, there are some standing here who will not experience death before they see the Son of Man coming in his kingdom." Matthew 16:24-28

Then Jesus called the crowd, along with his disciples, and said to them, "If anyone wants to become my follower, he must deny himself, take up his cross, and follow me. For whoever wants to save his life will lose it, but whoever loses his life for my sake and for the gospel will save it. For what benefit is it for a person to gain the whole world, yet forfeit his life? What can a person give in exchange for his life? For if anyone is ashamed of me and my words in this adulterous and sinful generation, the Son of Man will also be ashamed of him when he comes in the glory of his Father with the holy angels." And he said to them, "I tell you the truth, there are some standing here who will not experience death before they see the kingdom of God come with power." Mark 8:34 - 9:1

Then he said to them all, "If anyone wants to become my follower, he must deny himself, take up his cross daily, and follow me. For whoever wants to save his life will lose it, but whoever loses his life for my sake will save it. For what does it benefit a person if he gains the whole world but loses or forfeits himself? For whoever is ashamed of me and my words, the Son of Man will be ashamed of that person when he comes in his glory and in the glory of the Father and of the holy angels. But I tell you most certainly, there are some standing here who will not experience death before they see the kingdom of God." Luke 9:23-27

This is where this chapter ends, in a Roman city outside of Galilee with Jesus pointing to the cross. The cross of Calvary where Jesus is crucified and the cross we pick up as our old life dies to sin and we are raised renewed through faith in the sacrifice of Jesus.

It ends at the cross and begins anew for us at the cross.

CHAPTER 8

Transfiguration
Mount Tabor – Jordan River (32 AD)

The gospel story of Jesus now takes a dramatic turn. More than two years have passed, years of popularity and now growing opposition. Jesus has taught, healed, released, restored, convicted, challenged and above all expressed the coming kingdom of God, the fulfilment of the law through His shed blood.

Many have received the message and believed in Jesus as the Messiah. This included Jews, Samaritans, Canaanites, Romans and other tribes and groups east of the Jordan River. Jesus has started to seek greater solitude so He can teach the twelve disciples who are travelling with Him. It is almost as if Jesus is ramping up their preparation and training, knowing His time is now short – the cross less than two hundred days away. Jesus has given His message an edge of 'pick up your cross and follow me', resulting in many who were looking to Him as an earthly king fall away.

Now Jesus sets His mind resolutely to the cross.

The Transfiguration

It is not known how long Jesus spent in Caesarea Philippi, however six to eight days later the little band once again find themselves in familiar territory, back in Galilee. The disciples have spent a week with Jesus with few distractions, only the Master's voice. Their first stop is the Mount of Transfiguration, of which there is some discussion as to its location. The options are the traditional site of Mount Tabor to the east of the Sea of Galilee or Mount Hermon east of the Golan heights. Mount Tabor in Galilee at the eastern end of the Jezreel Valley, seventeen kilometres west of the Sea of Galilee seems the geographically and historically more obvious choice. Standing at 575 metres high, the mountain was seen as a sign of strength in ancient Israel. The Israelite tribes gathered on Mount Tabor in the days of Deborah the Judge of Israel when threatened by Sisera's army (Judges 4 and 5) and the prophet Jeremiah used the mountain as an example of the power and might of Nebuchadnezzar King of Babylon as his army came out to attack Egypt.

I the King, whose name is the LORD who rules over all, swear this: I swear as surely as I live that a conqueror is coming. He will be as imposing as Mount Tabor is among the mountains, as Mount Carmel is against the backdrop of the sea. Jeremiah 46:18

The photo above shows Mount Tabor, taken from Nazareth, and was taken by the American colony photo department between 1900 and 1920.

This may explain why Jesus chose this mountain to demonstrate His power and glory. Once again Jesus splits the disciples into two groups. Group one is the leadership group of Peter, John and his brother James (remember John and James are always mentioned together), which is the same three that went with Jesus into the room to raise Jarius's daughter from the dead and will go into the centre of the Garden of Gethsemane. The other nine disciples are in the second group. Jesus takes His close friends in group one up the mountain with Him whilst presumably group two camps at the bottom.

What transpires is breath taking and awe inspiring. Jesus is instantly, though briefly, transformed before their eyes into His future resurrection glory. God the Father speaks to the disciples and commands that they listen to Jesus, resulting in three prostrate, bumbling and terrified fishermen on the ground. I can imagine this state only worsened when Jesus was joined by Israel's two greatest prophets, Moses and Elijah. Greatest is always subjective and some could argue that other prophets may fit the bill. Considering Elijah didn't die, God just took him from the earth in a fiery angelic chariot (2 Kings 2:11) and Moses was personally buried by God on the plains of Moab (Deuteronomy 34:5-6), I think the word 'greatest' is apt. Let's not be too harsh on the three disciples though. It would have been a confronting, though gloriously amazing, scene for any of us.

Six days later Jesus took with him Peter, James, and John the brother of James, and led them privately up a high mountain. And he was transfigured before them. His face shone like the sun, and his clothes became white as light. Then Moses and Elijah also appeared before them, talking with him. So Peter said to Jesus, "Lord, it is good for us to be here. If you want, I will make three shelters-one for you, one for Moses, and one for Elijah." While he was still speaking, a bright cloud overshadowed them, and a voice from the cloud said, "This is my one dear Son, in whom I take great delight. Listen to him!" When the disciples heard this, they were overwhelmed with fear and threw themselves down with their faces to the ground. But Jesus came and touched them. "Get up," he said. "Do not be afraid." When they looked up, all they saw was Jesus alone. As they were coming down from the mountain, Jesus commanded them, "Do not tell anyone about the vision until the Son of Man is raised from the dead." The disciples asked him, "Why then do the experts in the law say that Elijah must come first?" He answered, "Elijah does indeed come first and will restore all things. And I tell you that Elijah has already come. Yet they did not recognize him, but did to him whatever they wanted. In the same way, the Son of Man will suffer at their hands." Then the disciples understood that he was speaking to them about John the Baptist. Matthew 17:1-13

Six days later Jesus took with him Peter, James, and John and led them alone up a high mountain privately. And he was transfigured before them, and his clothes became radiantly white, more so than any launderer in the world could bleach them. Then Elijah appeared before them along with Moses, and they were talking with Jesus. So Peter said to Jesus, "Rabbi, it is good for us to be here. Let us make three shelters-one for you, one for Moses, and one for Elijah." (For they were afraid, and he did not know what to say.) Then a cloud overshadowed them, and a voice came from the cloud, "This is my one dear Son. Listen to him!" Suddenly when they looked around, they saw no one with them any more except Jesus. As they were coming down from the mountain, he gave them orders not to tell anyone what they had seen until after the Son of Man had risen from the dead. They kept this statement to themselves, discussing what this rising from the dead meant. Then they asked him, "Why do the experts in the law say that Elijah must come first?" He said to them, "Elijah does indeed come first, and restores all things. And why is it written that the Son of Man must suffer many things and be despised? But I tell you that Elijah has certainly come, and they did to him whatever they wanted, just as it is written about him." Mark 9:2-13

Now about eight days after these sayings, Jesus took with him Peter, John, and James, and went up the mountain to pray. As he was praying, the appearance of his face was transformed, and his clothes became very bright, a brilliant white. Then two men, Moses and Elijah, began talking with him. They appeared in glorious splendor and spoke about his departure that he was about to carry out at Jerusalem. Now Peter and those with him were quite sleepy, but as they became fully awake, they saw his glory and the two men standing with him. Then as the men were starting to leave, Peter said to Jesus, "Master, it is good for us to be here. Let us make three shelters, one for you and one for Moses and one for Elijah"-not knowing what he was saying. As he was saying this, a cloud came and overshadowed them, and they were afraid as they entered the cloud. Then a voice came from the cloud, saying, "This is my Son, my Chosen One. Listen to him!" After the voice had spoken, Jesus was found alone. So they kept silent and told no one at that time anything of what they had seen. Luke 9:28-36

The twenty-seventh miracle – healing of a demon possessed boy

From solace and inspiration to the maddening crowds. The next day Jesus and His three closest friends descend the mountain to a melting pot scene of argument and adoration. The nine disciples at the bottom of the mountain were clearly no good at discretion, as the crowds had found them and the religious elite had also come. The disciples had earlier tried to cast out a demon with no effect and, rather than seek the God of the universe through prayer, they all decided to have an argument.

They had just spent a week with Jesus in the relative solitude of the northern Roman pagan cities. They had been sent out two by two whilst Jesus was in Jerusalem and had excitedly told Jesus about how, through them, people were healed and demons cast out. Yet here confronted with a particularly nasty demon they forget everything and start a verbal fight. I do feel for the disciples though. This was probably the first time they had seen the power of God not instantly heal or restore and couldn't understand why. The religious elite would also have been watching and immediately condemned them and Jesus when the demon wouldn't budge. Frustration must have been the order of the day. Be under no doubt this was a nasty demon. Much of the demonic when it sees Jesus acknowledges Him and flees, in some cases begging. Not this nasty thing. When it sees Jesus it torments the boy, and when commanded to leave, violently throws the boy around and then comes out. Jesus' words about 'this kind' of demon also point to a demonic order where some unclean spirits clearly have more power than others. This is another good lesson for the disciples, and us, that being grafted into the vine of Jesus is the only source of power and victory in our life and when in doubt, pray. It also reminds us that He, Jesus, who is in us, is eminently stronger than he, satan, who is in the world.

When they came to the disciples, they saw a large crowd around them and experts in the law arguing with them. When the whole crowd saw him, they were amazed and ran at once and greeted him. He asked them, "What are you arguing about with them?" A member of the crowd said to him, "Teacher, I brought you my son, who is possessed by a spirit that makes him mute. Whenever it seizes him, it throws him down, and he foams at the mouth, grinds his teeth, and becomes rigid. I asked your disciples to cast it out, but they were not able to do so." He answered them, "You unbelieving generation! How much longer must I be with you? How much longer must I endure you? Bring him to me." So they brought the boy to him. When the spirit saw him, it immediately threw the boy into a convulsion. He fell on the ground and rolled around, foaming at the mouth. Jesus asked his father, "How long has this been happening to him?" And he said, "From childhood. It has often thrown him into fire or water to destroy him. But if you are able to do anything, have compassion on us and help us." Then Jesus said to him, "If you are able?' All things are possible for the one who believes." Immediately the father of the boy cried out and said, "I believe; help my unbelief!"

Now when Jesus saw that a crowd was quickly gathering, he rebuked the unclean spirit, saying to it, "Mute and deaf spirit, I command you, come out of him and never enter him again." It shrieked, threw him into terrible convulsions, and came out. The boy looked so much like a corpse that many said, "He is dead!" But Jesus gently took his hand and raised him to his feet, and he stood up. Then, after he went into the house, his disciples asked him privately, "Why couldn't we cast it out?" He told them, "This kind can come out only by prayer." Mark 9:14-29

Now on the next day, when they had come down from the mountain, a large crowd met him. Then a man from the crowd cried out, "Teacher, I beg you to look at my son-he is my only child! A spirit seizes him, and he suddenly screams; it throws him into convulsions and causes him to foam at the mouth. It hardly ever leaves him alone, torturing him severely. I begged your disciples to cast it out, but they could not do so." Jesus answered, "You unbelieving and perverse generation! How much longer must I be with you and endure you? Bring your son here." As the boy was approaching, the demon threw him to the ground and shook him with convulsions. But Jesus rebuked the unclean spirit, healed the boy, and gave him back to his father. Then they were all astonished at the mighty power of God. Luke 9:37-43a

When they came to the crowd, a man came to him, knelt before him, and said, "Lord, have mercy on my son, because he has seizures and suffers terribly, for he often falls into the fire and into the water. I brought him to your disciples, but they were not able to heal him." Jesus answered, "You unbelieving and perverse generation! How much longer must I be with you? How much longer must I endure you? Bring him here to me." Then Jesus rebuked the demon and it came out of him, and the boy was healed from that moment. Then the disciples came to Jesus privately and said, "Why couldn't we cast it out?" He told them, "It was because of your little faith. I tell you the truth, if you have faith the size of a mustard seed, you will say to this mountain, 'Move from here to there,' and it will move; nothing will be impossible for you." Matthew 17:14-21

Jesus' death and resurrection foretold again

The party left Mount Tabor and continued through Galilee west en route to Capernaum, actively avoiding the people so Jesus could focus on His priority task, teaching his disciples and preparing them for their ministry once He had died and risen again. Once again Jesus explains to his disciples that He must die and will be raised from death. This is the same message Jesus told them the previous week in Caesarea Philippi. At least this time Peter had learnt that rebuking Jesus was not wise, though evidently they still did not understand what Jesus was saying.

They went out from there and passed through Galilee. But Jesus did not want anyone to know, for he was teaching his disciples and telling them, "The Son of Man will be betrayed into the hands of men. They will kill him, and after three days he will rise." But they did not understand this statement and were afraid to ask him. Mark 9:30-32

But while the entire crowd was amazed at everything Jesus was doing, he said to his disciples, "Take these words to heart, for the Son of Man is going to be betrayed into the hands of men." But they did not understand this statement; its meaning had been concealed from them, so that they could not grasp it. Yet they were afraid to ask him about this statement. Luke 9:43b-45

When they gathered together in Galilee, Jesus told them, "The Son of Man is going to be betrayed into the hands of men. They will kill him, and on the third day he will be raised." And they became greatly distressed. Matthew 17:22-23

The twenty-eighth miracle – the Temple tax

Arriving back in Capernaum, the place of so much healing and restoration, you would expect a hero's welcome. Apparently not, for the religious elite were once again desperately protecting their rules and regulations that defined their religion based on the law of Moses. Their latest affront was to demand that Jesus pay the Temple tax, something they had not bothered to ask in the preceding two and half years. Suddenly the tax is all very important, or was the religious elite's attempt to embarrass Jesus more important?

Firstly a little about the Temple tax. After the destruction of Jerusalem in 586 BC, there was a requirement to collect money to rebuild the Temple and provide for its sacrifices. The law of Moses allowed for such a collection (Exodus 30:11-16) of half a shekel per person. The Temple tax in the time of Jesus was a didrachma, or double drachma, and was a silver coin equal to the Jewish half shekel. The drachma represented an average pay for a day labourer, according to the parable of Matthew 20.

The question by the religious elite about whether Jesus pays the Temple tax implies that they half-thought that Jesus had evaded or would evade the payment. They were looking for another transgression of the law. As soon as Jesus entered Capernaum they tracked Him down, probably to Peter's house, and put the question to His disciple. Evidently the other disciples weren't there or they too may have been told to contribute. The result is remarkable. Jesus the fisher of men, uses a fish to pay the tax to not cause offence. As an aside, spare a thought for the poor person who lost that coin, worth two days wages, so Jesus could use it.

After they arrived in Capernaum, the collectors of the temple tax came to Peter and said, "Your teacher pays the double drachma tax, doesn't he?" He said, "Yes." When Peter came into the house, Jesus spoke to him first, "What do you think, Simon? From whom do earthly kings collect tolls or taxes-from their sons or from foreigners?" After he said, "From foreigners," Jesus said to him, "Then the sons are free. But so that we don't offend them, go to the lake and throw out a hook. Take the first fish that comes up, and when you open its mouth, you will find a four drachma coin. Take that and give it to them for me and you." Matthew 17:24-27

The discourses

In Capernaum, Jesus continued to teach His disciples. Six discourses are recorded that instruct the disciples on humility, inclusion, example, priority, accountability and forgiveness. They are timeless.

Discourse 1 - who is the greatest?

Then they came to Capernaum. After Jesus was inside the house he asked them, "What were you discussing on the way?" But they were silent, for on the way they had argued with one another about who was the greatest. After he sat down, he called the twelve and said to them, "If anyone wants to be first, he must be last of all and servant of all." He took a little child and had him stand among them. Taking him in his arms, he said to them, "Whoever welcomes one of these little children in my name welcomes me, and whoever welcomes me does not welcome me but the one who sent me." Mark 9:33-37

At that time the disciples came to Jesus saying, "Who is the greatest in the kingdom of heaven?" He called a child, had him stand among them, and said, "I tell you the truth, unless you turn around and become like little children, you will never enter the kingdom of heaven! Whoever then humbles himself like this little child is the greatest in the kingdom of heaven. And whoever welcomes a child like this in my name welcomes me. "But if anyone causes one of these little ones who believe in me to sin, it would be better for him to have a huge millstone hung around his neck and to be drowned in the open sea. Matthew 18:1-6

Now an argument started among the disciples as to which of them
might be the greatest. But when Jesus discerned their innermost
thoughts, he took a child, had him stand by his side, and said to
them, "Whoever welcomes this child in my name welcomes me, and
whoever welcomes me welcomes the one who sent me, for the one
who is least among you all is the one who is great." Luke 9:46-48

Discourse 2 - for and against

John said to him, "Teacher, we saw someone casting out demons in
your name, and we tried to stop him because he was not following
us." But Jesus said, "Do not stop him, because no one who does a
miracle in my name will be able soon afterward to say anything
bad about me. For whoever is not against us is for us. For I tell
you the truth, whoever gives you a cup of water because you bear
Christ's name will never lose his reward....Mark 9:38-41

John answered, "Master, we saw someone casting out demons
in your name, and we tried to stop him because he is not a
disciple along with us." But Jesus said to him, "Do not stop him,
for whoever is not against you is for you." Luke 9:49-50

Discourse 3 - stumbling blocks

Woe to the world because of stumbling blocks! It is necessary that
stumbling blocks come, but woe to the person through whom they come.
If your hand or your foot causes you to sin, cut it off and throw it away. It
is better for you to enter life crippled or lame than to have two hands or
two feet and be thrown into eternal fire. And if your eye causes you to sin,
tear it out and throw it away. It is better for you to enter into life with
one eye than to have two eyes and be thrown into fiery hell. "See that you
do not disdain one of these little ones. For I tell you that their angels in
heaven always see the face of my Father in heaven....Matthew 18:7-11

"If anyone causes one of these little ones who believe in me to sin, it would be better for him to have a huge millstone tied around his neck and to be thrown into the sea. If your hand causes you to sin, cut it off! It is better for you to enter into life crippled than to have two hands and go into hell, to the unquenchable fire. If your foot causes you to sin, cut it off! It is better to enter life lame than to have two feet and be thrown into hell. If your eye causes you to sin, tear it out! It is better to enter into the kingdom of God with one eye than to have two eyes and be thrown into hell, where their worm never dies and the fire is never quenched. Everyone will be salted with fire. Salt is good, but if it loses its saltiness, how can you make it salty again? Have salt in yourselves, and be at peace with each other." Mark 9:42-50

Discourse 4 - the hundred sheep

What do you think? If someone owns a hundred sheep and one of them goes astray, will he not leave the ninety-nine on the mountains and go look for the one that went astray? And if he finds it, I tell you the truth, he will rejoice more over it than over the ninety-nine that did not go astray. In the same way, your Father in heaven is not willing that one of these little ones be lost. Matthew 18:12-14

Discourse 5 - accountability

"If your brother sins, go and show him his fault when the two of you are alone. If he listens to you, you have regained your brother. But if he does not listen, take one or two others with you, so that at the testimony of two or three witnesses every matter may be established. If he refuses to listen to them, tell it to the church. If he refuses to listen to the church, treat him like a Gentile or a tax collector. "I tell you the truth, whatever you bind on earth will have been bound in heaven, and whatever you release on earth will have been released in heaven. Again, I tell you the truth, if two of you on earth agree about whatever you

ask, my Father in heaven will do it for you. For where two or three are assembled in my name, I am there among them." Matthew 18:15-20

Discourse 6 - forgiveness

Then Peter came to him and said, "Lord, how many times must I forgive my brother who sins against me? As many as seven times?" Jesus said to him, "Not seven times, I tell you, but seventy-seven times! "For this reason, the kingdom of heaven is like a king who wanted to settle accounts with his slaves. As he began settling his accounts, a man who owed ten thousand talents was brought to him. Because he was not able to repay it, the lord ordered him to be sold, along with his wife, children, and whatever he possessed, and repayment to be made. Then the slave threw himself to the ground before him, saying, 'Be patient with me, and I will repay you everything.' The lord had compassion on that slave and released him, and forgave him the debt. After he went out, that same slave found one of his fellow slaves who owed him one hundred silver coins. So he grabbed him by the throat and started to choke him, saying, 'Pay back what you owe me!' Then his fellow slave threw himself down and begged him, 'Be patient with me, and I will repay you.' But he refused. Instead, he went out and threw him in prison until he repaid the debt. When his fellow slaves saw what had happened, they were very upset and went and told their lord everything that had taken place. Then his lord called the first slave and said to him, 'Evil slave! I forgave you all that debt because you begged me! Should you not have shown mercy to your fellow slave, just as I showed it to you?' And in anger his lord turned him over to the prison guards to torture him until he repaid all he owed. So also my heavenly Father will do to you, if each of you does not forgive your brother from your heart." Matthew 18:21-35

The lonely road back to Jerusalem (six months to the cross)

Jesus now leaves Capernaum and the region of Galilee for the last time before He is crucified. Interestingly after His resurrection He meets the disciples again by the Sea of Galilee, however more of that later. Right now Jesus resolutely starts out on foot from his adopted home of Capernaum for His fourth post-baptism visit to Jerusalem to attend the final festival of the Jewish year, the feast of Tabernacles. The festival is held at the end of autumn (fall) starting on the 15th day of the Jewish seventh month, and is thus six months away from Passover where Jesus would lay down His life.

Now when Jesus finished these sayings, he left Galilee and went to the region of Judea beyond the Jordan River. Large crowds followed him, and he healed them there. Matthew 19:1-2

The gospels definitively record four visits and infer a possible fifth visit of Jesus to Jerusalem during His three years of ministry. The synoptic gospels and John all record the final visit (the triumphant entrance) into Jerusalem that would end with Jesus nailed to a Roman cross. Only John's gospel records the other three visits and infers a possible fourth. Whilst it is difficult to know for sure, there is a cogent argument to support Jesus visiting Jerusalem five times during His ministry:

- **Visit 1** - First Passover during the ministry year 30 AD and cleansing of the Temple (John 2:13);
- **Visit 2** - Feast of the Jews, probably the second Passover in 31 AD and the healing at the pool (John 5:1);
- **Visit 3** - Scripture says the Jewish Passover was near, indicating its importance to Jesus, but there is no definitive statement to say Jesus celebrated it in Jerusalem (John 6:4). Since Jesus came to complete the law it is likely He did attend Passover in Jerusalem in 32 AD as He had been raised to do so by His family and was required by the law.
- **Visit 4** - Both for the Feast of Tabernacles and Feast of Dedication (Hanukkah) in October and December 32 AD,

noting that Jesus moved around and taught in Judea between these two festivals. (John 7:14-10:39);

- **Visit 5** - All the gospels record Jesus' triumphant entry into Jerusalem and His crucifixion on Passover, Friday 3rd April 33 AD.

Before a discussion about Jesus' fourth visit to Jerusalem to celebrate the feast of Tabernacles, it is wise to learn a bit about the seven main festivals given by God for the Jews to observe. The Jews have since added other Festivals to their calendar based on their rich history and heritage, however seven Festivals were God ordained, three in the spring, one in the harvest and three in the autumn.

Three spring festivals

- Passover (Pesach)
  - Celebrated on the 14th day of the first month of the Jewish calendar, the month of Aviv.
  - Families will slay and eat a lamb to remember Israel's deliverance from Egypt.
  - Exodus 12:1-14; Leviticus 23:5; Numbers 9:1-14; Numbers 28:16 and Deuteronomy 16:1-3a and 4b-7.
- Unleavened Bread (Chag Hamotzi)
  - Celebrated for a week from 15-21 Aviv, starting on the day after Passover.
  - Families eat bread without yeast, hold a range of assemblies and make designated offering to remember Israel's deliverance from Egypt in haste.
  - Exodus 12:15-20, 13:3-10, 23:15, 34:18; Leviticus 23:6-8; Numbers 28:17-25 and Deuteronomy 16:3b, 4a and 8.
- First Fruits (Yom Habikkurim)

- Celebrated on the day after the Feast of Unleavened Bread commences (second day of the feast) 16 Aviv.
- A sheaf of the first of the barley harvest is presented as a wave offering to remember the Lord's bounty and blessing.
- Leviticus 23:9-14.

Harvest festival - Pentecost (Shavu'ot)

- Celebrated 50 days after Passover (including the Passover day) during the wheat harvest, 6 Sivan.
- The day the law was given at Mount Sinai.
- A festival to show joy and thankfulness for the Lord's blessing with a range of offerings.
- Exodus 23:16a, 34:22a; Leviticus 23:15-21; Numbers 28:26-31 and Deuteronomy 16:9-12.

Three autumn festivals

- Trumpets (Rosh Hashanah - New Year's Day)
  - Celebrated on Tishri 1.
  - A festival for Israel to present itself to the Lord for His favour, celebrated with trumpet blasts.
  - The Jewish new year.
  - Leviticus 23:23-25 and Numbers 29:1-6.
- Atonement (Yom Kippur)
  - Celebrated nine days after Trumpets, Tishri 10.
  - The one day of the year the priest goes into the Most Holy Place of the Temple, behind the curtain, to make atonement for all the sins of the people of Israel.
  - Leviticus 16, 23:26-32 and Numbers 29:7-11.
- Tabernacles (Sukkot)

- Celebrated for a week from Tishri 15 - 22, two weeks after Trumpets.
- A festival for Israel to live in booths to remember the journey from Egypt to the promised land of Canaan.
- Exodus 23:16b, 34:22b; Leviticus 23:33-36a, 39-43; Numbers 29:12-3; Deuteronomy 16:13-15 and Zechariah 14:16-19.

Just to add a little New Covenant fulfilment to these law based Old Covenant feasts, Jesus would be crucified on Passover, would be in the grave at the start of unleavened bread and would rise again on first fruits. Fifty days after crucifixion on Pentecost the promised Holy Spirit would be given. Where then does that leave the last three autumn feasts, that commence four months later, the feasts of Trumpets, Atonement and Tabernacles that occur over a twenty one day period? Perhaps their correlation to the New Covenant is linked to the second coming of Christ? What three events will occur over these twenty-one days of the second coming? I guess we'll all just have to wait and see.

Festival of Tabernacles
Back to the Feast of Tabernacles or Sukkot, the seventh (and final) feast given to Israel. This is the final celebration for autumn and the last of the three pilgrimage festivals where Jews went to Jerusalem to celebrate. Sukkot is observed from the 15th to the 22nd of Tishri (7th month) and was intended as a seven day feast. During this time many Jewish families construct a sukkah, a small hastily built hut in which meals are eaten throughout the festival. Sukkot is used to remember the huts Israel lived in during their forty-year sojourn in the desert after the exodus from Egypt. Later, after Israel entered the land of promise, Sukkot was associated with the fall harvest and came to be known as the 'festival of Ingathering' (of the harvest) at the end of the year.

As Jesus left Capernaum en route to Jerusalem to celebrate Sukkot, He once again took the road through Samaria rather than the traditional route via the Jordan Valley (remember the first time Jesus went to Jerusalem after His baptism, He walked back from Jerusalem to Galilee through Samaria).

I sense a little bit of frustration on the early part of this walk. Jesus is rejected from a Samaritan town, His disciples want to blow everything up and well-meaning people want to follow Jesus but have convenient excuses for why they can't follow Him now. I'd be frustrated by that.

Now when the days drew near for him to be taken up, Jesus set out resolutely to go to Jerusalem. He sent messengers on ahead of him. As they went along, they entered a Samaritan village to make things ready in advance for him, but the villagers refused to welcome him, because he was determined to go to Jerusalem. Now when his disciples James and John saw this, they said, "Lord, do you want us to call fire to come down from heaven and consume them?" But Jesus turned and rebuked them, and they went on to another village. Luke 9:51-56

Then an expert in the law came to him and said, "Teacher, I will follow you wherever you go." Jesus said to him, "Foxes have dens, and the birds in the sky have nests, but the Son of Man has no place to lay his head." Another of the disciples said to him, "Lord, let me first go and bury my father." But Jesus said to him, "Follow me, and let the dead bury their own dead." Matthew 8:19-22

As they were walking along the road, someone said to him, "I will follow you wherever you go." Jesus said to him, "Foxes have dens and the birds in the sky have nests, but the Son of Man has no place to lay his head." Jesus said to another, "Follow me." But he replied, "Lord, first let me go and bury my father." But Jesus said to him, "Let the dead bury their own dead, but as for you, go and proclaim the kingdom of

God." Yet another said, "I will follow you, Lord, but first let me say goodbye to my family." Jesus said to him, "No one who puts his hand to the plow and looks back is fit for the kingdom of God." Luke 9:57-62

The frustration of Jesus would not have been aided by His ungrateful younger brothers. They clearly saw the miracles that Jesus performed but didn't understand the purpose for which Jesus was on earth. If ever there was a case of familiarity breeding contempt, this would have to be it. His brothers went to Jerusalem but Jesus waited a few days and then left for Jerusalem, arriving around day four of the seven day festival.

Now the Jewish feast of Tabernacles was near. So Jesus' brothers advised him, "Leave here and go to Judea so your disciples may see your miracles that you are performing. For no one who seeks to make a reputation for himself does anything in secret. If you are doing these things, show yourself to the world." (For not even his own brothers believed in him.) So Jesus replied, "My time has not yet arrived, but you are ready at any opportunity! The world cannot hate you, but it hates me, because I am testifying about it that its deeds are evil. You go up to the feast yourselves. I am not going up to this feast because my time has not yet fully arrived." When he had said this, he remained in Galilee. John 7:2-9

But when his brothers had gone up to the feast, then Jesus himself also went up, not openly but in secret. John 7:10

Festival of Tabernacles (9 - 15 October 32 AD) five and a half months to the cross

When Jesus arrived in Jerusalem He went straight to the Temple and began to teach, as was His habit.

So the Jewish leaders were looking for him at the feast, asking, "Where is he?" There was a lot of grumbling about him among the crowds. Some were saying, "He is a good man," but others, "He deceives the common people." However, no one spoke openly about him for fear of the Jewish leaders. When the feast was half over, Jesus went up to the temple courts and began to teach. Then the Jewish leaders were astonished and said, "How does this man know so much when he has never had formal instruction?" So Jesus replied, "My teaching is not from me, but from the one who sent me. If anyone wants to do God's will, he will know about my teaching, whether it is from God or whether I speak from my own authority. The person who speaks on his own authority desires to receive honor for himself; the one who desires the honor of the one who sent him is a man of integrity, and there is no unrighteousness in him. Hasn't Moses given you the law? Yet not one of you keeps the law! Why do you want to kill me?" The crowd answered, "You're possessed by a demon! Who is trying to kill you?" Jesus replied, "I performed one miracle and you are all amazed. However, because Moses gave you the practice of circumcision (not that it came from Moses, but from the forefathers), you circumcise a male child on the Sabbath. But if a male child is circumcised on the Sabbath so that the law of Moses is not broken, why are you angry with me because I made a man completely well on the Sabbath? Do not judge according to external appearance, but judge with proper judgment." Then some of the residents of Jerusalem began to say, "Isn't this the man they are trying to kill? Yet here he is, speaking publicly, and they are saying nothing to him. Do the rulers really know that this man is the Christ? But we know where this man comes from. Whenever the Christ comes, no one will know where he comes from." Then Jesus, while teaching in the temple courts, cried out, "You both know me and know where I come from! And I have not come on my own initiative, but the one who sent me is true. You do not know him, but I know him, because I have come from him and he sent me." So then they tried to seize Jesus, but no one laid a hand on him, because his time had not yet come. Yet many of the crowd believed in him and said, "Whenever the Christ comes, he won't perform more miraculous signs than this man did, will he?" The Pharisees heard the crowd murmuring these things about Jesus, so the chief priests and the Pharisees sent officers to arrest him. Then Jesus said, "I will be with you for only a little while longer, and then I am going to the one who sent me. You will look for me but will not find me, and where I am you cannot come." Then the Jewish leaders said to one another, "Where is he going to go that we cannot find him? He is not going to go to the Jewish people dispersed among the Greeks and teach the Greeks, is he? What did he mean by saying, 'You will look for me but will not find me, and where I am you cannot come'?" On the last day of the feast, the greatest day, Jesus stood up and shouted out, "If anyone is thirsty, let him come to me, and let the one who believes in me drink. Just as the scripture says, 'From within him will flow rivers of living water.'" (Now he said this about the Spirit, whom those who believed in him were going to receive, for the Spirit had not yet been given, because Jesus was not yet glorified.) When they heard these words, some of the crowd began to say, "This really is the Prophet!" Others said, "This is the Christ!" But still others said, "No, for the Christ doesn't come from Galilee, does he? Don't the scriptures say that the Christ is a descendant of David and comes from Bethlehem, the village where David lived?" So there was a division in the crowd because of Jesus. Some of them were wanting to seize him, but no one laid a hand on him. Then the officers returned to the chief priests and Pharisees, who said to them, "Why didn't you bring him back with you?" The officers replied, "No one ever spoke like this man!" Then the Pharisees answered, "You haven't been deceived too, have you? None of the rulers or the Pharisees have believed in him, have they? But this rabble who do not know the law are accursed!" Nicodemus, who had gone to Jesus before and who was one of the rulers, said, "Our law doesn't condemn a man unless it first hears from him and learns what he is doing, does it?" They replied, "You aren't from Galilee too, are you? Investigate carefully and you will see that no prophet comes from Galilee!" And each one departed to his own house.... John 7:11-53

I've often wondered where Jesus and His disciples stayed when they visited Jerusalem as scripture says the Mount of Olives, but doesn't specify whether this is under the stars or in lodging. The Mount of

Olives is due east of Jerusalem across the Kidron Valley and is one of the seven mountains of Jerusalem. This ridge line east of Jerusalem has two other mountain peaks, Mount Scopus to the north, and the Mount of Corruption or Mount of Evil Counsel to the south (named because this is where Judas promised to betray Jesus for thirty pieces of silver). The last four peaks are Mount Ophel (2 Chronicles 27:3; 33:14 and Nehemiah 3:26-27) being the eastern ridge and south of the Temple, the original Mount Zion, the New Mount Zion and Mount Moriah (the Temple Mount), with the Antonia Fortress being built on the highest part.

The Mount of Olives was evidently covered in olive groves, hence its name and was less than a kilometre from the Temple, which made it technically within the confines of the city of Jerusalem. It also has an amazing view of the Temple. Jesus was born in a stable so I guess He was accustomed to sleeping a little rough if indeed that was what He did.

> *But Jesus went to the Mount of Olives. Early in the morning*
> *he came to the temple courts again. All the people came to him,*
> *and he sat down and began to teach them. John 8:1-2*

A despicable test
The next morning, probably day five of the Feast of Tabernacles, Jesus gets up early and is back in the Temple as the sun crests the Mount of Olives. The religious elite are not found sitting at the feet of Jesus but dragging a helpless woman, likely half stripped, into the Temple courts because she had been caught in adultery. The language in the gospels speaks of being caught in the very act, which begs questions like: where is the male offending party, how did the religious elite know where to look so early in the morning, and was it a set up and many more questions that reflect badly on the religious elite. Jesus loves people and His response is perfect.

The experts in the law and the Pharisees brought a woman who had been caught committing adultery. They made her stand in front of them and said to Jesus, "Teacher, this woman was caught in the very act of adultery. In the law Moses commanded us to stone to death such women. What then do you say?" (Now they were asking this in an attempt to trap him, so that they could bring charges against him.) Jesus bent down and wrote on the ground with his finger. When they persisted in asking him, he stood up straight and replied, "Whoever among you is guiltless may be the first to throw a stone at her." Then he bent over again and wrote on the ground. Now when they heard this, they began to drift away one at a time, starting with the older ones, until Jesus was left alone with the woman standing before him. Jesus stood up straight and said to her, "Woman, where are they? Did no one condemn you?" She replied, "No one, Lord." And Jesus said, "I do not condemn you either. Go, and from now on do not sin any more." John 8:3-11

As an aside, what was Jesus writing in the dirt? The law perhaps, maybe the Ten Commandments!

Having dealt with the murderous religious elite ready to sacrifice a distraught woman, Jesus returns to another discourse with the people about His purpose and His impending death and completion of the law, that John's gospel records so beautifully.

Then Jesus spoke out again, "I am the light of the world. The one who follows me will never walk in darkness, but will have the light of life." So the Pharisees objected, "You testify about yourself; your testimony is not true!" Jesus answered, "Even if I testify about myself, my testimony is true, because I know where I came from and where I am going. But you people do not know where I came from or where I am going. You people judge by outward appearances; I do not judge anyone. But if I judge, my evaluation is accurate, because I am not alone when I judge, but I and the Father who sent me do so together. It is written in your law that the testimony of two men is true. I testify about myself and the Father who sent me testifies about me." Then they began asking him, "Who is your father?" Jesus answered, "You do not know either me or my Father. If you knew me you would know my Father too." (Jesus spoke these words near the offering box while he was teaching in the temple courts. No one seized him because his time had not yet come.) Then Jesus said to them again, "I am going away, and you will look for me but will die in your sin. Where I am going you cannot come." So the Jewish leaders began to say, "Perhaps he is going to kill himself, because he says, 'Where I am going you cannot come.'" Jesus replied, "You people are from below; I am from above. You people are from this world; I am not from this world. Thus I told you that you will die in your sins. For unless you believe that I am he, you will die in your sins." So they said to him, "Who are you?" Jesus replied, "What I have told you from the beginning. I have many things to say and to judge about you, but the Father who sent me is truthful, and the things I have heard from him I speak to the world." (They did not understand that he was telling them about his Father.) Then Jesus said, "When you lift up the Son of Man, then you will know that I am he, and I do nothing on my own initiative, but I speak just what the Father taught me. And the one who sent me is with me. He has not left me alone, because I always do those things that please him." While he was saying these things, many people believed in him. Then Jesus said to those Judeans who had believed him, "If you continue to follow my teaching, you are really my disciples and you will know the truth, and the truth will set you free.""We are descendants of Abraham," they replied, "and have never been anyone's slaves! How can you say, 'You will become free'?" Jesus answered them, "I tell you the solemn truth, everyone who practices sin is a slave of sin. The slave does not remain in the family forever, but the son remains forever. So if the son sets you free, you will be really free. I know that you are Abraham's descendants. But you want to kill me, because my teaching makes no progress among you. I am telling you the things I have seen while with the Father; as for you, practice the things you have heard from the Father!" They answered him, "Abraham is our father!" Jesus replied, "If you are Abraham's children, you would be doing the deeds of Abraham. But now you are trying to kill me, a man who has told you the truth I heard from God. Abraham did not do this! You people are doing the deeds of your father." Then they said to Jesus, "We were not born as a result of immorality! We have only one Father, God himself." Jesus replied, "If God were your Father, you would love me, for I have come from God and am now here. I have not come on my own initiative, but he sent me. Why don't you understand what I am saying? It is because you cannot accept my teaching. You people are from your father the devil, and you want to do what your father desires. He was a murderer from the beginning, and does not uphold the truth, because there is no truth in him. Whenever he lies, he speaks according to his own nature, because he is a liar and the father of lies. But because I am telling you the truth, you do not believe me. Who among you can prove me guilty of any sin? If I am telling you the truth, why don't you believe me? The one who belongs to God listens and responds to God's words. You don't listen and respond, because you don't belong to God." The Judeans replied, "Aren't we correct in saying that you are a Samaritan and are possessed by a demon?" Jesus answered, "I am not possessed by a demon, but I honor my Father-and yet you dishonor me. I am not trying to get praise for myself. There is one who demands it, and he also judges. I tell you the solemn truth, if anyone obeys my teaching, he will never see death." Then the Judeans responded, "Now we know you're possessed by a demon! Both Abraham and the prophets died, and yet you say, 'If anyone obeys my teaching, he will never experience death.' You aren't greater than our father Abraham who died, are you? And the prophets died too! Who do you claim to be?" Jesus replied, "If I glorify myself, my glory is worthless. The one who glorifies me is my Father, about whom you people say, 'He is our God.' Yet you do not know him, but I know him. If I were to say that I do not know him, I would be a liar like you. But I do know him, and I obey his teaching. Your father Abraham was overjoyed to see my day, and he saw it and was glad." Then the Judeans replied, "You are not yet fifty years old! Have you seen Abraham?" Jesus *said to them, "I tell you the solemn truth, before Abraham came into existence, I am!" Then they picked up stones to throw at him, but Jesus was hidden from them and went out from the temple area. John 8:12-59*

Two months in Jerusalem and Judea

The feast of Tabernacles finished on the 15th October 32 AD so Jesus' subsequent healing actions and discourse occurred sometime between the end of Tabernacles and the start of the Festival of Dedication (Hanukkah) on 7th December 32 AD. For this two month period it is assumed that Jesus stayed in and around Jerusalem and Judea teaching and healing. Note that Hanukkah is not one of the seven festivals ordained by God, so what was Jesus doing there? A little more on that later.

The twenty-ninth miracle – healing the body

As Jesus travelled and taught during this two month period, He couldn't help but poke the religious elite in the eye once more (pun intended). Jesus is moving through Jerusalem and Judea and subsequently heals a blind man on the holy Sabbath day and He does it by working in direct contradiction to the Jewish law. Jesus spits on the ground and makes mud (which is defined as work on a Sabbath day) and puts the mud on the man's eyes and tells him to wash. An elaborate means to heal the man, to challenge the law and to reflect that Jesus is the light of the world.

Now as Jesus was passing by, he saw a man who had been blind from birth. His disciples asked him, "Rabbi, who committed the sin that caused him to be born blind, this man or his parents?" Jesus answered, "Neither this man nor his parents sinned, but he was born blind so that the acts of God may be revealed through what happens to him. We must perform the deeds of the one who sent me as long as it is daytime. Night is coming when no one can work. As long as I am in the world, I am the light of the world." Having said this, he spat on the ground and made some mud with the saliva. He smeared the mud on the blind man's eyes and said to him, "Go wash in the pool of Siloam" (which is translated "sent"). So the blind man went away and washed, and came back seeing.

Then the neighbors and the people who had seen him previously as a beggar began saying, "Is this not the man who used to sit and beg?" Some people said, "This is the man!" while others said, "No, but he looks like him." The man himself kept insisting, "I am the one!" So they asked him, "How then were you made to see?" He replied, "The man called Jesus made mud, smeared it on my eyes and told me, 'Go to Siloam and wash.' So I went and washed, and was able to see." They said to him, "Where is that man?" He replied, "I don't know." They brought the man who used to be blind to the Pharisees. (Now the day on which Jesus made the mud and caused him to see was a Sabbath.) So the Pharisees asked him again how he had gained his sight. He replied, "He put mud on my eyes and I washed, and now I am able to see." Then some of the Pharisees began to say, "This man is not from God, because he does not observe the Sabbath." But others said, "How can a man who is a sinner perform such miraculous signs?" Thus there was a division among them. So again they asked the man who used to be blind, "What do you say about him, since he caused you to see?" "He is a prophet," the man replied. Now the Jewish religious leaders refused to believe that he had really been blind and had gained his sight until at last they summoned the parents of the man who had become able to see. They asked the parents, "Is this your son, whom you say was born blind? Then how does he now see?" So his parents replied, "We know that this is our son and that he was born blind. But we do not know how he is now able to see, nor do we know who caused him to see. Ask him, he is a mature adult. He will speak for himself." (His parents said these things because they were afraid of the Jewish religious leaders. For the Jewish leaders had already agreed that anyone who confessed Jesus to be the Christ would be put out of the synagogue. For this reason his parents said, "He is a mature adult, ask him.") Then they summoned the man who used to be blind a second time and said to him, "Promise before God to tell the truth. We know *that this man is a sinner." He replied, "I do not know whether he is a sinner. I do know one thing-that although I was blind, now I can see." Then they said to him, "What did he do to you? How did he cause you to see?" He answered, "I told you already and you didn't listen. Why do you want to hear it again? You people don't want to become his disciples too, do you?" They heaped insults on him, saying, "You are his disciple! We are disciples of Moses! We know that God has spoken to Moses! We do not know where this man comes from!" The man replied, "This is a remarkable thing, that you don't know where he comes from, and yet he caused me to see! We know that God doesn't listen to sinners, but if anyone is devout and does his will, God listens to him. Never before has anyone heard of someone causing a man born blind to see. If this man were not from God, he could do nothing." They replied, "You were born completely in sinfulness, and yet you presume to teach us?" So they threw him out. Jesus heard that they had thrown him out, so he found the man and said to him, "Do you believe in the Son of Man?" The man replied, "And who is he, sir, that I may believe in him?" Jesus told him, "You have seen him; he is the one speaking with you." [He said, "Lord, I believe," and he worshiped him. Jesus said,] "For judgment I have come into this world, so that those who do not see may gain their sight, and the ones who see may become blind." Some of the Pharisees who were with him heard this and asked him, "We are not blind too, are we?" Jesus replied, "If you were blind, you would not be guilty of sin, but now because you claim that you can see, your guilt remains. John 9:1-41*

Having healed the man and confronted the Pharisees, Jesus continues his discourse.

"I tell you the solemn truth, the one who does not enter the sheepfold by the door, but climbs in some other way, is a thief and a robber. The one who enters by the door is the shepherd of the sheep. The doorkeeper opens the door for him, and the sheep hear his voice. He calls his own sheep by name and leads them out. When he has brought all his own sheep out,

he goes ahead of them, and the sheep follow him because they recognize his voice. They will never follow a stranger, but will run away from him, because they do not recognize the stranger's voice." Jesus told them this parable, but they did not understand what he was saying to them. So Jesus said again, "I tell you the solemn truth, I am the door for the sheep. All who came before me were thieves and robbers, but the sheep did not listen to them. I am the door. If anyone enters through me, he will be saved, and will come in and go out, and find pasture. The thief comes only to steal and kill and destroy; I have come so that they may have life, and may have it abundantly. "I am the good shepherd. The good shepherd lays down his life for the sheep. The hired hand, who is not a shepherd and does not own sheep, sees the wolf coming and abandons the sheep and runs away. So the wolf attacks the sheep and scatters them. Because he is a hired hand and is not concerned about the sheep, he runs away. "I am the good shepherd. I know my own and my own know me – just as the Father knows me and I know the Father – and I lay down my life for the sheep.

I have other sheep that do not come from this sheepfold. I must bring them too, and they will listen to my voice, so that there will be one flock and one shepherd. This is why the Father loves me-because I lay down my life, so that I may take it back again. No one takes it away from me, but I lay it down of my own free will. I have the authority to lay it down, and I have the authority to take it back again. This commandment I received from my Father." Another sharp division took place among the Jewish people because of these words. Many of them were saying, "He is possessed by a demon and has lost his mind! Why do you listen to him?" Others said, "These are not the words of someone possessed by a demon. A demon cannot cause the blind to see, can it?"... John 10:1-21

Festival of dedication (Hanukkah) 17th - 24th December 32 AD

Hanukkah remembers the last great deliverance for the Jewish people when a revolt occurred under Judas Maccabeus in December 165 BC to throw off the shackles of Antiochus IV Epiphanes. The festival of dedication remembers the cleansing of the Temple after Antiochus

Epiphanes sacrificed a pig's head on the altar. Hanukkah is observed for eight nights and days, starting on the 25th day of Kislev (17th December 32 AD). Jesus has just finished His two months in and around Judea and ends up in Jerusalem for Hanukkah. It is winter and cold.

Considering Hanukkah is not one of the seven God ordained festivals for the Jews, what is Jesus, the Son of God doing in Jerusalem at Hanukkah? There are plenty of ideas and theories and lots of people read lots of things into it. It could just be that Jesus loved being in His Father's house, the Temple, and here was an opportunity to reach more people. Maybe Jesus wanted to poke the religious elite in the eye again. Perhaps Jesus wanted to make the point that the deliverance Hanukkah celebrates is nothing compared to the deliverance Jesus would bring through His death and resurrection. Perhaps all of this and perhaps none of it. It makes you think though!

Then came the feast of the Dedication in Jerusalem. It was winter, and Jesus was walking in the temple area in Solomon's Portico. The Jewish leaders surrounded him and asked, "How long will you keep us in suspense? If you are the Christ, tell us plainly." Jesus replied, "I told you and you do not believe. The deeds I do in my Father's name testify about me. But you refuse to believe because you are not my sheep. My sheep listen to my voice, and I know them, and they follow me. I give them eternal life, and they will never perish; no one will snatch them from my hand. My Father, who has given them to me, is greater than all, and no one can snatch them from my Father's hand. The Father and I are one." The Jewish leaders picked up rocks again to stone him to death. Jesus said to them, "I have shown you many good deeds from the Father. For which one of them are you going to stone me?" The Jewish leaders replied, "We are not going to stone you for a good deed but for blasphemy, because you, a man, are claiming to be God." Jesus answered, "Is it not written in your law, 'I said, you are

gods'? If those people to whom the word of God came were called 'gods'
(and the scripture cannot be broken), do you say about the one whom
the Father set apart and sent into the world, 'You are blaspheming,'
because I said, 'I am the Son of God'? If I do not perform the deeds of my
Father, do not believe me. But if I do them, even if you do not believe
me, believe the deeds, so that you may come to know and understand
that I am in the Father and the Father is in me." Then they attempted
again to seize him, but he escaped their clutches.... John 10:22-39

Back to the Jordan River

After the festival of Hanukkah, Jesus leaves Jerusalem and heads back
to either the Jordan River or to Aenon near Salim, both within Judea.
Again Jesus touches the lives of people, this time mostly Judeans and
finished 32 AD down in the green valley by the flowing river.

Jesus went back across the Jordan River again to the place where
John had been baptizing at an earlier time, and he stayed
there. Many came to him and began to say, "John performed no
miraculous sign, but everything John said about this man was
true!" And many believed in Jesus there. John 10:40-42

CHAPTER 9

Travel diaries
(January - March 33 AD)

Jesus now begins what is sometimes referred to as the travel diaries, a period of three months (January - March 33 AD) prior to the final weeks of His life. They are so aptly named because the account is predominantly found in the Gospel of Luke chapters 10-20. These amazing ten chapters of Luke concern Jesus travels and teaching within Judea and Perea prior to the cross. Furthermore Jesus commissions and sends seventy-two special envoys in groups of two to prepare the ground in every town and village He would enter during this three month period. The envoys would have visited at least thirty-six villages if each pair only went to one village.

It is an intentional strategy that Jesus embarks on. The capacity to reach people is enhanced by having envoys go forward as a literal advance guard to every town and village. Whereas in Galilee Jesus visited many places multiple times, in these last months that was not to be. Jesus would pass through each town probably but once, hence the vanguard to prepare the way. Remember this is all in winter with average temperatures five to fifteen degrees centigrade.

Furthermore, Jesus evidently waited till the seventy-two had returned from their advance guard work before He set off to teach in those towns and villages, so the three months timeframe would now be compressed. So what did Jesus do whilst He waited for them? A good guess would be that Jesus spent the time teaching the twelve disciples as there is no evidence they joined the seventy-two in the vanguard mission.

Seventy-two go out

Jesus appoints the seventy-two 'others' and sends them to prepare the ground. He again refers to the evangelical triangle of Chorazin, Bethsaida and Capernaum, towns he spent his first two ministry years in, as an example of what not to be – hard hearted. The seventy-two then return jubilant and Jesus sets out to visit where the missionary vanguard have gone.

After this the Lord appointed seventy-two others and sent them on ahead of him two by two into every town and place where he himself was about to go. He said to them, "The harvest is plentiful, but the workers are few. Therefore ask the Lord of the harvest to send out workers into his harvest. Go! I am sending you out like lambs surrounded by wolves. Do not carry a money bag, a traveler's bag, or sandals, and greet no one on the road. Whenever you enter a house, first say, 'May peace be on this house!' And if a peace-loving person is there, your peace will remain on him, but if not, it will return to you. Stay in that same house, eating and drinking what they give you, for the worker deserves his pay. Do not move around from house to house. Whenever you enter a town and the people welcome you, eat what is set before you. Heal the sick in that town and say to them, 'The kingdom of God has come upon you!' But whenever you enter a town and the people do not welcome you, go into its streets and say, 'Even the dust of your town that clings to our feet we wipe off against you. Nevertheless know this: The kingdom of God has come.' I tell you, it will be more bearable on that day for Sodom than for that town! "Woe to you, Chorazin! Woe to you, Bethsaida! For if the miracles done in you had been done in Tyre and Sidon, they would have repented long ago, sitting in sackcloth and ashes. But it will be more bearable for Tyre and Sidon in the judgment than for you! And you, Capernaum, will you be exalted to heaven? No, you will be thrown down to Hades! "The one who listens to you listens to me, and the one who rejects you rejects me, and the one who rejects me rejects the one who sent me." Then the seventy-two returned with joy, saying, "Lord, even the demons submit to us in your name!" So he said to them, "I saw Satan fall like lightning from heaven. Look, I have given you authority to tread on snakes and scorpions and on the full force of the enemy, and nothing will hurt you. Nevertheless, do not rejoice that the spirits submit to you, but rejoice that your names stand written in heaven." On that same occasion Jesus rejoiced in the Holy Spirit and said, "I praise you, Father, Lord of heaven and earth, because you have hidden these things from the wise and intelligent, and revealed them to little children. Yes, Father, for this was your gracious will. All things have been given to me by my Father. No one knows who the Son is except the Father, or who the Father is except the Son and anyone to whom the Son decides to reveal him." Then Jesus turned to his disciples and said privately, "Blessed are the eyes that see what you see! For I tell you that many prophets and kings longed to see what you see but did not see it, and to hear what you hear but did not hear it." Luke 10:1-24

Parable of the good Samaritan

As Jesus commenced visiting the towns and villages the seventy-two had just returned from, He is confronted once more by the religious elite questioning Him, this time over 'who is my neighbour'. In reality they are trying to justify themselves using a situation on the road from Jerusalem to Jericho as the example. This is one of the more famous of Jesus' stories, often called the 'Parable of the Good Samaritan.'

Firstly what is this road from Jerusalem to Jericho and why does it feature in a parable about who my neighbour is? This is a common road that has been walked for thousands of years by literally everyone in Israel from the north (Galilee) journeying to Jerusalem. This road was the only main route to Jerusalem from the north if you wanted to avoid walking through the land of the 'half breeds' the Samaritans, as it followed the Jordan Valley to Jericho and then up to Jerusalem. Historically, David fled from Absalom on this road (2 Samuel 15:23–16:14); King Zedekiah of Judah fled from the advancing Babylonian hordes on this road in 586/587 BC (2 Kings 25:4); and 600 years later, Jesus would travel this road when He came to His final Passover in Jerusalem to be the ultimate Passover lamb (Mark 10:46–11:1). Josephus records that the Tenth Roman Legion used this Jericho – Jerusalem road on their way to besiege Jerusalem in 69 AD[26]. This is a well-travelled road.

Although Jericho is northeast of Jerusalem, travellers go 'down' to Jericho. Josephus explained that the first century road was approximately one hundred and fifty Roman stadioi, or about twenty-eight kilometres long[27]. A traveller descended from Jerusalem's height at 777 metres above sea level on Mount Moriah to Jericho's depth of 258 metres below sea level, a drop of 1035 metres or over 3000 feet. The climate changes rapidly in this journey with only a third of Jerusalem's annual rain fall occurring in the valley below. As the traveller slowly descends, trees disappear, followed by bushes until only a desert is left. It is a spectacular journey.

The road from Jerusalem goes down to the Kidron Valley, past the Mount of Olives, past Bethany and then starts to descend. At the twenty kilometre mark out from Jerusalem, having descended 500 metres, there is a pass that the Roman road would likely have gone through as it is it the shortest route. The Romans were nothing if not efficient. The name of the pass in Arabic is 'tal `at ed-damm', which means 'Ascent of Blood'. In Hebrew it means 'Ascent of Adummim' (Joshua 15:7 and 18:17). Adummim means red objects, which in this case most likely referred to the red rock found at the site. The Christian historian Eusebius (260–340 AD) argued that there was a castle here, and the

---

26 Josephus, The Wars of the Jews, Book V, Chapter I, Section 6
27 Josephus, The Wars of the Jews, Book V, Chapter I, Section 6

church patriarch Jerome (347–420 AD) named the area 'Maledomni' Greek for 'Ascent of the Red', because of the blood spilled by outlaws at that site. Jerome also argued that a castle or inn was located at the site and that it was strategically placed to aid travellers.[28]

At the bottom of this famous road from Jerusalem is the ancient city of Jericho, first mentioned when the Israelites camped opposite it, on the other side of the Jordan River after their forty years wandering in the wilderness (Numbers 22:1). This camp site was also the final camp prior to them entering the holy land as their inheritance (Numbers 33). Across from Jericho is Mount Nebo from where Moses would see the holy land and the plains of Moab where God would personally bury Moses (Numbers 34:6). When Joshua sent spies to look over the land, they specifically spied out Jericho (Joshua 2) and were hidden by Rahab the prostitute, yes the same Rahab in the genealogy of Jesus (Matthew 1:5). When God parted the Jordan River for the Israelites to walk into Canaan, the miraculous crossing occurred in front of Jericho (Joshua 3:16). The Israelites set up their first camp in the holy land at Gilgal, next to Jericho, and set up a stone reminder of the power and awe of God from stones taken from the Jordan River in front of Jericho (Joshua 4:19-24). There next to Jericho, the Israelites would circumcise every male and celebrate the first Passover in the promised land. Maybe there's something about Jericho, the 'city of palms' (Deuteronomy 34:3).

Jericho was the first city in the land of Canaan that would be miraculously taken by Israel. The city had high walls and strong defences and the people worshipped the moon god, depicted as a crescent moon[29]. The story of the destruction of Jericho by the hand of God is unparal-

---

[28]   http://bibleresources.americanbible.org/resource/from-jerusalem-to-jericho access on 25 Oct 16

[29]   Strong's Bible Dictionary, Htmlbible.com. Retrieved 28 November 2016.

leled anywhere in scripture (Joshua 5 and 6). A story of Joshua meeting the commander of the angelic host of heaven Himself, an arch-type of Jesus or maybe Jesus Himself considering Joshua was told he was standing on holy ground and was not asked to stand when he bowed in reverence (Joshua 5:13-15). It is a story of the walls not being smashed-in like a typical breach, but of the walls being pushed vertically into the ground from above, as if the hand of God reached down and squashed them after the Israelites shouted praise. It is a story of the Israelites resting in God's provision and God's timing to act.

After the destruction of Jericho, Joshua cursed the city to dissuade anyone from rebuilding it. Despite seeing what God did there, it was rebuilt and poor Hiel of Bethel felt the full force of the curse.

During Ahab's reign, Hiel the Bethelite rebuilt Jericho. Abiram, his firstborn son, died when he laid the foundation; Segub, his youngest son, died when he erected its gates, just as the LORD had warned through Joshua son of Nun. 1 Kings 16:34

Perhaps there was something about Jericho and it's moon god, depicted by the crescent moon, that saw such a move of the host of heaven and Jesus Himself, or at least an arch-type, coming personally to lead the fight? Perhaps it was just the first fight and God wanted to ensure the Israelites understood that it was never going to be their strength, their tactical brilliance or their performance that won the day. It was, is and always will be the unmerited, undeserved favour and grace of God.

Back to the pious self-righteous religious elite questioning Jesus about who their neighbour was and Jesus' masterful response that melded the geography, history and ethnography of the region. For the priest and the Levite both should have provided aid and did not. Yet the 'half cast, inbred and despised' Samaritan, who shouldn't have been on this road in the first place, showed the mercy and compassion others would not.

Now an expert in religious law stood up to test Jesus, saying, "Teacher, what must I do to inherit eternal life?" He said to him, "What is written in the law? How do you understand it?" The expert answered, "Love the Lord your God with all your heart, with all your soul, with all your strength, and with all your mind, and love your neighbor as yourself." Jesus said to him, "You have answered correctly; do this, and you will live." But the expert, wanting to justify himself, said to Jesus, "And who is my neighbor?" Jesus replied, "A man was going down from Jerusalem to Jericho, and fell into the hands of robbers, who stripped him, beat him up, and went off, leaving him half dead. Now by chance a priest was going down that road, but when he saw the injured man he passed by on the other side. So too a Levite, when he came up to the place and saw him, passed by on the other side. But a Samaritan who was traveling came to where the injured man was, and when he saw him, he felt compassion for him. He went up to him and bandaged his wounds, pouring oil and wine on them. Then he put him on his own animal, brought him to an inn, and took care of him. The next day he took out two silver coins and gave them to the innkeeper, saying, 'Take care of him, and whatever else you spend, I will repay you when I come back this way.' Which of these three do you think became a neighbor to the man who fell into the hands of the robbers?" The expert in religious law said, "The one who showed mercy to him." So Jesus said to him, "Go and do the same." Luke 10:25-37

Bethany (near Jerusalem)

Jesus continued his travels and arrives at the village of Bethany, three kilometres from Jerusalem and home to Martha, Mary and their brother Lazarus (John 11:1 and 11:18). Martha hears that Jesus has arrived and invites Him and His disciples in. What transpires is a beautiful picture of enjoying Jesus. This encounter also moves Jesus, as the next chapter outlines, to raise their brother Lazarus from the dead. All of this started by simply inviting Jesus into their home. There's a lesson there for us.

Firstly a little about Bethany. There is nothing special about this little town hanging off the back of the Mount of Olives, a stones throw from Jerusalem. The name Bethany is the English transliteration of the Greek name Bethania, which in turn comes from the Hebrew name Beth-aniah, which consists of two elements. The first part is identical to the common Hebrew word בית(bayit) meaning house. The second part comes from the extensive root cluster ענה(ana) meaning misery, sorrow or depression. Thus, Bethany is best understood as the 'house of sadness', perhaps referring to the events surrounding Lazarus's death.

The photo above is a view from the Mount of Olives to the village of Bethany taken by the American colony photo department between 1900 and 1920.

What makes Bethany so beautiful though is the hearts of some of its residents, particularly Mary, Martha and Lazarus. It has also become synonymous as an archetype of the two covenants, Martha who worked and Mary who rested. Martha was concerned about doing everything right and following the rules and Mary was concerned only with sitting at the feet of Jesus, knowing Jesus would do everything.

Now as they went on their way, Jesus entered a certain village where a woman named Martha welcomed him as a guest. She had a sister named Mary, who sat at the Lord's feet and listened to what he said. But Martha was distracted with all the preparations she had to make, so she came up to him and said, "Lord, don't you care that my sister has left me to do all the work alone? Tell her to help me." But the Lord answered her, "Martha, Martha, you are worried and troubled about many things, but one thing is needed. Mary has chosen the best part; it will not be taken away from her." Luke 10:38-42

Discourse on prayer

Jesus moved on from Bethany to reach more of the towns and villages in an around Judea. For Jesus had avoided Judea and Samaria for the first two years of His ministry and is now working overtime to reach this area. Remember He is going to a minimum of thirty-six villages and towns in less than three months, including travel time by foot in winter.

Now Jesus was praying in a certain place. When he stopped, one of his disciples said to him, "Lord, teach us to pray, just as John taught his disciples." So he said to them, "When you pray, say: Father, may your name be honored; may your kingdom come. Give us each day our daily bread, and forgive us our sins, for we also forgive everyone who sins against us. And do not lead us into temptation." Then he said to them, "Suppose one of you has a friend, and you go to him at midnight and say to him, 'Friend, lend me three loaves of bread, because a friend of mine has stopped here while on a journey, and I have nothing to set before him.' Then he will reply from inside, 'Do not bother me. The door is already shut, and my children and I are in bed. I cannot get up and give you anything.' I tell you, even though the man inside will not get up and give him anything because he is his friend, yet because of the first man's sheer persistence he will get up and give him whatever he needs. "So I tell you: Ask, and it will be given to you; seek, and you will find; knock, and the door will be opened for you. For everyone who asks receives, and the one who seeks finds, and to the one who knocks, the door will be opened. What father among you, if your son asks for a fish, will give him a snake instead of a fish? Or if he asks for an egg, will give him a scorpion? If you then, although you are evil, know how to give good gifts to your children, how much more will the heavenly Father give the Holy Spirit to those who ask him!" Luke 11:1-13

Six woes on the Pharisees

A Pharisee (those religious elite) listening to Jesus invited Him into his home for a meal. The Pharisee probably wasn't prepared for the six woes that Jesus levelled at him and his scoffing religious class. Jesus doesn't hold back either. He lines them up and all of their elite friends that have gone before them and lets them have it. Indeed Jesus makes it clear that from the first shedding of blood when Cain killed Abel (Genesis 4:8) through to the disgraceful murder of Zechariah the priest (2 Chronicles 24:17-27), it is the thinking of the religious elites that is responsible for it all. All in the Pharisee's home.

As he spoke, a Pharisee invited Jesus to have a meal with him, so he went in and took his place at the table. The Pharisee was astonished when he saw that Jesus did not first wash his hands before the meal. But the Lord said to him, "Now you Pharisees clean the outside of the cup and the plate, but inside you are full of greed and wickedness. You fools! Didn't the one who made the outside make the inside as well? But give from your heart to those in need, and then everything will be clean for you.

Woe 1

*"But woe to you Pharisees! You give a tenth of your mint, rue,
and every herb, yet you neglect justice and love for God! But you
should have done these things without neglecting the others.*

Woe 2

*Woe to you Pharisees! You love the best seats in the synagogues
and elaborate greetings in the marketplaces!*

Woe 3

*Woe to you! You are like unmarked graves, and people walk over them
without realizing it!" One of the experts in religious law answered him,
"Teacher, when you say these things you insult us too." But Jesus replied,*

Woe 4

*"Woe to you experts in religious law as well! You load people
down with burdens difficult to bear, yet you yourselves refuse
to touch the burdens with even one of your fingers!*

Woe 5

*Woe to you! You build the tombs of the prophets whom your ancestors
killed. So you testify that you approve of the deeds of your ancestors,
because they killed the prophets and you build their tombs! For this
reason also the wisdom of God said, 'I will send them prophets and
apostles, some of whom they will kill and persecute,' so that this
generation may be held accountable for the blood of all the prophets
that has been shed since the beginning of the world, from the blood of*

Abel to the blood of Zechariah, who was killed between the altar and the sanctuary. Yes, I tell you, it will be charged against this generation.

Woe 6

> *Woe to you experts in religious law! You have taken away the key to knowledge! You did not go in yourselves, and you hindered those who were going in." Luke 11:37-52*

Don't be fooled by the hypocrites

After delivering that up to the Pharisees and their religious mates, Jesus stepped outside to another maddening crowd, though firstly takes time to speak just to His disciples about the hypocrisy of the religious elite. Jesus then addresses the crowd and teaches them eight discourses. It is reasonable to assume that much of this would have been taught in all of the thirty-six odd towns and villages Jesus would be going to in Judea, although this teaching takes on a special significance, considering the blindness of the religious elite and their performance over lunch.

> *When he went out from there, the experts in the law and the Pharisees began to oppose him bitterly, and to ask him hostile questions about many things, plotting against him, to catch him in something he might say. Luke 11:53-54*

Meanwhile, when many thousands of the crowd had gathered so that they were trampling on one another, Jesus began to speak first to his disciples, "Be on your guard against the yeast of the Pharisees, which is hypocrisy. Nothing is hidden that will not be revealed, and nothing is secret that will not be made known. So then whatever you have said in the dark will be heard in the light, and what you have whispered in private rooms will be proclaimed from the housetops. "I tell you, my friends, do not be afraid of those who kill the body, and after that have nothing more they can do. But I will warn you whom you should fear: Fear the one who, after the killing, has authority to throw you into hell. Yes, I tell you, fear him! Aren't five sparrows sold for two pennies? Yet not one of them is forgotten before God. In fact, even the hairs on your head are all numbered. Do not be afraid; you are more valuable than many sparrows. "I tell you, whoever acknowledges me before men, the Son of Man will also acknowledge before God's angels. But the one who denies me before men will be denied before God's angels. And everyone who speaks a word against the Son of Man will be forgiven, but the person who blasphemes against the Holy Spirit will not be forgiven. But when they bring you before the synagogues, the rulers, and the authorities, do not worry about how you should make your defense or what you should say, for the Holy Spirit will teach you at that moment what you must say." Luke 12:1-12

Discourse 1 - Parable of the rich man

The Bible speaks about money more than any other topic (over 2500 verses), more than prayer, more than forgiveness. Could it be that God is trying to tell us something about dependence and who we should really be dependent upon, not what.

Then someone from the crowd said to him, "Teacher, tell my brother to divide the inheritance with me." But Jesus said to him, "Man, who made me a judge or arbitrator between you two?" Then he said to them, "Watch out and guard yourself from all types of greed, because one's life does not consist in the abundance of his possessions." He then told them a parable: "The land of a certain rich man produced an abundant crop, so he thought to himself, 'What should I do, for I have nowhere to store my crops?' Then he said, 'I will do this: I will tear down my barns and build bigger ones, and there I will store all my grain and my goods. And I will say to myself, "You have plenty of goods stored up for many years; relax, eat, drink, celebrate!"' But God said to him, 'You fool! This very night your life will be demanded back from you, but who will get what you have prepared for yourself?' So it is with the one who stores up riches for himself, but is not rich toward God." Luke 12:13-21

Discourse 2 - Do not worry

Then Jesus said to his disciples, "Therefore I tell you, do not worry about your life, what you will eat, or about your body, what you will wear. For there is more to life than food, and more to the body than clothing. Consider the ravens: They do not sow or reap, they have no storeroom or barn, yet God feeds them. How much more valuable are you than the birds! And which of you by worrying can add an hour to his life? So if you cannot do such a very little thing as this, why do you worry about the rest? Consider how the flowers grow; they do not work or spin. Yet I tell you, not even Solomon in all his glory was clothed like one of these! And if this is how God clothes the wild grass, which is here today and tomorrow is tossed into the fire to heat the oven, how much more will he clothe you, you people of little faith! So do not be overly concerned about what you will eat and what you will drink, and do not worry about such things. For all the nations of the world pursue these things, and your Father knows that you need them. Instead, pursue his kingdom, and these things will be given to you as well. "Do not be afraid, little flock, for your Father is well pleased to give you the kingdom. Sell your possessions and give to the poor. Provide yourselves purses that do not wear out-a treasure in heaven that never decreases, where no thief approaches and no moth destroys. For where your treasure is, there your heart will be also. Luke 12:22-34

Discourse 3 - Readiness

"Get dressed for service and keep your lamps burning; be like people waiting for their master to come back from the wedding celebration, so that when he comes and knocks they can immediately open the door for him. Blessed are those slaves whom their master finds alert when

he returns! I tell you the truth, he will dress himself to serve, have them take their place at the table, and will come and wait on them! Even if he comes in the second or third watch of the night and finds them alert, blessed are those slaves! But understand this: If the owner of the house had known at what hour the thief was coming, he would not have let his house be broken into. You also must be ready, because the Son of Man will come at an hour when you do not expect him." Then Peter said, "Lord, are you telling this parable for us or for everyone?" The Lord replied, "Who then is the faithful and wise manager, whom the master puts in charge of his household servants, to give them their allowance of food at the proper time? Blessed is that slave whom his master finds at work when he returns. I tell you the truth, the master will put him in charge of all his possessions. But if that slave should say to himself, 'My master is delayed in returning,' and he begins to beat the other slaves, both men and women, and to eat, drink, and get drunk, then the master of that slave will come on a day when he does not expect him and at an hour he does not foresee, and will cut him in two, and assign him a place with the unfaithful. That servant who knew his master's will but did not get ready or do what his master asked will receive a severe beating. But the one who did not know his master's will and did things worthy of punishment will receive a light beating. From everyone who has been given much, much will be required, and from the one who has been entrusted with much, even more will be asked. Luke 12:35-48

Discourse 4 - Division

"I have come to bring fire on the earth-and how I wish it were already kindled! I have a baptism to undergo, and how distressed I am until it is finished! Do you think I have come to bring peace on earth? No, I tell you, but rather division! For from now on there will be five in one household divided, three against two and two against three. They will be divided, father against son and son against father, mother against daughter

and daughter against mother, mother-in-law against her daughter-in-law and daughter-in-law against mother-in-law." Luke 12:49-53

Discourse 5 - Interpreting the signs

Jesus also said to the crowds, "When you see a cloud rising in the west, you say at once, 'A rainstorm is coming,' and it does. And when you see the south wind blowing, you say, 'There will be scorching heat,' and there is. You hypocrites! You know how to interpret the appearance of the earth and the sky, but how can you not know how to interpret the present time? Luke 12:54-56

Discourse 6 - Right judgements

"And why don't you judge for yourselves what is right? As you are going with your accuser before the magistrate, make an effort to settle with him on the way, so that he will not drag you before the judge, and the judge hand you over to the officer, and the officer throw you into prison. I tell you, you will never get out of there until you have paid the very last cent!" Luke 12:57-59

Discourse 7 - Repentance

Now there were some present on that occasion who told him about the Galileans whose blood Pilate had mixed with their sacrifices. He answered them, "Do you think these Galileans were worse sinners than all the other Galileans, because they suffered these things? No, I tell you! But unless you repent, you will all perish as well! Or those eighteen who were killed when the tower in Siloam fell on them, do you think they were worse offenders than all the others who live in Jerusalem? No, I tell you! But unless you repent you will all perish as well!" Luke 13:1-5

Discourse 8 - Unfruitful tree

Then Jesus told this parable: "A man had a fig tree planted in his vineyard, and he came looking for fruit on it and found none. So he said to the worker who tended the vineyard, 'For three years now, I have come looking for fruit on this fig tree, and each time I inspect it I find none. Cut it down! Why should it continue to deplete the soil?' But the worker answered him, 'Sir, leave it alone this year too, until I dig around it and put fertilizer on it. Then if it bears fruit next year, very well, but if not, you can cut it down.'" Luke 13:6-9

The thirtieth miracle – healing the body

Jesus continues to travel through this final winter of January – March 33 AD from village to village in Judea. As was His custom on the Sabbath, Jesus taught in whatever local synagogue He was in. Once again Jesus confronts the religious elite and this time calls out their utter hypocrisy and humiliates their moribund interpretation of the law.

Now he was teaching in one of the synagogues on the Sabbath, and a woman was there who had been disabled by a spirit for eighteen years. She was bent over and could not straighten herself up completely. When Jesus saw her, he called her to him and said, "Woman, you are freed from your infirmity." Then he placed his hands on her, and immediately she straightened up and praised God. But the president of the synagogue, indignant because Jesus had healed on the Sabbath, said to the crowd, "There are six days on which work should be done! So come and be healed on those days, and not on the Sabbath day." Then the Lord answered him, "You hypocrites! Does not each of you on the Sabbath untie his ox or his donkey from its stall, and lead it to water? Then shouldn't this woman, a daughter of Abraham whom Satan bound for eighteen long years, be released from this imprisonment on the Sabbath day?" When

he said this all his adversaries were humiliated, but the entire crowd
was rejoicing at all the wonderful things he was doing. Luke 13:10-17

Jesus continues to travel, town after town, synagogue after synagogue
on what is a circuitous route to Jerusalem through at least thirty-six
towns and villages, noting that He was just recently at Bethany in
Judea, which was only a thirty minute walk to Jerusalem.

Then Jesus traveled throughout towns and villages, teaching and making
his way toward Jerusalem. Someone asked him, "Lord, will only a few
be saved?" So he said to them, "Exert every effort to enter through the
narrow door, because many, I tell you, will try to enter and will not be
able to. Once the head of the house gets up and shuts the door, then you
will stand outside and start to knock on the door and beg him, 'Lord, let
us in!' But he will answer you, 'I don't know where you come from.' Then
you will begin to say, 'We ate and drank in your presence, and you taught
in our streets.' But he will reply, 'I don't know where you come from! Go
away from me, all you evildoers!' There will be weeping and gnashing
of teeth when you see Abraham, Isaac, Jacob, and all the prophets in the
kingdom of God but you yourselves thrown out. Then people will come
from east and west, and from north and south, and take their places
at the banquet table in the kingdom of God. But indeed, some are last
who will be first, and some are first who will be last." Luke 13:22-30

Jesus in Judea and Perea

Jesus was travelling not just in Judea, but also in Perea (north of the
Dead Sea) as apparently Herod Antipas, the Tetrach of Galilee and
Perea wanted to kill Jesus. Remember that Herod Antipas had form.
His father, Herod the Great had slaughtered every little boy two years
old and under in Bethlehem when trying to kill Jesus. Herod Antipas
had also killed John the Baptist in response to a pubescent erotic
dance so it is not surprising that he now wanted to kill Jesus. But Jesus

remains defiantly unafraid, knowing that He would lay down His life in Jerusalem and then rise again on the third day.

At that time, some Pharisees came up and said to Jesus, "Get away from here, because Herod wants to kill you." But he said to them, "Go and tell that fox, 'Look, I am casting out demons and performing healings today and tomorrow, and on the third day I will complete my work. Nevertheless I must go on my way today and tomorrow and the next day, because it is impossible that a prophet should be killed outside Jerusalem.' O Jerusalem, Jerusalem, you who kill the prophets and stone those who are sent to you! How often I have longed to gather your children together as a hen gathers her chicks under her wings, but you would have none of it! Look, your house is forsaken! And I tell you, you will not see me until you say, 'Blessed is the one who comes in the name of the Lord!'" Luke 13:31-35

The thirty-first miracle – healing on the Sabbath

Jesus continues His travels and His custom of teaching in synagogues and eating with and confronting the religious elite. This Sabbath is no different. Jesus heals on the Sabbath to confront the false authority of the religious elite and then uses the opportunity to teach two parables in the Pharisee's house.

Now one Sabbath when Jesus went to dine at the house of a leader of the Pharisees, they were watching him closely. There right in front of him was a man suffering from dropsy. So Jesus asked the experts in religious law and the Pharisees, "Is it lawful to heal on the Sabbath or not?" But they remained silent. So Jesus took hold of the man, healed him, and sent him away. Then he said to them, "Which of you, if you have a son or an ox that has fallen into a well on a Sabbath day, will not immediately pull him out?" But they could not reply to this. Luke 14:1-6

Parable 1 - of the guests

Then when Jesus noticed how the guests chose the places of honor, he told them a parable. He said to them, "When you are invited by someone to a wedding feast, do not take the place of honor, because a person more distinguished than you may have been invited by your host. So the host who invited both of you will come and say to you, 'Give this man your place.' Then, ashamed, you will begin to move to the least important place. But when you are invited, go and take the least important place, so that when your host approaches he will say to you, 'Friend, move up here to a better place.' Then you will be honored in the presence of all who share the meal with you. For everyone who exalts himself will be humbled, but the one who humbles himself will be exalted." He said also to the man who had invited him, "When you host a dinner or a banquet, don't invite your friends or your brothers or your relatives or rich neighbors so you can be invited by them in return and get repaid. But when you host an elaborate meal, invite the poor, the crippled, the lame, and the blind. Then you will be blessed, because they cannot repay you, for you will be repaid at the resurrection of the righteous." Luke 14:7-14

Parable 2 - of the dinner

When one of those at the meal with Jesus heard this, he said to him, "Blessed is everyone who will feast in the kingdom of God!" But Jesus said to him, "A man once gave a great banquet and invited many guests. At the time for the banquet he sent his slave to tell those who had been invited, 'Come, because everything is now ready.' But one after another they all began to make excuses. The first said to him, 'I have bought a field, and I must go out and see it. Please excuse me.' Another said, 'I have bought five yoke of oxen, and I am going out to examine them. Please excuse me.' Another said, 'I just got married, and I cannot come.' So the slave came back and reported this to his master. Then the master of the household was furious and said to his slave, 'Go out quickly to the streets and alleys of the city, and bring in the poor, the crippled, the blind, and the lame.' Then the slave said, 'Sir, what you instructed has been done, and there is still room.' So the master said to his slave, 'Go out to the highways and country roads and urge people to come in, so that my house will be filled. For I tell you, not one of those individuals who were invited will taste my banquet!'" Luke 14:15-24

Jesus spoke to them again in parables, saying: "The kingdom of heaven can be compared to a king who gave a wedding banquet for his son. He sent his slaves to summon those who had been invited to the banquet, but they would not come. Again he sent other slaves, saying, 'Tell those who have been invited, "Look! The feast I have prepared for you is ready. My oxen and fattened cattle have been slaughtered, and everything is ready. Come to the wedding banquet."' But they were indifferent and went away, one to his farm, another to his business. The rest seized his slaves, insolently mistreated them, and killed them. The king was furious! He sent his soldiers, and they put those murderers to death and set their city on fire. Then he said to his slaves, 'The wedding is ready, but the ones who had been invited were not worthy. So go into the main streets and invite everyone you find to the wedding banquet.' And those slaves went out into the streets and gathered all they found, both bad and good, and the wedding hall was filled with guests. But when the king came in to see the wedding guests, he saw a man there who was not wearing wedding clothes. And he said to him, 'Friend, how did you get in here without wedding clothes?' But he had nothing to say. Then the king said to his attendants, 'Tie him up hand and foot and throw him into the outer darkness, where there will be weeping and gnashing of teeth!' For many are called, but few are chosen." Matthew 22:1-14

The cost of following Jesus

Jesus continues travelling in Judea and Perea with large crowds following Him. In typical Jesus style, He challenges His follows to count the cost of discipleship.

*Now large crowds were accompanying Jesus, and turning to them he said,
"If anyone comes to me and does not hate his own father and mother, and
wife and children, and brothers and sisters, and even his own life, he cannot
be my disciple. Whoever does not carry his own cross and follow me cannot
be my disciple. For which of you, wanting to build a tower, doesn't sit
down first and compute the cost to see if he has enough money to complete
it? Otherwise, when he has laid a foundation and is not able to finish the
tower, all who see it will begin to make fun of him. They will say, 'This
man began to build and was not able to finish!' Or what king, going out
to confront another king in battle, will not sit down first and determine
whether he is able with ten thousand to oppose the one coming against him
with twenty thousand? If he cannot succeed, he will send a representative
while the other is still a long way off and ask for terms of peace. In the same
way therefore not one of you can be my disciple if he does not renounce all
his own possessions. "Salt is good, but if salt loses its flavor, how can its flavor
be restored? It is of no value for the soil or for the manure pile; it is to be
thrown out. The one who has ears to hear had better listen!" Luke 14:25-35*

The religious elite have still not given up confronting Jesus and again
they mingle with the crowds and mutter against Jesus. Jesus confronts
the elites head on and also manages to teach the tax collectors and sinners (the average person in the crowd) with five parables (stories), with
the first three focusing exclusively on God's love for the lost.

*Now all the tax collectors and sinners were coming to hear
him. But the Pharisees and the experts in the law were
complaining, "This man welcomes sinners and eats with
them." So Jesus told them this parable: Luke 15:1-3*

Parable 1 - The lost sheep

*"Which one of you, if he has a hundred sheep and loses one of them,
would not leave the ninety-nine in the open pasture and go look for*

the one that is lost until he finds it? Then when he has found it, he places it on his shoulders, rejoicing. Returning home, he calls together his friends and neighbors, telling them, 'Rejoice with me, because I have found my sheep that was lost.' I tell you, in the same way there will be more joy in heaven over one sinner who repents than over ninety-nine righteous people who have no need to repent. Luke 15:4-7

Parable 2 - The lost coin

"Or what woman, if she has ten silver coins and loses one of them, does not light a lamp, sweep the house, and search thoroughly until she finds it? Then when she has found it, she calls together her friends and neighbors, saying, 'Rejoice with me, for I have found the coin that I had lost.' In the same way, I tell you, there is joy in the presence of God's angels over one sinner who repents." Luke 15:8-10

Parable 3 - The lost son

This famous parable is so much more than what it seems. It is a story of a dad that loves his boys, even though the son says to his dad 'I wish you were dead, give me the money'. This is dishonourable in our societies, however to the ancient Jews they would have been aghast and would have thought the son was the devil himself. Then to find the son with pigs, that despised of animals, it was almost too much – what could top such horror? – The continuance of the story, that's what. The father took the fattened calf, the one reserved for that special day, and killed it to celebrate the son's return. Now that is scandalous grace writ large. This story would have been a show stopper. That's probably why Jesus told it.

Then Jesus said, "A man had two sons. The younger of them said to his father, 'Father, give me the share of the estate that will belong to me.' So he divided his assets between them. After a few days, the younger son gathered together all he had and left on a journey to a distant country, and there he squandered his wealth with a wild lifestyle. Then after he had spent everything, a severe famine took place in that country, and he began to be in need. So he went and worked for one of the citizens of that country, who sent him to his fields to feed pigs. He was longing to eat the carob pods the pigs were eating, but no one gave him anything. But when he came to his senses he said, 'How many of my father's hired workers have food enough to spare, but here I am dying from hunger! I will get up and go to my father and say to him, "Father, I have sinned against heaven and against you. I am no longer worthy to be called your son; treat me like one of your hired workers."' So he got up and went to his father. But while he was still a long way from home his father saw him, and his heart went out to him; he ran and hugged his son and kissed him. Then his son said to him, 'Father, I have sinned against heaven and against you; I am no longer worthy to be called your son.' But the father said to his slaves, 'Hurry! Bring the best robe, and put it on him! Put a ring on his finger and sandals on his feet! Bring the fattened calf and kill it! Let us eat and celebrate, because this son of mine was dead, and is alive again—he was lost and is found!' So they began to celebrate. "Now his older son was in the field. As he came and approached the house, he heard music and dancing. So he called one of the slaves and asked what was happening. The slave replied, 'Your brother has returned, and your father has killed the fattened calf because he got his son back safe and sound.' But the older son became angry and refused to go in. His father came out and appealed to him, but he answered his father, 'Look! These many years I have worked like a slave for you, and I never disobeyed your commands. Yet you never gave me even a goat so that I could celebrate with my friends! But when this son of yours came back, who has devoured your assets with prostitutes, you killed the fattened calf for him!' Then the father said to him, 'Son, you are always with me, and everything that belongs to me is yours. It was appropriate to celebrate and be glad, for your brother was dead, and is alive; he was lost and is found.'"... Luke 15:11-32

Parable 4 - The shrewd manager

Jesus also said to the disciples, "There was a rich man who was informed of accusations that his manager was wasting his assets. So he called the manager in and said to him, 'What is this I hear about you? Turn in the account of your administration, because you can no longer be my manager.' Then the manager said to himself, 'What should I do, since my master is taking my position away from me? I'm not strong enough to dig, and I'm too ashamed to beg. I know what to do so that when I am put out of management, people will welcome me into their homes.' So he contacted his master's debtors one by one. He asked the first, 'How much do you owe my master?' The man replied, 'A hundred measures of olive oil.' The manager said to him, 'Take your bill, sit down quickly, and write fifty.' Then he said to another, 'And how much do you owe?' The second man replied, 'A hundred measures of wheat.' The manager said to him, 'Take your bill, and write eighty.'

The master commended the dishonest manager because he acted shrewdly. For the people of this world are more shrewd in dealing with their contemporaries than the people of light. And I tell you, make friends for yourselves by how you use worldly wealth, so that when it runs out you will be welcomed into the eternal homes. Luke 16:1-9

Parable 5 - Faithful with money

"The one who is faithful in a very little is also faithful in much, and the one who is dishonest in a very little is also dishonest in much. If then you haven't been trustworthy in handling worldly wealth, who will entrust you with the true riches? And if you haven't been trustworthy with someone else's property, who will give you your own? No servant can serve two masters, for either he will hate the one and love the other, or he will be devoted to the one and despise the other. You cannot serve God and money." Luke 16:10-13

Jesus continues to teach in Judea and Perea and delivers three discourses to the religious elite and three to His disciples. The first three condemn, the last three instruct.

Discourse 1 - the Pharisees

The Pharisees (who loved money) heard all this and ridiculed him. But Jesus said to them, "You are the ones who justify yourselves in men's eyes, but God knows your hearts. For what is highly prized among men is utterly detestable in God's sight. "The law and the prophets were in force until John; since then, the good news of the kingdom of God has been proclaimed, and everyone is urged to enter it. But it is easier for heaven and earth to pass away than for one tiny stroke of a letter in the law to become void. Luke 16:14-17

Discourse 2 - Divorce

"Everyone who divorces his wife and marries someone else commits adultery, and the one who marries a woman divorced from her husband commits adultery. Luke 16:18

Discourse 3 - Wealth (Lazarus and the rich man)

"There was a rich man who dressed in purple and fine linen and who feasted sumptuously every day. But at his gate lay a poor man named Lazarus whose body was covered with sores, who longed to eat what fell from the rich man's table. In addition, the dogs came and licked his sores. "Now the poor man died and was carried by the angels to Abraham's side. The rich man also died and was buried. And in hell, as he was in torment, he looked up and saw Abraham far off with Lazarus at his side. So he called out, 'Father Abraham, have mercy on me, and send Lazarus to dip the tip of his finger in water and cool my tongue, because I am in anguish in this fire.' But Abraham

said, 'Child, remember that in your lifetime you received your good things and Lazarus likewise bad things, but now he is comforted here and you are in anguish. Besides all this, a great chasm has been fixed between us, so that those who want to cross over from here to you cannot do so, and no one can cross from there to us.' So the rich man said, 'Then I beg you, father-send Lazarus to my father's house (for I have five brothers) to warn them so that they don't come into this place of torment.' But Abraham said, 'They have Moses and the prophets; they must respond to them.' Then the rich man said, 'No, father Abraham, but if someone from the dead goes to them, they will repent.' He replied to him, 'If they do not respond to Moses and the prophets, they will not be convinced even if someone rises from the dead.'" Luke 16:19-31

Discourse 4 - Stumbling blocks

Jesus said to his disciples, "Stumbling blocks are sure to come, but woe to the one through whom they come! It would be better for him to have a millstone tied around his neck and be thrown into the sea than for him to cause one of these little ones to sin. Watch yourselves! If your brother sins, rebuke him. If he repents, forgive him. Even if he sins against you seven times in a day, and seven times returns to you saying, 'I repent,' you must forgive him." Luke 17:1-4

Discourse 5 - Faith

The apostles said to the Lord, "Increase our faith!" So the Lord replied, "If you had faith the size of a mustard seed, you could say to this black mulberry tree, 'Be pulled out by the roots and planted in the sea,' and it would obey you. Luke 17:5-6

Discourse 6 - Service

"Would any one of you say to your slave who comes in from the field after plowing or shepherding sheep, 'Come at once and sit down for a meal'? Won't the master instead say to him, 'Get my dinner ready, and make yourself ready to serve me while I eat and drink. Then you may eat and drink'? He won't thank the slave because he did what he was told, will he? So you too, when you have done everything you were commanded to do, should say, 'We are slaves undeserving of special praise; we have only done what was our duty.'" Luke 17:7-10

CHAPTER 10

Jesus sets out for Jerusalem
(March 33 AD)

As the final few months turn to the final few weeks, Jesus resolutely sets out for Jerusalem. He has been travelling through Judea and Perea and now turns into Samaria for the last time and heads to Jericho and the final climb up the infamous road to Jerusalem.

I wonder what Jesus was thinking. He had left Galilee for the final time pre-resurrection and now He would leave Perea, Samaria and shortly Judea for the last time. The next opportunity people in all of those towns and villages would have to hear the message of salvation would be through the disciples and those who had come to know Jesus. Sure, a whole cavalcade of people healed, released, restored and set free were roaming the countryside rejoicing, but it would be the post resurrection disciples that would commence, in the power of the Holy Spirit, to change the world.

The thirty-second miracle – healing of the ten Lepers
Jesus is travelling south and is on the northern border of the territory of the 'half bred' Samaritans, and the southern border of Galilee. In a village, ten desperate souls, suffering terribly from leprosy call out to Jesus. It appears likely that this group of outcasts were both Israelites and Samaritans. Again, Jesus heals with a response that is different

from what He had previously said and done. Jesus gives them the law, 'present yourself to the priests,' but as they turn to go, Jesus fulfils the law with healing grace. Jesus demonstrates through His own actions what He thought of the despised Samaritans. He loved them and He healed them.

> *Now on the way to Jerusalem, Jesus was passing along between Samaria and Galilee. Luke 17:11*

> *As he was entering a village, ten men with leprosy met him. They stood at a distance, raised their voices and said, "Jesus, Master, have mercy on us." When he saw them he said, "Go and show yourselves to the priests." And as they went along, they were cleansed. Then one of them, when he saw he was healed, turned back, praising God with a loud voice. He fell with his face to the ground at Jesus' feet and thanked him. (Now he was a Samaritan.) Then Jesus said, "Were not ten cleansed? Where are the other nine? Was no one found to turn back and give praise to God except this foreigner?" Then he said to the man, "Get up and go your way. Your faith has made you well." Luke 17:12-19*

As Jesus headed south He spent a greater amount of time teaching through long discourses and shorter parables in each Galilean and then Samaritan town and village. He shared stories and applied them to life and circumstances. He met and taught people where they were at and spent longer periods of time teaching the disciples.

Discourse to the Pharisees - on the coming of the kingdom of God

> *Now at one point the Pharisees asked Jesus when the kingdom of God was coming, so he answered, "The kingdom of God is not coming with signs to be observed, nor will they say, 'Look, here it is!' or 'There!' For indeed, the kingdom of God is in your midst." Luke 17:20-21*

Discourse to the disciples - on the second coming

Then he said to the disciples, "The days are coming when you will desire to see one of the days of the Son of Man, and you will not see it. Then people will say to you, 'Look, there he is!' or 'Look, here he is!' Do not go out or chase after them. For just like the lightning flashes and lights up the sky from one side to the other, so will the Son of Man be in his day. But first he must suffer many things and be rejected by this generation. Just as it was in the days of Noah, so too it will be in the days of the Son of Man. People were eating, they were drinking, they were marrying, they were being given in marriage-right up to the day Noah entered the ark. Then the flood came and destroyed them all. Likewise, just as it was in the days of Lot, people were eating, drinking, buying, selling, planting, building; but on the day Lot went out from Sodom, fire and sulfur rained down from heaven and destroyed them all. It will be the same on the day the Son of Man is revealed. On that day, anyone who is on the roof, with his goods in the house, must not come down to take them away, and likewise the person in the field must not turn back. Remember Lot's wife! Whoever tries to keep his life will lose it, but whoever loses his life will preserve it. I tell you, in that night there will be two people in one bed; one will be taken and the other left. There will be two women grinding grain together; one will be taken and the other left." Then the disciples said to him, "Where, Lord?" He replied to them, "Where the dead body is, there the vultures will gather." Luke 17:22-37

Parable to the disciples - of the persistent widow

Then Jesus told them a parable to show them they should always pray and not lose heart. He said, "In a certain city there was a judge who neither feared God nor respected people. There was also a widow in that city who kept coming to him and saying, 'Give me justice against my adversary.' For a while he refused, but later on he said to himself, 'Though I neither fear God nor have regard for people, yet because this widow keeps on bothering me, I will give her justice, or in the end she will wear me out by her unending pleas.'" And the Lord said, "Listen to what the unrighteous judge says! Won't God give justice to his chosen ones, who cry out to him day and night? Will he delay long to help them? I tell you, he will give them justice speedily. Nevertheless, when the Son of Man comes, will he find faith on earth?" Luke 18:1-8

Parable of the Pharisee and the publican

Jesus also told this parable to some who were confident that they were righteous and looked down on everyone else. "Two men went up to the temple to pray, one a Pharisee and the other a tax collector. The Pharisee stood and prayed about himself like this: 'God, I thank you that I am not like other people: extortionists, unrighteous people, adulterers-or even like this tax collector. I fast twice a week; I give a tenth of everything I get.' The tax collector, however, stood far off and would not even look up to heaven, but beat his breast and said, 'God, be merciful to me, sinner that I am!' I tell you that this man went down to his home justified rather than the Pharisee. For everyone who exalts himself will be humbled, but he who humbles himself will be exalted." Luke 18:9-14

Finally, Jesus leaves Samaria for the last time and enters Judea and continues to meet people and spend time with them. Something new started to happen – people brought their little children to Jesus and asked Him to put their hands on them. This probably commenced with one faithful mother and was then followed by many. People who were healed, restored and made whole again wanted that blessing of health and happiness spoken over their children. If the hands of Jesus could heal, they could also bless futures. Thus, a window opens to an image of unmerited, undeserved, unearned blessings that the New Covenant of Grace would bring.

*Then Jesus left that place and went to the region of Judea and
beyond the Jordan River. Again crowds gathered to him, and
again, as was his custom, he taught them. Mark 10:1*

Discourse to the Pharisees - divorce

*Then some Pharisees came, and to test him they asked, "Is it lawful
for a man to divorce his wife?" He answered them, "What did Moses
command you?" They said, "Moses permitted a man to write a certificate
of dismissal and to divorce her." But Jesus said to them, "He wrote
this commandment for you because of your hard hearts. But from the
beginning of creation he made them male and female. For this reason
a man will leave his father and mother, and the two will become one
flesh. So they are no longer two, but one flesh. Therefore what God has
joined together, let no one separate." In the house once again, the disciples
asked him about this. So he told them, "Whoever divorces his wife and
marries another commits adultery against her. And if she divorces her
husband and marries another, she commits adultery." Mark 10:2-12*

*Then some Pharisees came to him in order to test him. They asked, "Is
it lawful to divorce a wife for any cause?" He answered, "Have you not
read that from the beginning the Creator made them male and female,
and said, 'For this reason a man will leave his father and mother and
will be united with his wife, and the two will become one flesh'? So
they are no longer two, but one flesh. Therefore what God has joined
together, let no one separate." They said to him, "Why then did Moses
command us to give a certificate of dismissal and to divorce her?" Jesus
said to them, "Moses permitted you to divorce your wives because of
your hard hearts, but from the beginning it was not this way. Now I
say to you that whoever divorces his wife, except for immorality, and
marries another commits adultery." The disciples said to him, "If this
is the case of a husband with a wife, it is better not to marry!" He
said to them, "Not everyone can accept this statement, except those to*

whom it has been given. For there are some eunuchs who were that way from birth, and some who were made eunuchs by others, and some who became eunuchs for the sake of the kingdom of heaven. The one who is able to accept this should accept it." Matthew 19:3-12

Let the little children come

Now people were even bringing their babies to him for him to touch. But when the disciples saw it, they began to scold those who brought them. But Jesus called for the children, saying, "Let the little children come to me and do not try to stop them, for the kingdom of God belongs to such as these. I tell you the truth, whoever does not receive the kingdom of God like a child will never enter it." Luke 18:15-17

Then little children were brought to him for him to lay his hands on them and pray. But the disciples scolded those who brought them. But Jesus said, "Let the little children come to me and do not try to stop them, for the kingdom of heaven belongs to such as these." And he placed his hands on them and went on his way. Matthew 19:13-15

Now people were bringing little children to him for him to touch, but the disciples scolded those who brought them. But when Jesus saw this, he was indignant and said to them, "Let the little children come to me and do not try to stop them, for the kingdom of God belongs to such as these. I tell you the truth, whoever does not receive the kingdom of God like a child will never enter it." After he took the children in his arms, he placed his hands on them and blessed them. Mark 10:13-16

The rich young ruler

Something unique then occurs. A rich young ruler emerges from the crowd and asks a great question, *What must I do to inherit eternal life?* This is the question that everyone loves to hear asked and the answer is always laden with grace, "believe in the Lord Jesus and you will be saved." Yet Jesus, who came to bring grace didn't respond with grace, but responded with the law. Instead of telling the young ruler to believe in Him and accept His free offer of life, Jesus gave him the Ten Commandments. Jesus reminded him, "You know the commandments: 'Do not commit adultery'…'Do not steal'…'Honour your father and your mother.'" What's with that?

Jesus saw that the rich young ruler took pride in his ability to keep the law, to earn salvation and the favour of God when he replied, "all these I have kept since I was a boy." Jesus simply showed him that those who live by the law must realise that their best efforts can't save them. So Jesus told him, 'you still lack one thing…sell everything you have and give to the poor…and then come and follow Me.' When the young ruler heard that, he walked away saddened. When we boast of keeping the law, the law always points out something we lack or have failed to obey. The law is so perfect and holy that if we don't keep even one small part of it, the law has no choice but to judge and curse us (Galatians 3:10). That is what the law was designed to do.

God does not want us to boast in our abilities to keep the law. If we are to have confidence in anything at all, if we are to boast in anything at all, it is in the grace of God through Jesus. Only His grace can completely keep, save, heal, deliver and bless us.

Now a certain ruler asked him, "Good teacher, what must I do to inherit eternal life?" Jesus said to him, "Why do you call me good? No one is good except God alone. You know the commandments: 'Do not commit adultery, do not murder, do not steal, do not give false testimony, honor your father and mother.'" The man replied, "I have wholeheartedly obeyed all these laws since my youth." When Jesus heard this, he said to him, "One thing you still lack. Sell all that you have and give the money to the poor, and you will have treasure in heaven. Then come, follow me." But when the man heard this he became very sad, for he was extremely wealthy. When Jesus noticed this, he said, "How hard it is for the rich to enter the kingdom of God! In fact, it is easier for a camel to go through the eye of a needle than for a rich person to enter the kingdom of God." Those who heard this said, "Then who can be saved?" He replied, "What is impossible for mere humans is possible for God." Luke 18:18-27

Now someone came up to him and said, "Teacher, what good thing must I do to gain eternal life?" He said to him, "Why do you ask me about what is good? There is only one who is good. But if you want to enter into life, keep the commandments.""Which ones?" he asked. Jesus replied, "Do not murder, do not commit adultery, do not steal, do not give false testimony, honor your father and mother, and love your neighbor as yourself." The young man said to him, "I have wholeheartedly obeyed all these laws. What do I still lack?" Jesus said to him, "If you wish to be perfect, go sell your possessions and give the money to the poor, and you will have treasure in heaven. Then come, follow me." But when the young man heard this he went away sorrowful, for he was very rich. Then Jesus said to his disciples, "I tell you the truth, it will be hard for a rich person to enter the kingdom of heaven! Again I say, it is easier for a camel to go through the eye of a needle than for a rich person to enter into the kingdom of God." The disciples were greatly astonished when they heard this and said, "Then who can be saved?" Jesus looked at them and replied, "This is impossible for mere humans, but for God all things are possible." Matthew 19:16-26

Now as Jesus was starting out on his way, someone ran up to him, fell on his knees, and said, "Good teacher, what must I do to inherit eternal life?" Jesus said to him, "Why do you call me good? No one is good except God alone. You know the commandments: 'Do not murder, do not commit adultery, do not steal, do not give false testimony, do not defraud, honor your father and mother.'" The man said to him, "Teacher, I have wholeheartedly obeyed all these laws since my youth." As Jesus looked at him, he felt love for him and said, "You lack one thing. Go, sell whatever you have and give the money to the poor, and you will have treasure in heaven. Then come, follow me." But at this statement, the man looked sad and went away sorrowful, for he was very rich. Then Jesus looked around and said to his disciples, "How hard it is for the rich to enter the kingdom of God!" The disciples were astonished at these words. But again Jesus said to them, "Children, how hard it is to enter the kingdom of God! It is easier for a camel to go through the eye of a needle than for a rich person to enter the kingdom of God." They were even more astonished and said to one another, "Then who can be saved?" Jesus looked at them and replied, "This is impossible for mere humans, but not for God; all things are possible for God." Mark 10:17-27

Discourse to the disciples - on the cost of following Jesus

In typical Peter fashion after hearing this, and not yet grasping grace, he comes to Jesus with his own sacrificial story. Jesus wisely uses His answer to show the rewards on earth and heaven for those who follow the unforced rhythms of grace in Jesus.

And Peter said, "Look, we have left everything we own to follow you!" Then Jesus said to them, "I tell you the truth, there is no one who has left home or wife or brothers or parents or children for the sake of God's kingdom who will not receive many times more in this age-and in the age to come, eternal life." Luke 18:28-30

Then Peter said to him, "Look, we have left everything to follow you! What then will there be for us?" Jesus said to them, "I tell you the truth: In the age when all things are renewed, when the Son of Man sits on his glorious throne, you who have followed me will also sit on twelve thrones, judging the twelve tribes of Israel. And whoever has left houses or brothers or sisters or father or mother or children or fields for my sake will receive a hundred times as much and will inherit eternal life. But many who are first will be last, and the last first. Matthew 19:27-30

Peter began to speak to him, "Look, we have left everything to follow you!" Jesus said, "I tell you the truth, there is no one who has left home or brothers or sisters or mother or father or children or fields for my sake and for the sake of the gospel who will not receive in this age a hundred times as much-homes, brothers, sisters, mothers, children, fields, all with persecutions-and in the age to come, eternal life. But many who are first will be last, and the last first." Mark 10:28-31

Parable to the disciples - of the labourers in the vineyard

"For the kingdom of heaven is like a landowner who went out early in the morning to hire workers for his vineyard. And after agreeing with the workers for the standard wage, he sent them into his vineyard. When it was about nine o'clock in the morning, he went out again and saw others standing around in the marketplace without work. He said to them, 'You go into the vineyard too, and I will give you whatever is right.' So they went. When he went out again about noon and three o'clock that afternoon, he did the same thing. And about five o'clock that afternoon he went out and found others standing around, and said to them, 'Why are you standing here all day without work?' They said to him, 'Because no one hired us.' He said to them, 'You go and work in the vineyard too.' When it was evening the owner of the vineyard said to his manager, 'Call the workers and give the pay starting with the last hired until the first.' When those hired about five o'clock came, each received a full day's pay. And when those hired first came, they thought they would receive more. But each one also received the standard wage. When they received it, they began to complain against the landowner, saying, 'These last fellows worked one hour, and you have made them equal to us who bore the hardship and burning heat of the day.' And the landowner replied to one of them, 'Friend, I am not treating you unfairly. Didn't you agree with me to work for the standard wage? Take what is yours and go. I want to give to this last man the same as I gave to you. Am I not permitted to do what I want with what belongs to me? Or are you envious because I am generous?' So the last will be first, and the first last." Matthew 20:1-16

Jesus predicts His death

Jesus continues travelling south towards Jerusalem and at an opportune moment He takes the twelve aside to chat with them about what would happen. This may have been a challenge as there were numerous women travelling with the party caring for their needs, and crowds everywhere. Mark's gospel also points out that Jesus was personally leading the journey towards Jerusalem and there was a lot of fear in the followers and a lot of amazement, astonishment and bewilderment with the disciples. It is in this atmosphere that Jesus has something to share only with the twelve disciples about His impending arrest, mocking, flogging, death and resurrection. The disciples understood none of it, they were evidently still hoping for an earthly kingdom and had their minds elsewhere – on everything they had seen and done. I don't think they were coping that well.

As Jesus was going up to Jerusalem, he took the twelve aside privately and said to them on the way, "Look, we are going up to Jerusalem, and the Son of Man will be handed over to the chief priests and the experts in the law. They will condemn him to death, and will turn him over to the Gentiles to be mocked and flogged severely and crucified. Yet on the third day, he will be raised." Matthew 20:17-19

Then Jesus took the twelve aside and said to them, "Look, we are going up to Jerusalem, and everything that is written about the Son of Man by the prophets will be accomplished. For he will be handed over to the Gentiles; he will be mocked, mistreated, and spat on. They will flog him severely and kill him. Yet on the third day he will rise again." But the twelve understood none of these things. This saying was hidden from them, and they did not grasp what Jesus meant. Luke 18:31-34

They were on the way, going up to Jerusalem. Jesus was going ahead of them, and they were amazed, but those who followed were afraid. He took the twelve aside again and began to tell them what was going to happen to him. "Look, we are going up to Jerusalem, and the Son of Man will be handed over to the chief priests and experts in the law. They will condemn him to death and will turn him over to the Gentiles. They will mock him, spit on him, flog him severely, and kill him. Yet after three days, he will rise again." Mark 10:32-34

The request of the sons of thunder

The mother of James and John, the sons of thunder, was one of the women travelling with Jesus and caring for His needs. She also had a view of the kingdom of God only in earthly terms, hence her request of Jesus. This is one of those awkward but well-meaning moments when mums embarrass their children. Mums don't mean to, they're just being mums with their children's best interests at heart. However it becomes a teaching moment for Jesus on servant leadership and a reference point for the two sons on what was to come next. James would be the first disciple to be put to the sword and John the last disciple to die, of natural causes, though not before suffering severe privation through exile. The other disciples were less than impressed however.

Then the mother of the sons of Zebedee came to him with her sons, and kneeling down she asked him for a favor. He said to her, "What do you want?" She replied, "Permit these two sons of mine to sit, one at your right hand and one at your left, in your kingdom." Jesus answered, "You don't know what you are asking! Are you able to drink the cup I am about to drink?" They said to him, "We are able." He told them, "You will drink my cup, but to sit at my right and at my left is not mine to give. Rather, it is for those for whom it has been prepared by my Father." Now when the other ten heard this, they were angry with the two brothers. But Jesus called them and said, "You know that the rulers of the Gentiles lord it over them, and those in high positions use their authority over them. It must not be this way among you! Instead whoever wants to be great among you must be your servant, and whoever wants to be first among you must be your slave – just as the Son of Man did not come to be served but to serve, and to give his life as a ransom for many." Matthew 20:20-28

Then James and John, the sons of Zebedee, came to him and said, "Teacher, we want you to do for us whatever we ask." He said to them, "What do you want me to do for you?" They said to him, "Permit one of us to sit at your right hand and the other at your left in your glory." But Jesus said to them, "You don't know what you are asking! Are you able to drink the cup I drink or be baptized with the baptism I experience?" They said to him, "We are able." Then Jesus said to them, "You will drink the cup I drink, and you will be baptized with the baptism I experience, but to sit at my right or at my left is not mine to give. It is for those for whom it has been prepared." Now when the other ten heard this, they became angry with James and John. Jesus called them and said to them, "You know that those who are recognized as rulers of the Gentiles lord it over them, and those in high positions use their authority over them. But it is not this way among you. Instead whoever wants to be great among you must be your servant, and whoever wants to be first among you must be the slave of all. For even the Son of Man did not come to be served but to serve, and to give his life as a ransom for many." Mark 10:35-45

Message from Bethany

Some time after these events and presumably before Jesus arrives in Jericho, He receives word that Lazarus, the beloved brother of Mary and Martha, is dying. Yet Jesus waits, with a purpose, to glorify God through the miracle Jesus will do with Lazarus, and the miracle God will do with Jesus, both risen from the dead. Note that these events are only a few weeks from Jesus' crucifixion and the disciples are filled with bravado, especially Thomas the brave (or Thomas the doubter). The Garden of Gethsemane in the subsequent chapters will determine which of the two traits Thomas truly has.

Now a certain man named Lazarus was sick. He was from Bethany, the village where Mary and her sister Martha lived. (Now it was Mary who anointed the Lord with perfumed oil and wiped his feet dry with her hair, whose brother Lazarus was sick.) So the sisters sent a message to Jesus, "Lord, look, the one you love is sick." When Jesus heard this, he said, "This sickness will not lead to death, but to God's glory, so that the Son of God may be glorified through it." (Now Jesus loved Martha and her sister and Lazarus.) So when he heard that Lazarus was sick, he remained in the place where he was for two more days. Then after this, he said to his disciples, "Let us go to Judea again."The disciples replied, "Rabbi, the Jewish leaders were just now trying to stone you to death! Are you going there again?" Jesus replied, "Are there not twelve hours in a day? If anyone walks around in the daytime, he does not stumble, because he sees the light of this world. But if anyone walks around at night, he stumbles, because the light is not in him." After he said this, he added, "Our friend Lazarus has fallen asleep. But I am going there to awaken him." Then the disciples replied, "Lord, if he has fallen asleep, he will recover." (Now Jesus had been talking about his death, but they thought he had been talking about real sleep.) Then Jesus told them plainly, "Lazarus has died, and I am glad for your sake that I was not there, so that you may believe. But let us go to him." So Thomas (called Didymus) said to his fellow disciples, "Let us go too, so that we may die with him."... John 11:1-16

The thirty-third miracle – healing the blind

So Jesus waits and then continues His walk south till He reaches Jericho by the Jordan River. On the outskirts of the city of palms, Jesus heals in response to the impassioned plea for mercy by a blind man, Bartimaeus, the son of Timaeus. Bartimaeus was known by his condition. He was the son of Timaeus (Bar means 'son of' and Timaeus as a name can mean 'unclean'). It is not a great name. Here is the 'son of the unclean one' discarded on the side of the road and begging in a terrible city called Jericho. It doesn't get much lower in human misery than this.

To make matters worse, Bartimaeus called out to Jesus and was instantly rebuked by the crowd. Bartimaeus was told to be quiet, but faced with the Son of God, he was not going to be silent. He was not going to go quietly into the night when the Son of the living God was near. So he cried even louder, oblivious to the respectable folk who cared more for what others thought, than what Jesus thought. The son of the unclean one, faith astir, cried out to the Son of the holy living God. The result is of course inevitable.

They came to Jericho. As Jesus and his disciples and a large crowd were leaving Jericho, Bartimaeus the son of Timaeus, a blind beggar, was sitting by the road. When he heard that it was Jesus the Nazarene, he began to shout, "Jesus, Son of David, have mercy on me!" Many scolded him to get him to be quiet, but he shouted all the more, "Son of David, have mercy on me!" Jesus stopped and said, "Call him." So they called the blind man and said to him, "Have courage! Get up! He is calling you." He threw off his cloak, jumped up, and came to Jesus. Then Jesus said to him, "What do you want me to do for you?" The blind man replied, "Rabbi, let me see again." Jesus said to him, "Go, your faith has healed you." Immediately he regained his sight and followed him on the road. Mark 10:46-52

As Jesus approached Jericho, a blind man was sitting by the road begging. When he heard a crowd going by, he asked what was going on. They told him, "Jesus the Nazarene is passing by." So he called out, "Jesus, Son of David, have mercy on me!" And those who were in front scolded him to get him to be quiet, but he shouted even more, "Son of David, have mercy on me!" So Jesus stopped and ordered the beggar to be brought to him. When the man came near, Jesus asked him, "What do you want me to do for you?" He replied, "Lord, let me see again." Jesus said to him, "Receive your sight; your faith has healed you." And immediately he regained his sight and followed Jesus, praising God. When all the people saw it, they too gave praise to God. Luke 18:35-43

As they were leaving Jericho, a large crowd followed them. Two
blind men were sitting by the road. When they heard that Jesus
was passing by, they shouted, "Have mercy on us, Lord, Son of
David!" The crowd scolded them to get them to be quiet. But
they shouted even more loudly, "Lord, have mercy on us, Son of
David!" Jesus stopped, called them, and said, "What do you want
me to do for you?" They said to him, "Lord, let our eyes be opened."
Moved with compassion, Jesus touched their eyes. Immediately
they received their sight and followed him. Matthew 20:29-34

Zacchaeus comes to Jesus

Jesus entered the city and a large crowd has lined the streets and the
chief tax collector – short in statue and short of friends – climbed a tree
just to see Jesus. Unedifying for a senior bureaucrat, but when you want
to see Jesus, you'll do anything. You'll shout, you'll cry, you'll wave and
you'll climb. Once again Jesus' makes a mockery of the religious elite
and says to Zacchaeus, "I must stay at your house today". The effect on
Zacchaeus and his household is immediate, as is the effect on everyone
who invites Jesus into their house and their lives. Jesus then proceeds
to teach those gathered in Zacchaeus's house.

Jesus entered Jericho and was passing through it. Now a man named
Zacchaeus was there; he was a chief tax collector and was rich. He was
trying to get a look at Jesus, but being a short man he could not see over
the crowd. So he ran on ahead and climbed up into a sycamore tree to see
him, because Jesus was going to pass that way. And when Jesus came to
that place, he looked up and said to him, "Zacchaeus, come down quickly,
because I must stay at your house today." So he came down quickly and
welcomed Jesus joyfully. And when the people saw it, they all complained,
"He has gone in to be the guest of a man who is a sinner." But Zacchaeus
stopped and said to the Lord, "Look, Lord, half of my possessions I now
give to the poor, and if I have cheated anyone of anything, I am paying
back four times as much!" Then Jesus said to him, "Today salvation

has come to this household, because he too is a son of Abraham! For the Son of Man came to seek and to save the lost." Luke 19:1-10

Parable of the minas

While the people were listening to these things, Jesus proceeded to tell a parable, because he was near to Jerusalem, and because they thought that the kingdom of God was going to appear immediately. Therefore he said, "A nobleman went to a distant country to receive for himself a kingdom and then return. And he summoned ten of his slaves, gave them ten minas, and said to them, 'Do business with these until I come back.' But his citizens hated him and sent a delegation after him, saying, 'We do not want this man to be king over us!' When he returned after receiving the kingdom, he summoned these slaves to whom he had given the money. He wanted to know how much they had earned by trading. So the first one came before him and said, 'Sir, your mina has made ten minas more.' And the king said to him, 'Well done, good slave! Because you have been faithful in a very small matter, you will have authority over ten cities.' Then the second one came and said, 'Sir, your mina has made five minas.' So the king said to him, 'And you are to be over five cities.' Then another slave came and said, 'Sir, here is your mina that I put away for safekeeping in a piece of cloth. For I was afraid of you, because you are a severe man. You withdraw what you did not deposit and reap what you did not sow.' The king said to him, 'I will judge you by your own words, you wicked slave! So you knew, did you, that I was a severe man, withdrawing what I didn't deposit and reaping what I didn't sow? Why then didn't you put my money in the bank, so that when I returned I could have collected it with interest?' And he said to his attendants, 'Take the mina from him, and give it to the one who has ten.' But they said to him, 'Sir, he has ten minas already!' 'I tell you that everyone who has will be given more, but from the one who does not have, even what he has will be taken away. But as for these enemies of mine who did not want me to be their king, bring

them here and slaughter them in front of me!'" After Jesus had said
this, he continued on ahead, going up to Jerusalem. Luke 19:11-28

The thirty-fourth miracle – raising Lazarus from the dead

Jesus now leaves Jericho up the infamous road to Jerusalem, discussed
in the previous chapter. It is generally a steep, hot and dangerous climb,
though its winter, so cold. Furthermore what Jesus has to worry about
is not on the road, but in the destination, Jerusalem. Jesus arrives safely
in Bethany, a town situated on the eastern slope of the Mount of Olives,
three kilometres from Jerusalem, so less than an hour's walk from the
Temple (John 11:18). He is met by the two sisters, Mary and Martha,
who took Jesus into their home previously (Luke 10:38). Lazarus their
brother is dead and there is a lot of sorrow. Jesus knew all this and knew
what He would do next, yet He is still moved with compassion for this
beautiful, hurting family.

When Jesus arrived, he found that Lazarus had been in the tomb four
days already. (Now Bethany was less than two miles from Jerusalem, so
many of the Jewish people of the region had come to Martha and Mary
to console them over the loss of their brother.) So when Martha heard
that Jesus was coming, she went out to meet him, but Mary was sitting in
the house. Martha said to Jesus, "Lord, if you had been here, my brother
would not have died. But even now I know that whatever you ask from
God, God will grant you." Jesus replied, "Your brother will come back to
life again." Martha said, "I know that he will come back to life again in
the resurrection at the last day." Jesus said to her, "I am the resurrection
and the life. The one who believes in me will live even if he dies, and
the one who lives and believes in me will never die. Do you believe this?"
She replied, "Yes, Lord, I believe that you are the Christ, the Son of God
who comes into the world." And when she had said this, Martha went
and called her sister Mary, saying privately, "The Teacher is here and is
asking for you." So when Mary heard this, she got up quickly and went
to him. (Now Jesus had not yet entered the village, but was still in the

place where Martha had come out to meet him.) Then the people who were with Mary in the house consoling her saw her get up quickly and go out. They followed her, because they thought she was going to the tomb to weep there. Now when Mary came to the place where Jesus was and saw him, she fell at his feet and said to him, "Lord, if you had been here, my brother would not have died." When Jesus saw her weeping, and the people who had come with her weeping, he was intensely moved in spirit and greatly distressed. He asked, "Where have you laid him?" They replied, "Lord, come and see." Jesus wept. Thus the people who had come to mourn said, "Look how much he loved him!" But some of them said, "This is the man who caused the blind man to see! Couldn't he have done something to keep Lazarus from dying?" Jesus, intensely moved again, came to the tomb. (Now it was a cave, and a stone was placed across it.) Jesus said, "Take away the stone." Martha, the sister of the deceased, replied, "Lord, by this time the body will have a bad smell, because he has been buried four days." Jesus responded, "Didn't I tell you that if you believe, you would see the glory of God?" So they took away the stone. Jesus looked upward and said, "Father, I thank you that you have listened to me. I knew that you always listen to me, but I said this for the sake of the crowd standing around here, that they may believe that you sent me." When he had said this, he shouted in a loud voice, "Lazarus, come out!" The one who had died came out, his feet and hands tied up with strips of cloth, and a cloth wrapped around his face. Jesus said to them, "Unwrap him and let him go." John 11:17-44

Conspiracy to kill Jesus

Jesus performs a great miracle, (his last personally recorded except for poor Malchus's ear), so close to Jerusalem itself – the raising of a man from the dead. A man who had been dead for days and whose body had started to decay. This is a miraculous restoration of the body, soul and spirit. Understandably, the majority of those present believed in Jesus. How could you not? Yet amazingly (and not in a good way) some ran and informed the religious elite about what Jesus had done.

What is equally baffling is that the religious elite don't question the miracle, they believe it. They question their capacity to keep their rules and maintain their religious artifices against the Romans in their city. This is what drives their actions, not whether Jesus may be the Messiah, but the consequences on their world and world view if Jesus is allowed to continue to do what He has been doing. Apparently there was no immediate discussion about whether Jesus could actually be the Messiah, just how to kill Jesus. For that's what the law does, it brings death, compared to what the grace of Jesus brings, which is life.

Then many of the people, who had come with Mary and had seen the things Jesus did, believed in him. But some of them went to the Pharisees and reported to them what Jesus had done. So the chief priests and the Pharisees called the council together and said, "What are we doing? For this man is performing many miraculous signs. If we allow him to go on in this way, everyone will believe in him, and the Romans will come and take away our sanctuary and our nation." Then one of them, Caiaphas, who was high priest that year, said, "You know nothing at all! You do not realize that it is more to your advantage to have one man die for the people than for the whole nation to perish." (Now he did not say this on his own, but because he was high priest that year, he prophesied that Jesus was going to die for the Jewish nation, and not for the Jewish nation only, but to gather together into one the children of God who are scattered.) So from that day they planned together to kill him. John 11:45-53

Ephraim - the end of Jesus' public ministry'

Evidently the threat uttered from the high priest reaches Jesus' ears as here Jesus' public ministry ends, at a little village near the Judean wilderness called Ephraim. Here Jesus spent the last few days in quiet solitude with His disciples, a time of preparation for Him and them. A time of quiet prayer, a time of rest before ushering in the New Covenant of Grace.

Thus Jesus no longer went around publicly among the Judeans,
but went away from there to the region near the wilderness, to a
town called Ephraim, and stayed there with his disciples. Now
the Jewish feast of Passover was near, and many people went up
to Jerusalem from the rural areas before the Passover to cleanse
themselves ritually. Thus they were looking for Jesus, and saying to
one another as they stood in the temple courts, "What do you think?
That he won't come to the feast?" (Now the chief priests and the
Pharisees had given orders that anyone who knew where Jesus was
should report it, so that they could arrest him.) John 11:54-57

This village of Ephraim is not mentioned at any other time in the
Bible, not even in the Old Testament. It could be argued Ephraim is
the ancient town of Ephron mentioned in Chronicles, not far from
Bethel.

Abijah chased Jeroboam; he seized from him these cities: Bethel
and its surrounding towns, Jeshanah and its surrounding towns,
and Ephron and its surrounding towns. 2 Chronicles 13:19

Others argue it is the town of Taiyibeh perched on a conical hill on the
ancient tribal border between Benjamin and Ephraim[30]. The original
church historians Eusebius and Jerome argued Ephraim was seventeen
kilometres from Jerusalem, on the east of the road leading to Sichem.
Josephus speaks of 'two little towns of Bethela and Ephraim, through
which Vespasian passed and left garrisons' suggesting Ephraim was
close to Bethel[31].

Considering Jesus left Bethany for Ephraim (which is close to Bethel)
and was intent on going to Jerusalem, it is fair to conclude that Ephraim
was close to both Jerusalem and Bethany, in or near the Judean wilder-

---

[30] Robinson ('Bibl. Res.,' 2:127) and Stanley ('Sinai and Palestine,' p. 210)
[31] Josephus, The Wars of the Jews, Book 4, 9, 1

ness, noting that Bethel is sixteen kilometres north of Jerusalem and Bethany is three kilometres east of Jerusalem.

Mary anoints Jesus (Saturday 28th March 33 AD)

On the Sabbath, six days before Jesus would lay down His life, He leaves Ephraim and walks back to Bethany where Simon the Leper (unfortunate title) hosts dinner for Jesus and His disciples. I still think the gospels of Matthew and Mark are a little harsh here, as we can all agree that Simon would not have remained a leper if he had met Jesus. Indeed lepers were social outcasts and were not known for hosting dinners and if they had, it is unlikely that anyone would have turned up. Always untidy to have your soup served and the host has left his finger in the bowl. I think scripture should read 'Simon the previous leper' or 'Simon who was healed of leprosy', or maybe just 'Simon'. However I digress – Lazarus is reclining at the table (still thankful to be living I would think), Martha is once again serving (Martha, Martha, Martha) and in comes her sister, Mary, who has always only wanted to be near Jesus.

Mary arrives carrying with her an enormously expensive perfume, worth a year's wages. Mary also knows that there is nothing on earth of greater value than being with Jesus and Mary demonstrates this by anointing Jesus with the perfume. Like the Magi who bought myrrh to the King Priest Jesus to herald his birth, Mary now anoints Jesus with the most expensive of perfumes to prepare Him for death. The Magi there at the start with perfume, Mary there at the end with perfume. It's a beautiful bookend and a stark contrast with Judas the thief, the betrayer of the Son of God.

Then, six days before the Passover, Jesus came to Bethany, where Lazarus lived, whom he had raised from the dead. So they prepared a dinner for Jesus there. Martha was serving, and Lazarus was among those present at the table with him. Then Mary took three quarters of a pound of expensive aromatic oil from pure nard and anointed the feet of Jesus. She then wiped his feet dry with her hair. (Now the house was filled with the fragrance of the perfumed oil.) But Judas Iscariot, one of his disciples (the one who was going to betray him) said, "Why wasn't this oil sold for three hundred silver coins and the money given to the poor?" (Now Judas said this not because he was concerned about the poor, but because he was a thief. As keeper of the money box, he used to steal what was put into it.) So Jesus said, "Leave her alone. She has kept it for the day of my burial. For you will always have the poor with you, but you will not always have me!" Now a large crowd of Judeans learned that Jesus was there, and so they came not only because of him but also to see Lazarus whom he had raised from the dead. So the chief priests planned to kill Lazarus too, for on account of him many of the Jewish people from Jerusalem were going away and believing in Jesus. John 12:1-11

Now while Jesus was in Bethany at the house of Simon the leper, a woman came to him with an alabaster jar of expensive perfumed oil, and she poured it on his head as he was at the table. When the disciples saw this, they became indignant and said, "Why this waste? It could have been sold at a high price and the money given to the poor!" When Jesus learned of this, he said to them, "Why are you bothering this woman? She has done a good service for me. For you will always have the poor with you, but you will not always have me! When she poured this oil on my body, she did it to prepare me for burial. I tell you the truth, wherever this gospel is proclaimed in the whole world, what she has done will also be told in memory of her." Matthew 26:6-13

Now while Jesus was in Bethany at the house of Simon the leper, reclining at the table, a woman came with an alabaster jar of costly aromatic oil from pure nard. After breaking open the jar, she poured it on his head. But some who were present indignantly said to one another, "Why this waste of expensive ointment? It could have been sold for more than three hundred silver coins and the money given to the poor!" So they spoke angrily to her. But Jesus said, "Leave her alone. Why are you bothering her? She has done a good service for me. For you will always have the poor with you, and you can do good for them whenever you want. But you will not always have me! She did what she could. She anointed my body beforehand for burial. I tell you the truth, wherever the gospel is proclaimed in the whole world, what she has done will also be told in memory of her." Mark 14:3-9

And truly wherever the gospel has been preached, the story of Mary preparing Jesus for his impending death and burial has been told. For it is a story of self-sacrificial love. The alabaster jar of perfume was of such great value that it had not been used. Presumably the value was so great that Mary never countenanced using the perfume on herself, except perhaps for her wedding – or was it an investment –? Either way, it begs the question, how she had it and why? If the answer lies in the perfume being kept for family weddings, the gift of it all to anoint the Saviour demonstrates a heart prepared to sacrifice everything in response to the love of Jesus. Another lesson for us all.

Even as Mary was rebuked harshly she kept the perfume flowing, because to know Jesus means that nothing else matters. Wealth, property, belongings, words, wisdom and acceptance by the crowd all pale into insignificance compared to the passing greatness of Jesus. The apostle Paul says it best when he wrote to the church in Philippi and said…

More than that, I now regard all things as liabilities compared to the far greater value of knowing Christ Jesus my Lord, for whom I have suffered the loss of all things-indeed, I regard them as dung!-that I may gain Christ, Philippians 3:8

So this chapter closes with a room filled with the richest of aromas like in the days of old in the Temple when God dwelt between the cherubim above the mercy seat of the Ark. An aroma pleasing to God. Indeed Christ's sacrifice on the cross in the coming days would be the final pleasing aroma to God, the last sacrifice, the fulfilment of the law. Through that sacrifice, the shedding of blood, the New Covenant of Grace would be ushered in and the Old Covenant of Law fulfilled.

For we are a sweet aroma of Christ to God among those who are being saved and among those who are perishing. 2 Corinthians 2:15

CHAPTER 11

Triumphant entry
(Sunday 29th - Tuesday 31st March 33 AD)

Jesus rested the previous night in Bethany. He was richly anointed from an alabaster jar of perfume by Mary whilst reclining at the home of Simon the [previous] leper and it is likely that He spent this night where he previously had in Bethany, with Lazarus, Martha and Mary. A fragrant night no doubt, not just in aroma but in rich fellowship.

For the dawn, Jesus' last Sunday before the cross, would see Jesus wait in Bethany. Evidently He was in no hurry to make His triumphant entry into Jerusalem. Jesus would not traverse the three kilometres from Bethany to Jerusalem till the afternoon, arriving at the Temple late when all had gone home. So what was Jesus doing all morning in Bethany? Sounds like a question for you the reader to ask Jesus personally when your race is run on earth. If we had to guess what Jesus was doing before his entrance, seeking the Father through prayer would be a good guess.

From the triumphant entrance on what many call 'Palm Sunday' through to satan entering Judas, this final week is one of high drama. Temple tax tables will again be over turned, fig trees will wither, parables will be taught, questions answered, the religious elite maligned, the widow's mite honoured, the end time foretold, – all as Jesus taught openly and unafraid in the Temple. Each night Jesus would return to Bethany where he would stay overnight, presumably in that marvellous welcoming aromatic home of Lazarus, Martha and Mary. And I bet, every night poor Martha slaved in the kitchen whilst Mary sat at the feet of Jesus. Though I like to imagine that on the last night Martha got a glimpse of the grace of Jesus compared to the work of the law and instead asked Lazarus to cook, whilst she joined Mary at the feet of Jesus, listening, learning, loving, worshipping and being truly fulfilled. Oh, I hope Martha did that!

Triumphant Entry (Sunday 29th March)

After staying overnight in Bethany, Jesus now enters Jerusalem past the Mount of Olives, past the town of Bethphage (now just part of Jerusalem) covering the distance of three kilometres riding on a donkey that is miraculously provided to fulfil scripture. It is less than an hour's journey, even with cloaks and palm branches spread liberally around as people mistakenly expected the return of the earthly king. It is afternoon, it is cool and the crowd is loud.

Now when they approached Jerusalem and came to Bethphage, at the Mount of Olives, Jesus sent two disciples, telling them, "Go to the village ahead of you. Right away you will find a donkey tied there, and a colt with her. Untie them and bring them to me. If anyone says anything to you, you are to say, 'The Lord needs them,' and he will send them at once." This took place to fulfill what was spoken by the prophet: "Tell the people of Zion, 'Look, your king is coming to you, unassuming and seated on a donkey, and on a colt, the foal of a donkey.'" So the disciples went and did as Jesus had instructed them. They brought the donkey and the colt and placed their cloaks on them, and he sat on them. A very large crowd spread their cloaks on the road. Others cut branches from the trees and spread them on the road. The crowds that went ahead of him and those following kept shouting, "Hosanna to the Son of David! Blessed is the one who comes in the name of the Lord! Hosanna in the highest!" As he entered Jerusalem the whole city was thrown into an uproar, saying, "Who is this?" And the crowds were saying, "This is the prophet Jesus, from Nazareth in Galilee." Matthew 21:1-11

After Jesus had said this, he continued on ahead, going up to Jerusalem. Now when he approached Bethphage and Bethany, at the place called the Mount of Olives, he sent two of the disciples, telling them, "Go to the village ahead of you. When you enter it, you will find a colt tied there that has never been ridden. Untie it and bring it here. If anyone asks you, 'Why are you untying it?' just say, 'The Lord needs it.'" So those who were sent ahead found it exactly as he had told them. As they were untying the colt, its owners asked them, "Why are you untying that colt?" They replied, "The Lord needs it." Then they brought it to Jesus, threw their cloaks on the colt, and had Jesus get on it. As he rode along, they spread their cloaks on the road. As he approached the road leading down from the Mount of Olives, the whole crowd of his disciples began to rejoice and praise God with a loud voice for all the mighty works they had seen: "Blessed is the king who comes in the name of the Lord! Peace in heaven and glory in the highest!" But some of the Pharisees in the crowd said to him, "Teacher, rebuke your disciples." He answered, "I tell you, if they keep silent, the very stones will cry out!" Now when Jesus approached and saw the city, he wept over it, saying, "If you had only known on this day, even you, the things that make for peace! But now they are hidden from your eyes. For the days will come upon you when your enemies will build an embankment against you and surround you and close in on you from every side. They will demolish you-you and your children within your walls-and they will not leave within you one stone on top of another, because you did not recognize the time of your visitation from God." Luke 19:28-44

The next day the large crowd that had come to the feast heard that Jesus was coming to Jerusalem. So they took branches of palm trees and went out to meet him. They began to shout, "Hosanna! Blessed is the one who comes in the name of the Lord! Blessed is the king of Israel!" Jesus found a young donkey and sat on it, just as it is written, "Do not be afraid, people of Zion; look, your king is coming, seated on a donkey's colt!" (His disciples did not understand these things when they first happened, but when Jesus was glorified, then they remembered that these things were written about him and that these things had happened to him.) So the crowd who had been with him when he called Lazarus out of the tomb and raised him from the dead were continuing to testify about it. Because they had heard that Jesus had performed this miraculous sign, the crowd went out to meet him. Thus the Pharisees said to one another, "You see that you can do nothing. Look, the world has run off after him!" John 12:12-19

Now as they approached Jerusalem, near Bethphage and Bethany, at the Mount of Olives, Jesus sent two of his disciples and said to them, "Go to the village ahead of you. As soon as you enter it, you will find a colt tied there that has never been ridden. Untie it and bring it here. If anyone says to you, 'Why are you doing this?' say, 'The Lord needs it and will send it back here soon.'" So they went and found a colt tied at a door, outside in the street, and untied it. Some people standing there said to them, "What are you doing, untying that colt?" They replied as Jesus had told them, and the bystanders let them go. Then they brought the colt to Jesus, threw their cloaks on it, and he sat on it. Many spread their cloaks on the road and others spread branches they had cut in the fields. Both those who went ahead and those who followed kept shouting, "Hosanna! Blessed is the one who comes in the name of the Lord! Blessed is the coming kingdom of our father David! Hosanna in the highest!" Mark 11:1-10

Jesus enters to a hero's welcome, fit for a king. I imagine the disciples walking behind were also fairly upbeat, a roaring crowd can do that. Jesus would have entered the Temple through the east or golden gate, the only original gate from the time of Christ still visible as part of Jerusalem's current wall. He would have alighted the donkey at the

Temple wall though, as the photos show it would have been difficult for the donkey to navigate the stairs inside the gate. Jesus would have walked through the golden gate and up the stairs into the Temple complex. Yet Jesus, of all men, knows that it is palm branches one week, the cross the next. Jesus entered the Temple to find little activity due to the lateness of the hour, so He back tracked to Bethany to spend the night.

The photo above is of the eastern (golden) gate into the Temple taken by Maison Bonfills between 1867 and 1899.

The photo above is of the eastern (golden) gate's exit onto the Temple Mount. Jesus would have walked through this gate and up these stairs to enter the Temple. The photo was taken by the Hon Stuart Robert.

Then Jesus entered Jerusalem and went to the temple. And after looking around at everything, he went out to Bethany with the twelve since it was already late. Mark 11:11

Monday 30th March

The next morning Jesus again heads for Jerusalem from Bethany on the same road, evidently before breakfast. Not so many palm branches this time and the donkey has been returned to its grateful owner. What I can't believe though, is that Martha didn't feed Jesus in the morning, because Jesus gets hungry on his stroll into town. Martha is renowned for her work ethic, but perhaps it is really early, or perhaps Martha grasped the truth, that it is better to sit at the feet of Jesus in restful awe, than to slave in work based effort. Either way, can someone please feed the Saviour of the world?

Now the next day, as they went out from Bethany, he was hungry. After noticing in the distance a fig tree with leaves, he went to see if he could find any fruit on it. When he came to it he found nothing but leaves, for it was not the season for figs. He said to it, "May no one ever eat fruit from you again." And his disciples heard it. Mark 11:12-14

Just like the first time when Jesus entered the Temple courts after His baptism, His righteous anger burns against those who had turned the worship of God into a profit-making business. The scene of clearing the Temple is repeated with the same zeal as the first time Jesus visited the Temple during His ministry years, three years earlier.

Then Jesus entered the temple courts and began to drive out those who were selling things there, saying to them, "It is written, 'My house will be a house of prayer,' but you have turned it into a den of robbers!" Luke 19:45-46

Then they came to Jerusalem. Jesus entered the temple area and began to drive out those who were selling and buying in the temple courts. He turned over the tables of the money changers and the chairs of those selling doves, and he would not permit anyone to carry merchandise through the temple courts. Then he began to teach them and said, "Is it not written: 'My house will be called a house of prayer for all nations'? But you have turned it into a den of robbers!" The chief priests and the experts in the law heard it and they considered how they could assassinate him, for they feared him, because the whole crowd was amazed by his teaching. Mark 11:15-18

Then Jesus entered the temple area and drove out all those who were selling and buying in the temple courts, and turned over the tables of the money changers and the chairs of those selling doves. And he said to them, "It is written, 'My house will be called a house of prayer,' but you are turning it into a den of robbers!" Matthew 21:12-13

You can imagine the scene. Uproar over Jesus wrecking the businesses of the money changers and animal sellers, compared with sheer joy of those healed and restored. What a comparison between religion and relationship, between Old Covenant Law and the New Covenant Grace that Jesus would implement. As an aside, considering Jesus showed this same righteous anger exactly three years previously in exactly the same place, how is it that no one learnt? How is it that the religious elite kept the Temple so defiled and did nothing? That unfortunately is the way of dead religion. It is about rules, permits, permissions to trade in the outer court and control.

The blind and lame came to him in the temple courts, and he healed them. But when the chief priests and the experts in the law saw the wonderful things he did and heard the children crying out in the temple courts, "Hosanna to the Son of David," they became indignant and said to him, "Do you hear what they are saying?" Jesus said to them, "Yes. Have you never read, 'Out of the mouths of children and nursing infants you have prepared praise for yourself'?" Matthew 21:14-16

Jesus was teaching daily in the temple courts. The chief priests and the experts in the law and the prominent leaders among the people were seeking to assassinate him, but they could not find a way to do it, for all the people hung on his words. Luke 19:47-48

After a big day of healing, restoring, teaching and offending the religious elite, Jesus heads back for the night to Bethany. I only hope Martha fed Jesus that evening and remembered breakfast the next morning.

And leaving them, he went out of the city to Bethany
and spent the night there. Matthew 21:17

When evening came, Jesus and his disciples
went out of the city. Mark 11:19

Tuesday 31st March (thirty-fifth miracle – power over the environment)

The sun is rising and Jesus is back on the three kilometre, forty-five minute walk to Jerusalem, again very early. Can I say this is also good advice for us today that work hard. Do some exercise in the morning, although without cursing fig trees or over turning tables.

Now early in the morning, as he returned to the city, he was hungry.
After noticing a fig tree by the road he went to it, but found nothing
on it except leaves. He said to it, "Never again will there be fruit
from you!" And the fig tree withered at once. When the disciples
saw it they were amazed, saying, "How did the fig tree wither so
quickly?" Jesus answered them, "I tell you the truth, if you have
faith and do not doubt, not only will you do what was done to
the fig tree, but even if you say to this mountain, 'Be lifted up
and thrown into the sea,' it will happen. And whatever you ask
in prayer, if you believe, you will receive." Matthew 21:18-22

In the morning as they passed by, they saw the fig tree withered from
the roots. Peter remembered and said to him, "Rabbi, look! The fig
tree you cursed has withered." Jesus said to them, "Have faith in
God. I tell you the truth, if someone says to this mountain, 'Be lifted
up and thrown into the sea,' and does not doubt in his heart but

believes that what he says will happen, it will be done for him. For
this reason I tell you, whatever you pray and ask for, believe that you
have received it, and it will be yours. Whenever you stand praying,
if you have anything against anyone, forgive him, so that your
Father in heaven will also forgive you your sins." Mark 11:20-26

As was Jesus' habit, He went straight back to the Temple. We can probably assume that the quasi-religious businesses selling animals for profit didn't come back into the Temple courtyards this day. However the religious elites, those that previously had vowed to kill Jesus were back with a vengeance, once again questioning Jesus' authority (like being the Son of God isn't enough?). Jesus' loaded response is perfect to combat those who believe in their own self righteousness.

Now after Jesus entered the temple courts, the chief priests and elders
of the people came up to him as he was teaching and said, "By what
authority are you doing these things, and who gave you this authority?"
Jesus answered them, "I will also ask you one question. If you answer
me then I will also tell you by what authority I do these things. Where
did John's baptism come from? From heaven or from people?" They
discussed this among themselves, saying, "If we say, 'From heaven,' he will
say, 'Then why did you not believe him?' But if we say, 'From people,'
we fear the crowd, for they all consider John to be a prophet." So they
answered Jesus, "We don't know." Then he said to them, "Neither will I
tell you by what authority I am doing these things. Matthew 21:23-27

They came again to Jerusalem. While Jesus was walking in the temple
courts, the chief priests, the experts in the law, and the elders came up
to him and said, "By what authority are you doing these things? Or
who gave you this authority to do these things?" Jesus said to them,
"I will ask you one question. Answer me and I will tell you by what
authority I do these things: John's baptism-was it from heaven or
from people? Answer me." They discussed with one another, saying,

"If we say, 'From heaven,' he will say, 'Then why did you not believe him?' But if we say, 'From people-'" (they feared the crowd, for they all considered John to be truly a prophet). So they answered Jesus, "We don't know." Then Jesus said to them, "Neither will I tell you by what authority I am doing these things." Mark 11:27-33

Now one day, as Jesus was teaching the people in the temple courts and proclaiming the gospel, the chief priests and the experts in the law with the elders came up and said to him, "Tell us: By what authority are you doing these things? Or who is it who gave you this authority?" He answered them, "I will also ask you a question, and you tell me: John's baptism-was it from heaven or from people?" So they discussed it with one another, saying, "If we say, 'From heaven,' he will say, 'Why did you not believe him?' But if we say, 'From people,' all the people will stone us, because they are convinced that John was a prophet." So they replied that they did not know where it came from. Then Jesus said to them, "Neither will I tell you by whose authority I do these things." Luke 20:1-8

After dealing with the religious elite, Jesus goes back to teaching the people, again in story or parable form. Each parable was both a thorn for the elite and a rose for the people as again Jesus confronts the law that brings death compared to His grace that brings life.

Parable 1 - of the two sons

"What do you think? A man had two sons. He went to the first and said, 'Son, go and work in the vineyard today.' The boy answered, 'I will not.' But later he had a change of heart and went. The father went to the other son and said the same thing. This boy answered, 'I will, sir,' but did not go. Which of the two did his father's will?" They said, "The first." Jesus said to them, "I tell you the truth, tax collectors and prostitutes will go ahead of you into the kingdom of God! For John came to you in the way of righteousness, and you did not believe him. But

the tax collectors and prostitutes did believe. Although you saw this, you did not later change your minds and believe him. Matthew 21:28-32

Parable 2 - of the vine growers

"Listen to another parable: There was a landowner who planted a vineyard. He put a fence around it, dug a pit for its winepress, and built a watchtower. Then he leased it to tenant farmers and went on a journey. When the harvest time was near, he sent his slaves to the tenants to collect his portion of the crop. But the tenants seized his slaves, beat one, killed another, and stoned another. Again he sent other slaves, more than the first, and they treated them the same way. Finally he sent his son to them, saying, 'They will respect my son.' But when the tenants saw the son, they said to themselves, 'This is the heir. Come, let's kill him and get his inheritance!' So they seized him, threw him out of the vineyard, and killed him. Now when the owner of the vineyard comes, what will he do to those tenants?" They said to him, "He will utterly destroy those evil men! Then he will lease the vineyard to other tenants who will give him his portion at the harvest." Jesus said to them, "Have you never read in the scriptures: 'The stone the builders rejected has become the cornerstone. This is from the Lord, and it is marvelous in our eyes'? For this reason I tell you that the kingdom of God will be taken from you and given to a people who will produce its fruit. The one who falls on this stone will be broken to pieces, and the one on whom it falls will be crushed." Matthew 21:33-44

Then he began to speak to them in parables: "A man planted a vineyard. He put a fence around it, dug a pit for its winepress, and built a watchtower. Then he leased it to tenant farmers and went on a journey. At harvest time he sent a slave to the tenants to collect from them his portion of the crop. But those tenants seized his slave, beat him, and sent him away empty-handed. So he sent another slave to them again. This one they struck on the head and treated outrageously. He sent another, and that one they killed. This happened to many others, some of whom were beaten, others killed. He had one left, his one dear son. Finally he sent him to them, saying, 'They will respect my son.' But those tenants said to one another, 'This is the heir. Come, let's kill him and the inheritance will be ours!' So they seized him, killed him, and threw his body out of the vineyard. What then will the owner of the vineyard do? He will come and destroy those tenants and give the vineyard to others. Have you not read this scripture: 'The stone the builders rejected has become the cornerstone. This is from the Lord, and it is marvelous in our eyes'?" Mark 12:1-11

Then he began to tell the people this parable: "A man planted a vineyard, leased it to tenant farmers, and went on a journey for a long time. When harvest time came, he sent a slave to the tenants so that they would give him his portion of the crop. However, the tenants beat his slave and sent him away empty-handed. So he sent another slave. They beat this one too, treated him outrageously, and sent him away empty-handed. So he sent still a third. They even wounded this one, and threw him out. Then the owner of the vineyard said, 'What should I do? I will send my one dear son; perhaps they will respect him.' But when the tenants saw him, they said to one another, 'This is the heir; let's kill him so the inheritance will be ours!' So they threw him out of the vineyard and killed him. What then will the owner of the vineyard do to them? He will come and destroy those tenants and give the vineyard to others." When the people heard this, they said, "May this never happen!" But Jesus looked straight at them and said, "Then what is the meaning of that which is written: 'The stone the builders rejected has become the cornerstone'? Everyone who falls on this stone will be broken to pieces, and the one on whom it falls will be crushed." Luke 20:9-18

Parable 3 - of the marriage feast

Jesus spoke to them again in parables, saying: "The kingdom of heaven can be compared to a king who gave a wedding banquet for his son. He sent his slaves to summon those who had been invited to the banquet, but they would not come. Again he sent other slaves, saying, 'Tell those who have been invited, "Look! The feast I have prepared for you is ready. My oxen and fattened cattle have been slaughtered, and everything is ready. Come to the wedding banquet."' But they were indifferent and went away, one to his farm, another to his business. The rest seized his slaves, insolently mistreated them, and killed them. The king was furious! He sent his soldiers, and they put those murderers to death and set their city on fire. Then he said to his slaves, 'The wedding is ready, but the ones who had been invited were not worthy. So go into the main streets and invite everyone you find to the wedding banquet.' And those slaves went out into the streets and gathered all they found, both bad and good, and the wedding hall was filled with guests. But when the king came in to see the wedding guests, he saw a man there who was not wearing wedding clothes. And he said to him, 'Friend, how did you get in here without wedding clothes?' But he had nothing to say. Then the king said to his attendants, 'Tie him up hand and foot and throw him into the outer darkness, where there will be weeping and gnashing of teeth!' For many are called, but few are chosen." Matthew 22:1-14

It appears the teaching makes no difference to the hearts of the religious elite as their first response is to look for a way to arrest Jesus.

Now they wanted to arrest him (but they feared the crowd), because they realized that he told this parable against them. So they left him and went away. Mark 12:12

When the chief priests and the Pharisees heard his parables, they realized that he was speaking about them. They wanted to arrest him, but they were afraid of the crowds, because the crowds regarded him as a prophet. Matthew 21:45-46

Lacking a spine, the self righteous conspired a cunning plan through three questions on the law designed to trip up Jesus. I know what you're thinking, surely after their first question on His authority in the morning they would have learnt their lesson. Apparently not, as hours later they have regrouped with even more desperate measures. They now conspire with their hated enemy the Herodians, those despised Jews who had sold their souls to the Romans. Apparently hate and self righteousness knows no bounds and become strange bed fellows.

The problem is that the religious elite have not worked out that Jesus came to complete the law by ushering in grace – that Jesus was with the Father when the law was given at Mt Sinai, that Jesus was with the Father in the beginning (John 1:1) and that Jesus is the author of life (Acts 3:15). So it is always going to be a hard sell to trip up the author of the law who has now come to complete it by ushering in a New Covenant of Grace. All of this was missed by the assembly of teachers of the law, chief priests, Pharisees, Sadducees and Herodians. Jesus' response to their three questions on the law is so powerful, thorough and incisive that this ends their questions. They know they have been soundly beaten and that Jesus' authority and credibility is now unquestioned and they reconcile to themselves that there is only one path left for them, to seek the death of the Saviour of the world.

Question 1 - A question on the law (tax)

Whilst this first question on tax was designed to discredit Jesus by aligning Him with the dreaded occupying power of Rome, it is also the only time Jesus spoke about politics. Imagine coming into the world at the time of the most powerful political empire in history and not mentioning it once except to say give to them what is theirs and to God what is His.

Then the experts in the law and the chief priests wanted to arrest him that very hour, because they realized he had told this parable against them. But they were afraid of the people. Then they watched him carefully and sent spies who pretended to be sincere. They wanted to take advantage of what he might say so that they could deliver him up to the authority and jurisdiction of the governor. Thus they asked him, "Teacher, we know that you speak and teach correctly, and show no partiality, but teach the way of God in accordance with the truth. Is it right for us to pay the tribute tax to Caesar or not?" But Jesus perceived their deceit and said to them, "Show me a denarius. Whose image and inscription are on it?" They said, "Caesar's." So he said to them, "Then give to Caesar the things that are Caesar's, and to God the things that are God's." Thus they were unable in the presence of the people to trap him with his own words. And stunned by his answer, they fell silent. Luke 20:19-26

Then the Pharisees went out and planned together to entrap him with his own words. They sent to him their disciples along with the Herodians, saying, "Teacher, we know that you are truthful, and teach the way of God in accordance with the truth. You do not court anyone's favor because you show no partiality. Tell us then, what do you think? Is it right to pay taxes to Caesar or not?" But Jesus realized their evil intentions and said, "Hypocrites! Why are you testing me? Show me the coin used for the tax." So they brought him a denarius. Jesus said to them, "Whose image is this, and whose inscription?" They replied, "Caesar's." He said to them, "Then give to Caesar the things that are Caesar's, and to God the things that are God's." Now when they heard this they were stunned, and they left him and went away. Matthew 22:15-22

Then they sent some of the Pharisees and Herodians to trap him with his own words. When they came they said to him, "Teacher, we know that you are truthful and do not court anyone's favor, because you show no partiality but teach the way of God in accordance with the truth. Is it right to pay taxes to Caesar or not? Should we pay or shouldn't we?" But he saw through their hypocrisy and said to them, "Why are you testing me? Bring me a denarius and let me look at it." So they brought one, and he said to them, "Whose image is this, and whose inscription?" They replied, "Caesar's." Then Jesus said to them, "Give to Caesar the things that are Caesar's, and to God the things that are God's." And they were utterly amazed at him. Mark 12:13-17

Question 2 - A question on the law (resurrection)

The same day Sadducees (who say there is no resurrection) came to him and asked him, "Teacher, Moses said, 'If a man dies without having children, his brother must marry the widow and father children for his brother.' Now there were seven brothers among us. The first one married and died, and since he had no children he left his wife to his brother. The second did the same, and the third, down to the seventh. Last of all, the woman died. In the resurrection, therefore, whose wife of the seven will she be? For they all had married her." Jesus answered them, "You are deceived, because you don't know the scriptures or the power of God. For in the resurrection they neither marry nor are given in marriage, but are like angels in heaven. Now as for the resurrection of the dead, have you not read what was spoken to you by God, 'I am the God of Abraham, the God of Isaac, and the God of Jacob'? He is not the God of the dead but of the living!" When the crowds heard this, they were amazed at his teaching. Matthew 22:23-33

Sadducees (who say there is no resurrection) also came to him and asked him, "Teacher, Moses wrote for us: 'If a man's brother dies and leaves a wife but no children, that man must marry the widow and father children for his brother.' There were seven brothers. The first one married, and when he died he had no children. The second married her and died without any children, and likewise the third. None of the seven had children. Finally, the woman died too. In the resurrection, when they rise again, whose wife will she be? For all seven had married her." Jesus said to them, "Aren't you deceived for this reason, because you don't know the scriptures or the power of God? For when they rise from the dead, they neither marry nor are given in marriage, but are like angels in heaven. Now as for the dead being raised, have you not read in the book of Moses, in the passage about the bush, how God said to him, 'I am the God of Abraham, the God of Isaac, and the God of Jacob'? He is not the God of the dead but of the living. You are badly mistaken!" Mark 12:18-27

Now some Sadducees (who contend that there is no resurrection) came to him. They asked him, "Teacher, Moses wrote for us that if a man's brother dies leaving a wife but no children, that man must marry the widow and father children for his brother. Now there were seven brothers. The first one married a woman and died without children. The second and then the third married her, and in this same way all seven died, leaving no children. Finally the woman died too. In the resurrection, therefore, whose wife will the woman be? For all seven had married her." So Jesus said to them, "The people of this age marry and are given in marriage. But those who are regarded as worthy to share in that age and in the resurrection from the dead neither marry nor are given in marriage. In fact, they can no longer die, because they are equal to angels and are sons of God, since they are sons of the resurrection. But even Moses revealed that the dead are raised in the passage about the bush, where he calls the Lord the God of Abraham and the God of Isaac and the God of Jacob. Now he is not God of the dead, but of the living, for all live before him." Then some of the experts in the law answered, "Teacher, you have spoken well!" For they did not dare any longer to ask him anything. Luke 20:27-40

Question 3 - A question on the law (greatest commandment)

Now when the Pharisees heard that he had silenced the Sadducees, they assembled together. And one of them, an expert in religious law, asked him a question to test him: "Teacher, which commandment in the law is the greatest?" Jesus said to him, "'Love the Lord your

God with all your heart, with all your soul, and with all your mind.' This is the first and greatest commandment. The second is like it: 'Love your neighbor as yourself.' All the law and the prophets depend on these two commandments." Matthew 22:34-40

Now one of the experts in the law came and heard them debating. When he saw that Jesus answered them well, he asked him, "Which commandment is the most important of all?" Jesus answered, "The most important is: 'Listen, Israel, the Lord our God, the Lord is one. Love the Lord your God with all your heart, with all your soul, with all your mind, and with all your strength.' The second is: 'Love your neighbor as yourself.' There is no other commandment greater than these." The expert in the law said to him, "That is true, Teacher; you are right to say that he is one, and there is no one else besides him. And to love him with all your heart, with all your mind, and with all your strength and to love your neighbor as yourself is more important than all burnt offerings and sacrifices." When Jesus saw that he had answered thoughtfully, he said to him, "You are not far from the kingdom of God." Then no one dared any longer to question him. Mark 12:28-34

Jesus asks a question

Now that the questioners have been silenced and the three questions answered, Jesus is faced with a despondent and frustrated, but captive, religious elite audience and He strikes back. He has answered every question asked of Him, now Jesus asks one simple question back, about the Messiah that they were all waiting expectantly for. Could they answer just one simple question about a topic they had devoted their lives to?

While the Pharisees were assembled, Jesus asked them a question: "What do you think about the Christ? Whose son is he?" They said, "The son of David." He said to them, "How then does David by the Spirit call him 'Lord,' saying,'The Lord said to my lord, "Sit at my right hand, until I put your enemies under your feet"'? If David then calls him 'Lord,' how can he be his son?" No one was able to answer him a word, and from that day on no one dared to question him any longer. Matthew 22:41-46

While Jesus was teaching in the temple courts, he said, "How is it that the experts in the law say that the Christ is David's son? David himself, by the Holy Spirit, said, 'The Lord said to my lord, "Sit at my right hand, until I put your enemies under your feet."' If David himself calls him 'Lord,' how can he be his son?" And the large crowd was listening to him with delight. Mark 12:35-37

But he said to them, "How is it that they say that the Christ is David's son? For David himself says in the book of Psalms, 'The Lord said to my lord, "Sit at my right hand, until I make your enemies a footstool for your feet."' If David then calls him 'Lord,' how can he be his son?" Luke 20:41-44

Jesus' warning against the scribes

Having publicly answered the three questions on the law asked by the elite that left them dumb founded and then asking His own question only to be met with silence, Jesus turns back to the crowd who have watched this unfold and launches both barrels at the religious elite. The crowd undoubtedly would have been silent during this time having learnt through painful means that crossing the elite never ended well. Just ask the early church, persecuted by Saul before he met Jesus. However the crowd had just witnessed Jesus excoriate the religious elites, the Pharisees, Saducees, scribes, teachers of the law, chief priests and elders. It is no wonder that from this point, the religious elite do not ask any more questions of Jesus and only have one thing on their mind - murder. It is also no wonder that the crowd loved Jesus even more.

Then Jesus said to the crowds and to his disciples, "The experts in the law and the Pharisees sit on Moses' seat. Therefore pay attention to what they tell you and do it. But do not do what they do, for they do not practice what they teach. They tie up heavy loads, hard to carry, and put them on men's shoulders, but they themselves are not willing even to lift a finger to move them. They do all their deeds to be seen by people, for they make their phylacteries wide and their tassels long. They love the place of honor at banquets and the best seats in the synagogues and elaborate greetings in the marketplaces, and to have people call them 'Rabbi.' But you are not to be called 'Rabbi,' for you have one Teacher and you are all brothers. And call no one your 'father' on earth, for you have one Father, who is in heaven. Nor are you to be called 'teacher,' for you have one teacher, the Christ. The greatest among you will be your servant. And whoever exalts himself will be humbled, and whoever humbles himself will be exalted. Matthew 23:1-12

In his teaching Jesus also said, "Watch out for the experts in the law. They like walking around in long robes and elaborate greetings in the marketplaces, and the best seats in the synagogues and the places of honor at banquets. They devour widows' property, and as a show make long prayers. These men will receive a more severe punishment." Mark 12:38-40

As all the people were listening, Jesus said to his disciples, "Beware of the experts in the law. They like walking around in long robes, and they love elaborate greetings in the marketplaces and the best seats in the synagogues and the places of honor at banquets. They devour widows' property, and as a show make long prayers. They will receive a more severe punishment." Luke 20:45-47

Seven woes against the scribes

For the final time Jesus turns to the religious elite and calls them to task. He unleashes seven 'woe to you', 'what sorrow awaits you', 'you're hopeless' statements and they are in your face. For this is the last opportunity Jesus will have to call out the religious elite. Remember, Jesus loves these blind guides and He wants them to grasp the fulfilment of the law through grace and this is His last ditch effort to reach them. Sadly, it will fall on deaf ears as scripture shows only two of the seventy-one members of the Great Sanhedrin would put their faith in Jesus as the Son of God.

Woe 1

"But woe to you, experts in the law and you Pharisees, hypocrites! You keep locking people out of the kingdom of heaven! For you neither enter nor permit those trying to enter to go in. Matthew 23:13-14

Woe 2

"Woe to you, experts in the law and you Pharisees, hypocrites! You cross land and sea to make one convert, and when you get one, you make him twice as much a child of hell as yourselves! Matthew 23:15

Woe 3

"Woe to you, blind guides, who say, 'Whoever swears by the temple is bound by nothing. But whoever swears by the gold of the temple is bound by the oath.' Blind fools! Which is greater, the gold or the temple that makes the gold sacred? And, 'Whoever swears by the altar is bound by nothing. But if anyone swears by the gift on it he is bound by the oath.' You are blind! For which is greater, the gift or the altar that makes the gift sacred? So whoever swears by the altar swears by it and by everything on it. And whoever swears by the temple swears by it and the one who dwells in it. And whoever swears by heaven swears by the throne of God and the one who sits on it. Matthew 23:16-22

Woe 4

"Woe to you, experts in the law and you Pharisees, hypocrites! You give a tenth of mint, dill, and cumin, yet you neglect what is more important in the law-justice, mercy, and faithfulness! You should have done these things without neglecting the others. Blind guides! You strain out a gnat yet swallow a camel! Matthew 23:23-24

Woe 5

"Woe to you, experts in the law and you Pharisees, hypocrites! You clean the outside of the cup and the dish, but inside they are full of greed and self-indulgence. Blind Pharisee! First clean the inside of the cup, so that the outside may become clean too! Matthew 23:25-26

Woe 6

"Woe to you, experts in the law and you Pharisees, hypocrites! You are like whitewashed tombs that look beautiful on the outside but inside are full of the bones of the dead and of everything unclean. In the same way, on the outside you look righteous to people, but inside you are full of hypocrisy and lawlessness. Matthew 23:27-28

Woe 7

"Woe to you, experts in the law and you Pharisees, hypocrites! You build tombs for the prophets and decorate the graves of the righteous. And you say, 'If we had lived in the days of our ancestors, we would not have participated with them in shedding the blood of the prophets.' By saying this you testify against yourselves that you are descendants of those who murdered the prophets. Fill up then the measure of your ancestors! You snakes, you offspring of vipers! How will you escape being condemned to hell? "For this reason I am sending you prophets and wise men and

experts in the law, some of whom you will kill and crucify, and some
you will flog in your synagogues and pursue from town to town, so that
on you will come all the righteous blood shed on earth, from the blood
of righteous Abel to the blood of Zechariah son of Barachiah, whom you
murdered between the temple and the altar. I tell you the truth, this
generation will be held responsible for all these things! Matthew 23:29-36

The religious elite were supposed to be the shepherds of the Jewish people, yet had failed for hundreds of years. Jesus felt that failure deeply.

"O Jerusalem, Jerusalem, you who kill the prophets and stone those
who are sent to you! How often I have longed to gather your children
together as a hen gathers her chicks under her wings, but you would
have none of it! Look, your house is left to you desolate! For I tell
you, you will not see me from now until you say, 'Blessed is the
one who comes in the name of the Lord!'" Matthew 23:37-39

The widows gift

The comparison between the confrontation Jesus had with the elites
and what He does now is breath taking. Jesus has just lambasted the
rulers with His disciples and the crowds of people in attendance. Now
Jesus rests and turns His attention to the giving in the Temple of the
tithes and offerings. In the Temple there was a chest with a hole in it
where people deposited their ten percent tithe. Jesus was watching,
but not in the way we watch events. Jesus was looking through people
into their hearts and motivations. What He saw was people giving out
of their wealth with no sacrifice involved, until He saw a poor widow.
Jesus was so moved He called His disciples over to explain this singu-
lar act of sacrificial giving, a poor widow giving everything she had,
her last coin (the veritable widow's mite). Trust Jesus who would give
everything He had on the cross for us, to point out a widow who gave
out of her poverty everything she had. Something tells me such faithfulness did not go unrewarded.

Then he sat down opposite the offering box, and watched the crowd putting coins into it. Many rich people were throwing in large amounts. And a poor widow came and put in two small copper coins, worth less than a penny. He called his disciples and said to them, "I tell you the truth, this poor widow has put more into the offering box than all the others. For they all gave out of their wealth. But she, out of her poverty, put in what she had to live on, everything she had." Mark 12:41-44

Jesus looked up and saw the rich putting their gifts into the offering box. He also saw a poor widow put in two small copper coins. He said, "I tell you the truth, this poor widow has put in more than all of them. For they all offered their gifts out of their wealth. But she, out of her poverty, put in everything she had to live on." Luke 21:1-4

Discourse on the end times

Jesus now leaves the Temple, probably back towards Bethany across the Kidron Valley and up to the Mount of Olives. From this vantage point you have a stunning view of the Temple Mount built by Herod the Great with the massive kotel stones and the magnificent Temple itself. As the sun was setting the light reflecting off the golden exterior would have been breath taking. Jesus uses this sight to engage in a lengthy discourse with the disciples as they walk forty-five minutes back to their lodging (presumably in Bethany). A discussion that starts in wonder at the large limestone blocks that built the Temple and ends in shock and awe at what the end times look like when Jesus returns in power to reclaim the world. This discourse is broken into three sections: the end times; five parables on keeping watch and being faithful, and a look at the final judgement. The end times section is further divided into five parts:

View of the Temple Mount from the Mount of Olives. Photo courtesy of the Hon Stuart Robert

- Introduction. A quick interlude into the end times that includes both the Temple's destruction in 70 AD and then the future end of the world.
- Beginning of birth pains. What comes prior to the ultimate end of the world.
- Abomination that causes desolation. Pointing to a sign, last seen in the Maccabean revolt when Antiochus IV Epiphanes, the eighth Hellenistic Greek King of the Seleucid Empire from 175 BC until his death in 164 BC devastated Jerusalem in 168 BC. He defiled the Temple by offering a pig on its altar and erecting an altar to Jupiter, prohibited Temple worship, forbade circumcision on pain of death, sold thousands of Jewish families into slavery, destroyed all copies of scripture that could be found, and slaughtered everyone discov-

ered in possession of such copies, and resorted to every conceivable torture to force Jews to renounce their religion[32].
- Second coming of Jesus. What occurs when Jesus returns.
- Sign of the end times. Signs to look out for that herald the end times.

The five 'Be' parables all deal with being cognisant that the end will come and Jesus is looking for spirit filled believers who will be found doing the Master's work when He returns:

- Be watchful
- Be on guard
- Be careful
- Be wise
- Be faithful

The final section is a glimpse on the judgement of the world after Jesus returns.

Introduction

Now as Jesus was going out of the temple courts and walking away, his disciples came to show him the temple buildings. And he said to them, "Do you see all these things? I tell you the truth, not one stone will be left on another. All will be torn down!" As he was sitting on the Mount of Olives, his disciples came to him privately and said, "Tell us, when will these things happen? And what will be the sign of your coming and of the end of the age?" Matthew 24:1-3

Now as Jesus was going out of the temple courts, one of his disciples said to him, "Teacher, look at these tremendous stones and buildings!" Jesus

---

[32] http://www.bible-history.com/archaeology/greece/2-antiochus-iv-bust-bb.html, accessed on 1 Feb 2017.

said to him, "Do you see these great buildings? Not one stone will be left on another. All will be torn down!" So while he was sitting on the Mount of Olives opposite the temple, Peter, James, John, and Andrew asked him privately, "Tell us, when will these things happen? And what will be the sign that all these things are about to take place?" Mark 13:1-4

Now while some were speaking about the temple, how it was adorned with beautiful stones and offerings, Jesus said, "As for these things that you are gazing at, the days will come when not one stone will be left on another. All will be torn down!" So they asked him, "Teacher, when will these things happen? And what will be the sign that these things are about to take place?" Luke 21:5-7

Beginning of birth pains

Jesus answered them, "Watch out that no one misleads you. For many will come in my name, saying, 'I am the Christ,' and they will mislead many. You will hear of wars and rumors of wars. Make sure that you are not alarmed, for this must happen, but the end is still to come. For nation will rise up in arms against nation, and kingdom against kingdom. And there will be famines and earthquakes in various places. All these things are the beginning of birth pains. "Then they will hand you over to be persecuted and will kill you. You will be hated by all the nations because of my name. Then many will be led into sin, and they will betray one another and hate one another. And many false prophets will appear and deceive many, and because lawlessness will increase so much, the love of many will grow cold. But the person who endures to the end will be saved. And this gospel of the kingdom will be preached throughout the whole inhabited earth as a testimony to all the nations, and then the end will come. Matthew 24:4-14

Jesus began to say to them, "Watch out that no one misleads you. Many will come in my name, saying, 'I am he,' and they will mislead many.

When you hear of wars and rumors of wars, do not be alarmed. These things must happen, but the end is still to come. For nation will rise up in arms against nation, and kingdom against kingdom. There will be earthquakes in various places, and there will be famines. These are but the beginning of birth pains. "You must watch out for yourselves. You will be handed over to councils and beaten in the synagogues. You will stand before governors and kings because of me, as a witness to them. First the gospel must be preached to all nations. When they arrest you and hand you over for trial, do not worry about what to speak. But say whatever is given you at that time, for it is not you speaking, but the Holy Spirit. Brother will hand over brother to death, and a father his child. Children will rise against parents and have them put to death. You will be hated by everyone because of my name. But the one who endures to the end will be saved. Mark 13:5-13

He said, "Watch out that you are not misled. For many will come in my name, saying, 'I am he,' and, 'The time is near.' Do not follow them! And when you hear of wars and rebellions, do not be afraid. For these things must happen first, but the end will not come at once." Then he said to them, "Nation will rise up in arms against nation, and kingdom against kingdom. There will be great earthquakes, and famines and plagues in various places, and there will be terrifying sights and great signs from heaven. But before all this, they will seize you and persecute you, handing you over to the synagogues and prisons. You will be brought before kings and governors because of my name. This will be a time for you to serve as witnesses. Therefore be resolved not to rehearse ahead of time how to make your defense. For I will give you the words along with the wisdom that none of your adversaries will be able to withstand or contradict. You will be betrayed even by parents, brothers, relatives, and friends, and they will have some of you put to death. You will be hated by everyone because of my name. Yet not a hair of your head will perish. By your endurance you will gain your lives. Luke 21:8-19

Abomination that causes desolation

"So when you see the abomination of desolation-spoken about by Daniel the prophet-standing in the holy place" (let the reader understand), "then those in Judea must flee to the mountains. The one on the roof must not come down to take anything out of his house, and the one in the field must not turn back to get his cloak. Woe to those who are pregnant and to those who are nursing their babies in those days! Pray that your flight may not be in winter or on a Sabbath. For then there will be great suffering unlike anything that has happened from the beginning of the world until now, or ever will happen. And if those days had not been cut short, no one would be saved. But for the sake of the elect those days will be cut short. Then if anyone says to you, 'Look, here is the Christ!' or 'There he is!' do not believe him. For false messiahs and false prophets will appear and perform great signs and wonders to deceive, if possible, even the elect. Remember, I have told you ahead of time. So then, if someone says to you, 'Look, he is in the wilderness,' do not go out, or 'Look, he is in the inner rooms,' do not believe him. For just like the lightning comes from the east and flashes to the west, so the coming of the Son of Man will be. Wherever the corpse is, there the vultures will gather. Matthew 24:15-28

"But when you see the abomination of desolation standing where it should not be" (let the reader understand), "then those in Judea must flee to the mountains. The one on the roof must not come down or go inside to take anything out of his house. The one in the field must not turn back to get his cloak. Woe to those who are pregnant and to those who are nursing their babies in those days! Pray that it may not be in winter. For in those days there will be suffering unlike anything that has happened from the beginning of the creation that God created until now, or ever will happen. And if the Lord had not cut short those days, no one would be saved. But because of the elect, whom he chose, he has cut them short. Then if anyone says to you, 'Look, here is the Christ!' or 'Look, there he is!' do not believe him. For false messiahs and false prophets will

appear and perform signs and wonders to deceive, if possible, the elect. Be careful! I have told you everything ahead of time. Mark 13:14-23

"But when you see Jerusalem surrounded by armies, then know that its desolation has come near. Then those who are in Judea must flee to the mountains. Those who are inside the city must depart. Those who are out in the country must not enter it, because these are days of vengeance, to fulfill all that is written. Woe to those who are pregnant and to those who are nursing their babies in those days! For there will be great distress on the earth and wrath against this people. They will fall by the edge of the sword and be led away as captives among all nations. Jerusalem will be trampled down by the Gentiles until the times of the Gentiles are fulfilled. Luke 21:20-24

Second coming of Jesus

"Immediately after the suffering of those days, the sun will be darkened, and the moon will not give its light; the stars will fall from heaven, and the powers of heaven will be shaken. Then the sign of the Son of Man will appear in heaven, and all the tribes of the earth will mourn. They will see the Son of Man arriving on the clouds of heaven with power and great glory. And he will send his angels with a loud trumpet blast, and they will gather his elect from the four winds, from one end of heaven to the other. Matthew 24:29-31

"But in those days, after that suffering, the sun will be darkened and the moon will not give its light;the stars will be falling from heaven, and the powers in the heavens will be shaken. Then everyone will see the Son of Man arriving in the clouds with great power and glory. Then he will send angels and they will gather his elect from the four winds, from the ends of the earth to the ends of heaven. Mark 13:24-27

"And there will be signs in the sun and moon and stars, and on the earth nations will be in distress, anxious over the roaring of the sea and the surging waves. People will be fainting from fear and from the expectation of what is coming on the world, for the powers of the heavens will be shaken. Then they will see the Son of Man arriving in a cloud with power and great glory. Luke 21:25-27

Signs of the end times

"Learn this parable from the fig tree: Whenever its branch becomes tender and puts out its leaves, you know that summer is near. So also you, when you see all these things, know that he is near, right at the door. I tell you the truth, this generation will not pass away until all these things take place. Heaven and earth will pass away, but my words will never pass away. "But as for that day and hour no one knows it-not even the angels in heaven-except the Father alone. For just like the days of Noah were, so the coming of the Son of Man will be. For in those days before the flood, people were eating and drinking, marrying and giving in marriage, until the day Noah entered the ark. And they knew nothing until the flood came and took them all away. It will be the same at the coming of the Son of Man. Then there will be two men in the field; one will be taken and one left. There will be two women grinding grain with a mill; one will be taken and one left. Matthew 24:32-41

"Learn this parable from the fig tree: Whenever its branch becomes tender and puts out its leaves, you know that summer is near. So also you, when you see these things happening, know that he is near, right at the door. I tell you the truth, this generation will not pass away until all these things take place. Heaven and earth will pass away, but my words will never pass away. "But as for that day or hour no one knows it-neither the angels in heaven, nor the Son-except the Father. Mark 13:28-32

But when these things begin to happen, stand up and raise your heads, because your redemption is drawing near." Then he told them a parable: "Look at the fig tree and all the other trees. When they sprout leaves, you see for yourselves and know that summer is now near. So also you, when you see these things happening, know that the kingdom of God is near. I tell you the truth, this generation will not pass away until all these things take place. Heaven and earth will pass away, but my words will never pass away. Luke 21:28-33

Five 'Be' parables
Parable 1 - Be watchful

"Therefore stay alert, because you do not know on what day your Lord will come. But understand this: If the owner of the house had known at what time of night the thief was coming, he would have been alert and would not have let his house be broken into. Therefore you also must be ready, because the Son of Man will come at an hour when you do not expect him. "Who then is the faithful and wise slave, whom the master has put in charge of his household, to give the other slaves their food at the proper time? Blessed is that slave whom the master finds at work when he comes. I tell you the truth, the master will put him in charge of all his possessions. But if that evil slave should say to himself, 'My master is staying away a long time,' and he begins to beat his fellow slaves and to eat and drink with drunkards, then the master of that slave will come on a day when he does not expect him and at an hour he does not foresee, and will cut him in two, and assign him a place with the hypocrites, where there will be weeping and gnashing of teeth. Matthew 24:42-51

Parable 2 - Be on guard

Watch out! Stay alert! For you do not know when the time will come. It is like a man going on a journey. He left his house and put his slaves in charge, assigning to each his work, and commanded the doorkeeper to stay alert. Stay alert, then, because you do not know when the owner of the house will return-whether during evening, at midnight, when the rooster crows, or at dawn – or else he might find you asleep when he returns suddenly. What I say to you I say to everyone: Stay alert!" Mark 13:33-37

Parable 3 - Be careful

"But be on your guard so that your hearts are not weighed down with dissipation and drunkenness and the worries of this life, and that day close down upon you suddenly like a trap. For it will overtake all who live on the face of the whole earth. But stay alert at all times, praying that you may have strength to escape all these things that must happen, and to stand before the Son of Man." Luke 21:34-36

Parable 4 - Be wise

"At that time the kingdom of heaven will be like ten virgins who took their lamps and went out to meet the bridegroom. Five of the virgins were foolish, and five were wise. When the foolish ones took their lamps, they did not take extra olive oil with them. But the wise ones took flasks of olive oil with their lamps. When the bridegroom was delayed a long time, they all became drowsy and fell asleep. But at midnight there was a shout, 'Look, the bridegroom is here! Come out to meet him.' Then all the virgins woke up and trimmed their lamps. The foolish ones said to the wise, 'Give us some of your oil, because our lamps are going out.' No,' they replied. 'There won't be enough for you and for us. Go instead to those who sell oil and buy some for yourselves.' But while they had gone to buy it, the bridegroom arrived, and those who were ready went inside with him to the wedding banquet. Then the door was shut. Later, the other virgins came too, saying, 'Lord, lord! Let

us in!' But he replied, 'I tell you the truth, I do not know you!' Therefore stay alert, because you do not know the day or the hour. Matthew 25:1-13

Parable 5 - Be faithful

"For it is like a man going on a journey, who summoned his slaves and entrusted his property to them. To one he gave five talents, to another two, and to another one, each according to his ability. Then he went on his journey. The one who had received five talents went off right away and put his money to work and gained five more. In the same way, the one who had two gained two more. But the one who had received one talent went out and dug a hole in the ground and hid his master's money in it. After a long time, the master of those slaves came and settled his accounts with them. The one who had received the five talents came and brought five more, saying, 'Sir, you entrusted me with five talents. See, I have gained five more.' His master answered, 'Well done, good and faithful slave! You have been faithful in a few things. I will put you in charge of many things. Enter into the joy of your master.' The one with the two talents also came and said, 'Sir, you entrusted two talents to me. See, I have gained two more.' His master answered, 'Well done, good and faithful slave! You have been faithful with a few things. I will put you in charge of many things. Enter into the joy of your master.' Then the one who had received the one talent came and said, 'Sir, I knew that you were a hard man, harvesting where you did not sow, and gathering where you did not scatter seed, so I was afraid, and I went and hid your talent in the ground. See, you have what is yours.' But his master answered, 'Evil and lazy slave! So you knew that I harvest where I didn't sow and gather where I didn't scatter? Then you should have deposited my money with the bankers, and on my return I would have received my money back with interest! Therefore take the talent from him and give it to the one who has ten. For the one who has will be given more, and he will have more than enough. But the one who does not have, even what he has will be

taken from him. And throw that worthless slave into the outer darkness, where there will be weeping and gnashing of teeth." Matthew 25:14-30

Judgement at the second coming of Jesus

"When the Son of Man comes in his glory and all the angels with him, then he will sit on his glorious throne. All the nations will be assembled before him, and he will separate people one from another like a shepherd separates the sheep from the goats. He will put the sheep on his right and the goats on his left. Then the king will say to those on his right, 'Come, you who are blessed by my Father, inherit the kingdom prepared for you from the foundation of the world. For I was hungry and you gave me food, I was thirsty and you gave me something to drink, I was a stranger and you invited me in, I was naked and you gave me clothing, I was sick and you took care of me, I was in prison and you visited me.' Then the righteous will answer him, 'Lord, when did we see you hungry and feed you, or thirsty and give you something to drink? When did we see you a stranger and invite you in, or naked and clothe you? When did we see you sick or in prison and visit you?' And the king will answer them, 'I tell you the truth, just as you did it for one of the least of these brothers or sisters of mine, you did it for me.' "Then he will say to those on his left, 'Depart from me, you accursed, into the eternal fire that has been prepared for the devil and his angels! For I was hungry and you gave me nothing to eat, I was thirsty and you gave me nothing to drink. I was a stranger and you did not receive me as a guest, naked and you did not clothe me, sick and in prison and you did not visit me.' Then they too will answer, 'Lord, when did we see you hungry or thirsty or a stranger or naked or sick or in prison, and did not give you whatever you needed?' Then he will answer them, 'I tell you the truth, just as you did not do it for one of the least of these, you did not do it for me.' And these will depart into eternal punishment, but the righteous into eternal life." Matthew 25:31-46

When Jesus had finished saying all these things, he told his disciples, "You know that after two days the Passover is coming, and the Son of Man will be handed over to be crucified." Matthew 26:1-2

CHAPTER 12

Passover
(Wednesday 1st - Thursday 2nd April 33 AD)

Jesus and his disciples again overnighted on the Mount of Olives, either out in the open or more likely in Bethany, on the eastern side of the mountain, thus still technically on the mountain. Considering the last few nights Jesus had gone back to Bethany, it is reasonable to conclude He did so again this time.

It is once again dawn and odds are Jesus rose early to pray before breakfast. It is Wednesday, the day before the first day of the Feast of Unleavened Bread. Tomorrow night the Jews, including Jesus, would celebrate the Passover and Jesus would be arrested. Devout families would take the little lamb that had been playing in their homes for the past two days, as required by the law outlined in Exodus below, and would slaughter it and eat it as a family to remember the miracle of God rescuing the ancient Jewish people from Egypt.

Tell the whole community of Israel, 'In the tenth day of this month they each must take a lamb for themselves according to their families-a lamb for each household. If any household is too small for a lamb, the man and his next-door neighbor are to take a lamb according to the number of people-you will make your count for the lamb according to how much each one can eat. Your lamb must be perfect, a male, one year old; you may take it from the sheep or from the goats. You must care for it until the fourteenth day of this month, and then the whole community of Israel will kill it around sundown. Exodus 12:3-6

But today and tomorrow the lamb still plays in the Jewish houses and the lamb of God still reaches out to the people.

As was the practice of the last few days, Jesus heads to the Temple early to teach the people. I'm still hopeful Lazarus cooked breakfast and Martha sat with Mary at the feet of Jesus.

So every day Jesus was teaching in the temple courts, but at night he went and stayed on the Mount of Olives. And all the people came to him early in the morning to listen to him in the temple courts. Luke 21:37-38

A Grecian interlude

There is a marvellous interlude at the end of the final week, where foreigners who came to see Jesus were not turned away but were included. Just like when Jesus went to the Samaritans, the Phoenicians, the Romans and the pagans in the Decapolis east of the Jordan River, Jesus now includes the Greeks who had travelled from even further afield. The message is the same, grace is freely available to all, to every person even to the very ends of the earth. It is a final message to all the people of the world, reinforced at Pentecost fifty days later, that the salvation found in the New Covenant is for everyone.

Evidently Philip didn't feel comfortable asking Jesus if the Greeks could say hello, so he went to Andrew (Peter's brother) and then both Philip and Andrew came to ask Jesus. It appears that even at this late stage, Philip still didn't believe that salvation was available to such as the Greeks.

Now some Greeks were among those who had gone up to worship at the feast. So these approached Philip, who was from Bethsaida in Galilee, and requested, "Sir, we would like to see Jesus." Philip went and told Andrew, and they both went and told Jesus. John 12:20-22

Jesus final discourse – foretelling His death to the crowd in the Temple

Jesus responds to the request at this late hour by delivering His final public discourse that is authenticated with the audible voice of God Himself from heaven. There is a crowd listening that included Jews and Gentiles, Israelites and Greeks. It is a picture of inclusion, of all people being there at the final discourse, the final public word from heaven, the moment Jesus talks publicly of the cross. This word from heaven is the final public teaching of Jesus. From this moment, Jesus will withdraw to Bethany and will venture to Jerusalem only the following evening for the Passover dinner.

Jesus replied, "The time has come for the Son of Man to be glorified. I tell you the solemn truth, unless a kernel of wheat falls into the ground and dies, it remains by itself alone. But if it dies, it produces much grain. The one who loves his life destroys it, and the one who hates his life in this world guards it for eternal life. If anyone wants to serve me, he must follow me, and where I am, my servant will be too. If anyone serves me, the Father will honor him. "Now my soul is greatly distressed. And what should I say? 'Father, deliver me from this hour'? No, but for this very reason I have come to this hour. Father, glorify your name." Then a voice came from heaven, "I have glorified it, and I will glorify it again." The crowd that stood there and heard the voice said that it had thundered. Others said that an angel had spoken to him. Jesus said, "This voice has not come for my benefit but for yours. Now is the judgment of this world; now the ruler of this world will be driven out. And I, when I am lifted up from the earth, will draw all people to myself." (Now he said this to indicate clearly what kind of death he was going to die.) Then the crowd responded, "We have heard from the law that the Christ will remain forever. How can you say, 'The Son of Man must be lifted up'? Who is this Son of Man?" Jesus replied, "The light is with you for a little while longer. Walk while you have the light, so that the darkness may not overtake you. The one who walks in the darkness does not know where he is going. While you have the light, believe in the light, so that you may become sons of light." John 12:23-36a

When Jesus had said these things, he went away and hid himself from them. Although Jesus had performed so many miraculous signs before them, they still refused to believe in him, so that the word of Isaiah the prophet would be fulfilled. He said, "Lord, who has believed our message, and to whom has the arm of the Lord been revealed?" For this reason they could not believe, because again Isaiah said, "He has blinded their eyes and hardened their heart, so that they would not see with their eyes and understand with their heart, and turn to me, and I would heal them." Isaiah said these things because he saw Christ's glory, and spoke about him. Nevertheless, even among the rulers many believed in him, but because of the Pharisees they would not confess Jesus to be the Christ, so that they would not be put out of the synagogue. For they loved praise from men more than praise from God. But Jesus shouted out, "The one who believes in me does not believe in me, but in the one who sent me, and the one who sees me sees the one who sent me. I have come as a light into the world, so that everyone who believes in me should not remain in darkness. If anyone hears my words and does not obey them, I do not judge him. For I have not come to judge the world, but to save the world. The one who rejects me and does not accept my words has a judge; the word I have spoken will judge him at the last day. For I have not spoken from my own authority, but the Father himself who sent me has commanded me what I should say and what I should speak. And I know that his commandment is eternal life. Thus the things I say, I say just as the Father has told me." John 12:36b-50

The religious elite move in

Whilst Jesus was including everyone in His salvation offered by grace, the religious elite were behind closed doors plotting murder. It appears they were at a loose end as to how to arrest Jesus as they couldn't anticipate His movements to arrest Him secretly.

Then the chief priests and the elders of the people met together in the palace of the high priest, who was named Caiaphas. They planned to arrest Jesus by stealth and kill him. But they said, "Not during the feast, so that there won't be a riot among the people." Matthew 26:3-5

Two days before the Passover and the Feast of Unleavened Bread, the chief priests and the experts in the law were trying to find a way to arrest Jesus by stealth and kill him. For they said, "Not during the feast, so there won't be a riot among the people." Mark 14:1-2

Now the Feast of Unleavened Bread, which is called the Passover, was approaching. The chief priests and the experts in the law were trying to find some way to execute Jesus, for they were afraid of the people. Luke 22:1-2

This was until one of the disciples, Judas offered up Jesus for money. Judas, who had travelled the last few years with Jesus. Judas who had gone out in one of the pairs of disciples teaching, healing and restoring. Judas who had watched Jesus raise people from the dead and cast out the demonic. Judas, the lone disciple from Judea agreed to betray Jesus for money.

Then one of the twelve, the one named Judas Iscariot, went to the chief priests and said, "What will you give me to betray him into your hands?" So they set out thirty silver coins for him. From that time on, Judas began looking for an opportunity to betray him. Matthew 26:14-16

Then Satan entered Judas, the one called Iscariot, who was one of the twelve. He went away and discussed with the chief priests and officers of the temple guard how he might betray Jesus, handing him over to them. They were delighted and arranged to give him money. So Judas agreed and began looking for an opportunity to betray Jesus when no crowd was present. Luke 22:3-6

Then Judas Iscariot, one of the twelve, went to the chief priests to betray Jesus into their hands. When they heard this, they were delighted and promised to give him money. So Judas began looking for an opportunity to betray him. Mark 14:10-11

So Wednesday draws to a close and with it Jesus' teaching of the people and responding to and rebuking of the religious elite. Jesus had entered Jerusalem on Sunday and then spent the next three days teaching in the Temple. He has presented, argued and passionately pleaded. He has countered every attack, responded to every aspect of the law, included every race of people in the city and talked openly about the future of the world. Here ends His public ministry in the Temple.

From here satan has some control over Judas who subsequently offered to sell out the Son of God, to show the religious elite where they could arrest Jesus outside of the Temple. Those charged with protecting the flock now become the wolves as they seek to murder Jesus. The people are blessed, the elite are cursed and tomorrow is the preparation day for the Passover.

The following day, Thursday 2nd April 33 AD, would start with the disciples asking Jesus about where He would like to eat the Passover meal. Presumably Jesus and His disciples would have been invited by Mary, Martha and Lazarus to share Passover at their home, that would have been customary. Surely that is the least Lazarus could offer since Jesus raised him from the dead. Apparently Jesus had other ideas that involved a large room and just the disciples, for Jesus to break bread with for the very last time.

What did Jesus do all day whilst two of His disciples sorted out the Passover? Nothing is recorded. It is fair to say He prayed and rested and maybe played with the little lamb running freely in the home of Mary, Martha and Lazarus before it became dinner. The ultimate lamb of God gently holding the little lamb. I'd like to think that before ushering in the New Covenant of Grace, of unmerited, undeserved favour, of a light yoke, of rest in the finished work of the cross, I can see the Saviour resting in the love of the Father.

Preparations for the last supper

On this day of preparation for the Passover, the two disciples closest to Jesus, Peter and John were sent to a divine appointment in the walled city of Jerusalem. The two disciples who represent the Old and New Covenants were sent to organise the Passover where the Old would be fulfilled and the New Covenant announced. Peter who boasted of his love for Jesus, his work (Old Covenant) and John who boasted of Jesus' love for him, Jesus' work (New Covenant). It is a beautiful picture of both covenants walking into Jerusalem where that evening one would be fulfilled and the new commenced.

First thing was the divine appointment to chat to an unnamed man carrying a water jar who led them to another unnamed man who owned a house with an upstairs room. This man would then be led by the Spirit of God to prepare everything for the Passover meal.

Many people in scripture are led by the Spirit of God and they generally have a name, think Ananias from Straight Street in Damascus who was sent to the Apostle Paul (Acts 9:10-17). At this critical juncture, the last supper of Jesus where communion, the bread and wine, is given to symbolise the New Covenant, there is no name for the host. There is no distraction from the crucial event of what Jesus will do. This man is known only to eternity, and like Mary, where the gospel is preached, the actions of this man will be told.

It is reasonable to assume that the upstairs room was within the walls of the city of Jerusalem. It would be strange for a man carrying a jar of water to leave Jerusalem and walk to another town close by that would have had its own water source. Thus the upstairs room was probably in Jerusalem, with the historical site being on Mount Zion.

Historically 'Zion' was the name given to the City of David (Jerusalem) in the book of Samuel, when David conquered the city from the Jebusites, and the word is still used to refer to Jerusalem as a whole. In the time of Samuel, the city was built on the lower reaches of Jerusalem's eastern hill, where King David would build his palace.

But David captured the fortress of Zion (that
is, the City of David). 2 Samuel 5:7

From this early mention, Zion is mentioned another 164 times in the Bible. Over time Jerusalem grew to include the northern reaches of the eastern hill where the Temple was eventually built on Mount Moriah. The term Zion then migrated north to include the Temple area. The city further expanded over time across the Tyropean Valley or Valley of the Cheesemakers to include the western hill and in the time of Jesus this hill was known as Mount Zion[33]. The Tyropean valley, as seen in this 1858 map, joined the Hinnom valley. Herod's massive platform, on which 'Herod's Temple' stood, with its over 130 feet high walls started at the bottom of the Tyropean valley, and a number of bridges crossed over the valley from the western hill to the Temple mount for ease of access. One of those bridges was called the 'Zion Bridge.'

---

[33] Name given to this valley between Mount Moriah ands Zion by Josephus in his books 'Wars of the Jews' 5.140

ANCIENT JERUSALEM.

Map of Jerusalem, published in 1858 by J. T. Barclay
in the book City of the Great King, p. 56.

*Now on the first day of the feast of Unleavened Bread the disciples
came to Jesus and said, "Where do you want us to prepare for you to
eat the Passover?" He said, "Go into the city to a certain man and tell
him, 'The Teacher says, "My time is near. I will observe the Passover
with my disciples at your house."'" So the disciples did as Jesus had
instructed them, and they prepared the Passover. Matthew 26:17-19*

*Now on the first day of the feast of Unleavened Bread, when the
Passover lamb is sacrificed, Jesus' disciples said to him, "Where do*

333

you want us to prepare for you to eat the Passover?" He sent two of his disciples and told them, "Go into the city, and a man carrying a jar of water will meet you. Follow him. Wherever he enters, tell the owner of the house, 'The Teacher says, "Where is my guest room where I may eat the Passover with my disciples?"' He will show you a large room upstairs, furnished and ready. Make preparations for us there." So the disciples left, went into the city, and found things just as he had told them, and they prepared the Passover. Mark 14:12-16

Then the day for the feast of Unleavened Bread came, on which the Passover lamb had to be sacrificed. Jesus sent Peter and John, saying, "Go and prepare the Passover for us to eat." They said to him, "Where do you want us to prepare it?" He said to them, "Listen, when you have entered the city, a man carrying a jar of water will meet you. Follow him into the house that he enters, and tell the owner of the house, 'The Teacher says to you, "Where is the guest room where I may eat the Passover with my disciples?"' Then he will show you a large furnished room upstairs. Make preparations there." So they went and found things just as he had told them, and they prepared the Passover. Luke 22:7-13

The last supper

Before dark, Jesus and His disciples leave Bethany for the last time. I can imagine there would have been some hugs all round. Jesus knew He would not see Mary, Martha and Lazarus all together again prior to His resurrection. They would have walked the three kilometres towards Jerusalem as the setting sun struck the magnificent Temple sending its light reflecting in all directions. By dusk they would have entered the city, greeted the unnamed host and walked upstairs to the Passover meal. The host's family and servants would have served Jesus and His disciples and it is probable that the host celebrated the Passover downstairs with His own family.

There is a part of me that sees this godly humble family in their home, so humble that their name is not recorded in scripture yet they served the King of Kings His last meal. This little family that themselves broke bread that night and ate the Passover lamb whilst serving Jesus upstairs, the final, completed, fulfilled Passover lamb for the sins of the world. What faithfulness is rewarded with such honour?

When it was evening, he took his place at the table with the twelve. Matthew 26:20

Then, when it was evening, he came to the house with the twelve. Mark 14:17

Now when the hour came, Jesus took his place at the table and the apostles joined him. And he said to them, "I have earnestly desired to eat this Passover with you before I suffer. For I tell you, I will not eat it again until it is fulfilled in the kingdom of God." Luke 22:14-16

There is something authentic about what follows next because it is so human. Jesus has just told the disciples that He wanted to share one last meal before He would suffer and die and the disciples response is to argue over who is the greatest. Unfathomable I know! I don't know if Jesus rolled His eyes, but that would have been a fair response. Such is the grace of Jesus, that He uses the moment to both teach and then encourage. The basin and the towel have become such a powerful metaphor for service because Jesus used it in this moment. The disciple's dusty dirty feet were washed by Jesus after they argued about who is the greatest. Jesus showed them true greatness is through service and if service is beneath you, leadership is beyond you.

A dispute also started among them over which of them was to be regarded as the greatest. So Jesus said to them, "The kings of the Gentiles lord it over them, and those in authority over them are called 'benefactors.'

Not so with you; instead the one who is greatest among you must become like the youngest, and the leader like the one who serves. For who is greater, the one who is seated at the table, or the one who serves? Is it not the one who is seated at the table? But I am among you as one who serves." You are the ones who have remained with me in my trials. Thus I grant to you a kingdom, just as my Father granted to me, that you may eat and drink at my table in my kingdom, and you will sit on thrones judging the twelve tribes of Israel. Luke 22:24-30

Just before the Passover feast, Jesus knew that his time had come to depart from this world to the Father. Having loved his own who were in the world, he now loved them to the very end. The evening meal was in progress, and the devil had already put into the heart of Judas Iscariot, Simon's son, that he should betray Jesus. Because Jesus knew that the Father had handed all things over to him, and that he had come from God and was going back to God, he got up from the meal, removed his outer clothes, took a towel and tied it around himself. He poured water into the washbasin and began to wash the disciples' feet and to dry them with the towel he had wrapped around himself. Then he came to Simon Peter. Peter said to him, "Lord, are you going to wash my feet?" Jesus replied, "You do not understand what I am doing now, but you will understand after these things." Peter said to him, "You will never wash my feet!" Jesus replied, "If I do not wash you, you have no share with me." Simon Peter said to him, "Lord, wash not only my feet, but also my hands and my head!" Jesus replied, "The one who has bathed needs only to wash his feet, but is completely clean. And you disciples are clean, but not every one of you." (For Jesus knew the one who was going to betray him. For this reason he said, "Not every one of you is clean.") So when Jesus had washed their feet and put his outer clothing back on, he took his place at the table again and said to them, "Do you understand what I have done for you? You call me 'Teacher' and 'Lord,' and do so correctly, for that is what I am. If I then, your Lord and Teacher, have washed your feet, you too ought to wash one another's feet. For I have given you an example-you should do just as I have done for you. I tell you the solemn truth, the slave is not greater than his master, nor is the one who is sent as a messenger greater than the one who sent him. If you understand these things, you will be blessed if you do them. "What I am saying does not refer to all of you. I know the ones I have chosen. But this is to fulfill the scripture, 'The one who eats my bread has turned against me.' I am telling you this now, before it happens, so that when it happens you may believe that I am he. I tell you the solemn truth, whoever accepts the one I send accepts me, and whoever accepts me accepts the one who sent me." John 13:1-20

I think supper might have gone a little quiet after this object lesson in leadership and greatness. I think it went quieter still when Jesus spoke of betrayal.

And while they were eating he said, "I tell you the truth, one of you will betray me." They became greatly distressed and each one began to say to him, "Surely not I, Lord?" He answered, "The one who has dipped his hand into the bowl with me will betray me. The Son of Man will go as it is written about him, but woe to that man by whom the Son of Man is betrayed! It would be better for him if he had never been born." Then Judas, the one who would betray him, said, "Surely not I, Rabbi?" Jesus replied, "You have said it yourself." Matthew 26:21-25

While they were at the table eating, Jesus said, "I tell you the truth, one of you eating with me will betray me." They were distressed, and one by one said to him, "Surely not I?" He said to them, "It is one of the twelve, one who dips his hand with me into the bowl. For the Son of Man will go as it is written about him, but woe to that man by whom the Son of Man is betrayed! It would be better for him if he had never been born." Mark 14:18-21

"But look, the hand of the one who betrays me is with me on the table. For the Son of Man is to go just as it has been determined, but woe to that

*man by whom he is betrayed!" So they began to question one another as
to which of them it could possibly be who would do this. Luke 22:21-23*

*When he had said these things, Jesus was greatly distressed in spirit,
and testified, "I tell you the solemn truth, one of you will betray me."
The disciples began to look at one another, worried and perplexed to
know which of them he was talking about. One of his disciples, the one
Jesus loved, was at the table to the right of Jesus in a place of honor.
So Simon Peter gestured to this disciple to ask Jesus who it was he was
referring to. Then the disciple whom Jesus loved leaned back against
Jesus' chest and asked him, "Lord, who is it?" Jesus replied, "It is the
one to whom I will give this piece of bread after I have dipped it in
the dish." Then he dipped the piece of bread in the dish and gave it
to Judas Iscariot, Simon's son. And after Judas took the piece of bread,
Satan entered into him. Jesus said to him, "What you are about to
do, do quickly." (Now none of those present at the table understood
why Jesus said this to Judas. Some thought that, because Judas had the
money box, Jesus was telling him to buy whatever they needed for the
feast, or to give something to the poor.) Judas took the piece of bread
and went out immediately. (Now it was night.) John 13:21-30*

So Judas gets up and leaves dinner. He had already been tempted by
satan to thieve, then to betray Jesus and is now literally possessed by
the prince of darkness. Jesus, who is fully man and fully God, must
have sensed and/or known of the presence of such darkness entering
the room and entering Judas. The disciples apparently did not, though
all of that would change in fifty days at Pentecost when the Holy Spirit
would come upon them.

What an extraordinary dinner.

Jesus has gently but firmly confronted and dealt with the disciples pride,
one of them has betrayed Him and He now points out, prophetically,

that they will all desert Him. This must have been a low point seeing such isolation not just from His friends, but knowing that in a short time, His Father who He has been with for eternity, would shortly turn His back on Him for the first time ever. A mere mortal could be forgiven for thinking of themselves and their trial at this moment. Jesus though is only thinking of us, as He gives a new commandment, 'to love one another as Christ has loved us'.

Another fascinating aside has also occurred to indicate the impending New Covenant that this Passover dinner will introduce. John's gospel, written by John, refers to himself the following five times as the 'disciple whom Jesus loved', with the first reference being at this Passover dinner:

- John 13:23 when he asked Jesus who was going to betray Him,
- John 19:26 when Jesus said this is your mother,
- John 20:2 when Peter and John ran to the empty tomb,
- John 21:7 when Jesus met them at the beach, and
- John 21:20 when Jesus told Peter he'd suffer.

You'd be forgiven for thinking that the disciple John has a few tickets on himself, but in reality he is speaking the truth of the New Covenant. Peter was renowned for speaking of his love for Jesus, his dying with Jesus and his not denying Jesus. Peter spoke of his efforts, his work, his love, all of which he failed at. John only spoke of Jesus' love for him, all of which Jesus succeeded at. A part of me thinks that at this moment, John grasps the truth that it would not be nails that kept Jesus on the cross the following day, it would be His love for all humanity.

When Judas had gone out, Jesus said, "Now the Son of Man is glorified, and God is glorified in him. If God is glorified in him, God will also glorify him in himself, and he will glorify him right away. Children,

I am still with you for a little while. You will look for me, and just as I said to the Jewish religious leaders, 'Where I am going you cannot come,' now I tell you the same. "I give you a new commandment-to love one another. Just as I have loved you, you also are to love one another. Everyone will know by this that you are my disciples-if you have love for one another." Simon Peter said to him, "Lord, where are you going?" Jesus replied, "Where I am going, you cannot follow me now, but you will follow later." Peter said to him, "Lord, why can't I follow you now? I will lay down my life for you!" Jesus answered, "Will you lay down your life for me? I tell you the solemn truth, the rooster will not crow until you have denied me three times! John 13:31-38

Then Jesus said to them, "This night you will all fall away because of me, for it is written: 'I will strike the shepherd, and the sheep of the flock will be scattered.' But after I am raised, I will go ahead of you into Galilee." Peter said to him, "If they all fall away because of you, I will never fall away!" Jesus said to him, "I tell you the truth, on this night, before the rooster crows, you will deny me three times." Peter said to him, "Even if I must die with you, I will never deny you." And all the disciples said the same thing. Matthew 26:31-35

Then Jesus said to them, "You will all fall away, for it is written, 'I will strike the shepherd, and the sheep will be scattered.' But after I am raised, I will go ahead of you into Galilee." Peter said to him, "Even if they all fall away, I will not!" Jesus said to him, "I tell you the truth, today-this very night-before a rooster crows twice, you will deny me three times." But Peter insisted emphatically, "Even if I must die with you, I will never deny you." And all of them said the same thing. Mark 14:27-31

"Simon, Simon, pay attention! Satan has demanded to have you all, to sift you like wheat, but I have prayed for you, Simon, that your faith may not fail. When you have turned back, strengthen your brothers." But Peter said to him, "Lord, I am ready to go with you both to prison and

*to death!" Jesus replied, "I tell you, Peter, the rooster will not crow today
until you have denied three times that you know me." Luke 22:31-34*

*Then Jesus said to them, "When I sent you out with no money bag,
or traveler's bag, or sandals, you didn't lack anything, did you?" They
replied, "Nothing." He said to them, "But now, the one who has a money
bag must take it, and likewise a traveler's bag too. And the one who has
no sword must sell his cloak and buy one. For I tell you that this scripture
must be fulfilled in me, 'And he was counted with the transgressors.' For
what is written about me is being fulfilled." So they said, "Look, Lord,
here are two swords." Then he told them, "It is enough." Luke 22:35-38*

Bread and wine

The Passover meal now reaches its history-dividing penultimate juncture of pointing to the impending cross and the establishment of the New Covenant of Grace. Jesus would take two simple elements that were on the table, bread and wine and use them reflectively to usher in a simple analogous remembrance service. Jesus would break bread to symbolise that His body would be broken so ours could be healed. Jesus would then drink wine to indicate His shed blood would replace the blood of the Passover lamb as the fulfilment of the law and the final sacrifice to reconcile fallen mankind back to God the Father. Jesus would then command that we too break bread and drink wine every time we come together to remember the New Covenant of Grace that is upon us, the unmerited favour that surrounds us and the physical healing available to us through Jesus' sacrifice on the cross.

*While they were eating, he took bread, and after giving thanks
he broke it, gave it to them, and said, "Take it. This is my body."
And after taking the cup and giving thanks, he gave it to them,
and they all drank from it. He said to them, "This is my blood, the
blood of the covenant, that is poured out for many. I tell you the*

truth, I will no longer drink of the fruit of the vine until that day when I drink it new in the kingdom of God." Mark 14:22-25

While they were eating, Jesus took bread, and after giving thanks he broke it, gave it to his disciples, and said, "Take, eat, this is my body." And after taking the cup and giving thanks, he gave it to them, saying, "Drink from it, all of you, for this is my blood, the blood of the covenant, that is poured out for many for the forgiveness of sins. I tell you, from now on I will not drink of this fruit of the vine until that day when I drink it new with you in my Father's kingdom." Matthew 26:26-29

Then he took a cup, and after giving thanks he said, "Take this and divide it among yourselves. For I tell you that from now on I will not drink of the fruit of the vine until the kingdom of God comes." Then he took bread, and after giving thanks he broke it and gave it to them, saying, "This is my body which is given for you. Do this in remembrance of me." And in the same way he took the cup after they had eaten, saying, "This cup that is poured out for you is the new covenant in my blood. Luke 22:17-20

For I received from the Lord what I also passed on to you, that the Lord Jesus on the night in which he was betrayed took bread, and after he had given thanks he broke it and said, "This is my body, which is for you. Do this in remembrance of me." In the same way, he also took the cup after supper, saying, "This cup is the new covenant in my blood. Do this, every time you drink it, in remembrance of me." 1 Corinthians 11:23-25

Jesus' final teaching

Jesus now teaches his disciples for the last time. Final words are always interesting because they reflect perhaps what is most important. In Jesus' final words to His disciples He provides a rich array of comforting truths, teaches three discourses, promises the Holy Spirit, talks of His death and resurrection, promises to answer prayer and provide peace and then ultimately prays for Himself and His disciples. After His final word of prayer, the little party descends down to the Valley of Hinnom and into the Garden of Gethsemane, a distance of less than one kilometre. What an extraordinary dinner.

Jesus' final words are rich in truths and promises that include:

- My Father's house has many rooms.
- I am the way, the truth and the life. No one comes to the Father except through me.
- Anyone who has seen me, has seen the Father.
- I am in the Father and the Father is in me.
- I will do whatever you ask in my name.
- I will ask the Father, and he will give you another advocate to help you and be with you forever.... the Spirit of Truth.
- Because I live, you also will live.
- The Holy Spirit, whom the Father will send in my name, will teach you all things and will remind you of everything I have said to you.
- Peace I leave with you; my peace I give you.
- Do not let your hearts be troubled and do not be afraid.

"Do not let your hearts be distressed. You believe in God; believe also in me. There are many dwelling places in my Father's house. Otherwise, I would have told you, because I am going away to make ready a place for you. And if I go and make ready a place for you, I will come again and take you to be with me, so that where I am you may be too. And you know the way where I am going." Thomas said, "Lord, we don't know where you are going. How can we know the way?" Jesus replied, "I am the way, and the truth, and the life. No one comes to the Father except through me. If you have known me, you will know my Father too. And from now on you do know him and have seen him." Philip said, "Lord, show us the Father, and we will be content." Jesus replied, "Have I been

with you for so long, and you have not known me, Philip? The person who has seen me has seen the Father! How can you say, 'Show us the Father'? Do you not believe that I am in the Father, and the Father is in me? The words that I say to you, I do not speak on my own initiative, but the Father residing in me performs his miraculous deeds. Believe me that I am in the Father, and the Father is in me, but if you do not believe me, believe because of the miraculous deeds themselves. I tell you the solemn truth, the person who believes in me will perform the miraculous deeds that I am doing, and will perform greater deeds than these, because I am going to the Father. And I will do whatever you ask in my name, so that the Father may be glorified in the Son. If you ask me anything in my name, I will do it. "If you love me, you will obey my commandments. Then I will ask the Father, and he will give you another Advocate to be with you forever – the Spirit of truth, whom the world cannot accept, because it does not see him or know him. But you know him, because he resides with you and will be in you."I will not abandon you as orphans, I will come to you. In a little while the world will not see me any longer, but you will see me; because I live, you will live too. You will know at that time that I am in my Father and you are in me and I am in you. The person who has my commandments and obeys them is the one who loves me. The one who loves me will be loved by my Father, and I will love him and will reveal myself to him.""Lord," Judas (not Judas Iscariot) said, "what has happened that you are going to reveal yourself to us and not to the world?" Jesus replied, "If anyone loves me, he will obey my word, and my Father will love him, and we will come to him and take up residence with him. The person who does not love me does not obey my words. And the word you hear is not mine, but the Father's who sent me. "I have spoken these things while staying with you. But the Advocate, the Holy Spirit, whom the Father will send in my name, will teach you everything, and will cause you to remember everything I said to you."Peace I leave with you; my peace I give to you; I do not give it to you as the world does. Do not let your hearts be distressed or lacking in courage. You heard me say to you, 'I am going away and I am coming back to you.' If you loved me, you would be glad that I am going to the Father, because the Father is greater than I am. I have told you now before it happens, so that when it happens you may believe. I will not speak with you much longer, for the ruler of this world is coming. He has no power over me, but I am doing just what the Father commanded me, so that the world may know that I love the Father. Get up, let us go from here. John 14:1-31

Jesus now teaches three discourses that revolve around His impending suffering. The first discourse concerns pruning, often painful, but fruit only grows on pruned vines. The second discourse concerns the ultimate expression of love, that of laying down your life for your friends. The third discourse is on the nature of the world, that it will cause you and I to suffer as Jesus suffered.

Discourse 1 - on the vine

"I am the true vine and my Father is the gardener. He takes away every branch that does not bear fruit in me. He prunes every branch that bears fruit so that it will bear more fruit. You are clean already because of the word that I have spoken to you. Remain in me, and I will remain in you. Just as the branch cannot bear fruit by itself, unless it remains in the vine, so neither can you unless you remain in me. "I am the vine; you are the branches. The one who remains in me-and I in him-bears much fruit, because apart from me you can accomplish nothing. If anyone does not remain in me, he is thrown out like a branch, and dries up; and such branches are gathered up and thrown into the fire, and are burned up. If you remain in me and my words remain in you, ask whatever you want, and it will be done for you. My Father is honored by this, that you bear much fruit and show that you are my disciples. "Just as the Father has loved me, I have also loved you; remain in my love. If you obey my commandments, you will remain in my love, just as I have obeyed my Father's commandments

and remain in his love. I have told you these things so that my joy may be in you, and your joy may be complete. John 15:1-11

Discourse 2 - on loving one another

My commandment is this-to love one another just as I have loved you. No one has greater love than this-that one lays down his life for his friends. You are my friends if you do what I command you. I no longer call you slaves, because the slave does not understand what his master is doing. But I have called you friends, because I have revealed to you everything I heard from my Father. You did not choose me, but I chose you and appointed you to go and bear fruit, fruit that remains, so that whatever you ask the Father in my name he will give you. This I command you-to love one another. John 15:12-17

Discourse 3 - on persecution

"If the world hates you, be aware that it hated me first. If you belonged to the world, the world would love you as its own. However, because you do not belong to the world, but I chose you out of the world, for this reason the world hates you. Remember what I told you, 'A slave is not greater than his master.' If they persecuted me, they will also persecute you. If they obeyed my word, they will obey yours too. But they will do all these things to you on account of my name, because they do not know the one who sent me. If I had not come and spoken to them, they would not be guilty of sin. But they no longer have any excuse for their sin. The one who hates me hates my Father too. If I had not performed among them the miraculous deeds that no one else did, they would not be guilty of sin. But now they have seen the deeds and have hated both me and my Father. Now this happened to fulfill the word that is written in their law, 'They hated me without reason.' When the Advocate comes, whom I will send you from the Father-the Spirit of truth who goes out from the Father-he will testify about me, and you also will testify,

because you have been with me from the beginning." I have told you all these things so that you will not fall away. They will put you out of the synagogue, yet a time is coming when the one who kills you will think he is offering service to God. They will do these things because they have not known the Father or me. But I have told you these things so that when their time comes, you will remember that I told you about them. "I did not tell you these things from the beginning because I was with you. But now I am going to the one who sent me, and not one of you is asking me, 'Where are you going?' Instead your hearts are filled with sadness because I have said these things to you. John 15:18 - John 16:6

Jesus now promises the disciples that after He lays down His life, the person of the Holy Spirit, the Counsellor, the Comforter, the Spirit of Truth, the Advocate will come to convince those of Christ, Christians, of their righteousness and the world of their sin. This is a promise to the disciples and to all who believe that the Holy Spirit will guide us in all truth and He will speak to us the very words of God.

Jesus then promises His disciples that God will raise Him from the dead and they will see Him again. He further promises answered prayer and peace with a healthy dose of reality. His final words prior to His last prayer with them are instructive, final words always are. Jesus tells them to have peace through Him knowing that the world will make them all suffer, but to be brave, for Jesus has defeated the world.

I have told you these things so that in me you may have peace. In the world you have trouble and suffering, but take courage – I have conquered the world." John 16:33

What extraordinary final words to hear. After three years of teaching and training Jesus looks them in the eye and says that the world will make them suffer, but to be brave, for Jesus will indeed overcome the world. And because Jesus reigns, we can also.

Promise of the Holy Spirit

*But I tell you the truth, it is to your advantage that I am going away.
For if I do not go away, the Advocate will not come to you, but if I go,
I will send him to you. And when he comes, he will prove the world
wrong concerning sin and righteousness and judgment – concerning sin,
because they do not believe in me; concerning righteousness, because I
am going to the Father and you will see me no longer; and concerning
judgment, because the ruler of this world has been condemned. "I have
many more things to say to you, but you cannot bear them now. But
when he, the Spirit of truth, comes, he will guide you into all truth.
For he will not speak on his own authority, but will speak whatever he
hears, and will tell you what is to come. He will glorify me, because he
will receive from me what is mine and will tell it to you. Everything
that the Father has is mine; that is why I said the Spirit will receive
from me what is mine and will tell it to you. John 16:7-15*

Jesus death and resurrection foretold

*In a little while you will see me no longer; again after a little while, you
will see me." Then some of his disciples said to one another, "What is
the meaning of what he is saying, 'In a little while you will not see me;
again after a little while, you will see me,' and, 'because I am going to
the Father'?" So they kept on repeating, "What is the meaning of what
he says, 'In a little while'? We do not understand what he is talking
about." Jesus could see that they wanted to ask him about these things,
so he said to them, "Are you asking each other about this-that I said, 'In
a little while you will not see me; again after a little while, you will see
me'? I tell you the solemn truth, you will weep and wail, but the world
will rejoice; you will be sad, but your sadness will turn into joy. When
a woman gives birth, she has distress because her time has come, but
when her child is born, she no longer remembers the suffering because
of her joy that a human being has been born into the world. So also*

you have sorrow now, but I will see you again, and your hearts will rejoice, and no one will take your joy away from you. John 16:16-22

Promise of answered prayer and peace

At that time you will ask me nothing. I tell you the solemn truth, whatever you ask the Father in my name he will give you. Until now you have not asked for anything in my name. Ask and you will receive it, so that your joy may be complete. "I have told you these things in obscure figures of speech; a time is coming when I will no longer speak to you in obscure figures, but will tell you plainly about the Father. At that time you will ask in my name, and I do not say that I will ask the Father on your behalf. For the Father himself loves you, because you have loved me and have believed that I came from God. I came from the Father and entered into the world, but in turn, I am leaving the world and going back to the Father." His disciples said, "Look, now you are speaking plainly and not in obscure figures of speech! Now we know that you know everything and do not need anyone to ask you anything. Because of this we believe that you have come from God." Jesus replied, "Do you now believe? Look, a time is coming-and has come-when you will be scattered, each one to his own home, and I will be left alone. Yet I am not alone, because my Father is with me. I have told you these things so that in me you may have peace. In the world you have trouble and suffering, but take courage-I have conquered the world." John 16:23-33

Jesus prays for Himself and His disciples

Jesus' last dialogue to His disciples is one of prayer, the longest prayer recorded in scripture. How incredibly fitting that Jesus lifts up holy voices of praise and petition to His Father God at this hour. Jesus prays essentially about three matters. First, He prays for Himself that He may be glorified, then He prays for the eleven apostles, that they may be protected and sanctified, and, finally, He prays for the whole church down through the centuries, that they all may be unified. It is a prayer for the moment, a prayer for the establishment of the church and a prayer for the ages.

When Jesus had finished saying these things, he looked upward to heaven and said, "Father, the time has come. Glorify your Son, so that your Son may glorify you – just as you have given him authority over all humanity, so that he may give eternal life to everyone you have given him. Now this is eternal life-that they know you, the only true God, and Jesus Christ, whom you sent. I glorified you on earth by completing the work you gave me to do. And now, Father, glorify me at your side with the glory I had with you before the world was created. "I have revealed your name to the men you gave me out of the world. They belonged to you, and you gave them to me, and they have obeyed your word. Now they understand that everything you have given me comes from you, because I have given them the words you have given me. They accepted them and really understand that I came from you, and they believed that you sent me. I am praying on behalf of them. I am not praying on behalf of the world, but on behalf of those you have given me, because they belong to you. Everything I have belongs to you, and everything you have belongs to me, and I have been glorified by them. I am no longer in the world, but they are in the world, and I am coming to you. Holy Father, keep them safe in your name that you have given me, so that they may be one just as we are one. When I was with them I kept them safe and watched over them in your name that you have given me. Not one of them was lost except the one destined for destruction, so that the scripture could be fulfilled. But now I am coming to you, and I am saying these things in the world, so they may experience my joy completed in themselves. I have given them your word, and the world has hated them, because they do not belong to the world, just as I do not belong to the world. I am not asking you to take them out of the world, but that you keep them safe from the evil one. They do not belong to the world just as I do not belong to the world. Set them apart in the truth; your word is truth. Just as you sent me into the world, so I sent them into the world. And I set myself apart on their behalf, so that they too may be truly set apart. "I am not praying only on their behalf, but also on behalf of those who believe in me through their testimony, that they will all be one, just as you, Father, are in me and I am in you. I pray that they will be in us, so that the world will believe that you sent me. The glory you gave to me I have given to them, that they may be one just as we are one – I in them and you in me – that they may be completely one, so that the world will know that you sent me, and you have loved them just as you have loved me. «Father, I want those you have given me to be with me where I am, so that they can see my glory that you gave me because you loved me before the creation of the world. Righteous Father, even if the world does not know you, I know you, and these men know that you sent me. I made known your name to them, and I will continue to make it known, so that the love you have loved me with may be in them, and I may be in them." John 17:1-26

The Passover has drawn to a close. The meal is eaten, no bones are broken. Jesus encourages His disciples one last time and reminds them of the Father's provision. I can hear them singing in the upper room and I see the little unnamed family downstairs also quietly singing as they finish their meal. I see Jesus and His disciples walking downstairs and greeting the little family, blessing them and shaking the hand of the unnamed man who gave his house to the Master before they walked down to the Kidron Valley and to the lower reaches of the Mount of Olives into an olive grove complete with an olive press. I see the little family watching them walk away, a father hugging his family and thankful for the opportunity to have served the Son of God this night. Thankful for the protection provided by Jesus, as satan walked the halls of his house. I see a family legacy of service that began with a touch from Jesus. I also see a dark night outside, an evil night, a night where satan erroneously saw victory, not knowing the full measure of God's love for His created mankind. All this on Mount Zion.

After singing a hymn, they went out to the
Mount of Olives. Matthew 26:30

After singing a hymn, they went out to the Mount of Olives. Mark 14:26

Then Jesus went out and made his way, as he customarily did, to
the Mount of Olives, and the disciples followed him. Luke 22:39

When he had said these things, Jesus went out with his
disciples across the Kidron Valley. There was an orchard
there, and he and his disciples went into it. John 18:1

In Gethsemane (the olive grove and wine press)

Jesus and His disciples walk less than a kilometre across the Kidron Valley to the lower part of the Mount of Olives into the Garden of Gethsemane. Except it is not a garden as we know it, a veritable flower patch, but an olive grove. The Greek for garden 'keros' means a cultivated tract of land. In a traditional olive grove is an olive press where the olives are crushed and their juices flow. Gethsemane is Greek for 'press of oils' and close to the Hebrew word for the same 'Gat Shemanim'. Thus the picture is of Jesus in an olive grove. Within this grove, He takes His three closest friends into the centre of the grove, where there was usually an olive press and there at the symbolic place of crushing, red juice flowing and transforming, Jesus prays to Abba Father, literally His Daddy. The Aramaic word 'Abba' is an intimate form only mentioned three times in the Word of God, once here in the garden and twice more in the apostle Paul's letters to the church in Rome (Romans 8:15) and Galatia (Galatians 4:6).

Then Jesus went with them to a place called Gethsemane, and he said to
the disciples, "Sit here while I go over there and pray." He took with him
Peter and the two sons of Zebedee, and became anguished and distressed.

Then he said to them, "My soul is deeply grieved, even to the point of death. Remain here and stay awake with me." Matthew 26:36-38

Then they went to a place called Gethsemane, and Jesus said to his disciples, "Sit here while I pray." He took Peter, James, and John with him, and became very troubled and distressed. He said to them, "My soul is deeply grieved, even to the point of death. Remain here and stay alert." Mark 14:32-34

When he came to the place, he said to them, "Pray that you will not fall into temptation." Luke 22:40

Jesus' first prayer

Jesus is now at the centre of the olive grove, quite probably near the olive press with His three closest friends. Jesus moves a little further away from His friends and I believe kneels at the olive press to pray in anguish for the cup to be taken from Him, but not His will, but that of the Father. There at the place where olives are crushed and red juice flows, the gospel writer, Luke the doctor says Jesus sweated blood in His anguish. Such a condition is very real and can manifest in times of enormous stress, like you're about to be punished with the sins of the entire earth; past, present and future. The condition is called hematidrosis and is where capillaries in the sweat glands rupture causing bleeding.[34] At the place of crushing in the olive grove, Jesus feels personally the crushing that is to come.

When Jesus returns to His three closest friends He finds them asleep. It has been a big night at the Passover dinner so in a human sense the disciple's tiredness is understandable. Only Jesus knows what comes next, so His desire for His close friends to pray with Him is understandable. What is interesting is that Jesus singles Peter out and calls him to pray

---

[34] Sutton, R.L. Jr. (1956), *Diseases of the Skin* (St. Louis, MO: Mosby College Publishing), eleventh edition, pp 1393-94.

so that he won't fall into temptation. Advice that Peter probably should have heeded a little more.

> *Going a little farther, he threw himself to the ground and prayed that if it were possible the hour would pass from him. He said, "Abba, Father, all things are possible for you. Take this cup away from me. Yet not what I will, but what you will." Then he came and found them sleeping, and said to Peter, "Simon, are you sleeping? Couldn't you stay awake for one hour? Stay awake and pray that you will not fall into temptation. The spirit is willing, but the flesh is weak." Mark 14:35-38*

> *Going a little farther, he threw himself down with his face to the ground and prayed, "My Father, if possible, let this cup pass from me! Yet not what I will, but what you will." Then he came to the disciples and found them sleeping. He said to Peter, "So, couldn't you stay awake with me for one hour? Stay awake and pray that you will not fall into temptation. The spirit is willing, but the flesh is weak." Matthew 26:39-41*

> *He went away from them about a stone's throw, knelt down, and prayed, "Father, if you are willing, take this cup away from me. Yet not my will but yours be done." [Then an angel from heaven appeared to him and strengthened him. And in his anguish he prayed more earnestly, and his sweat was like drops of blood falling to the ground.] When he got up from prayer, he came to the disciples and found them sleeping, exhausted from grief. So he said to them, "Why are you sleeping? Get up and pray that you will not fall into temptation!" Luke 22:41-46*

Jesus' second prayer

Jesus walked a little way away a second time from the disciples and prayed, and once more returned to sleepy disciples.

> *He went away a second time and prayed, "My Father, if this cup cannot be taken away unless I drink it, your will must*

*be done." He came again and found them sleeping; they
could not keep their eyes open. Matthew 26:42-43*

*He went away again and prayed the same thing. When he came
again he found them sleeping; they could not keep their eyes open.
And they did not know what to tell him. Mark 14:39-40*

Jesus' third prayer

Jesus then withdrew a third time and prayed the same prayer a third time to take this trial from Him if possible, but also prayed not His will, but that of God the Father's be done. A third time Jesus returns to finds His three best friends sleeping.

*So leaving them again, he went away and prayed for the third time,
saying the same thing once more. Then he came to the disciples and said
to them, "Are you still sleeping and resting? Look, the hour is approaching,
and the Son of Man is betrayed into the hands of sinners. Get up,
let us go. Look! My betrayer is approaching!" Matthew 26:44-46*

*He came a third time and said to them, "Are you still sleeping
and resting? Enough of that! The hour has come. Look, the Son
of Man is betrayed into the hands of sinners. Get up, let us
go. Look! My betrayer is approaching!" Mark 14:41-42*

Judas arrives with soldiers

Jesus has now prayed three times with His closest friends, albeit whilst they were sleepy. The other eight disciples were at the edge of the olive grove and would have been the first to see the maddening crowd arrive. Suffice to say Jesus has joined them quickly with Peter, James and John in tow, all wide awake now as the scene is frightening. A large number of soldiers, the religious elite and their cheer squads turn up with flaming torches, lanterns and an array of weapons and hand made clubs. They have come in physical power, yet know nothing of real power.

Jesus never resisted, but gave an object lessons in the power of the Word of God when the mere mention of the great 'I AM' floored hardened soldiers, saw them reel back and fall to the ground. A mere word from The Word of Life, Jesus the Christ, God's Son and the hardest of the hard can do nothing but involuntarily bend their knees and fall to the ground. The image is stark and prophesies a time at the end of the world when…

> For it is written, "As I live, says the Lord, every knee will bow to me, and every tongue will give praise to God." Romans 14:11

The armed crowd will gather themselves from the ground, shake the dust from their clothes, ask one another what just happened and then take Jesus, after Judas greets Him and kisses Him. The scene has shown clearly that no one is capturing Jesus because of their power, their fall to the ground (including Judas) shows they have none. They are capturing Jesus because this perfect lamb of God is voluntarily laying down His life to be the final sacrifice to reconcile us all (those soldiers and elders included) back to God.

> (Now Judas, the one who betrayed him, knew the place too, because Jesus had met there many times with his disciples.) So Judas obtained a squad of soldiers and some officers of the chief priests and Pharisees. They came to the orchard with lanterns and torches and weapons. Then Jesus, because he knew everything that was going to happen to him, came and asked them, "Who are you looking for?" They replied, "Jesus the Nazarene." He told them, "I am he." (Now Judas, the one who betrayed him, was standing there with them.) So when Jesus said to them, "I am he," they retreated and fell to the ground. Then Jesus asked them again, "Who are you looking for?" And they said, "Jesus the Nazarene." Jesus replied, "I told you that I am he. If you are looking for me, let these men go." He said this to fulfill the word he had spoken, "I have not lost a single one of those whom you gave me." John 18:2-9

While he was still speaking, Judas, one of the twelve, arrived. With him was a large crowd armed with swords and clubs, sent by the chief priests and elders of the people. (Now the betrayer had given them a sign, saying, "The one I kiss is the man. Arrest him!") Immediately he went up to Jesus and said, "Greetings, Rabbi," and kissed him. Jesus said to him, "Friend, do what you are here to do." Then they came and took hold of Jesus and arrested him. Matthew 26:47-50

While he was still speaking, suddenly a crowd appeared, and the man named Judas, one of the twelve, was leading them. He walked up to Jesus to kiss him. But Jesus said to him, "Judas, would you betray the Son of Man with a kiss?" Luke 22:47-48

Right away, while Jesus was still speaking, Judas, one of the twelve, arrived. With him came a crowd armed with swords and clubs, sent by the chief priests and experts in the law and elders. (Now the betrayer had given them a sign, saying, "The one I kiss is the man. Arrest him and lead him away under guard.") When Judas arrived, he went up to Jesus immediately and said, "Rabbi!" and kissed him. Then they took hold of him and arrested him. Mark 14:43-46

The thirty-sixth miracle – power over flesh

Faced with such opposition, what does Peter do? He cleaves the high priest's representative, Malchus, cutting off his right ear. The name Malchus has two meanings: ruler and counsellor. This may have been his original name or a title given to him because of his close position to the high priest Caiaphas, as his personal assistant. This was a prominent position in the religious order of the priesthood. So I can imagine when Peter saw Malchus in the garden, replete in the regalia of a high ranking religious official, he saw red.

I don't think for a second Peter meant to cut off the high priest's servant's ear. I see Peter, in the half dark with torches flaming, afraid and volatile, widely swinging his sword at the high priest's servant intent on killing him by cleaving his head in two. It is highly likely the servant was wearing a traditional steel pointed helmet so that any weapon strike to the head would deflect off the helmet leaving the ear exposed. The Roman soldiers sensibly had side flaps on their helmets and then shoulder and arm protection so a blow to the head would slide down the helmet, over the ear flat and shoulder protection and down beside the arm. Not so the priestly class or their servants. That's the impetuous Peter we all know, strike first, think later. Ready, Fire, Aim!

We tend to focus on the recklessness of Peter, the one-eared servant and the miracle of Jesus' healing touch. In doing so, we miss perhaps another purpose of this episode, the last chance to reach God's apparent priest on earth, the high priest. When the blow cleaved the servant's ear there would have been cries, lots of blood and confusion. What does Jesus do, He reaches out and heals, right in front of everyone. I bet the servant was changed that night having personally felt the healing touch of Jesus. Yet on his return, bloodied and shocked, his master the high priest apparently ignored the miraculous. It didn't fit in with his world view of harmony with the occupying power of Rome. The high priest was given one last chance to embrace the miraculous of Jesus, one last chance through the healing of his personal servant, and he ignored it. What amazing grace from Jesus, what hard-heartedness from the high priest.

> *But one of those with Jesus grabbed his sword, drew it out, and struck the high priest's slave, cutting off his ear. Then Jesus said to him, "Put your sword back in its place! For all who take hold of the sword will die by the sword. Or do you think that I cannot call on my Father, and that he would send me more than twelve legions of angels right now? How then would the scriptures that say it must happen this way be fulfilled?" Matthew 26:51-54*

Then Simon Peter, who had a sword, pulled it out and struck the high priest's slave, cutting off his right ear. (Now the slave's name was Malchus.) But Jesus said to Peter, "Put your sword back into its sheath! Am I not to drink the cup that the Father has given me?" John 18:10-11

One of the bystanders drew his sword and struck the high priest's slave, cutting off his ear. Mark 14:47

When those who were around him saw what was about to happen, they said, "Lord, should we use our swords?" Then one of them struck the high priest's slave, cutting off his right ear. But Jesus said, "Enough of this!" And he touched the man's ear and healed him. Luke 22:49-51

The glory of Jesus' response

So the perfect lamb of God, the Word through whom all things were created puts Himself into the hands of His creation. As He does so, he makes it clear that this is an hour of darkness and of evil but also that this is what was prophesied and predicted in the writings of the prophets. This was the will of God.

At that moment Jesus said to the crowd, "Have you come out with swords and clubs to arrest me like you would an outlaw? Day after day I sat teaching in the temple courts, yet you did not arrest me. But this has happened so that the scriptures of the prophets would be fulfilled." Matthew 26:55-56a

Then Jesus said to the chief priests, the officers of the temple guard, and the elders who had come out to get him, "Have you come out with swords and clubs like you would against an outlaw? Day after day when I was with you in the temple courts, you did not arrest me. But this is your hour, and that of the power of darkness!" Luke 22:52-53

Jesus said to them, "Have you come with swords and clubs to arrest me like you would an outlaw? Day after day I was with you, teaching in the temple courts, yet you did not arrest me. But this has happened so that the scriptures would be fulfilled." Mark 14:48-49

The disciples leg it

The disciples with all their bravado about dying with Jesus all leg it. They run, afraid, lost and confused. They never really understood what was going to happen, though Jesus had told them plainly. This would all change at Pentecost when the Holy Spirit arrives, but this night, Jesus is alone. The mob tried to arrest Jesus' followers, including a young man who managed to escape by sliding out of his one-piece garment. Only Mark's gospel includes this vignette which leads to the view that Mark is writing about himself as the young man witnessing such events.

Then all the disciples left him and fled. Matthew 26:56b

Then all the disciples left him and fled. A young man was following him, wearing only a linen cloth. They tried to arrest him, but he ran off naked, leaving his linen cloth behind. Mark 14:50-52

Then the squad of soldiers with their commanding officer and the officers of the Jewish leaders arrested Jesus and tied him up. John 18:12

The unfairness and injustice of what Jesus now endures on His journey to the cross is breathtaking. He will undergo six trials, six being the number of man (one less than seven, the perfect prime number of God signifying completeness). He will be mocked and beaten by both the religious elite and the Roman guard. He will be flogged mercilessly to the point that the prophesy of Isaiah 53:2b says there would be nothing in His appearance that we should desire him. His freedom would be offered up to the maddening crowd to give, but they would demand a murderer be released. The crowd would proclaim Caesar as their king whilst demanding the King of Kings be killed and then the Word of Life would be crucified as a common criminal, indeed between two criminals.

All of this commencing on the Passover evening. The subsequent six trials and merciless punishment of Jesus would take no more than twelve hours from that evening till the hammer blow of crucifixion nails at nine in the morning (Mark 15:25). Darkness can indeed move quickly.

Jewish trial no. 1 - Annas (father-in-law of the high priest Caiaphas)
The first trial is with Annas, the father-in-law of the current high priest Caiaphas. Annas had previously been high priest for ten years, deposed in 15 AD at the age of 36 by the Roman procurator Gratus. Being removed from office meant little reduction in power and influence however, both of which he exercised vicariously through his five sons and his son-in-law Caiaphas. The historian Josephus even made the point that "It is said that the elder Ananus was extremely fortunate. For he had five sons, all of whom, after he himself had previously enjoyed the office for a very long period, became high priests of God - a thing that had never happened to any other of our high priests."[35] This trial is small as only Annas, some Jewish officials and soldiers are present, but they question Jesus about what He taught and whom He led and they beat Him.

> *They brought him first to Annas, for he was the father-in-law of Caiaphas, who was high priest that year. (Now it was Caiaphas who had advised the Jewish leaders that it was to their advantage that one man die for the people.) John 18:13-14*

---

[35] Josephus, Jewish Antiquities XX, 9.1

While this was happening, the high priest questioned Jesus about his disciples and about his teaching. Jesus replied, "I have spoken publicly to the world. I always taught in the synagogues and in the temple courts, where all the Jewish people assemble together. I have said nothing in secret. Why do you ask me? Ask those who heard what I said. They know what I said." When Jesus had said this, one of the high priest's officers who stood nearby struck him on the face and said, "Is that the way you answer the high priest?" Jesus replied, "If I have said something wrong, confirm what is wrong. But if I spoke correctly, why strike me?" John 18:19-23

Jewish trial no. 2 - The high priest Caiaphas

The second trial is one where Jesus is questioned, beaten, tortured and mocked. It is dark and very late, quite probably before or around midnight. The high priest has assembled everyone, the entire Sanhedrin of seventy-one plus other teachers of the law and elders. The high priest speaks directly with Jesus at this late hour, and allows Jesus to be beaten, quite probably in front of him. It is also clear that the Sanhedrin members spoke amongst themselves and determined a course of action that would result in Jesus being formally brought before them at dawn complete with a host of false witnesses. This is a kangaroo court if ever such a beast existed.

Then Annas sent him, still tied up, to Caiaphas the high priest. John 18:24

Now the ones who had arrested Jesus led him to Caiaphas, the high priest, in whose house the experts in the law and the elders had gathered. Matthew 26:57

Then they led Jesus to the high priest, and all the chief priests and elders and experts in the law came together. Mark 14:53

Then they arrested Jesus, led him away, and brought him into the high priest's house. But Peter was following at a distance. Luke 22:54

The chief priests and the whole Sanhedrin were trying to find false testimony against Jesus so that they could put him to death. But they did not find anything, though many false witnesses came forward. Finally two came forward and declared, "This man said, 'I am able to destroy the temple of God and rebuild it in three days.'" So the high priest stood up and said to him, "Have you no answer? What is this that they are testifying against you?" But Jesus was silent. The high priest said to him, "I charge you under oath by the living God, tell us if you are the Christ, the Son of God." Jesus said to him, "You have said it yourself. But I tell you, from now on you will see the Son of Man sitting at the right hand of the Power and coming on the clouds of heaven." Then the high priest tore his clothes and declared, "He has blasphemed! Why do we still need witnesses? Now you have heard the blasphemy! What is your verdict?" They answered, "He is guilty and deserves death." Then they spat in his face and struck him with their fists. And some slapped him, saying, "Prophesy for us, you Christ! Who hit you?" Matthew 26:59-68

The chief priests and the whole Sanhedrin were looking for evidence against Jesus so that they could put him to death, but they did not find anything. Many gave false testimony against him, but their testimony did not agree. Some stood up and gave this false testimony against him: "We heard him say, 'I will destroy this temple made with hands and in three days build another not made with hands.'" Yet even on this point their testimony did not agree. Then the high priest stood up before them and asked Jesus, "Have you no answer? What is this that they are testifying against you?" But he was silent and did not answer. Again the high priest questioned him, "Are you the Christ, the Son of the Blessed One?" "I am," said Jesus, "and you will see the Son of Man sitting at the right hand of the Power and coming with the clouds of heaven." Then the high priest tore his clothes and said, "Why do we still need witnesses? You have heard the blasphemy! What is your verdict?" They all condemned him as deserving death. Then some began to spit

on him, and to blindfold him, and to strike him with their fists, saying,
"Prophesy!" The guards also took him and beat him. Mark 14:55-65

Now the men who were holding Jesus under guard began to
mock him and beat him. They blindfolded him and asked
him repeatedly, "Prophesy! Who hit you?" They also said many
other things against him, reviling him. Luke 22:63-65

Peter's first denial

At this dark hour, where are the disciples, who in the words of Thomas
promised to go to Jerusalem and die with Jesus? Words can be cheap, as
only two of the disciples are anywhere near Jesus, John son of Zebedee
and Peter. Evidently John was sufficiently known to be allowed into
the high priest's courtyard and he would then smuggle Peter in. What
is interesting is that John was known and still allowed into the courtyard 'with Jesus' and there is no indication that John was afraid or in
danger or denied Jesus. Peter on the other hand felt sufficiently uneasy
that he would deny knowing Jesus when questioned by the humblest
of servants.

Simon Peter and another disciple followed them as they brought Jesus to
Annas. (Now the other disciple was acquainted with the high priest, and
he went with Jesus into the high priest's courtyard.) But Simon Peter was
left standing outside by the door. So the other disciple who was acquainted
with the high priest came out and spoke to the slave girl who watched
the door, and brought Peter inside. The girl who was the doorkeeper said
to Peter, "You're not one of this man's disciples too, are you?" He replied,
"I am not." (Now the slaves and the guards were standing around a
charcoal fire they had made, warming themselves because it was cold.
Peter also was standing with them, warming himself.) John 18:15-18

But Peter was following him from a distance, all the way to the high priest's courtyard. After going in, he sat with the guards to see the outcome. Matthew 26:58

Now Peter was sitting outside in the courtyard. A slave girl came to him and said, "You also were with Jesus the Galilean." But he denied it in front of them all: "I don't know what you're talking about!" Matthew 26:69-70

And Peter had followed him from a distance, up to the high priest's courtyard. He was sitting with the guards and warming himself by the fire. Mark 14:54

Now while Peter was below in the courtyard, one of the high priest's slave girls came by. When she saw Peter warming himself, she looked directly at him and said, "You also were with that Nazarene, Jesus." But he denied it: "I don't even understand what you're talking about!" Then he went out to the gateway, and a rooster crowed. Mark 14:66-68

When they had made a fire in the middle of the courtyard and sat down together, Peter sat down among them. Then a slave girl, seeing him as he sat in the firelight, stared at him and said, "This man was with him too!" But Peter denied it: "Woman, I don't know him!" Luke 22:55-57

So the Passover night ends with Jesus in chains, beaten and questioned and Peter warming himself by the fire denying he ever knew the Saviour of the world, the one to whom he walked on water to reach. Two trials have finished and the dawn and early morning will bring four more. Fairness will be thrown out, justice will be extinguished and thirty years of growing and three years of ministry will come to an end. And the world will be changed, forever.

CHAPTER 13

Crucifixion
(Friday 3rd April 33 AD)

After the darkest night, the sun always rises to herald a new day, though on this crucifixion Friday the spiritual darkness extends into the dawn. As the first rays were striking the gold-encrusted Temple built to worship the living God, the one whom they worshipped was dragged, battered and bleeding into their presence. The religious elite who had hours before consumed the meat of the Passover lamb, failed to recognise the final lamb of God in their midst. It is one of the saddest ironies in history, dead religion (man's attempt to get to God) missing the opportunity for a relationship with Jesus (God's attempt to get to man).

Two unfair, unjust and rigged Jewish trials occurred the previous evening before the past and current high priest, God's apparent representative on earth in the tradition, though not line, of Aaron. Four more trials, one Jewish and three Roman would follow that lead directly to the cross.

Jewish trial no. 3 - Sanhedrin

The high priest Caiphias who on the previous night questioned Jesus and allowed him to be beaten, has now assembled the entire seventy-one members of the Great Sanhedrin. This would have included

Nicodemus and Joseph of Arimathea, the only two members of the great council that are known to have believed in Jesus as Messiah. Jesus is then dragged forward to face this third Jewish trial, whose members have been working through the night to build a case against the sinless lamb of God. Their case will fail, but the truth from Jesus' own mouth, that He is the Son of God, will send Him to the cross.

When day came, the council of the elders of the people gathered together, both the chief priests and the experts in the law. Then they led Jesus away to their council and said, "If you are the Christ, tell us." But he said to them, "If I tell you, you will not believe, and if I ask you, you will not answer. But from now on the Son of Man will be seated at the right hand of the power of God." So they all said, "Are you the Son of God, then?" He answered them, "You say that I am." Then they said, "Why do we need further testimony? We have heard it ourselves from his own lips!" Luke 22:66-71

When it was early in the morning, all the chief priests and the elders of the people plotted against Jesus to execute him. They tied him up, led him away, and handed him over to Pilate the governor. Matthew 27:1-2

Early in the morning, after forming a plan, the chief priests with the elders and the experts in the law and the whole Sanhedrin tied Jesus up, led him away, and handed him over to Pilate. Mark 15:1

Then the whole group of them rose up and brought Jesus before Pilate. Luke 23:1

Peter's second denial

Peter courageously went with John to the house of Caiphias to see what would become of Jesus, and warming himself by the fire he denied knowing Jesus the first time when the servant girl asked. Apparently a little uncomfortable, Peter leaves the fire and walks to the gateway, perhaps looking to leave in fear for his safety or to avoid the nosey servant girl. Here by the gateway Peter is challenged by another servant girl and denies knowing the One who was transformed in his presence on Mount Tabor, a second time.

Then a little later someone else saw him and said, "You are one of them too." But Peter said, "Man, I am not!" Luke 22:58

When he went out to the gateway, another slave girl saw him and said to the people there, "This man was with Jesus the Nazarene." He denied it again with an oath, "I do not know the man!" Matthew 26:71-72

When the slave girl saw him, she began again to say to the bystanders, "This man is one of them." But he denied it again. Mark 14:69-70a

Meanwhile Simon Peter was standing in the courtyard warming himself. They said to him, "You aren't one of his disciples too, are you?" Peter denied it: "I am not!" John 18:25

Peter's third denial

Finally after an hour of Peter talking with those around him at the gateway his broad northern Galilean accent gives him away and those with him challenge him. The challenge also comes from a friend of Malchus, the servant whose ear Peter cleaved from his skull, who was with Malchus in the garden. You'd think that friend would reflect on the healing touch of Jesus, but apparently hard heartedness runs right through the high priest's office and their friends. Peter again denies Jesus, the author of life, the one he saw raise people from death, a third time.

... and a rooster crows…. and he remembers Jesus' words…and the author of life looks straight at him…. and Peter leaves devastated.

One of the high priest's slaves, a relative of the man whose ear Peter had cut off, said, "Did I not see you in the orchard with him?" Then Peter denied it again, and immediately a rooster crowed. John 18:26-27

A short time later the bystanders again said to Peter, "You must be one of them, because you are also a Galilean." Then he began to curse, and he swore with an oath, "I do not know this man you are talking about!" Immediately a rooster crowed a second time. Then Peter remembered what Jesus had said to him: "Before a rooster crows twice, you will deny me three times." And he broke down and wept. Mark 14:70b-72

After a little while, those standing there came up to Peter and said, "You really are one of them too-even your accent gives you away!" At that he began to curse, and he swore with an oath, "I do not know the man!" At that moment a rooster crowed. Then Peter remembered what Jesus had said: "Before the rooster crows, you will deny me three times." And he went outside and wept bitterly. Matthew 26:73-75

And after about an hour still another insisted, "Certainly this man was with him, because he too is a Galilean." But Peter said, "Man, I don't know what you're talking about!" At that moment, while he was still speaking, a rooster crowed. Then the Lord turned and looked straight at Peter, and Peter remembered the word of the Lord, how he had said to him, "Before a rooster crows today, you will deny me three times." And he went outside and wept bitterly. Luke 22:59-62

Judas' remorse

Remorse is a funny thing. Judas suddenly became overwhelmed with guilt after he saw Jesus condemned. Perhaps satan has left him and thus allowed him a shred of conscience. Perhaps Judas reflected on everything he saw and did whilst with Jesus. Whatever the reason his remorse was not reciprocated by the religious elite and would ultimately lead to him taking his own life.

Now when Judas, who had betrayed him, saw that Jesus had been condemned, he regretted what he had done and returned the thirty silver coins to the chief priests and the elders, saying, "I have sinned by betraying innocent blood!" But they said, "What is that to us? You take care of it yourself!" So Judas threw the silver coins into the temple and left. Then he went out and hanged himself. The chief priests took the silver and said, "It is not lawful to put this into the temple treasury, since it is blood money." After consulting together they bought the Potter's Field with it, as a burial place for foreigners. For this reason that field has been called the "Field of Blood" to this day. Then what was spoken by Jeremiah the prophet was fulfilled: "They took the thirty silver coins, the price of the one whose price had been set by the people of Israel, and they gave them for the potter's field, as the Lord commanded me." Matthew 27:3-10

"A Brothers, the scripture had to be fulfilled that the Holy Spirit foretold through David concerning Judas-who became the guide for those who arrested Jesus – for he was counted as one of us and received a share in this ministry." (Now this man Judas acquired a field with the reward of his unjust deed, and falling headfirst he burst open in the middle and all his intestines gushed out. This became known to all who lived in Jerusalem, so that in their own language they called that field Hakeldama, that is, "Field of Blood.") "For it is written in the book of Psalms, 'Let his house become deserted, and let there be no one to live in it,' and 'Let another take his position of responsibility." Acts 1:16-20

Trial no. 4 - Jesus before Pilate (the first time)

Fresh from three Jewish trials, Jesus is now dragged before the Roman leadership, in this case the prefect of Judea, Pontius Pilate. Pilate was the fifth prefect of the Roman province of Judaea and served from 26 - 36 AD. Apart from the gospel accounts, there is a key piece of archeological evidence that confirms that Pilate was prefect. This is a Latin inscription on a limestone block relating to Pilate's tribute to Tiberius, discovered in 1961 at the ancient Roman theatre of Caesarea.

The inscription states that Pilate was a prefect of Judeae and reads *praefectus Iudaeae.*

Pilate is not interested in this trial and not interested in Jesus. Accordingly this trial will not be about justice as Pilate tells the religious elite to judge Jesus by their own law and they respond with their true motives 'we have no right to execute anyone'. So Pilate questions Jesus, but is clearly looking to move the 'problem' on, not wanting to be embroiled in a question of Jewish law. Once he realised Jesus was a Galilean, Pilate sent Jesus to Herod Antipas tetrarch of Galilee and Perea, a man Pilate did not like. Herod was in Jerusalem for the Passover.

Then they brought Jesus from Caiaphas to the Roman governor's residence. (Now it was very early morning.) They did not go into the governor's residence so they would not be ceremonially defiled, but could eat the Passover meal. So Pilate came outside to them and said, "What accusation do you bring against this man?" They replied, "If this man were not a criminal, we would not have handed him over to you." Pilate told them, "Take him yourselves and pass judgment on him according to your own law!" The Jewish leaders replied, "We cannot legally put anyone to death." (This happened to fulfill the word Jesus had spoken when he indicated what kind of death he was going to die.) John 18:28-32

So Pilate went back into the governor's residence, summoned Jesus, and asked him, "Are you the king of the Jews?" Jesus replied, "Are you saying this on your own initiative, or have others told you about me?" Pilate answered, "I am not a Jew, am I? Your own people and your chief priests handed you over to me. What have you done?" Jesus replied, "My kingdom is not from this world. If my kingdom were from this world, my servants would be fighting to keep me from being handed over to the Jewish authorities. But as it is, my kingdom is not from here." Then Pilate said, "So you are a king!" Jesus replied, "You say that I am a king. For this reason I was born, and for this reason I came into the world-to testify to the truth. Everyone who belongs to the truth listens to my voice." Pilate asked, "What is truth?" John 28:33-38a

They began to accuse him, saying, "We found this man subverting our nation, forbidding us to pay the tribute tax to Caesar and claiming that he himself is Christ, a king." So Pilate asked Jesus, "Are you the king of the Jews?" He replied, "You say so." Then Pilate said to the chief priests and the crowds, "I find no basis for an accusation against this man." But they persisted in saying, "He incites the people by teaching throughout all Judea. It started in Galilee and ended up here!" Luke 23:2-5

So Pilate asked him, "Are you the king of the Jews?" He replied, "You say so." Then the chief priests began to accuse him repeatedly. So Pilate asked him again, "Have you nothing to say? See how many charges they are bringing against you!" But Jesus made no further reply, so that Pilate was amazed. Mark 15:2-5

Then Jesus stood before the governor, and the governor asked him, "Are you the king of the Jews?" Jesus said, "You say so." But when he was accused by the chief priests and the elders, he did not respond. Then Pilate said to him, "Don't you hear how many charges they are bringing against you?" But he did not answer even one accusation, so that the governor was quite amazed. Matthew 27:11-14

Trial no. 5 - Jesus before Herod

Herod Antipas had wanted to speak with Jesus for quite a while, more out of curiosity and miracle seeking than any sense of learning the truth. Now he had his chance, yet Jesus remained quiet and all that could be heard in the audience chamber was the roar of the accusations. Herod probably felt a little silly, hence his resort to appease the crowd with ridicule and mocking. Weak leaders do that. They have no capacity to rise above popularism to seek the truth and are easily swayed by the false applause of the crowd.

What is interesting is the statement that Herod and Pilate became friends this day. What was it that overturned years of enmity to bridge the divide between Jewish governor and Roman prefect? Clearly it had something to do with Jesus, or appeasing the crowds or something more sinister perhaps? Either way, the second Roman trial is a farce and Jesus is bounced back to Pilate, complete with a mocking robe.

Now when Pilate heard this, he asked whether the man was a Galilean. When he learned that he was from Herod's jurisdiction, he sent him over to Herod, who also happened to be in Jerusalem at that time. When Herod saw Jesus, he was very glad, for he had long desired to see him, because he had heard about him and was hoping to see him perform some miraculous sign. So Herod questioned him at considerable length; Jesus gave him no answer. The chief priests and the experts in the law were there, vehemently accusing him. Even Herod with his soldiers treated him with contempt and mocked him. Then, dressing him in elegant clothes, Herod sent him back to Pilate. That very day Herod and Pilate became friends with each other, for prior to this they had been enemies. Luke 23:6-12

The people gather before Pilate

Pilate knows Jesus is not guilty of anything and that it is out of pure self interest that the Jewish leaders sought to kill Jesus. Herod returned Jesus to Pilate also having not reached any conclusions as to guilt. Pilate therefore, as a matter of law and justice, has to release Jesus. Strong leaders do the right thing, regardless of the crowd. Pilate is not strong. He tries to bargain with the crowd saying that he will 'punish' Jesus and release Him, hoping the crowd will accept this as a compromise knowing full well the Roman punishment by flogging, killed as many as survived it. The crowd is not buying it. Pilate then tries to use the customary release of a prisoner on Passover, as an occupying power's act of good will, to set Jesus free and ends up releasing a notorious murderer, Barabbas. Weak leadership always leads to weak outcomes.

A personal crescendo then builds in Pilates life with the entrance of his wife. I dare say it was not customary for the prefect's wife to be involved in matters of trial or law, certainly not when the crowds are on the verge of revolt. Yet here is a picture of Pilate sitting on the judgement seat of Rome, facing the mob and a message from his wife is bought to him. A message from God in a dream to his wife to say that Jesus is innocent. What a picture of grace. It is clear that Jesus is fault-less in every way. It is clear that Pilate knows this yet lacks the strength to act. It is clear the religious elite are acting out of self interest. It is clear that God is ensuring that everyone knows the truth that Jesus is the innocent lamb of God sent to pay our penalty for sin.

Though the LORD desired to crush him and make him ill, once restitution is made, he will see descendants and enjoy long life, and the LORD's purpose will be accomplished through him. Isaiah 53:10

I wonder what Pilate's wife did and thought from that moment on? What did it mean that she suffered a great deal in a dream because of the innocence of Jesus? How did she respond? Questions without answers, but questions still.

Then Pilate called together the chief priests, the rulers, and the people, and said to them, "You brought me this man as one who was misleading the people. When I examined him before you, I did not find this man guilty of anything you accused him of doing. Neither did Herod, for he sent him back to us. Look, he has done nothing deserving death. I will therefore have him flogged and release him." Luke 23:13-16

Again Pilate went out and said to the Jewish leaders, "Look, I am bringing him out to you, so that you may know that I find no reason for an accusation against him." So Jesus came outside, wearing the crown of thorns and the purple robe. Pilate said to them, "Look, here is the man!" When the chief priests and their officers saw him, they shouted out, "Crucify him! Crucify him!" Pilate said, "You take him and crucify him! Certainly I find no reason for an accusation against him!" The Jewish leaders replied, "We have a law, and according to our law he ought to die, because he claimed to be the Son of God!" John 19:4-7

When he had said this [what is truth?] he went back outside to the Jewish leaders and announced, "I find no basis for an accusation against him. But it is your custom that I release one prisoner for you at the Passover. So do you want me to release for you the king of the Jews?" Then they shouted back, "Not this man, but Barabbas!" (Now Barabbas was a revolutionary.) John 18:38b-40

But they all shouted out together, "Take this man away! Release Barabbas for us!" (This was a man who had been thrown into prison for an insurrection started in the city, and for murder.) Pilate addressed them once again because he wanted to release Jesus. But they kept on shouting, "Crucify, crucify him!" A third time he said to them, "Why? What wrong has he done? I have found him guilty of no crime deserving death. I will therefore flog him and release him." Luke 23:17-22

During the feast it was customary to release one prisoner to the people, whomever they requested. A man named Barabbas was imprisoned with rebels who had committed murder during an insurrection. Then the crowd came up and began to ask Pilate to release a prisoner for them, as was his custom. Mark 15:6-8

During the feast the governor was accustomed to release one prisoner to the crowd, whomever they wanted. At that time they had in custody a notorious prisoner named Jesus Barabbas. So after they had assembled, Pilate said to them, "Whom do you want me to release for you, Jesus Barabbas or Jesus who is called the Christ?" (For he knew that they had handed him over because of envy.) As he was sitting on the judgment seat, his wife sent a message to him:

"Have nothing to do with that innocent man; I have suffered greatly as a result of a dream about him today." Matthew 27:15-19

But the chief priests and the elders persuaded the crowds to ask for Barabbas and to have Jesus killed. The governor asked them, "Which of the two do you want me to release for you?" And they said, "Barabbas!" Pilate said to them, "Then what should I do with Jesus who is called the Christ?" They all said, "Crucify him!" He asked, "Why? What wrong has he done?" But they shouted more insistently, "Crucify him!" Matthew 27:20-23

So Pilate asked them, "Do you want me to release the king of the Jews for you?" (For he knew that the chief priests had handed him over because of envy.) But the chief priests stirred up the crowd to have him release Barabbas instead. So Pilate spoke to them again, "Then what do you want me to do with the one you call king of the Jews?" They shouted back, "Crucify him!" Pilate asked them, "Why? What has he done wrong?" But they shouted more insistently, "Crucify him!" Mark 15:9-14

Trial no. 6 - Jesus before Pilate (the second time)

Pilate is vexed beyond all reason. He is a Roman and the law is the law. He knows Jesus is innocent and questions Jesus one more time, hoping to find the loophole to set Him free. Yet a weak leader always gives in when his allegiance and authority is challenged. The crowd manipulates Pilate by questioning his loyalty to Caesar, to Rome. An occupying power only maintains authority when it's right to rule is unquestioned.

When Pilate heard what they said, he was more afraid than ever, and he went back into the governor's residence and said to Jesus, "Where do you come from?" But Jesus gave him no answer. So Pilate said, "Do you refuse to speak to me? Don't you know I have the authority to release you, and to crucify you?" Jesus replied, "You would have no authority over me at all, unless it was given to you from above. Therefore the one who handed me over to you is guilty of greater sin." From this point on, Pilate tried to release him. But the Jewish leaders shouted out, "If you release this man, you are no friend of Caesar! Everyone who claims to be a king opposes Caesar!" When Pilate heard these words he brought Jesus outside and sat down on the judgment seat in the place called "The Stone Pavement" (Gabbatha in Aramaic). (Now it was the day of preparation for the Passover, about noon.) Pilate said to the Jewish leaders, "Look, here is your king!" Then they shouted out, "Away with him! Away with him! Crucify him!" Pilate asked, "Shall I crucify your king?" The high priests replied, "We have no king except Caesar!" John 19:8-15

Pilate hands Jesus over

Pilate caves in. The authority of Rome is questioned, his allegiance to Rome is in doubt, the mob is getting out of hand and frankly Pilate doesn't care. Jesus is a Jew and His own people want Him dead, what is that to Rome? Indeed the Jews are even swearing responsibility for the death of Jesus on themselves and their children. They are making oaths and literally indemnifying Rome. Pilate has had enough, the sixth trial has ended and Jesus is sent to be crucified.

But they were insistent, demanding with loud shouts that he be crucified. And their shouts prevailed. So Pilate decided that their demand should be granted. He released the man they asked for, who had been thrown in prison for insurrection and murder. But he handed Jesus over to their will. Luke 23:23-25

When Pilate saw that he could do nothing, but that instead a riot was starting, he took some water, washed his hands before the crowd and said, "I am innocent of this man's blood. You take care of it yourselves!" In reply all the people said, "Let his blood be on us and on our children!" Then he released Barabbas for them. Matthew 27:24-26a

Because he wanted to satisfy the crowd, Pilate
released Barabbas for them. Mark 15:15a

Then Pilate handed him over to them to be crucified. John 19:16a

Pilate's soldiers mock Jesus

Rome maintained its power through application of its law and brutality to any who stepped outside of it. Indeed the word fascism is drawn from the Roman word 'fasces' which in turn is drawn from the Latin word 'fascis' meaning bundle. The Roman fasces was an axe surrounded by bundles of sticks. This was a symbol that was deposited in the towns and cities of the nations conquered by Rome to indicate that Rome was the axe, the conquered people are now bonded to Rome like the sticks and there is strength in unity. Likewise any disobedience would also see the axe fall. It was a powerful symbol of occupation to nations and individuals.

Jesus would now feel the weight of the axe fall as He is handed over to the Roman soldiers. The Roman Governor's personal guard would drag Jesus into their barracks, the Praetorian and would mock and torture Him. A crown of thorns would crush into His skull and He would be flogged at the post till almost unrecognisable. He would then be led to the cross.

Why a crown of thorns? If the Praetorian wished to mock Jesus they could have used a jester's hat. A crown of thorns is an elaborate measure to mock a kingly crown. I believe the answer lies in the redemptive work of the impending cross. When Adam disobey God in the Garden of Eden, the ground was cursed to produce thorns. Literally mankind would have to struggle and work would be hard, where prior to the fall, Adam worked in the Garden of Eden, but it was easy and light.

But to Adam he said, "Because you obeyed your wife and ate from
the tree about which I commanded you, 'You must not eat from it,'
cursed is the ground thanks to you; in painful toil you will eat of it all
the days of your life. It will produce thorns and thistles for you, but
you will eat the grain of the field. By the sweat of your brow you will
eat food until you return to the ground, for out of it you were taken;
for you are dust, and to dust you will return." Genesis 3:17-19

As the New Covenant of Grace was instituted in the blood of Jesus, the
crown of thorns is a picture of Jesus taking the curse, the thorns and
struggles of our life on His head. Jesus wore the full curse of the fall on
His head so we can wear His righteousness on ours. Jesus was pierced
by the thorns so we could once again experience New Covenant living
that is light and easy.

So they [soldiers] took Jesus, John 19:16b

Then, after he had Jesus flogged, he handed him
over to be crucified. Mark 15:15b

But after he had Jesus flogged, he handed him
over to be crucified. Matthew 27:26b

Then Pilate took Jesus and had him flogged severely. The soldiers braided
a crown of thorns and put it on his head, and they clothed him in a
purple robe. They came up to him again and again and said, "Hail, king
of the Jews!" And they struck him repeatedly in the face. John 19:1-3

So the soldiers led him into the palace (that is, the governor's
residence) and called together the whole cohort. They put a purple
cloak on him and after braiding a crown of thorns, they put it on
him. They began to salute him: "Hail, king of the Jews!" Again and

again they struck him on the head with a staff and spit on him.
Then they knelt down and paid homage to him. Mark 15:16-19

Then the governor's soldiers took Jesus into the governor's residence and
gathered the whole cohort around him. They stripped him and put a
scarlet robe around him, and after braiding a crown of thorns, they put it
on his head. They put a staff in his right hand, and kneeling down before
him, they mocked him: "Hail, king of the Jews!" They spat on him and
took the staff and struck him repeatedly on the head. Matthew 27:27-30

When they had finished mocking him, they stripped him
of the purple cloak and put his own clothes back on him.
Then they led him away to crucify him. Mark 15:20

When they had mocked him, they stripped him of the
robe and put his own clothes back on him. Then they
led him away to crucify him. Matthew 27:31

Carrying the cross

Evidently the punishment of Jesus was so severe He was unable to carry His cross so a man was randomly plucked from the crowd and forced to help. The man's name was Simon from a place called Cyrene in north Africa. Cyrene is mentioned a number of times in scripture, notably in Acts 2:10 on the day of Pentecost where people from parts of Libya near Cyrene heard the gospel in their own language. The city is modern day Tripoli, at the time called Cyrenaica, lying between Carthage and Egypt. Though on the African coast, it was a Greek city, and Jews were settled there in large numbers by Ptolemy, because he thought they would contribute to the security of the region. It is probable that Simon was walking on the Via Delarosa at that instant with his two sons Alexander and Rufus and was oblivious to what was occurring. Yet he is forced to carry the Saviour's cross behind Jesus, walking in the bloodied footsteps of the Son of God. He has picked up the cross and followed Jesus. Simon's sons walked behind, probably trying to make sense of it all, or perhaps crucifixion was so common this was just what happened.

As they were going out, they found a man from Cyrene named Simon, whom they forced to carry his cross. Matthew 27:32

The soldiers forced a passerby to carry his cross, Simon of Cyrene, who was coming in from the country (he was the father of Alexander and Rufus). Mark 15:21

As they led him away, they seized Simon of Cyrene, who was coming in from the country. They placed the cross on his back and made him carry it behind Jesus. Luke 23:26

A great number of the people followed him, among them women who were mourning and wailing for him. But Jesus turned to them and said, "Daughters of Jerusalem, do not weep for me, but weep for yourselves and for your children. For this is certain: The days are coming when they will say, 'Blessed are the barren, the wombs that never bore children, and the breasts that never nursed!' Then they will begin to say to the mountains, 'Fall on us!' and to the hills, 'Cover us!' For if such things are done when the wood is green, what will happen when it is dry?" Luke 23:27-31

Simon's task of carrying the cross was either completed at Golgotha, the place of the skull or shortly before. The Romans may well have made Jesus carry His cross the last little way. The cross would have been taken from Him and secured to an existing anchor, probably a place where numerous poor souls had met their death. The cross would probably have been as low to the ground as made sense. Logistically this was easier for the Romans to manage and it also served as a cruel form of street signage as a warning to others thinking about breaking Roman law. Two self-confessed criminals were crucified with Jesus, their crime not in dispute, their own mouths would testify that. Jesus was indeed numbered amongst the transgressors.

> *and carrying his own cross he went out to the place called "The Place of the Skull" (called in Aramaic Golgotha). There they crucified him along with two others, one on each side, with Jesus in the middle. John 19:17-18*

> *Two other criminals were also led away to be executed with him.So when they came to the place that is called "The Skull," they crucified him there, along with the criminals, one on his right and one on his left. Luke 23:32-33*

> *They came to a place called Golgotha (which means "Place of the Skull") and offered Jesus wine mixed with gall to drink. But after tasting it, he would not drink it.....Then two outlaws were crucified with him, one on his right and one on his left. Matthew 27:33-34 & 38*

> *They brought Jesus to a place called Golgotha (which is translated, "Place of the Skull"). They offered him wine mixed with myrrh, but he did not take it.... It was nine o'clock in the morning when they crucified him..... And they crucified two outlaws with him, one on his right and one on his left. Mark 15:22-23 & 25 &27-28*

Crucified at Golgotha

The crucifixion site would have been close to the city walls and outside one of the main gates on a major thoroughfare as a warning to others not to cross the might and power of Rome. There are two generally accepted locations for the crucifixion site. They are often referred to as the Catholic and Protestant sites, but they are better described as the traditional versus the modern sites as the 'Catholic' site is also accepted by the Greek Orthodox, the Armenian and Ethiopian churches.

The traditional site is the Church of the Holy Sepulchre that stands over both the crucifixion site and the tomb. Now within the 15th century walls of Jerusalem, but in the time of Jesus this was outside the city walls. There is some history to suggest that Roman emperor Hadrian in the 2nd century AD built a temple dedicated to the goddess Aphrodite in order to bury the tomb in which Jesus had been buried. In 325 AD Emperor Constantine allegedly accepted Jesus as Lord and ordered the temple be replaced by a church. His mother Helena was also dispatched to investigate holy sites and allegedly rediscovered the tomb. Tradition says that Constantine had the top of the tomb all removed so that only the rock slab that Jesus lay on was left. This was subsequently covered by a marble sheath and then a rotunda placed above it, all within the church.

The modern site is just outside the original location of the city walls if you walk through the Damascus gate, and is thus close to a major thoroughfare. The site known as 'skull hill' was identified in the mid-19th century but it wasn't until the influential British General Charles Gordon, on leave in Jerusalem, published in London about the possibility in 1883 that the idea caught on. Just like the women who were last at the cross and first at the tomb, it was two women, Charlotte Hussey and Louisa Hope who were instrumental in preserving the site. On 22 September 1892 a notice was placed in the *London Times* asking people to donate so that they could purchase the site. The Garden Tomb Association was then formally established in 1893 and the property purchased in 1894[36]. The property is an ancient olive grove or garden with a tomb cut into the rock close to the base of skull rock, a possible site for Golgotha (place of the skull). The tomb had a weeping and burial chamber and is of sufficient size to have been owned by a wealthy man. It also has a large channel at the door where a very large stone would have sat to be rolled across the entrance. There is

---

[36] www.gardentomb.com/about/brief-history accessed on 1 Feb 2017.

also a crack in the outside of the tomb caused by seismic activity or an earthquake.

I personally prefer the modern site, though perhaps for different reasons to others. The location is now the local bus depot, is concreted, smells of diesel and is not appealing at all, compared with the beautifully serene olive grove next door. The scene screams that the cross is not the end, merely the means, to focus on the empty tomb. The stone that was rolled away, that is the real power.

The photo above is a view from the Damascus gate in Jerusalem looking at skull hill and to the left, the garden tomb, taken by the American colony photo department between 1900 and 1920.

Whenever I travel to Jerusalem I run around the old city and stop, tired and exhausted in the bus depot, dodging traffic, in front of skull rock, with the olive garden to my left. I stand and look at where the cross might have been in the middle of this bus depot, in all its obscurity and commonness. The Son of Man, the Son of God, died in such a common place for all of us, the common man.

Or it could be that I like to avoid the crowds at the Church of the Holy Sepulchre. In reality it doesn't matter. My Jesus lives in me, my body is 'a' temple of the Holy Spirit. The bus depot does remind me of Isaiah's prophetic words in that it has no beauty, it is not held in high esteem and it is not desired. Yet the resurrection peace in the garden next door required the sadness of the cross. The unforced rhythms of grace in my life required Jesus to be crushed for my iniquity. Jesus took my sin and I was freely given His righteousness. Unbelievable, but true!

He sprouted up like a twig before God, like a root out of parched soil; he had no stately form or majesty that might catch our attention, no special appearance that we should want to follow him. He was despised and rejected by people, one who experienced pain and was acquainted with illness; people hid their faces from him; he was despised, and we considered him insignificant. But he lifted up our illnesses, he carried our pain; even though we thought he was being punished, attacked by God, and afflicted for something he had done. He was wounded because of our rebellious deeds, crushed because of our sins; he endured punishment that made us well; because of his wounds we have been healed. Isaiah 53:2-5

Jesus' clothes divided up

If being flogged almost to death and then nailed to a cross wasn't enough, the Roman guards then stole Jesus' clothes. Whilst His mother and other faithful supporters look on in tears and anguish the soldiers unashamedly strip Jesus and then haggle over who will steal the most from Him. The price for our sin and shame was high.

Now when the soldiers crucified Jesus, they took his clothes and made four shares, one for each soldier, and the tunic remained. (Now the tunic was seamless, woven from top to bottom as a single piece.) So the soldiers said to one another, "Let's not tear it, but throw dice to see who will get it." This took place to fulfill the scripture that says, "They divided my garments among them, and for my clothing they threw dice." So the soldiers did these things. John 19:23-24

Then they crucified him and divided his clothes, throwing dice for them, to decide what each would take. Mark 15:24

When they had crucified him, they divided his clothes by throwing dice. Then they sat down and kept guard over him there. Matthew 27:35-36

[But Jesus said, "Father, forgive them, for they don't know what they are doing."] Then they threw dice to divide his clothes. Luke 23:34

Pilate's inscription

In one last attempt to ease his soul, Pilate places a sign on the cross above Jesus' head saying 'The King of the Jews'. It is doubtful that Pilate believed this, but he knew it was out of jealousy and self-interest that the crowd demanded Jesus' death, so the sign was more of a poke in the eye to the religious elite and the crowds rather than any sense of proclaiming the truth. I still wonder how Pilate slept at night after this? How did his wife sleep?

Pilate also had a notice written and fastened to the cross, which read: "Jesus the Nazarene, the king of the Jews." Thus many of the Jewish residents of Jerusalem read this notice, because the place where Jesus was crucified was near the city, and the notice was written in Aramaic, Latin, and Greek. Then the chief priests of the Jews said to Pilate, "Do not write, 'The king of the Jews,' but rather, 'This man said, I am king of the Jews.'" Pilate answered, "What I have written, I have written." John 19:19-22

The inscription of the charge against him read,
"The king of the Jews." Mark 15:26

Above his head they put the charge against him, which read:
"This is Jesus, the king of the Jews." Matthew 27:37

There was also an inscription over him, "This
is the king of the Jews." Luke 23:38

Derision of the people

The Roman custom of crucifying people on thoroughfares as a warning to others meant large numbers of people always passed by the suffering souls. In this case, many of them derided Jesus including everyday people passing by, the religious elite, the soldiers and one of the criminals. Many of those hurling abuse possibly sat under His teaching, saw His miraculous hand at work and marvelled at His words and deeds. But they all expected an earthly Davidic king and did not recognise the establishment of the New Covenant of Grace. Jesus' death was thus not part of their plan, but it was always part of God's plan.

Those who passed by defamed him, shaking their heads and saying, "You
who can destroy the temple and rebuild it in three days, save yourself!
If you are God's Son, come down from the cross!" Matthew 27:39-40

Those who passed by defamed him, shaking their heads and saying,
"Aha! You who can destroy the temple and rebuild it in three days,
save yourself and come down from the cross!" Mark 15:29-30

The people also stood there watching, but the rulers ridiculed
him, saying, "He saved others. Let him save himself if he
is the Christ of God, his chosen one!" Luke 23:35

Derision of the religious elite

In the same way even the chief priests-together with the experts in the law and elders-were mocking him: "He saved others, but he cannot save himself! He is the king of Israel! If he comes down now from the cross, we will believe in him! He trusts in God-let God, if he wants to, deliver him now because he said, 'I am God's Son'!" Matthew 27:41-43

In the same way even the chief priests-together with the experts in the law-were mocking him among themselves: "He saved others, but he cannot save himself! Let the Christ, the king of Israel, come down from the cross now, that we may see and believe!" Mark 15:31-32a

Derision of the soldiers

The soldiers also mocked him, coming up and offering him sour wine, and saying, "If you are the king of the Jews, save yourself!" Luke 23:36-37

Derision of the two criminals

Within all the abuse, one guilty dying criminal hanging on a cross reached out his heart to Jesus. One heart felt cry of 'remember me' was all it took to guarantee this man's eternity with Jesus. Indeed, this one man would die soon after Jesus, courtesy of the Romans breaking his legs and thus causing his suffocation. He was, therefore, quite probably the first person to enter heaven's rest under the New Covenant of Grace, saved through faith and most certainly not of works. What a marvellous act of unmerited favour.

The robbers who were crucified with him also spoke abusively to him. Matthew 27:44

Those who were crucified with him also spoke abusively to him. Mark 15:32b

*One of the criminals who was hanging there railed at him,
saying, "Aren't you the Christ? Save yourself and us!" But the other
rebuked him, saying, "Don't you fear God, since you are under
the same sentence of condemnation? And we rightly so, for we are
getting what we deserve for what we did, but this man has done
nothing wrong." Then he said, "Jesus, remember me when you
come in your kingdom." And Jesus said to him, "I tell you the
truth, today you will be with me in paradise." Luke 23:39-43*

Jesus' love for His mother

The scene now moves from the large number who hurled abuse at Jesus to the faithful women and one faithful man who remained at Jesus' side. His mother, Mary, her sister, Mary the wife of Clopas and the indomitable Mary Magdalene. Faithful to the end.

The only disciple and the one faithful man there was John – the son of thunder, the disciple whom Jesus loved. John was also in the court-yard of Caiphias so it is reasonable to assume he stayed close to Jesus through this ordeal, quite possible by the side of Mary the mother of Jesus. The other disciples are nowhere to be seen. Peter's courage failed him at the second and third trials and Thomas, who so famously encouraged the other disciples to go back to Judea with Jesus to die with Him (John 11:16), is conspicuous by his absence. Two powerful men would stump up at the end, Joseph of Arimathea and Nicodemus, men who had a lot to lose but knew in their hearts that through Christ they had gained so much more. That stills leave four women compared to three men who publicly stood up for Jesus.

Just before darkness covered the land, as God turned His back on His son who bore your sin and mine, Jesus looks to His mother's welfare. This is such an incredible act of human decency. Jesus is about to cement the New Covenant in His blood and one of His final thoughts is to ensure the well being of His mum. What a picture of grace.

Now standing beside Jesus' cross were his mother, his mother's sister,
Mary the wife of Clopas, and Mary Magdalene. So when Jesus
saw his mother and the disciple whom he loved standing there,
he said to his mother, "Woman, look, here is your son!" He then
said to his disciple, "Look, here is your mother!" From that very
time the disciple took her into his own home. John 19:25-27

Darkness over the land

Jesus is slowly dying on the cross, one labouring breath after another, carrying the full weight of our sin past, present and future. The sinless lamb of God is being slain as the final Passover lamb to reconcile mankind back to God. The final Adam repairing what the first Adam created. The New Covenant in blood fulfilling the Old Covenant's requirement. For this to occur God had to judge our sin and accept the sacrifice of Jesus. Thus for three hours, God literally turned His back on His son bearing our sin, and it was dark. The Godhead becomes separated for the first time in eternity, and Jesus was truly alone.

Now from noon until three, darkness came
over all the land. Matthew 27:45

Now when it was noon, darkness came over the whole
land until three in the afternoon. Mark 15:33

It was now about noon, and darkness came over the whole land until
three in the afternoon, because the sun's light failed. Luke 23:44-45a

Jesus cries out and dies

As the darkness lifted, Jesus cried out four times from the cross:

'My God, my God, why have you forsaken me'. Jesus has been separated from God the Father for three hours as your and my sin was atoned for and the full measure of judgement poured out on Jesus. The loneliness was palpable, Jesus was indeed forsaken.

'I am thirsty.' Jesus ensured the prophetic scripture of Psalm 69:21 was fulfilled.

'Father, into your hands I commit my spirit.' As Jesus finished His earthly life, His Spirit is placed into the hands of His Father. His earthly ministry is complete, our sins forgiven, our salvation won, our perfection through the shed blood of Jesus obtained, our righteousness obtained through the finished work on the cross. Jesus paid completely for our forgiveness, our righteousness and every blessing in the heavenly realms.

'It is completed.' Jesus speaks of the end of His life and the beginning of ours. The fulfilment of the Old Covenant and the beginning of the New Covenant. The end of the law and the beginning of grace. The words 'it is completed', come from one Greek word 'teleo', that has a range of uses including a servant reporting to his master: 'I have completed the work you gave me to do' (John 17:4) and was also used by traders to say, 'the debt has been paid in full'. 'Teleo' literally means it stands finished and can not be unfinished. That is why the cross words of Jesus, 'It is completed' is so appropriate as Jesus fully met the requirements of the law and paid yours and my debt in full. Sin's hold on us is finished. Our forgiveness is finished. Our imputed righteousness from Jesus is completed.

Today, it is not our works that will bring us the blessings, it is Christ's finished work. Christian living is not about doing, but believing in His finished work. Under the law, we must do. Under grace, Jesus did. It is finished.

At about three o'clock Jesus shouted with a loud voice, "Eli, Eli, lema sabachthani?" that is, "My God, my God, why have you forsaken me?" When some of the bystanders heard it, they said, "This man is calling for Elijah." Immediately one of them ran and got a sponge, filled it with sour wine, put it on a stick, and gave it to him to drink. But the rest said, "Leave him alone! Let's see if Elijah will come to save him." Matthew 27:46-49

Around three o'clock Jesus cried out with a loud voice, "Eloi, Eloi, lema sabachthani?" which means, "My God, my God, why have you forsaken me?" When some of the bystanders heard it they said, "Listen, he is calling for Elijah!" Then someone ran, filled a sponge with sour wine, put it on a stick, and gave it to him to drink, saying, "Leave him alone! Let's see if Elijah will come to take him down!" Mark 15:34-36

After this Jesus, realizing that by this time everything was completed, said (in order to fulfill the scripture), "I am thirsty!" A jar full of sour wine was there, so they put a sponge soaked in sour wine on a branch of hyssop and lifted it to his mouth. John 19:28-29

Then Jesus, calling out with a loud voice, said, "Father, into your hands I commit my spirit!" And after he said this he breathed his last. Luke 23:46

When he had received the sour wine, Jesus said, "It is completed!" Then he bowed his head and gave up his spirit. John 19:30

Then Jesus cried out again with a loud voice and gave up his spirit. Matthew 27:50

But Jesus cried out with a loud voice and breathed his last. Mark 15:37

Events of Jesus' death

The moment Jesus died three things occurred:

- The curtain of the temple was torn in half from top to bottom.
- There was an earthquake that rocked the ground, split rocks and broke open tombs (that were generally in rock structures of some type).
- Many 'holy people' were raised from the dead and went into Jerusalem.

The curtain

Firstly, what is the curtain in the Temple? Moses was instructed by God in the Sinai Desert to construct a portable tabernacle (Exodus 26) where God would meet with the Israelites and where sacrifices would be made. The tabernacle was literally a structure made from cloth. Once in the promised land King Solomon would replace the cloth structure with a permanent Temple on Mount Moriah. This Temple would be destroyed by the Babylonians and would be rebuilt under the guidance of the priest Ezra (Ezra 6:15) during the time of the Persian King Darius. Over time this second Temple would fall into disrepair and would be largely replaced by the third Temple, known colloquially as Herod's Temple, which stood during the time of Jesus.

Within the Temple the Ark of the Covenant, where God would meet the Israelites, was in the 'Most Holy Place', a room the priest could enter once a year on the Day of Atonement. To separate the Most Holy Place from 'The Holy Place', where the Priest would enter daily to offer sacrifices, was hung a curtain (Exodus 26:31-33).

"You are to make a special curtain of blue, purple, and scarlet yarn and fine twisted linen; it is to be made with cherubim, the work of an artistic designer. You are to hang it with gold hooks on four posts

of acacia wood overlaid with gold, set in four silver bases. You are to hang this curtain under the clasps and bring the ark of the testimony in there behind the curtain. The curtain will make a division for you between the Holy Place and the Most Holy Place. Exodus 26:31-33

When the cloth tabernacle was replaced by a Temple of stone, timber and precious metals, the heavy woven curtain separating the two rooms remained. This curtain separated man from God, indicative of the separation that occurred when the original Adam sinned in the Garden of Eden (Genesis 3). The moment Jesus died, paying the price for our sin and fulfilling all the righteous requirements of the law, mankind was no longer separated from God. Because at that instant, Jesus became the way, the truth and the life. Accordingly the heavy curtain was torn in two, fully exposing the Most Holy Place where God dwelt, to the Holy Place where man entered. If ever there was a powerful message to the Jews, this was it. Furthermore the curtain was torn top to bottom. Normally when cloth is ripped, we start at the bottom and work our way up. In this instance, God reached down from heaven and tore the heavy curtain apart from the top, for God had made a way for us to be reconciled back with Him.

When the religious elite entered the Temple either that evening or the next day to offer the daily sacrifice they would have seen the curtain ripped in two. They would have known that no one had entered the Temple, because it is guarded, and even if someone had, how would they have torn this thick curtain from the top to the bottom. Apparently the religious elite thought nothing of it, repaired the curtain and went on with their religious observance. Hard heartedness will do that.

The earthquake and the holy men

The earth literally shook as the Son of God died. Not only did this serve as a sign to the Roman guards and others, it also broke open many tombs of prophets and holy men from ages past. How many is unknown but the term 'many' means more than a few.

Try and picture the scene. Ancient men in ancient cloths rose from the dead and went into Jerusalem. Matthew's gospel says they appeared to many people, indicating they presented themselves as once dead and now raised to life. It's a fair bet they communicated with all of these people about what had just occurred, the fulfilment of the law that they once served and the commencement of grace that they once looked forward to. If that wasn't enough to shake people, I don't know what would have been.

This of course raises far more questions. Did these holy men then live out the rest of their lives or did they go back to their split tombs? If they did live out their lives did they have to pay their life insurance back and how did their families feel when dad came back to claim the family house? What if they were hundreds of years old and now their great grand son is older than them, and the list of crazy questions goes on…. The point is that this was a tumultuous, life changing event that did not, could not, go unnoticed. The hardened Centurion was changed. The Roman soldiers who knew death as a daily event were changed. The people standing around were changed.

Just then the temple curtain was torn in two, from top to bottom. The earth shook and the rocks were split apart. And tombs were opened, and the bodies of many saints who had died were raised. (They came out of the tombs after his resurrection and went into the holy city and appeared to many people.) Matthew 27:51-53

And the temple curtain was torn in two, from top to bottom. Mark 15:38

The temple curtain was torn in two. Luke 23:45b

Witness of the Centurion and people

Now when the centurion and those with him who were guarding Jesus saw the earthquake and what took place, they were extremely terrified and said, "Truly this one was God's Son!" Matthew 27:54

Now when the centurion, who stood in front of him, saw how he died, he said, "Truly this man was God's Son!" Mark 15:39

Now when the centurion saw what had happened, he praised God and said, "Certainly this man was innocent!" And all the crowds that had assembled for this spectacle, when they saw what had taken place, returned home beating their breasts. Luke 23:47-48

Jesus' side is pierced

I feel for the Roman soldiers. They are terrified, perplexed, and possibly fundamentally changed. But they are still Roman soldiers and they have been given an order to remove anyone on crosses prior to the Sabbath. I can see them, still shaking, going through the time-honoured procedure of breaking the leg bones of the poor souls hanging on the crosses so they would suffocate without any leg support to keep their bodies upright and their lungs unconstrained. Oblivious to the screams and horrific sounds of bones breaking, this was their daily chore. Yet Jesus was already dead. Though to be sure, a soldier was ordered to use a spear to test the reaction of Jesus. The sword was thrust into Jesus' side, either under or between the ribs and evidently pierced His heart.

Jesus bled from His head from the thorns, His body from the lash, both hands and both feet from the nails, six times in total whilst He was alive. Yet when the spear entered His heart, causing blood and water to come forth, He bled a seventh time. Medical science points to this meaning His heart had ruptured. Jesus died literally of a broken heart so that out heart could be filled with joy. Seven times He bled, the number of completion, the number of God.

God put Adam to sleep in the Garden of Eden and opened his side to create his bride, Eve. In the same manner, God allowed Jesus to die so the bride of Christ, His church, could come forth from Jesus' pierced side.

Then, because it was the day of preparation, so that the bodies should not stay on the crosses on the Sabbath (for that Sabbath was an especially important one), the Jewish leaders asked Pilate to have the victims' legs broken and the bodies taken down. So the soldiers came and broke the legs of the two men who had been crucified with Jesus, first the one and then the other. But when they came to Jesus and saw that he was already dead, they did not break his legs. But one of the soldiers pierced his side with a spear, and blood and water flowed out immediately. And the person who saw it has testified (and his testimony is true, and he knows that he is telling the truth), so that you also may believe. For these things happened so that the scripture would be fulfilled, "Not a bone of his will be broken." And again another scripture says, "They will look on the one whom they have pierced." John 19:31-37

Those who were present

A number of woman and the apostle John were there at the cross when Jesus died. The women now receive a second mention, as faithfulness generally does. But how many women were there? You may be amazed to find it could have been dozens. Seven are specifically named or referred to, three of them are only ever mentioned here at the cross, at least three are called Mary and then Mark's gospel notes that there were 'many' more. These amazing women included:

- Mary, the mother of Jesus.
- Mary's sister (only mentioned in John 19:25).

- Mary, the wife of Clopas (only mentioned in John 19:25).
- Mary Magdalene.
- Mary, the mother of James and Joseph.
- The mother of John and James Zebedee (the sons of thunder), a woman whose name we are never told.
- Salome (only mentioned by Mark's gospel and only mentioned at the cross and bringing spices on resurrection Sunday).
- Many other women who had come up with Jesus from Jerusalem, that probably included Joanna, most likely the wife of Chuza (Luke 8:3) who was with Mary Magdalene, Mary the mother of James and others at the tomb on Sunday (Luke 24:10).

This list asks many questions such as: what is the name of Mary's sister, who is Salome and what is the name of the wife of Zebedee? The answer is no one knows. Some argue that Mary the wife of Clopas was Mary's sister, though having two daughters named Mary in one family could be confusing. Others suggest Salome was both Mary's sister and the wife of Zebedee, thus James and John's mother. All interesting speculation but not definitive. If this later point was true, than James and John Zebedee would be Jesus' cousins (like John the Baptist), which may explain why they were two of the three disciples closest to Jesus.

Many women who had followed Jesus from Galilee and given him support were also there, watching from a distance. Among them were Mary Magdalene, Mary the mother of James and Joseph, and the mother of the sons of Zebedee. Matthew 27:55-56

There were also women, watching from a distance. Among them were Mary Magdalene, and Mary the mother of James the younger and of Joses, and Salome. When he was in Galilee, they had followed

him and given him support. Many other women who had come
up with him to Jerusalem were there too. Mark 15:40-41

And all those who knew Jesus stood at a distance, and the women
who had followed him from Galilee saw these things. Luke 23:49

Jesus' burial

Sometimes courage comes at the very end. This was the case of the two powerful members of the Sanhedrin, the ruling council of the Jews, Joseph of Arimathea and Nicodemus. Nicodemus has been discussed in a previous chapter, though this is the first time that Joseph is mentioned. Little is known of him except for a few passages of scripture. He was from the Judean town of Arimathea which means 'city of the Jews'. The two early church historians Eusebius and Jerome, identify Arimathea with Ramah in the hills of Ephraim, the city where the prophet Samuel was born (1 Samuel 1:19)[37]. Joseph was considered good and upright and was also rich and a prominent member of the Sanhedrin, thus senior in the religious elite ranks. Interestingly as such a senior member of the Sanhedrin, he was one of two of its members mentioned in the Bible to be disciples of Jesus, the other being Nicodemus, who it can be presumed by his public actions with Joseph and his prior defence of Jesus (John 7:50) was also a follower. Luke's gospel says Joseph did not consent to the Sanhedrin's decision and action, indicating his disapproval was verbal and public. No wonder scripture says he went boldly to Pilate to ask for the body of Jesus. Joseph had previously been a secret disciple (John 19:38), fearing the Jews, but now he publicly disagrees with the Sanhedrin, goes boldly to the prefect and personally takes Jesus down from the cross and openly buries Him in his own tomb. Such an act world have invited the scorn and ridicule of the religious elite and possible expulsion from the Sanhedrin. Such worldly derision means little to the true disciples

---

[37] www.biblehub.com/topical/a/Arimathea.htm access 1 Feb 2017

of the Saviour of the world though. Sometimes courage comes at the very end.

The scene here is one of speed. There is no time for the customary lengthy burial arrangements, though spices were brought and the body was wrapped in a clean white cloth. Jesus was laid in Joseph's tomb because it was close, as the Sabbath was 'about to begin'. A large stone was then rolled in front indicating a stone of such size it could not be lifted. This was therefore a large tomb with a large stone and thus a large stone channel for it to be rolled in. As an aside, this all fits the evidence for the garden tomb.

Now when it was evening, there came a rich man from Arimathea, named Joseph, who was also a disciple of Jesus. He went to Pilate and asked for the body of Jesus. Then Pilate ordered that it be given to him. Joseph took the body, wrapped it in a clean linen cloth, and placed it in his own new tomb that he had cut in the rock. Then he rolled a great stone across the entrance of the tomb and went away. (Now Mary Magdalene and the other Mary were sitting there, opposite the tomb.) Matthew 27:57-60

Now when evening had already come, since it was the day of preparation (that is, the day before the Sabbath), Joseph of Arimathea, a highly regarded member of the council, who was himself looking forward to the kingdom of God, went boldly to Pilate and asked for the body of Jesus. Pilate was surprised that he was already dead. He called the centurion and asked him if he had been dead for some time. When Pilate was informed by the centurion, he gave the body to Joseph. After Joseph bought a linen cloth and took down the body, he wrapped it in the linen and placed it in a tomb cut out of the rock. Then he rolled a stone across the entrance of the tomb. Mark 15:42-46

Now there was a man named Joseph who was a member of the council,
a good and righteous man. (He had not consented to their plan and
action.) He was from the Judean town of Arimathea, and was looking
forward to the kingdom of God. He went to Pilate and asked for the body
of Jesus. Then he took it down, wrapped it in a linen cloth, and placed it
in a tomb cut out of the rock, where no one had yet been buried. It was
the day of preparation and the Sabbath was beginning. Luke 23:50-54

After this, Joseph of Arimathea, a disciple of Jesus (but secretly, because
he feared the Jewish leaders), asked Pilate if he could remove the body
of Jesus. Pilate gave him permission, so he went and took the body
away. Nicodemus, the man who had previously come to Jesus at night,
accompanied Joseph, carrying a mixture of myrrh and aloes weighing
about seventy-five pounds. Then they took Jesus' body and wrapped it,
with the aromatic spices, in strips of linen cloth according to Jewish
burial customs. Now at the place where Jesus was crucified there was
a garden, and in the garden was a new tomb where no one had yet
been buried. And so, because it was the Jewish day of preparation and
the tomb was nearby, they placed Jesus' body there. John 19:38-42

Preparations by the women

I am still in awe of these women at the cross. They have not left the
side of Jesus. They watched Joseph and Nicodemus take the body of
Jesus, hastily spice and wrap Him and then lay Him in the new tomb.
Because the Sabbath was looming they rushed home in obedience to
the law but spent their time preparing the spices and perfumes that
they intended to use to 'properly' prepare the body. My goodness were
they in for a shock when they returned on what we now call Sunday
morning.

(Now Mary Magdalene and the other Mary were sitting
there, opposite the tomb.) Matthew 27:61

*Mary Magdalene and Mary the mother of Joses saw
where the body was placed. Mark 15:47*

*The women who had accompanied Jesus from Galilee followed,
and they saw the tomb and how his body was laid in it. Then they
returned and prepared aromatic spices and perfumes. On the Sabbath
they rested according to the commandment. Luke 23:55-56*

Guard placed at the tomb

So the scene closes with a Roman guard placed at the tomb. The religious elite are cautious to the end to ensure their closed shop religiosity continues under the occupation. They are taking no chances and want to ensure the body is not snatched away as a final act of deception. So the prefect orders not just a full armed Roman guard but the tomb to be sealed. For someone to take the body they would have to defeat trained soldiers and then break the seal and incur the wrath of the occupying power. This would have been almost inconceivable, which is why the religious elite were satisfied that a Roman guard was in place.

*The next day (which is after the day of preparation) the chief priests and
the Pharisees assembled before Pilate and said, "Sir, we remember that
while that deceiver was still alive he said, 'After three days I will rise
again.' So give orders to secure the tomb until the third day. Otherwise
his disciples may come and steal his body and say to the people, 'He has
been raised from the dead,' and the last deception will be worse than
the first." Pilate said to them, "Take a guard of soldiers. Go and make
it as secure as you can." So they went with the soldiers of the guard
and made the tomb secure by sealing the stone. Matthew 27:62-66*

No mortal came for the body of Jesus. The guards remained at their post through the Sabbath day and night and into the following, third day. And then everything changed......

CHAPTER 14

Resurrection
(Sunday 5th April 33 AD)

I've always preferred visiting the garden tomb in Jerusalem rather than the Church of the Holy Sepulchre. There is no definitive proof that either one is the actual burial spot and both are the result of the historical and theological passion of either Constantine and his mother Helena or the British General Charles Gordon. The garden tomb site is quieter, the tomb how I pictured it, the channel for the entrance stone to sit in to be rolled away large and the whole site an olive grove, literally a garden. There is peace in the garden, resurrection peace.

It's Sunday morning and the Roman guards are watching the tomb. Romans were good at watching stuff and keeping things safe. They did it with a degree of firmness we struggle to understand. The Jews were not their people so their level of compassion was zero. They were as accustomed to death as we are going to the movies so suffice to say the doctrine of minimum force whilst guarding stuff was not their modus operandi. They were Rome, they had defeated all in their path and they were not afraid. Until they met the host of heaven. Shepherds rejoiced at such a sight, the fiercest warriors in the world trembled.

And the host of heaven came.

The stone is rolled away

The soldiers of the mightiest conquering power the world had ever encountered had met fierce foes on the battlefield and had seen sights unimaginable. They had never experienced the shock and awe of the host of heaven and the soldiers shook violently and froze still as dead men. So much so that during the entire encounter between the woman at the tomb and the angel, the fierce and battle-hardened armed Roman guards literally stood still, as silent witnesses to all that transpired. They were told to guard the tomb and not leave their post, so remain they did, completely terrified.

It was Mary Magdalene; Mary, the mother of James and John; Salome; Joanna and other women who came to the tomb with spices to properly treat the body of Jesus. Where, you ask, are our brave disciples? Good question. They are holed up in a room, afraid. But not these women. Not Joseph and Nicodemus who buried Jesus and not these women. When they arrived they saw two things – the stone rolled away and terrified, speechless, mortified, Roman guards.

> *Now after the Sabbath, at dawn on the first day of the week, Mary Magdalene and the other Mary went to look at the tomb. Suddenly there was a severe earthquake, for an angel of the Lord descending from heaven came and rolled away the stone and sat on it. His appearance was like lightning, and his clothes were white as snow. The guards were shaken and became like dead men because they were so afraid of him. Matthew 28:1-4*

> *When the Sabbath was over, Mary Magdalene, Mary the mother of James, and Salome bought aromatic spices so that they might go and anoint him. And very early on the first day of the week, at sunrise, they went to the tomb. They had been asking each other, "Who will roll away the stone for us from the entrance to*

the tomb?" But when they looked up, they saw that the stone,
which was very large, had been rolled back. Mark 16:1-4

Now on the first day of the week, at early dawn, the women went to
the tomb, taking the aromatic spices they had prepared. They found
that the stone had been rolled away from the tomb, Luke 24:1-2

Now very early on the first day of the week, while it was still
dark, Mary Magdalene came to the tomb and saw that the
stone had been moved away from the entrance. John 20:1

Angel(s) appears to the women

As the guards stood motionless, the angel(s) said to the women, 'Do
not be afraid', a statement not given to the Roman guards. And then
the angel(s) spoke about the risen Christ and pointed them to the
empty tomb and the waiting risen Messiah in Galilee, 160 kilometres
north. I see a picture of the mighty host of heaven with compassion
in their eyes for these godly women and the odd glance of terrifying
power towards the guards.

But the angel said to the women, "Do not be afraid; I know that
you are looking for Jesus, who was crucified. He is not here, for
he has been raised, just as he said. Come and see the place where
he was lying. Then go quickly and tell his disciples, 'He has been
raised from the dead. He is going ahead of you into Galilee. You
will see him there.' Listen, I have told you!" Matthew 28:5-7

Then as they went into the tomb, they saw a young man dressed
in a white robe sitting on the right side; and they were alarmed.
But he said to them, "Do not be alarmed. You are looking for Jesus
the Nazarene, who was crucified. He has been raised! He is not
here. Look, there is the place where they laid him. But go, tell his

disciples, even Peter, that he is going ahead of you into Galilee.
You will see him there, just as he told you." Mark 16:5-7

but when they went in, they did not find the body of the Lord Jesus. While
they were perplexed about this, suddenly two men stood beside them in
dazzling attire. The women were terribly frightened and bowed their faces
to the ground, but the men said to them, "Why do you look for the living
among the dead? He is not here, but has been raised! Remember how
he told you, while he was still in Galilee, that the Son of Man must be
delivered into the hands of sinful men, and be crucified, and on the third
day rise again." Then the women remembered his words, Luke 24:3-8

The reports

Two groups rushed from the tomb that morning. Godly faithful women, tearful, joyful, fearful and excited – ran back to tell the disciples. At the same time, and probably in a different direction, some of the guards ran to tell the chief priests what had happened. So what were the other guards doing? Remember, they are still Roman soldiers who understand the penalty for disobeying orders. I see them running back to their headquarters and telling their Centurion what had happened, the same Centurion who was changed a few days previously as he stood at the foot of the cross. I see this Centurion quietly sitting, listening and praising God. There is no indication anywhere in scripture that the soldiers were punished for what happened at the tomb, even after they allowed the lie to spread that they fell asleep on duty, a crime punishable by death. Roman authority is built on disciple and order so how could such a lie be allowed to propagate. Only one thing makes sense, a Centurion changed at the foot of the cross after hearing the words of his soldiers tell of the resurrection of the Son of God. Such things change the hardest of men. Such things lead to forgiveness.

So they left the tomb quickly, with fear and great joy,
and ran to tell his disciples. Matthew 28:8

*While they were going, some of the guard went into the city and
told the chief priests everything that had happened. After they had
assembled with the elders and formed a plan, they gave a large sum
of money to the soldiers, telling them, "You are to say, 'His disciples
came at night and stole his body while we were asleep.' If this matter
is heard before the governor, we will satisfy him and keep you out of
trouble." So they took the money and did as they were instructed. And
this story is told among the Jews to this day. Matthew 28:11-15*

*and when they returned from the tomb they told all these things to
the eleven and to all the rest. Now it was Mary Magdalene, Joanna,
Mary the mother of James, and the other women with them who
told these things to the apostles. But these words seemed like pure
nonsense to them, and they did not believe them. Luke 24:9-11*

*So she [Mary Magdalene] went running to Simon Peter and the other
disciple whom Jesus loved and told them, "They have taken the Lord
from the tomb, and we don't know where they have put him!" John 20:2*

*Then they [Mary Magdalene, Mary the mother of James,
and Salome] went out and ran from the tomb, for terror
and bewilderment had seized them. And they said nothing
to anyone, because they were afraid. Mark 16:8*

Peter and John visit the tomb and Jesus' first appearance

Evidently those beautiful women, including Mary Magdalene, saw the
angels, ran to tell the disciples and then some of the women ran back
with Peter and John and waited outside. Peter and John went into the
tomb, saw it empty and then went back to where they were staying.
Mary and some other of the women remained at the tomb, crying, and
that's where Mary became the first person on earth to meet the risen
Saviour, Jesus the Christ.

Then Peter and the other disciple set out to go to the tomb. The two were running together, but the other disciple ran faster than Peter and reached the tomb first. He bent down and saw the strips of linen cloth lying there, but he did not go in. Then Simon Peter, who had been following him, arrived and went right into the tomb. He saw the strips of linen cloth lying there, and the face cloth, which had been around Jesus' head, not lying with the strips of linen cloth but rolled up in a place by itself. Then the other disciple, who had reached the tomb first, came in, and he saw and believed. (For they did not yet understand the scripture that Jesus must rise from the dead.) So the disciples went back to their homes. John 20:3-10

But Peter got up and ran to the tomb. He bent down and saw only the strips of linen cloth; then he went home, wondering what had happened. Luke 24:12

So the disciples went back to their homes. But Mary stood outside the tomb weeping. As she wept, she bent down and looked into the tomb. And she saw two angels in white sitting where Jesus' body had been lying, one at the head and one at the feet. They said to her, "Woman, why are you weeping?" Mary replied, "They have taken my Lord away, and I do not know where they have put him!" When she had said this, she turned around and saw Jesus standing there, but she did not know that it was Jesus. Jesus said to her, "Woman, why are you weeping? Who are you looking for?" Because she thought he was the gardener, she said to him, "Sir, if you have carried him away, tell me where you have put him, and I will take him." Jesus said to her, "Mary." She turned and said to him in Aramaic, "Rabboni" (which means Teacher). Jesus replied, "Do not touch me, for I have not yet ascended to my Father. Go to my brothers and tell them, 'I am ascending to my Father and your Father, to my God and your God.'" Mary Magdalene came and informed the disciples, "I have seen the Lord!" And she told them what Jesus had said to her. John 20:11-18

[[Early on the first day of the week, after he arose, he appeared first to Mary Magdalene, from whom he had driven out seven demons. She went out and told those who were with him, while they were mourning and weeping. And when they heard that he was alive and had been seen by her, they did not believe. Mark 16:9-11

But Jesus met them, saying, "Greetings!" They came to him, held on to his feet and worshiped him. Then Jesus said to them, "Do not be afraid. Go and tell my brothers to go to Galilee. They will see me there." Matthew 28:9-10

The road to Emmaus

This incredible history-shattering story then moves to modern Highway 1 from Jerusalem to Tel Aviv, which 2000 years ago was in and around the road to a village called Emmaus. No one knows exactly where the ancient town of Emmaus was and therefore which route the road took. Our old Jewish friend and historian, Josephus, writes about two towns called Emmaus. In his book '*Antiquities of the Jews*' he refers to a city called Emmaus, later called Emmaus Nicopolis, located 170 Roman stadia (thirty kilometres) from Jerusalem[38]. In his other work '*The Jewish War*' he writes about another town called Emmaus, just sixty Roman stadia (ten kilometres) from Jerusalem, where Vespasian settled 800 Roman legionnaires after the First Jewish Revolt[39]. If you had to choose you would go with the closer town, though the location is far less important than the conversation en route. For those seeking to emulate the spiritual journey from Jerusalem to Emmaus, my strong recommendation is to stay off the road, as it is really busy.

---

[38]   Thiede, Carsten Peter (2005). „Die Wiederentdeckung von Emmaus bei Jerusalem" [Rediscovering Emmaus near Jerusalem]. *Zeitschrift für antikes Christentum* (in German). Walter de Gruyter. 8: 593–599

[39]   Josephus, The Jewish War, Chapter 6

The story of Jesus appearing to two disciples on the road to Emmaus is covered extensively in Luke's gospel, with a passing comment in Mark about a couple of blokes walking in the countryside. It is an incredible piece of scripture as Jesus explains the gospel of grace starting from Moses, right the way through to the prophets. So incredible that the hearts of the two disciples burned inside them. Jesus then cements His words about the New Covenant by breaking bread. The last meal He shared with the eleven disciples included breaking bread to herald the coming New Covenant. Now the first meal He has with believers is to break bread to reveal that the New Covenant has come.

So who was walking to Emmaus? It is two believers – one of them is identified as Cleopas and because they report to the eleven disciples, neither of them is one of the eleven but are close to them as they knew where they were hiding. The key is that they were believers. Jesus broke bread only with the eleven before His death, now He breaks bread with all believers after his resurrection.

Now that very day two of them were on their way to a village called Emmaus, about seven miles from Jerusalem. They were talking to each other about all the things that had happened. While they were talking and debating these things, Jesus himself approached and began to accompany them (but their eyes were kept from recognizing him). Then he said to them, "What are these matters you are discussing so intently as you walk along?" And they stood still, looking sad. Then one of them, named Cleopas, answered him, "Are you the only visitor to Jerusalem who doesn't know the things that have happened there in these days?" He said to them, "What things?""The things concerning Jesus the Nazarene," they replied, "a man who, with his powerful deeds and words, proved to be a prophet before God and all the people; and how our chief priests and rulers handed him over to be condemned to death, and crucified him. But we had hoped that he was the one who was going to redeem Israel. Not only this, but it is now the third day since these things happened.

Furthermore, some women of our group amazed us. They were at the tomb early this morning, and when they did not find his body, they came back and said they had seen a vision of angels, who said he was alive. Then some of those who were with us went to the tomb, and found it just as the women had said, but they did not see him." So he said to them, "You foolish people-how slow of heart to believe all that the prophets have spoken! Wasn't it necessary for the Christ to suffer these things and enter into his glory?" Then beginning with Moses and all the prophets, he interpreted to them the things written about himself in all the scriptures. So they approached the village where they were going. He acted as though he wanted to go farther, but they urged him, "Stay with us, because it is getting toward evening and the day is almost done." So he went in to stay with them. When he had taken his place at the table with them, he took the bread, blessed and broke it, and gave it to them. At this point their eyes were opened and they recognized him. Then he vanished out of their sight. They said to each other, "Didn't our hearts burn within us while he was speaking with us on the road, while he was explaining the scriptures to us?" So they got up that very hour and returned to Jerusalem. They found the eleven and those with them gathered together.....Then they told what had happened on the road, and how they recognized him when he broke the bread. Luke 24:13-33 & 35

After this he appeared in a different form to two of them while they were on their way to the country. They went back and told the rest, but they did not believe them. Mark 16:12-13

Jesus appears to Peter

Jesus has now appeared to Mary Magdalene and other faithful women. He has appeared to two believers on the road to Emmaus, and broken bread of the New Covenant with them. He then appears to Peter before meeting with the rest of the disciples. Only Luke's gospel states this, backed up by the apostle Paul in his letter to the church at Corinth. Mark's gospel, written mostly as Peter's account is silent on this meeting, which is odd. Surely Peter would have shouted from the roof tops about the risen Lord coming to see him before any of the other disciples and Mark would have recorded it?

The bottom line is that no one knows what was said in that meeting between Jesus and Peter. What we can assume is that Jesus was pure love, grace, peace and forgiveness and that Peter was both joyful at seeing Jesus and remorseful for denying Him. However, since Peter was considered the leader of the early church, how gracious of Jesus to see Peter first, a silent message of Peter's continued leadership.

> *and saying, "The Lord has really risen, and has appeared to Simon!" Luke 24:34*

> *and that he appeared to Cephas, then to the twelve. 1 Corinthians 15:5*

Jesus appears to the ten disciples (excluding Thomas)

On that Sunday evening, Jesus appears to the rest of the disciples, who are still holed up behind locked doors. At this stage the disciples had received three reports about the risen Saviour: from the women, from Cleopas and his mate on the road to Emmaus, and from Peter. Now Jesus, in His post-resurrection perfect body that allows Him to appear whenever and wherever He wants, joins the disciples. Their response is still one of fear until He explains everything, as He did to Cleopas and his friend and then shows them the crucifixion marks on His hands and feet. The disciples were overjoyed, but one was missing, Thomas.

> *While they were saying these things, Jesus himself stood among them and said to them, "Peace be with you." But they were startled and terrified, thinking they saw a ghost. Then he said to them, "Why are you frightened, and why do doubts arise in your hearts? Look at my hands and my feet; it's me! Touch me and see; a ghost does not have flesh and bones like you see I have." When he had said this, he showed them his*

hands and his feet. And while they still could not believe it (because of their joy) and were amazed, he said to them, "Do you have anything here to eat?" So they gave him a piece of broiled fish, and he took it and ate it in front of them. Then he said to them, "These are my words that I spoke to you while I was still with you, that everything written about me in the law of Moses and the prophets and the psalms must be fulfilled."

Then he opened their minds so they could understand the scriptures, and said to them, "Thus it stands written that the Christ would suffer and would rise from the dead on the third day, and repentance for the forgiveness of sins would be proclaimed in his name to all nations, beginning from Jerusalem. You are witnesses of these things. And look, I am sending you what my Father promised. But stay in the city until you have been clothed with power from on high." Luke 24:36-49

On the evening of that day, the first day of the week, the disciples had gathered together and locked the doors of the place because they were afraid of the Jewish leaders. Jesus came and stood among them and said to them, "Peace be with you." When he had said this, he showed them his hands and his side. Then the disciples rejoiced when they saw the Lord. So Jesus said to them again, "Peace be with you. Just as the Father has sent me, I also send you." And after he said this, he breathed on them and said, "Receive the Holy Spirit. If you forgive anyone's sins, they are forgiven; if you retain anyone's sins, they are retained." John 20:19-23

Now Thomas (called Didymus), one of the twelve, was not with them when Jesus came. The other disciples told him, "We have seen the Lord!" But he replied, "Unless I see the wounds from the nails in his hands, and put my finger into the wounds from the nails, and put my hand into his side, I will never believe it!" John 20:24-25

A week later.....

Jesus appears to the eleven disciples and then others

A week later, the doors are still locked, and Jesus appears and specifically addresses Thomas. Furthermore, Jesus outlines the task, the great commission, for believers to go into the world and preach the gospel of grace. Jesus would then appear to over 500 believers including, graciously, to members of His own family.

Eight days later the disciples were again together in the house, and Thomas was with them. Although the doors were locked, Jesus came and stood among them and said, "Peace be with you!" Then he said to Thomas, "Put your finger here, and examine my hands. Extend your hand and put it into my side. Do not continue in your unbelief, but believe." Thomas replied to him, "My Lord and my God!" Jesus said to him, "Have you believed because you have seen me? Blessed are the people who have not seen and yet have believed." John 20:26-29

Then he appeared to the eleven themselves, while they were eating, and he rebuked them for their unbelief and hardness of heart, because they did not believe those who had seen him resurrected. He said to them, "Go into all the world and preach the gospel to every creature. The one who believes and is baptized will be saved, but the one who does not believe will be condemned. These signs will accompany those who believe: In my name they will drive out demons; they will speak in new languages; they will pick up snakes with their hands, and whatever poison they drink will not harm them; they will place their hands on the sick and they will be well." Mark 16:14-18

Then he appeared to more than five hundred of the brothers and sisters at one time, most of whom are still alive, though some have fallen asleep. Then he appeared to James, then to all the apostles. 1 Corinthians 15:6-7

The thirty-seventh and final miracle – Jesus in Galilee with power over nature

Jesus now returns to Galilee for the first time since He left the previous year to teach in the Judean, Samaritan and Perean towns and cities. The disciples also head to Galilee for that is where they were told to go to see Jesus. When they arrive back in Galilee they return to their fishing roots, which is where Jesus found them, on the Sea of Galilee. They were unsuccessfully fishing and had been at it all night until Jesus turned up and said to let down their nets on the right side.

This is not the first time that Jesus asked His disciples to let down their nets. On a previous occasion Jesus had told Peter to throw his nets into the water and when Peter threw just one net down, he caught so many fish that the net 'was breaking' (Luke 5:4-7). To save the haul of fish, the other disciples quickly gathered the fish into their boats to keep the net from breaking.

Now with the post-resurrection Jesus, a similar incident takes place. Once again, Jesus asked His disciples to cast their net out and they caught a multitude of fish. However, "It was full of large fish, 153, but even with so many the net was not torn"(John 21:11). Notice that in the first case, the net was breaking. In the second case, it was not! Something supernatural happened to their nets after Jesus rose from the dead! Favour descended on those who knew Jesus. Because of the death and resurrection of Jesus, not only were the disciples blessed but all who know Jesus are blessed (Ephesians 1:3).

Nothing symbolises this blessing more than the abundance of fish, 153 to be precise. The Bible states the disciples marvelled at the fact that their net held together even though it contained so many large fish (John 21:11). Additionally, the catching of such a large amount of fish happened only after Jesus became involved in the work. This is a subtle (or perhaps not so subtle!) reminder that without Jesus the disciples' (and any believer's) attempts to accomplish something great in their own strength, will fail, but that with Jesus all things are possible (John 15:5).

As a fascinating aside, 153 is the grand total of people directly named as being blessed through healing, restoration and/or wholeness in the forty-eight seperate incidents mentioned in the gospels. Only thirty-seven of these forty-eight events were classed as miracles though. The book of Mark records three occasions where Jesus blessed three people, healing a man with an unclean spirit (Mark 1:23), healing a man who was deaf (Mark 7:32) and making whole another who was blind (Mark 8:22). Matthew records twenty-three occasions where Jesus blessed a total of forty-seven people, including a leper (Matthew 8:2), a non-Israelite woman and her daughter (Matthew 15:22), Mary Magdalene (Matthew 27:56) and Joseph of Arimathea (Matthew 27:57). Luke records fourteen occasions where ninety-four people were blessed, including the seventy disciples sent out to preach and heal (Luke 10:1), ten lepers cleansed at the same time (Luke 17:12) and Zaccheus (Luke 19:2). Lastly, John records eight incidents where nine people were blessed by Jesus, including Nicodemus (John 3:1), the woman accused of adultery (John 8:11) and Lazarus (John 11).

After this Jesus revealed himself again to the disciples by the Sea of Tiberias. Now this is how he did so. Simon Peter, Thomas (called Didymus), Nathanael (who was from Cana in Galilee), the sons of Zebedee, and two other disciples of his were together. Simon Peter told them, "I am going fishing.""We will go with you," they replied. They went out and got into the boat, but that night they caught nothing. When it was already very early morning, Jesus stood on the beach, but the disciples did not know that it was Jesus. So Jesus said to them, "Children, you don't have any fish, do you?" They replied, "No." He told them, "Throw your net on the right side of the boat, and you will find some." So they threw the net, and were not able to pull it in because of the large number of fish. Then the disciple whom Jesus loved said to Peter, "It is the Lord!" So Simon Peter, when he heard that it was the Lord, tucked in his outer garment (for he had nothing on underneath it), and plunged into the sea. Meanwhile the other disciples came with the boat, dragging the net full of fish, for they were not far from land, only about a hundred yards. When they got out on the beach, they saw a charcoal fire ready with a fish placed on it, and bread. Jesus said, "Bring some of the fish you have just now caught." So Simon Peter went aboard and pulled the net to shore. It was full of large fish, one hundred fifty-three, but although there were so many, the net was not torn. "Come, have breakfast," Jesus said. But none of the disciples dared to ask him, "Who are you?" because they knew it was the Lord. Jesus came and took the bread and gave it to them, and did the same with the fish. This was now the third time Jesus was revealed to the disciples after he was raised from the dead. Then when they had finished breakfast, Jesus said to Simon Peter, "Simon, son of John, do you love me more than these do?" He replied, "Yes, Lord, you know I love you." Jesus told him, "Feed my lambs." Jesus said a second time, "Simon, son of John, do you love me?" He replied, "Yes, Lord, you know I love you." Jesus told him, "Shepherd my sheep." Jesus said a third time, "Simon, son of John, do you love me?" Peter was distressed that Jesus asked him a third time, "Do you love me?" and said, "Lord, you know everything. You know that I love you." Jesus replied, "Feed my sheep. I tell you the solemn truth, when you were young, you tied your clothes around you and went wherever you wanted, but when you are old, you will stretch out your hands, and others will tie you up and bring you where you do not want to go." (Now Jesus said this to indicate clearly by what kind of death Peter was going to glorify God.) After he said this, Jesus told Peter, "Follow me." Peter turned around and saw the disciple whom Jesus loved following them. (This was the disciple who had leaned back against Jesus' chest at the meal and asked, "Lord, who is the one who is going to betray you?") So when Peter saw him, he asked Jesus, "Lord, what about him?" Jesus replied, "If I want him to live until I come back, what concern is that of yours? You follow me!" So the saying circulated among the brothers and sisters that this disciple was not going to die. But Jesus did not say to him that he was not going to die, but rather, "If I want him to live until I come back, what concern is that of yours?" John 21:1-23

Last words and ascension

Jesus walked the earth for forty days after his resurrection, the same amount of time He was in the wilderness after His baptism and one day for each year the ancient Jews wandered in the desert after leaving Egypt. I think post-resurrection fellowship was probably more pleasant than post-baptism Judean wilderness temptation though, but you couldn't have the earlier without the latter. During this time Jesus met with His disciples, encouraged them, reminded them of what He had taught and then left them with two final words.

Last words are always instructive. I would like to think that my last words on earth would be to try and encapsulate all I lived for, wrapped up in a few sentences. Not an enigma encased in a riddle but full of wisdom and indisputable truth. Jesus of course nails it, as He leaves what is known as the 'Great Commission', to be witnesses to Jesus in all the world. Literally to go. Yet Jesus knows His disciples only too well, especially the impetuous Peter. Before they go, they must wait. I know what you're thinking, we're back to this enigma wrapped in a riddle.

To understand, we have to head back to the seven Jewish festivals or holy days. Jesus was crucified on the first festival day of Passover. He was in the grave at the second festival, that of the thanks giving offering. He rose again at the third festival, that of the Feast of Weeks. Fifty days from Passover was the fourth festival, that of Pentecost. When Jesus ascended to heaven, Pentecost was only days away. Jesus asked His disciples to wait for the new Pentecost under the New Covenant, to arrive, where the promised Holy Spirit would descend on the disciples and they would receive power to go, power to be His witnesses, power to change the world.

Jesus would ascend from a mountain in the vicinity of Bethany, which would likely be the Mount of Olives. Why was Bethany important? Perhaps because it was near the home of Mary, Martha and Lazarus, the home in which Jesus stayed most nights during the final week, the home of the two covenants, Martha at work, Mary at rest.

To the same apostles also, after his suffering, he presented himself alive with many convincing proofs. He was seen by them over a forty-day period and spoke about matters concerning the kingdom of God. While he was with them, he declared, "Do not leave Jerusalem, but wait there for what my Father promised, which you heard about from me. For John baptized with water, but you will be baptized with the Holy Spirit not many days from now." So when they had gathered together, they began to ask him, "Lord, is this the time when you are restoring the kingdom to Israel?" He told them, "You are not permitted to know the times or periods that the Father has set by his own authority. But you will receive power when the Holy Spirit has come upon you, and you will be my witnesses in Jerusalem, and in all Judea and Samaria, and to the farthest parts of the earth." After he had said this, while they were watching, he was lifted up and a cloud hid him from their sight. As they were still staring into the sky while he was going, suddenly two men in white clothing stood near them and said, "Men of Galilee, why do you stand here looking up into the sky? This same Jesus who has been taken up from you into heaven will come back in the same way you saw him go into heaven." Acts 1:3-11

So the eleven disciples went to Galilee to the mountain Jesus had designated. When they saw him, they worshiped him, but some doubted. Then Jesus came up and said to them, "All authority in heaven and on earth has been given to me. Therefore go and make disciples of all nations, baptizing them in the name of the Father and the Son and the Holy Spirit, teaching them to obey everything I have commanded you. And remember, I am with you always, to the end of the age." Matthew 28:16-20

After the Lord Jesus had spoken to them, he was taken up into heaven and sat down at the right hand of God. Mark 16:19

Then Jesus led them out as far as Bethany, and lifting up his hands, he blessed them. Now during the blessing he departed and was taken up into heaven. Luke 24:50-51

What did the disciples do next?

I'm always intrigued by what the disciples did next. Next steps show where the heart is. After the death of Jesus, the disciples walked back to Galilee and back to fishing, for Jesus had appeared to them and told them He'd meet them there. There is no indication they shared the good news en route, and no indication that they didn't. It appears possible that they just went back to their nets. Post-ascension the disciples head to Jerusalem, worshipping, praising, teaching and preaching. They are a different bunch and post Pentecost they are a powerful Spirit filled world-changing evangelical force for good.

So they worshiped him and returned to Jerusalem with great joy, and were continually in the temple courts blessing God. Luke 24:52-53

They went out and proclaimed everywhere, while the Lord worked with them and confirmed the word through the accompanying signs. Mark 16:20

So ends the rollicking gospel account of the Son of God, the greatest story ever told. A story that began with the beginning of the world when Jesus, the Word of Life created our world and us. We became separated from our creator God by the actions of the first man, Adam, and now through the actions of the second Adam, Jesus, we are once again made right with God.

God made a covenant of law with man at Sinai, through the prophet Moses. Mankind was never able to keep it and ended up receiving the curses of the law, not its blessings. God then made a New Covenant of Grace to complete the Old Covenant. This New Covenant was made between two infallible beings, God the Father and God the Son and is therefore a covenant that can never be broken, will always be fulfilled and will never change. This New Covenant was that Jesus, the sinless Son of God, would pay the penalty for our sin on the Roman cross and die as our atoning sacrifice therefore satisfying the righteous wrath of God and making us right with God. Jesus took our sin and paid our price on that cross of death and we received His righteousness, so that whenever God looks at us, He sees Jesus. That is why there is no longer any condemnation for those who believe, because we are now the very righteousness of God in Christ Jesus.

There is therefore now no condemnation for those who are in Christ Jesus. For the law of the life-giving Spirit in Christ Jesus has set you free from the law of sin and death. For God achieved what the law could not do because it was weakened through the flesh. By sending his own Son in the likeness of sinful flesh and concerning sin, he condemned sin in the flesh, so that the righteous requirement of the law may be fulfilled in us, who do not walk according to the flesh but according to the Spirit. Romans 8:1-4

Not everything Jesus did was recorded. There are only thirty-seven recorded miraculous events and only forty-eight stories of blessing have names, dates, people and places attached to them. But Jesus healed, restored and released thousands of desperate souls. This ministry of healing and restoring was both to authenticate His message and to show the compassion of a loving God. Such healing and restoration is available to us today, now.

Now Jesus performed many other miraculous signs in the presence of the disciples, which are not recorded in this book. But these are recorded so that you may believe that Jesus is the Christ, the Son of God, and that by believing you may have life in his name. John 20:30-31

This is the disciple who testifies about these things and has written these things, and we know that his testimony is true. There are many other things that Jesus did. If every one of them were written down, I suppose the whole world would not have room for the books that would be written. John 21:24-25

Conclusion

There are many other things that Jesus did. If every one of them were written down, I suppose the whole world would not have room for the books that would be written. John 21:25

There is something initially sad about coming to the end of a book and realising you haven't even started. This can be the feeling at the end of the 64,766 words of the four gospels when confronted with the last line in John's gospel stating that Jesus did so much more. Then again perhaps we should have expected such a thing from the beginning. The creator and Saviour of the world was always going to be bigger than what we could ever hope to imagine. Jesus, who in His very nature is God, living outside time and space, who through all things in heaven and earth were created, was always a big ask to confine to mere words. How blessed are we that the Word became flesh as a baby, grew into a man and died to reconcile us back to the Father.

That, my friends is called grace, transacted at the cross. We gain the righteousness of Jesus and He gains our sin. Unearned, unmerited, highly favoured grace. A grace that calls us to rest in His love, to pick up His light burden (Mathew 11:28-30) and soar, sail, glide and love effortlessly through life. This is the principle story of the gospels. Four different accounts, written to different audiences at different times with different emphasises and all screaming the same scandal of grace.

This book has attempted to harmonise all 64,766 words into a chronological order to present a modern narrative of the gospel of Jesus without losing a single word of scripture. It has taken nothing away from the gospels as they are, and my prayer is that this book will be a blessing for those looking for a new fresh insight into our Saviour Jesus.

This book is not a commentary but an opportunity to read every word of the four Gospels woven into the time and setting of the historical truth of the Saviour of the world. To present the fact that all that Jesus is in heaven today, we are in this world. That all that belongs to Him, belongs to us. That we are an heir of the most high God and a joint heir with Christ Jesus. Within these pages I hope you have seen Jesus a fresh in all His glory and beauty as you journey further into all the blessings that your rich inheritance affords. I hope you enjoyed this marvellous journey of walking with Jesus, and may it spur you on in your own relationship and personal walk with the Saviour of the world.

About the Author

Stuart currently serves his nation as a member of the Australian Parliament representing the northern Gold Coast electorate of 'Fadden' in the House of Representatives, a seat he has held since 2007. He has been a Minister of State, serving at different times as the Assistant Minister for Defence, the Minister for Veterans' Affairs, Minister for Human Services and the Minister Assisting the Prime Minister for the Centenary of ANZAC.

Prior to entering Parliament, he co-owned a medium sized Information Technology company that was twice named as one of the fastest growing 100 companies in Australia. He previously served in the Australian Army for twelve years as an infantry and intelligence corps officer and is a graduate of the Australian Defence Force Academy and a top ten graduate of the Royal Military College Duntroon. He saw operational service in 1998 on the PNG Island of Bougainville following the devastating civil war.

He was a founding director of Watoto Australia and a member of the Watoto International board. Based in Uganda, Watoto operates the world's largest non-institutional orphan care program and is now exporting this program globally.

He holds a Masters in Business Administration, Masters in Information Technology and a Bachelor of Arts (Hons).

Stuart's previous books include 'Hope the Watoto Journey' and 'The trial of Lieutenant General Hiroshi Tamura: a question of command responsibility'.

He is married to his beautiful wife Chantelle and has three sons. He loves four wheel driving with his family, paragliding, learning Chinese, playing the piano and serving in his local church.

www.ingramcontent.com/pod-product-compliance
Lightning Source LLC
Chambersburg PA
CBHW062356090426
42740CB00010B/1303